Instructor's Manual

to Accompany

THE ART OF
PUBLIC SPEAKING

ELEVENTH EDITION

Stephen E. Lucas
University of Wisconsin

Paul Stob
Vanderbilt University

McGraw-Hill Higher Education

Instructor's Manual to accompany
THE ART OF PUBLIC SPEAKING
Stephen E. Lucas

Published by McGraw-Hill, an imprint of The McGraw-Hill Companies, Inc., 1221 Avenue of the Americas, New York, NY 10020. Copyright © 2012, 2009, 2007, 2004, 2001, 1998, 1995, 1992 by Stephen E. Lucas. All rights reserved. Printed in the United States of America.

1 2 3 4 5 6 7 8 9 0 QDB/QDB 1 0 9 8 7 6 5 4 3 2 1

ISBN: 978-0-07-742816-7
MHID: 0-07-742816-1

www.mhhe.com

Contents

Preface   xiv

A Guide to Instructional Resources   xvi
for *The Art of Public Speaking*

PART ONE: Suggested Course Outlines   1

    Outline for a 15-Week, 45-Hour Semester   3

    Outline for a One-Semester Course with a Unit on Group Discussion   8

    Outline for a 10-Week, 30-Hour Quarter OR a 15-Week, 30-Hour Semester   13

    Outline for a 10-Week, 40-Hour Quarter   17

PART TWO: Speaking Assignments   23

  Introductory Speeches   24

    Option A: A Two-Minute Speech Introducing a Classmate   24

    Option B: A Two-Minute Speech Introducing a Classmate   24

    Option C: A Two-Minute Speech of Self-Introduction   25

    Option D: A Two-Minute Speech of Self-Introduction   25

    Option E: A Two-Minute Speech of Self-Introduction Based on   26
           a Newspaper or Magazine Article

    Option F: A Two-Minute Speech of Self-Introduction Based on   26
           a Personal Object

  Informative Speeches   27

    Option A: A Speech of 5 to 6 Minutes About an Object, Process,   27
           Concept, or Event

Option B: A Speech of 5 to 6 Minutes About an Object, Process, Concept, or Event   27

Option C: A Speech of 5 to 6 Minutes About the Steps of a Process   27

Option D: A Speech of 5 to 6 Minutes About a Culture Different from the Speaker's Own   28

Persuasive Speeches   28

Option A: A Speech of 7 to 8 Minutes For or Against a Question of Policy   28

Option B: A Speech of 7 to 8 Minutes on a Question of Fact or a Question of Value   29

Commemorative Speech   29

Final Speeches   29

Option A: A Speech of 8 to 10 Minutes That Is Informative or Persuasive   29

Option B: A Speech of 8 to 10 Minutes Revising an Informative or Persuasive Speech from Earlier in the Term   30

Option C: A Speech of 8 to 10 Minutes About a Prominent Public Speaker   30

Impromptu Speech   31

Problem-Solving Group Discussion with Symposium   31

PART THREE: Evaluation and Grading   33

Criteria, Exams, and Grading Scales   34

Evaluation Forms   35

Strategies of Evaluation   36

Evaluations by Students   36

Criteria Used for Evaluating Speeches   38

Speech Evaluation Form A   39

Speech Evaluation Form B   40

Speech Evaluation Form C   41

Policy Speech Evaluation Form   42

Monroe's Motivated Sequence Evaluation Form   43

Commemorative Speech Evaluation Form   44

PART FOUR: Chapter-by-Chapter Guide to *The Art of Public Speaking*   45

Chapter 1   Speaking in Public

Chapter Objectives   47

Chapter Outline   48

Exercises for Critical Thinking   50

Using Public Speaking in Your Career   51

Additional Exercises and Activities   52

Student Introduction Questionnaire   56

Chapter 2   Ethics and Public Speaking

Chapter Objectives   57

Chapter Outline   57

Exercises for Critical Thinking   58

Using Public Speaking in Your Career   60

Additional Exercises and Activities   61

Chapter 3   Listening

Chapter Objectives   65

Chapter Outline   65

Exercises for Critical Thinking   67

Additional Exercises and Activities   68

Listening Self-Evaluation Worksheet   71

Speech Listening Worksheet   72

Chapter 4   Giving Your First Speech

Chapter Objectives   73

Chapter Outline   73

Exercises for Critical Thinking   74

Additional Exercises and Activities   76

Chapter 5   Selecting a Topic and a Purpose

Chapter Objectives   78

Chapter Outline   78

Exercises for Critical Thinking   80

Using Public Speaking in Your Career   82

Additional Exercises and Activities   83

Chapter 6   Analyzing the Audience

Chapter Objectives   87

Chapter Outline   87

Exercises for Critical Thinking   90

Using Public Speaking in Your Career   92

Additional Exercises and Activities   93

Questionnaire for Demographic Audience Analysis   96

Audience Analysis and Adaptation Worksheet, Part I   97

Audience Analysis and Adaptation Worksheet, Part II   98

Chapter 7   Gathering Materials

Chapter Objectives   99

Chapter Outline   99

Exercises for Critical Thinking   101

Using Public Speaking in Your Career   102

Additional Exercises and Activities   103

Library Research Worksheet   104

Internet Research Worksheet   105

Chapter 8   Supporting Your Ideas

Chapter Objectives   106

Chapter Outline   106

Exercises for Critical Thinking   108

Additional Exercises and Activities   113

Chapter 9   Organizing the Body of the Speech

Chapter Objectives   116

Chapter Outline   116

Exercises for Critical Thinking   118

Using Public Speaking in Your Career   120

Additional Exercises and Activities   121

Connectives Worksheet   125

Chapter 10   Beginning and Ending the Speech

Chapter Objectives   126

Chapter Outline   126

Exercises for Critical Thinking   128

Using Public Speaking in Your Career   131

Additional Exercises and Activities   131

Chapter 11   Outlining the Speech

Chapter Objectives   134

Chapter Outline   134

Exercises for Critical Thinking   136

Using Public Speaking in Your Career   138

Additional Exercises and Activities   139

Chapter 12   Using Language

Chapter Objectives   146

Chapter Outline   146

Exercises for Critical Thinking   148

Using Public Speaking in Your Career   152

Additional Exercises and Activities   153

Chapter 13   Delivery

Chapter Objectives   159

Chapter Outline   160

Exercises for Critical Thinking   162

Using Public Speaking in Your Career   163

Additional Exercises and Activities   164

Out-of-Class Speech Observation Worksheet   172

Chapter 14　Using Visual Aids

Chapter Objectives	173
Chapter Outline	173
Exercises for Critical Thinking	175
Using Public Speaking in Your Career	176
Additional Exercises and Activities	177

Chapter 15　Speaking to Inform

Chapter Objectives	179
Chapter Outline	179
Exercises for Critical Thinking	181
Using Public Speaking in Your Career	184
Additional Exercises and Activities	185
Informative Speech Preparation Worksheet	191
Informative Speech Self-Assessment	193

Chapter 16　Speaking to Persuade

Chapter Objectives	194
Chapter Outline	195
Exercises for Critical Thinking	198
Using Public Speaking in Your Career	203
Additional Exercises and Activities	204
Persuasive Speech Preparation Worksheet	211
Fact, Value, Policy Worksheet	213
Persuasive Speech Self-Assessment	214

Chapter 17　Methods of Persuasion

Chapter Objectives	215
Chapter Outline	216
Exercises for Critical Thinking	219
Using Public Speaking in Your Career	224
Additional Exercises and Activities	226
Fallacies Worksheet	231

Chapter 18   Speaking on Special Occasions

Chapter Objectives   232

Chapter Outline   232

Exercises for Critical Thinking   234

Additional Exercises and Activities   235

Speech of Introduction Observation Worksheet   239

Special Occasion Speech Self-Assessment   240

Chapter 19   Speaking in Small Groups

Chapter Objectives   241

Chapter Outline   241

Exercises for Critical Thinking   244

Additional Exercises and Activities   245

"Lost on the Moon" Individual Worksheet   250

"Lost on the Moon" Group Worksheet   251

"Hostages" Individual Worksheet   252

"Hostages" Group Worksheet   254

Classroom Speech Deliberation Worksheet   255

Group Discussion Self-Assessment   256

Group Discussion Participation Evaluation Worksheet   257

PART FIVE: Speeches for Analysis and Discussion

259

Introductory Speeches and Commentaries

New Game, New Life (*Self-Introduction*)   260

A Heart Worn on My Hand (*Self-Introduction*)   262

Pot, Soil, Water: Needs Improvement (*Self-Introduction*)   264

Pot, Soil, Water: Final Version (*Self-Introduction*)   267

My Life from Toe to Head (*Self-Introduction*)   269

My Eye on the World (*Self-Introduction*)   271

The Rare Phobia (*Self-Introduction*)   273

A Mile in My Shoes (*Self-Introduction*)   275

Kiyomi and Me (*Self-Introduction*)   277

Brooklyn Roads (*Introducing a Classmate*)   279

Rhymes with Orange (*Introducing a Classmate*)   281

Steady and True (*Introducing a Classmate*)   283

A Family Tradition (*Introducing a Classmate*)   285

Informative Speeches and Commentaries

Yoga: Uniting Mind, Body, and Spirit   288

Sign Language   292

Securing Yourself Online: Needs Improvement   296

Securing Yourself Online: Final Version   299

The Hidden World of Chili Peppers: Needs Improvement   303

The Hidden World of Chili Peppers: Final Version   308

Acupuncture: New Uses for an Ancient Remedy   312

Feng Shui   317

Dying to Be Thin   322

Cryonics   327

Dandelions: The Uncommon Weed   332

Edible Insects   336

Nothing to Sneeze At   340

Persuasive Speeches and Commentaries

Making a Difference Through the Special Olympics   345

Putting the Brakes on Teenage Driving   350

The Ultimate Gift   355

Self-Defense on Campus   360

To Save a Child   366

The Problem with Pennies   371

Multicultural, Multilingual   376

The Dangers of Chewing Tobacco   382

Boxing: The Most Dangerous Sport   388

Seatbelts: A Habit That Could Save Your Life   394

Capital Punishment   399

Responsible Drinking   403

Making Campus Accessible for Disabled Students   408

A Whisper of AIDS (Mary Fisher)   412

Commemorative Speeches and Commentaries

Choices and Change (Barbara Bush)   419

The Massachusetts 54th   424

James "Cool Papa" Bell   428

The Survivors   432

My Grandfather   436

Evaluation and Instructional Forms

Criteria Used for Evaluating Speeches   38

Speech Evaluation Form A   39

Speech Evaluation Form B   40

Speech Evaluation Form C   41

Policy Speech Evaluation Form   42

Monroe's Motivated Sequence Evaluation Form   43

Commemorative Speech Evaluation Form   44

Student Introduction Questionnaire   56

Listening Self-Evaluation Worksheet   71

Speech Listening Worksheet   72

Questionnaire for Demographic Audience Analysis   96

Audience Analysis and Adaptation Worksheet, Part I   97

Audience Analysis and Adaptation Worksheet, Part II   98

Library Research Worksheet   104

Internet Research Worksheet   105

Connectives Worksheet   125

Out-of-Class Speech Observation Worksheet   172

Informative Speech Preparation Worksheet   191

Informative Speech Self-Assessment   193

Persuasive Speech Preparation Worksheet   211

Fact, Value, Policy Worksheet   213

Persuasive Speech Self-Assessment   214

Fallacies Worksheet   231

Speech of Introduction Observation Worksheet   239

Special Occasion Speech Self-Assessment   240

"Lost on the Moon" Individual Worksheet   250

"Lost on the Moon" Group Worksheet   251

"Hostages" Individual Worksheet   252

"Hostages" Group Worksheet   254

Classroom Speech Deliberation Worksheet   255

Group Discussion Self-Assessment   256

Group Discussion Participation Evaluation Worksheet   257

Analyses of Speeches from *The Art of Public Speaking* and Student Speech DVD

There's an App for That (*Self-Introduction*)   75

Fork in the Road (*Introducing a Classmate*)   75

Bursting the Antibacterial Bubble (*Persuasive*)   110

I Have a Dream (*Commemorative*)   149

Questions of Culture (*Commemorative*)   165

Ramadan (*Informative*)   182

Medical Robots: From Science Fiction to Science Fact (*Informative*)   185

Phony Pharmaceuticals: Final Version (*Persuasive*)   201

Phony Pharmaceuticals: Needs Improvement (*Persuasive*)   205

The Horrors of Puppy Mills (*Persuasive*)   223

The Dangers of Cell Phones (*Persuasive*)   226

Elie Wiesel (*Commemorative*)   234

My Crazy Aunt Sue (*Commemorative*)   235

New Game, New Life (*Self-Introduction*)   260

A Heart Worn on My Hand (*Self-Introduction*)   262

Pot, Soil, Water: Needs Improvement (*Self-Introduction*)   264

Pot, Soil, Water: Final Version (*Self-Introduction*)   267

Rhymes with Orange (*Introducing a Classmate*)   281

Yoga: Uniting Mind, Body, and Spirit (*Informative*)   288

Securing Yourself Online: Needs Improvement (*Informative*)   296

Securing Yourself Online: Final Version (*Informative*)   299

The Hidden World of Chili Peppers: Needs Improvement (*Informative*)   303

The Hidden World of Chili Peppers: Final Version (*Informative*)   308

Acupuncture: New Uses for an Ancient Remedy (*Informative*)   312

Making a Difference Through the Special Olympics (*Persuasive*)   345

The Massachusetts 54th (*Commemorative*)   424

Preface

This manual is a guide to teaching from *The Art of Public Speaking*. It is intended primarily for the benefit of new and less experienced instructors, but I hope you will find it valuable even if you have been teaching public speaking for many years.

The first part of the manual presents course outlines based on *The Art of Public Speaking* for both the semester and quarter systems. Part II explains the speech assignments included in the course outlines and offers alternative assignments as well. Part III discusses evaluation and grading and includes several forms for evaluating student speeches.

Part IV is a chapter-by-chapter guide to *The Art of Public Speaking*. For each chapter of the book, it provides a statement of objectives, a chapter outline, discussions of the critical-thinking exercises presented in the book, and additional suggestions for exercises and classroom activities.

In addition to the exercises in the book and in this manual, instructors will find more than 380 speech assignments and classroom activities in the six anthologies of *Selections from the Communication Teacher* that are on the Instructor's Resource CD-ROM that accompanies this edition of *The Art of Public Speaking*. Written by teachers for teachers, these articles offer a wealth of practical ideas for classroom use.

Part V of this manual contains 45 speeches for analysis and evaluation. They supplement the speeches in the appendix that follows Chapter 19 of the textbook, and each is followed by a brief guide for classroom discussion.

The Art of Public Speaking also includes an Annotated Instructor's Edition, which provides a wealth of teaching aids for each chapter in the book. These aids include instructional strategies, class activities, discussion questions, speech assignments, worksheets, and related readings. The Annotated Instructor's Edition is designed to complement the *Instructor's Manual*, and it is cross-referenced with the *Manual* as well as with other supplements that accompany *The Art of Public Speaking*.

To help instructors construct examinations, I have prepared a separate volume titled *Test Bank to Accompany The Art of Public Speaking*. The Test Bank contains 2,600 true-false, multiple-choice, short-answer, and essay questions—all of which are also available electronically for computerized test construction. In addition, the Test Bank provides a preconstructed true-false quiz for each chapter, as well as three sample final examinations. As a special feature, it also includes a guest essay by Professor Anita Vangelisti of the University of Texas on test construction and assessment.

The *Instructor's Manual* has again been printed on 8½ x 11 tear-out pages, so instructors can easily reproduce exercises, speeches, and evaluation forms for use in the classroom.

In preparing this manual, my aim has been to provide the most helpful resource of its kind available with any public speaking textbook. If you have questions about the manual, or suggestions for improving it, please contact me at selucas@wisc.edu.

Stephen E. Lucas
University of Wisconsin

A Guide to Instructional Resources for *The Art of Public Speaking*

Every aspect of the textbook, print supplements, video program, and online resources have been carefully developed to ensure that they work together as an integrated teaching and learning system. Each element of the system is explained below. By summarizing them here, my aim is to provide a clear sense of the teaching and learning resources available with *The Art of Pubic Speaking* so individual instructors can determine which are best suited to meeting the needs of their students.

Connect

A revolutionary digital resource, *Connect* (formerly *Connect Lucas*) provides online access to all the teaching and learning materials available with *The Art of Public Speaking* at a single Web site. Specially marked icons in the book direct readers to appropriate items at the site.

Connect can be used by students, on their own, as they read the book, prepare their speeches, and study for exams. Instructors can also integrate *Connect* with their reading assignments and classroom discussions—either by requiring that students access the appropriate items in preparation for class or by using it directly in the classroom. *Connect* can be used with equal effectiveness in traditional courses and online courses.

Connect provides more than a dozen resources. Let me say a word about each.

Speech Videos

Connect contains more than 60 video clips that demonstrate the principles of public speaking in action. As students read the book, icons in the margins guide them to the appropriate clips at *Connect*. Each clip has been chosen to illustrate a specific aspect of speechmaking, and each is fully coordinated with the book. So, for example, in the section of Chapter 10 that deals with preview statements, students can go to *Connect* and see how the preview statements they are reading in the book were delivered by the original speakers. The same is true of subjects from ethics to visual aids, supporting materials to extemporaneous delivery, introductions and conclusions to language use and audience adaptation.

Running in length from twenty seconds to a minute and a half, the video clips are distributed throughout the book. To help students prepare their classroom speeches, more than three-fourths are from student presentations. The remainder are from public figures and include such models of rhetorical excellence as Winston Churchill, Martin Luther King Jr., Ronald Reagan, Barbara Jordan, Barack Obama, and John F. Kennedy. In addition to helping students develop their skills, these clips give them an opportunity to experience some of the finest and most important speeches of recent time.

In addition to the video clips, *Connect* includes 27 full student presentations—eight introductory speeches, nine informative speeches, six persuasive speeches, and four commemorative speeches—all with a closed-captioning option. Each is accompanied by an outline of the speech and by critical-thinking questions that can be used for classroom discussion or out-of-class assignments.

Interactive Study Questions

To reinforce key principles and ideas, *Connect* contains a comprehensive set of study questions. These questions are interactive, use a variety of formats, and systematically cover all the major concepts discussed in the book. Entirely different from items in the *Test Bank,* the questions are designed both to gauge students' knowledge and to help them learn. After students enter their answer for each question, they receive not just an indication of whether the answer is right or wrong, but *feedback* that explains the correct answer.

LearnSmart

LearnSmart is a new diagnostic study tool that helps students absorb and internalize key ideas from the book. LearnSmart adapts to individual students and, based on their responses to questions about key concepts in the book, identifies strengths and weaknesses in their grasp of core content. By tracking student responses, instructors can use class time to focus on subjects that students find most challenging.

Outline Tool

In addition to video clips and study questions, *Connect* includes a speech outliner that guides students systematically through the process of organizing and outlining their speeches. As students use the outliner, they move step by step through each element of the speech from title through bibliography. Tutorial screens explain the organizational methods involved in composing each part of the speech, and the outliner automatically formats the speech in accordance with proper outlining principles. It also allows students to save, revise, and print their work, as well as to export it to their own word processors.

Outline Exercises

Interactive outlining exercises give students additional help in developing their skills of speech organization. These exercises present scrambled outlines that students can rearrange in the correct order by using standard drag-and-drop procedures. As with other features at *Connect,* the aim of these exercises is to put online technology to the best possible pedagogical use. The exercises can also be used in the classroom to facilitate the discussion of outlining principles.

EasyBib

EasyBib is a Web-based tool that automatically formats bibliographic entries in MLA or APA style. Students can use it when creating bibliographies for their speech outlines.

Worksheets

More than 20 worksheets deal with such topics as listening, audience analysis and adaptation, library and Internet research, informative and persuasive speech preparation, and out-of-class speech observations. Students can print the worksheets or complete them electronically and e-mail them to their instructor.

Self-Assessments

Self-assessment forms for the informative, persuasive, and commemorative speeches direct students in reflecting on their presentations and what they need to work on in the future. A self-assessment form is also available for group discussion projects. Like other elements of *Connect*, the self-assessments are designed for online courses as well as for traditional classrooms.

Speech Capture

This cutting-edge tool lets instructors evaluate speeches live using a fully customizable rubric. Instructors can insert comments at any point in the video, thereby allowing for precise, pinpointed feedback. Speech Capture can also be used by students for peer review in conjunction with the self-assessment forms discussed above.

Speech Preparation Checklists

All of the speech checklists printed in the book are also available at *Connect*. In addition to helping students keep on track as they prepare their speeches, the checklists can be printed or e-mailed in case instructors want students to submit them with their speeches.

Glossary of Key Terms

Throughout the book, key terms are defined in the margin as they appear in the text. Those key terms are also available at *Connect,* where they can be accessed via a master glossary arranged in alphabetical order. Whether students are reviewing for exams or working with the study questions, they can instantly check the meaning of any key term at the click of a mouse.

Course Management System

Another advantage of *Connect* is that it allows instructors to create, administer, and grade assignments completely online. It also provides a single site for posting syllabi, course announcements, assignments, grades, and discussion forums. New to this edition is McGraw-Hill's partnership with Blackboard, which allows for full integration of course content and digital tools into Blackboard. Students and faculty have single sign-on capability

ConnectLucas.com contains everything available with *Connect*, but goes beyond it to provide a media-rich electronic version of the textbook itself. Identical in content to the print version of *The Art of Public Speaking*, it embeds in the text all the teaching and learning resources discussed above as part of *Connect*. Rather than switching between the printed page and *Connect*, students can read the book online and link instantly to all its resources.

Although designed primarily to meet the needs of students and instructors in online courses, the electronic *Art of Public Speaking* is also perfectly suitable for use in traditional classes. Students can choose the print version or the electronic version based on their personal preferences. In either case, they will receive the same content and the same access to all the resources integral to this edition.

Annotated Instructor's Edition

The *Annotated Instructor's Edition* provides a wealth of teaching aids for each chapter in the book. These aids include instructional strategies, class activities, discussion questions, speech assignments, and related readings. The *Annotated Instructor's Edition* is also cross-referenced with the *Instructor's Manual* and the other supplements that accompany *The Art of Public Speaking*.

Instructor's Manual

Running close to 450 pages, the *Instructor's Manual* provides a comprehensive guide to teaching from *The Art of Public Speaking*. It contains outlines for each chapter of the book, discusses the end-of chapter exercises, furnishes supplementary exercises and classroom activities, offers suggested course outlines and speaking assignments, and provides 45 additional speeches for discussion and analysis.

Test Bank

The *Test Bank* furnishes 2,600 examination questions based on *The Art of Public Speaking*; more than 300 are new to this edition. As a special feature, the *Test Bank* offers preconstructed true-false quizzes for each chapter in the book, as well as three complete final examinations.

Introductions, Conclusions, and Visual Aids

Because speeches are performative acts, students need to be able to view speakers in action as well as read their words on the printed page. *Introductions, Conclusions, and Visual Aids* is a 30-minute DVD that uses excerpts from a wide range of speeches to illustrate the principles of effective introductions, conclusions, and visual aids. Produced exclusively to accompany *The Art of Public Speaking*, it is based on the principles of visual learning and provides a valuable resource that instructors can use to help students understand and apply key principles discussed in the book. It is available on *Connect* as well as on DVD.

Student Speech DVD

Speeches for Analysis and Discussion contains 27 full student presentations, nine of which are new to this edition of the book. Here is a listing of the speeches. Those marked with an asterisk are printed in the book; the others are printed in this manual. All the speeches are also available to instructors at *Connect*.

*There's an App for That (Self-Introduction)

New Game, New Life (Self-Introduction)

Pot, Soil, Water: Needs Improvement (Self-Introduction)

Pot, Soil, Water: Final Version (Self-Introduction)

A Heart Worn on My Hand (Self-Introduction)

*Fork in the Road (Introducing a Classmate)

Brooklyn Roads (Introducing a Classmate)

Rhymes with Orange (Introducing a Classmate)

Medical Robots: From Science Fiction to Science Fact: Needs Improvement (Informative)

*Medical Robots: Science Fiction to Science Fact: Final Version (Informative)

*Ramadan

Yoga: Uniting Mind, Body, and Spirit (Informative: Demonstration)

Securing Yourself Online: Needs Improvement (Informative)

Securing Yourself Online: Final Version (Informative)

The Hidden World of Chili Peppers: Needs Improvement (Informative)

The Hidden World of Chili Peppers: Final Version (Informative)

Acupuncture: New Uses for an Ancient Remedy (Informative)

Phony Pharmaceuticals: Needs Improvement (Persuasive)

*Phony Pharmaceuticals: Final Version (Persuasive)

*The Dangers of Cell Phones (Persuasive)

*The Horrors of Puppy Mills (Persuasive)

Making a Difference Through the Special Olympics (Persuasive: Motivated Sequence)

Bursting the Antibacterial Bubble (Persuasive)

*Elie Wiesel (Commemorative)

*My Crazy Aunt Sue (Commemorative)

The Massachusetts 54th (Commemorative)

*Questions of Culture (Commemorative)

The speeches reflect the diversity of today's society and college classroom. They are presented by speakers of many backgrounds, deal with a wide range of topics, and employ several kinds of visual aids. All are meant to illustrate the principles of organization, audience analysis, supporting materials, creativity, and language that are discussed throughout the book and that are central to effective public speaking in any context.

The speeches also include five sets of paired Needs Improvement and Final Version presentations: "Medical Robots: From Science Fiction to Science Fact," "Phony Pharmaceuticals," "The Hidden World of Chili Peppers," "Securing Yourself Online," and "Pot, Soil, Water." In all five cases, the needs improvement version contains many of the flaws that typically appear in student presentations early in the term—inadequate preparation, underdevelopment of ideas, sloppy organization, ineffective use of visual aids, and the like. My aim is to show students—rather than just tell them—the things to avoid when seeking to craft a successful speech. Once students have seen the needs improvement version, instructors can show the final version, in which the flaws have been corrected.

Student Workbook

The *Student Workbook* contains a host of exercises, checklists, worksheets, and other materials that give students additional opportunities to work with the major elements of effective speechmaking. It also contains evaluation forms that students can use when evaluating the speeches of their classmates. Integrated with the book and the *Instructor's Manual*, it enables teachers to make daily assignments without having to strain department budgets by copying page upon page of materials. Instructors teaching online courses have found it highly valuable, but it has become a staple in many traditional classes as well.

PowerPoint Slides with Video Clips

There is also a collection of more than 450 slides for instructors who use PowerPoint in their lectures and discussions. Fully revised for this edition, the slides include photographs and video clips as well as text. Instructors can use the slides just as they are, or they can modify them to fit the special needs of individual classes. The slides can be found both at *Connect* and on the Instructor's Resource CD-ROM described below.

Instructor's Resource CD-ROM

For the convenience of instructors, the *Instructor's Manual*, *Test Bank*, and PowerPoint slides are all available on the Instructor's Resource CD-ROM. The CD also includes *Selections from the Communication Teacher*, *Teaching Public Speaking*, *Teaching Public Speaking Online*, and the *Handbook for Teachers of Non-Native Speakers of English*—all of which are described below.

Selections from the Communication Teacher

Over the years, I have compiled six volumes of *Selections from the Communication Teacher* to accompany *The Art of Public Speaking*. All six are available on the Instructor's Resource CD-ROM. They cover a host of topics related to the teaching of public speaking, including audience analysis, critical thinking, diversity and multiculturalism, informative speaking, persuasion, and general instructional methods. Taken together, they reprint more than 380 brief articles that offer a wealth of practical ideas for classroom use.

Teaching Public Speaking

Written primarily for beginning instructors, *Teaching Public Speaking* reprints my essay of the same title from *Teaching Communication: Theory, Research, and Methods* (Lawrence Erlbaum Associates). This essay presents an overview of the pedagogical philosophy behind *The Art of Public Speaking* and discusses a number of practical classroom issues.

Teaching Public Speaking Online

Written by Professor Jennifer Cochrane of Indiana University and Purdue University at Indianapolis, *Teaching Public Speaking Online* has been fully updated for the eleventh edition. Available on the Instructor's Resource CD-ROM and at *Connect*, it provides a wealth of practical guidance for instructors who are using *The Art of Public Speaking* in an online course. It draws upon Professor Cochrane's pioneering experience with online instruction to explore how one can teach an intellectually rich, practically rewarding public speaking course via the Internet.

Handbook for Teachers of Non-Native Speakers of English

Developed for instructors who have ESL students in their public speaking classes, this 60-page handbook focuses on the central issues that should be considered when working with students from different linguistic and cultural backgrounds.

Part One

Suggested
Course Outlines

*T*he Art of Public Speaking* is easily adapted to a wide variety of class schedules and teaching methods. The following class outlines reflect one approach to the course. They take students through a series of reading, application, and speaking assignments that build systematically upon one another. They are also designed to allow students to undertake their first graded speaking assignment without having to read practically the whole book. Reading assignments are structured to give students adequate preparation time for each speech.

The first part of the syllabus culminates in the informative speech and focuses on such basic matters as analyzing the audience, choosing a topic and specific purpose, and organizing the speech. The second part culminates in the persuasive speech and focuses on more complex matters such as the target audience, building credibility, and using evidence and reasoning. The third part culminates in the commemorative speech and focuses on the effective use of language. By the fourth part, which culminates in the final speech, students have been exposed to all the major skills of speechmaking discussed in the textbook. Now the instructor can concentrate on strengthening students' command of those skills.

The course outlines presented here are for a class of roughly twenty students. If you have an appreciably higher enrollment, you will probably have to reduce the length of the speeches or increase the number of class sessions devoted to the presentation of student speeches.

Finally, although these outlines include suggestions for classroom discussion based on the Exercises for Critical Thinking in *The Art of Public Speaking*, there are many more exercises in the Annotated Instructor's Edition of the book and in this manual. *Connect* makes many of the exercises assignable and interactive. You should have no trouble choosing the ones that best fit your teaching emphases and the needs of your students.

The speaking assignments indicated in the course outlines are explained in Part Two of this manual.

OUTLINE FOR A 15-WEEK, 45-HOUR SEMESTER

Class Meeting	Topic—Activity	Reading
1	**Course Overview** Introduce yourself; hand out syllabi; explain grading and attendance policies. Assign introductory speeches.	
2	**Basic Principles of Speech Communication** Focus class discussion on selected exercises, text pp. 26–27 and 75, or additional exercises from pp. 52–55 and 76–77 of this manual. Explain introductory speeches; show "There's an App for That" and "Fork in the Road" from the DVD of student speeches that accompanies this edition of *The Art of Public Speaking*.	Chapter 1 and Chapter 4
3	**Ethics and Public Speaking** Focus class discussion on exercises 1 and 3, text p. 45. Have students develop a code of ethical speaking for their classroom as explained in additional exercise 1 on p. 61 of this manual.	Chapter 2
4	**Introductory Speeches**	
5	**Introductory Speeches**	
6	**Speaking to Inform** Assign informative speeches. Focus class discussion on kinds of informative speeches and guidelines for informative speaking. Show the needs improvement and final versions of "Medical Robots: From Science Fiction to Science Fact" and "The Hidden World of Chili Peppers" from the DVD of student speeches that accompanies this edition of *The Art of Public Speaking*. For discussion of "Medical Robots," see pp. 294–296 of the textbook and 185–188 of this manual; for "Chili Peppers," see pp. 303–311 of this manual.	Chapter 15
7	**Choosing Topics and Purposes** Focus class discussion on exercises 2 and 3, text pp. 94–95, and Using Public Speaking in Your Career, text p. 83.	Chapter 5

Class Meeting	Topic—Activity	Reading
8	**Analyzing the Audience** Focus class discussion on exercise 2, text p. 117, and Using Public Speaking in Your Career, text p. 110. Use additional exercise 1 or 4 on pp. 93–95 of this manual as a classroom activity.	Chapter 6
9	**Organizing the Body of the Speech** Focus class discussion on exercises 1–3 and Using Public Speaking in Your Career, text pp. 173, 181–182. Use additional exercises as needed from pp. 121–124 of this manual.	Chapter 9
10	**Introductions and Conclusions** Focus class discussion on exercise 1 and Using Public Speaking in Your Career, text pp. 198–203. Use additional exercise 1 or 2 on pp. 131–132 of this manual as a classroom activity. Show Part One of *Introductions, Conclusions, and Visual Aids*, which accompanies *The Art of Public Speaking*.	Chapter 10
11	**Outlining the Speech** Focus class discussion on exercise 1, text pp. 218–219, and Using Public Speaking in Your Career, text p. 215. Have students do the interactive outlining exercises in Chapter 11 at *Connect* as a homework assignment; discuss the results in class.	Chapter 11
12	**Delivering the Speech** Focus class discussion on principles of effective delivery. Select from exercises 1–3, text p. 257, or the additional exercises on pp. 164–171 of this manual.	Chapter 13
13	**Using Visual Aids** Focus class discussion on exercise 2, text p. 275. Use additional exercise 2 on p. 177 of this manual as a classroom activity. Show Part Two of *Introductions, Conclusions, and Visual Aids*, which accompanies *The Art of Public Speaking*. If time allows, show a full speech that uses visual aids from the DVD of student speeches that accompanies this edition. Good candidates include "Medical Robots: From Science Fiction to Science Fact," "Yoga: Uniting Mind, Body, and Spirit," and "Securing Yourself Online."	Chapter 14

Class Meeting	Topic—Activity	Reading
14	**Informative Speeches**	
15	**Informative Speeches**	
16	**Informative Speeches**	
17	**Informative Speeches**	
18	**Introduction to Persuasive Speaking** Assign persuasive speeches. Focus class discussion on selected exercises and Using Public Speaking in Your Career, text p. 317. Show "Phony Pharmaceuticals" from the DVD of student speeches that accompanies this edition of *The Art of Public Speaking*. For commentary on the speech, see textbook pp. 318–320 and pp. 201–207 of this manual.	Chapter 16
19	**Gathering Materials** Take a library tour—see additional exercise 1 on p. 103 of this manual. Assign selected exercises from text p. 139 or from p. 103 of this manual.	Chapter 7
20	**Using Supporting Materials** Focus class discussion on exercises 1–2, text p. 163. Or select from among the additional exercises on pp. 113–115 of this manual.	Chapter 8
21	**Methods of Persuasion** Focus class discussion on selected exercises and Using Public Speaking in Your Career, text pp. 342 and 351. Use additional exercise 3 on pp. 229–230 of this manual as a classroom activity. Show "The Dangers of Cell Phones" from the DVD of student speeches that accompanies this edition of *The Art of Public Speaking*. For commentary on the speech, see textbook pp. 346–349 and pp. 226–227 of this manual.	Chapter 17
22	**Analysis of Persuasive Speeches** Have students prepare brief analyses of the assigned speech or speeches. Good candidates for analysis include "The Horrors of Puppy Mills" and "Bursting the Antibacterial Bubble." See pp. 222–224 and 110–113 of this manual for analyses of these speeches.	Selections from "Speeches for Analysis and Discussion," pp. A1–A15

Class Meeting	Topic—Activity	Reading
23	**Listening to Speeches** Focus class discussion on exercise 2, text p. 61. (The Listening Self-Evaluation Worksheet is available on p. 71 of this manual, or you can assign it from the assignments available on *Connect*.) Choose from additional exercises on pp. 68–70 of this manual for classroom activities.	Chapter 3
24	**Persuasive Speeches**	
25	**Persuasive Speeches**	
26	**Persuasive Speeches**	
27	**Persuasive Speeches**	
28	**Midterm Examination**	
29	**Commemorative Speaking** Assign commemorative speech. Focus class discussion on exercise 3, text p. 363. Show "Elie Wiesel," "My Crazy Aunt Sue," or "The Massachusetts 54th" from the DVD of student speeches that accompanies this edition of *The Art of Public Speaking*. See pp. 234–235, 235–236, and 424–427 of this manual for commentary on these speeches.	Chapter 18, especially pp. 358–361
30	**Return and Review Midterm Examinations**	
31	**Using Language Effectively** Focus class discussion on selections from exercises 1–3, text p. 237; Using Public Speaking in Your Career, text p. 231; and additional exercises on pp. 153–158 of this manual.	Chapter 12
32	**Using Language Effectively** Have students prepare a brief analysis of King's speech as directed in exercise 4, text p. 237. Show the video of "I Have a Dream" in class and focus discussion on King's use of language. For analysis of King's speech, see pp. 149–152 of this manual.	Martin Luther King, "I Have a Dream," pp. A2–A5

Class Meeting	Topic—Activity	Reading
33	**Commemorative Speeches**	
34	**Commemorative Speeches**	
35	**Commemorative Speeches**	
36	**The Final Speech** Assign final speeches and begin review of elements students most need to work on in preparing the final speech. Major items usually are supporting materials, organization and outlining, and delivery.	
37	**Preparing for the Final Speech: Supporting Materials** Focus class discussion on selected exercises from Chapter 8 of the text, or on analyzing speeches from pp. A1–A15 of the text or from Part Five of this manual.	Review Chapter 8
38	**Preparing for the Final Speech: Organization and Outlining** Focus class discussion on selected exercises from Chapters 9–11 and additional exercises from this manual.	Review Chapters 9–11
39	**Preparing for the Final Speech: Delivery** By this point in the course, many students are ready to work on polishing their delivery skills. Choose from among the exercises in Chapter 13 of the text or the additional exercises on pp. 164–171 of this manual.	Review Chapter 13
40	**Final Speeches**	
41	**Final Speeches**	
42	**Final Speeches**	
43	**Final Speeches**	
44	**Final Speeches**	
45	**Summary and Review for Final Examination**	

OUTLINE FOR A ONE-SEMESTER COURSE WITH A UNIT ON GROUP DISCUSSION

Class Meeting	Topic—Activity	Reading
1	**Course Overview** Introduce yourself; hand out syllabi; explain grading and attendance policies. Assign introductory speeches.	
2	**Basic Principles of Speech Communication** Focus class discussion on selected exercises, text pp. 26–27 and 75, or additional exercises from pp. 52–55 and 76–77 of this manual. Explain introductory speeches; show "There's an App for That" and "Fork in the Road" from the DVD of student speeches that accompanies this edition of *The Art of Public Speaking*.	Chapter 1 and Chapter 4
3	**Ethics and Public Speaking** Focus class discussion on exercises 1 and 3, text p. 45. Have students develop a code of ethical speaking for their classroom as explained in additional exercise 1 on p. 61 of this manual.	Chapter 2
4	**Introductory Speeches**	
5	**Introductory Speeches**	
6	**Speaking to Inform** Assign informative speeches. Focus class discussion on kinds of informative speeches and guidelines for informative speaking. Show the needs improvement and final versions of "Medical Robots: From Science Fiction to Science Fact" and "The Hidden World of Chili Peppers" from the DVD of student speeches that accompanies this edition of *The Art of Public Speaking*. For discussion of "Medical Robots," see pp. 294–296 of the textbook and 185–188 of this manual; for discussion of "Chili Peppers," see pp. 303–311 of this manual.	Chapter 15
7	**Choosing Topics and Purposes** Focus class discussion on exercises 2 and 3, text pp. 94–95, and Using Public Speaking in Your Career, text p. 83.	Chapter 5

Class Meeting	Topic—Activity	Reading
8	**Analyzing the Audience** Focus class discussion on exercise 2, text p. 117, and Using Public Speaking in Your Career, text p. 110. Use additional exercise 1 or 4 on pp. 93–95 of this manual as a classroom activity.	Chapter 6
9	**Organizing the Body of the Speech** Focus class discussion on exercises 1–3 and Using Public Speaking in Your Career, text pp. 173, 181–182. Use additional exercises as needed from pp. 121–124 of this manual.	Chapter 9
10	**Introductions and Conclusions** Focus class discussion on exercise 1 and Using Public Speaking in Your Career, text pp. 198 and 203. Use additional exercise 1 or 2 on pp. 131–133 of this manual as a classroom activity. Show Part One of *Introductions, Conclusions, and Visual Aids*, which accompanies *The Art of Public Speaking*.	Chapter 10
11	**Outlining the Speech** Focus class discussion on exercise 1, text pp. 218–219, and Using Public Speaking in Your Career, text p. 215. Have students do the interactive outlining exercises in Chapter 11 at *Connect* as a homework assignment; discuss the results in class.	Chapter 11
12	**Delivering the Speech** Focus class discussion on principles of effective delivery. Select from exercises 1–3, text p. 257, or the additional exercises on pp. 164–171 of this manual.	Chapter 13
13	**Using Visual Aids** Focus class discussion on exercise 2, text p. 275. Use additional exercise 2 on p. 177 of this manual as a classroom activity. Show Part Two of *Introductions, Conclusions, and Visual Aids*, which accompanies *The Art of Public Speaking*. If time allows, show a full speech that uses visual aids from the DVD of student speeches that accompanies this edition. Good candidates include "Medical Robots: From Science Fiction to Science Fact," "Yoga: Uniting Mind, Body, and Spirit," and "Securing Yourself Online."	Chapter 14

Class Meeting	Topic—Activity	Reading
14	**Informative Speeches**	
15	**Informative Speeches**	
16	**Informative Speeches**	
17	**Informative Speeches**	
18	**Introduction to Persuasive Speaking** Assign persuasive speeches. Focus class discussion on selected exercises and Using Public Speaking in Your Career, text p. 317. Show "Phony Pharmaceuticals" from the DVD of student speeches that accompanies this edition of *The Art of Public Speaking*. For commentary on the speech, see textbook pp. 318–320 and pp. 201–207 of this manual.	Chapter 16
19	**Gathering Materials** Take a library tour—see additional exercise 1 on p. 103 of this manual. Assign selected exercises from text p. 139 or from p. 103 of this manual.	Chapter 7
20	**Using Supporting Materials** Focus class discussion on exercises 1–2, text p. 163. Or select from among the additional exercises on pp. 113–115 of this manual.	Chapter 8
21	**Methods of Persuasion** Focus class discussion on selected exercises and Using Public Speaking in Your Career, text pp. 342 and 351. Use additional exercise 3 on pp. 229–230 of this manual as a classroom activity. Show "The Dangers of Cell Phones" from the DVD of student speeches that accompanies this edition of *The Art of Public Speaking*. For commentary on the speech, see textbook pp. 346–349 and pp. 226–227 of this manual.	Chapter 17
22	**Analysis of Persuasive Speeches** Have students prepare brief analyses of the assigned speech or speeches. Good candidates for analysis include "The Horrors of Puppy Mills," and "Bursting the Antibacterial Bubble." See pp. 222–224 and 110–113 of this manual for analyses of these speeches.	Selections from "Speeches for Analysis and Discussion," pp. A1–A15

Class Meeting	Topic—Activity	Reading
23	**Listening to Speeches** Focus class discussion on exercise 2, text p. 61. (The Listening Self-Evaluation Worksheet is available on p. 71 of this manual, or you can assign it from the assignments available on *Connect*.) Choose from additional exercises on pp. 68–70 of this manual for classroom activities.	Chapter 3
24	**Persuasive Speeches**	
25	**Persuasive Speeches**	
26	**Persuasive Speeches**	
27	**Persuasive Speeches**	
28	**Midterm Examination**	
29	**Commemorative Speaking** Assign commemorative speech. Focus class discussion on exercise 3, text p. 363. Show "Elie Wiesel," "My Crazy Aunt Sue," or "The Massachusetts 54th" from the DVD of student speeches that accompanies this edition of *The Art of Public Speaking*. See pp. 234–235, 235–236, and 424–427 of this manual for commentary on these speeches.	Chapter 18, especially pp. 358–361
30	**Return and Review Midterm Examinations**	
31	**Using Language Effectively** Focus class discussion on selections from exercises 1–3, text p. 237; Using Public Speaking in Your Career, text p. 231; and additional exercises on pp. 153–158 of this manual.	Chapter 12
32	**Using Language Effectively** Have students prepare a brief analysis of King's speech as directed in exercise 4, text p. 237. Show the video of "I Have a Dream" in class and focus discussion on King's use of language. For analysis of King's speech, see pp. 149–152 of this manual.	Martin Luther King, "I Have a Dream," pp. A2–A5
33	**Commemorative Speeches**	
34	**Commemorative Speeches**	
35	**Commemorative Speeches**	

Class Meeting	Topic—Activity	Reading
36	**Introduction to Small-Group Discussion** Assign group discussion projects. Discuss Chapter 19, with special emphasis on pp. 365–372.	Chapter 19, especially pp. 365–372
37	**Problem Solving in Small Groups** Focus class discussion on the reflective-thinking method; use exercises 1 and 3, text p. 381.	Chapter 19 especially, pp. 373–380
38	**Decision-Making Processes in Small Groups** Do "Lost on the Moon" or "Hostages" activity from pp. 245–247 of this manual.	
39	**Group Project Work** Have groups work on their projects in class. This will give you a chance to meet briefly with each group to assess its progress and to offer guidance.	
40	**Group Presentations**	
41	**Group Presentations**	
42	**Group Presentations**	
43	**Group Presentations**	
44	**Group Presentations**	
45	**Summary and Review for Final Examinations**	

OUTLINE FOR A 10-WEEK, 30-HOUR QUARTER
OR
A 15-WEEK, 30-HOUR SEMESTER

Class Meeting	Topic—Activity	Reading
1	**Course Overview** Introduce yourself; hand out syllabi; explain grading and attendance policies. Assign introductory speeches.	
2	**Basic Principles of Speech Communication** Focus class discussion on selected exercises, text pp. 26–27, or additional exercises from pp. 52–55 and 76–77 of this manual. Explain introductory speeches; show "There's an App for That" and "Fork in the Road" from the DVD of student speeches that accompanies this edition of *The Art of Public Speaking*.	Chapter 1 and Chapter 4
3	**Ethics and Public Speaking** Focus class discussion on exercises 1 and 3, text p. 45. Have students develop a code of ethical speaking for their classroom as explained in additional exercise 1 on p. 61 of this manual.	Chapter 2
4	**Introductory Speeches**	
5	**Introductory Speeches**	
6	**Speaking to Inform** Assign informative speeches. Focus class discussion on kinds of informative speeches and guidelines for informative speaking. Show the needs improvement and final versions of "Medical Robots: From Science Fiction to Science Fact" and "The Hidden World of Chili Peppers" from the DVD that accompanies this edition of *The Art of Public Speaking*. For discussion of "Medical Robots," see pp. 294–296 of the textbook and 185–188 of this manual; for "Chili Peppers," see pp. 303–311 of this manual.	Chapter 15
7	**Choosing Topics and Purposes** Focus class discussion on exercises 2 and 3, text pp. 94–95, and Using Public Speaking in Your Career, text p. 83.	Chapter 5

Class Meeting	Topic—Activity	Reading
8	**Analyzing the Audience** Focus class discussion on exercise 2, text p. 117, and Using Public Speaking in Your Career, text p. 119. Use additional exercise 1 or 4 on pp. 93–95 of this manual as a classroom activity.	Chapter 6
9	**Organizing the Speech** Focus class discussion on exercises 1–3 and Using Public Speaking in Your Career, text pp. 173, 181–182, and exercise 1, text p. 203. Use additional exercises as needed from pp. 121–124 and 131–133 of this manual. Show Part One of *Introductions, Conclusions, and Visual Aids*, which accompanies *The Art of Public Speaking*.	Chapters 9–10
10	**Outlining the Speech** Focus class discussion on exercise 1, text pp. 218–219, and Using Public Speaking in Your Career, text p. 215. Have students do the interactive outlining exercises in Chapter 11 at *Connect* as a homework assignment; discuss the results in class.	Chapter 11
11	**Delivering the Speech and Using Visual Aids** Select from exercises 1–3, text p. 257, or the additional exercises on pp. 164–171 of this manual. If visual aids are required for the informative speech, discuss exercise 2, text p. 275. Use additional exercise 2 on p. 177 of this manual as a classroom activity. Show Part Two of *Introductions, Conclusions, and Visual Aids*, which accompanies *The Art of Public Speaking*. If time allows, show a full speech that uses visual aids from the DVD of student speeches that accompanies this edition. Good candidates include "Medical Robots: From Science Fiction to Science Fact," "Yoga: Uniting Mind, Body, and Spirit," and "Securing Yourself Online."	Chapters 13–14
12	**Informative Speeches**	
13	**Informative Speeches**	
14	**Informative Speeches**	

Class Meeting	Topic—Activity	Reading
15	**Introduction to Persuasive Speaking** Assign persuasive speeches. Focus class discussion on selected exercises and Using Public Speaking in Your Career, text p. 317. Show "Phony Pharmaceuticals" from the DVD of student speeches that accompanies this edition of *The Art of Public Speaking*. For commentary on the speech, see textbook pp. 318–320 and pp. 201–207 of this manual.	Chapter 16
16	**Gathering Materials** Take a library tour—see additional exercise 1 on p. 103 of this manual. Assign selected exercises from text p. 139 or from p. 103 of this manual.	Chapter 7
17	**Using Supporting Materials** Focus class discussion on exercises 1–2, text p. 163. Or select from among the additional exercises on pp. 113–115 of this manual.	Chapter 8
18	**Methods of Persuasion** Focus class discussion on selected exercises and Using Public Speaking in Your Career, text pp. 342–351. Use additional exercise 3 on pp. 229–230 of this manual as a classroom activity. Show "The Dangers of Cell Phones" from the DVD of student speeches that accompanies this edition of *The Art of Public Speaking*. For commentary on the speech, see textbook pp. 346–349 and pp. 226–227 of this manual.	Chapter 17
19	**Listening to Speeches** Focus class discussion on exercise 2, text p. 61. (The Listening Self-Evaluation Worksheet is available on p. 71 of this manual, or you can assign it from the assignments available on *Connect*.) Choose from additional exercises on pp. 68–70 of this manual for classroom activities.	Chapter 3
20	**Persuasive Speeches**	
21	**Persuasive Speeches**	
22	**Persuasive Speeches**	
23	**Persuasive Speeches**	

Class Meeting	Topic—Activity	Reading
24	**Commemorative Speaking** Assign commemorative speech. Focus class discussion on exercise 3, text p. 363. Show "Elie Wiesel," "My Crazy Aunt Sue," or "The Massachusetts 54th" from the DVD of student speeches that accompanies this edition of *The Art of Public Speaking*. See pp. 234–235, 235–236, and 424–427 of this manual for commentary on these speeches.	Chapter 18, especially pp. 358–361
25	**Using Language Effectively** Focus class discussion on selections from exercises 1–3, text p. 237; Using Public Speaking in Your Career, text p. 231; and additional exercises on pp. 153–158 of this manual.	Chapter 12
26	**Using Language Effectively** Have students prepare a brief analysis of King's speech as directed in exercise 4, text p. 237. Show the video of "I Have a Dream" in class and focus discussion on King's use of language. For analysis of King's speech, see pp. 149–152 of this manual.	Martin Luther King, "I Have a Dream," pp. A2–A5
27	**Commemorative Speeches**	
28	**Commemorative Speeches**	
29	**Commemorative Speeches**	
30	**Summary and Review for Final Examination**	

OUTLINE FOR A 10-WEEK, 40-HOUR QUARTER

Class Meeting	Topic—Activity	Reading
1	**Course Overview** Introduce yourself; hand out syllabi; explain grading and attendance policies. Assign introductory speeches.	
2	**Basic Principles of Speech Communication** Focus class discussion on selected exercises, text pp. 26–27, or additional exercises from pp. 52–55 of this manual. Explain introductory speeches; show "There's an App for That" and "Fork in the Road" from the DVD of student speeches that accompanies this edition of *The Art of Public Speaking*.	Chapter 1 and Chapter 4
3	**Ethics and Public Speaking** Focus class discussion on exercises 1 and 3, text p. 45. Have students develop a code of ethical speaking for their classroom as explained in additional exercise 1 on p. 61 of this manual.	Chapter 2
4	**Introductory Speeches**	
5	**Introductory Speeches**	
6	**Speaking to Inform** Assign informative speeches. Focus class discussion on kinds of informative speeches and guidelines for informative speaking. Show the needs improvement and final versions of "Medical Robots: From Science Fiction to Science Fact" and "The Hidden World of Chili Peppers" from the DVD of student speeches that accompanies this edition of *The Art of Public Speaking*. For discussion of "Medical Robots," see pp. 294–296 of the textbook and 185–188 of this manual; for discussion of "Chili Peppers," see pp. 303–311 of this manual.	Chapter 15
7	**Choosing Topics and Purposes** Focus class discussion on exercises 2–4, text pp. 94–95, and Using Public Speaking in Your Career, text p. 83.	Chapter 5

Class Meeting	Topic—Activity	Reading
8	**Analyzing the Audience** Focus class discussion on exercise 2, text p. 117, and Using Public Speaking in Your Career, text p. 119. Use additional exercise 1 or 4 on pp. 93–95 of this manual as a classroom activity.	Chapter 6
9	**Organizing the Speech** Focus class discussion on exercises 1–3 and Using Public Speaking in Your Career, text pp. 173, 181–182, and exercise 1, text p. 203. Use additional exercises as needed from pp. 121–124 and 131–133 of this manual. Show Part One of *Introductions, Conclusions, and Visual Aids*, which accompanies *The Art of Public Speaking*.	Chapters 9–10
10	**Outlining the Speech** Focus class discussion on exercise 1, text pp. 218–219, and Using Public Speaking in Your Career, text p. 215. Have students do the interactive outlining exercises in Chapter 11 at *Connect* as a homework assignment; discuss the results in class.	Chapter 11
11	**Delivering the Speech and Using Visual Aids** Select from exercises 1–3, text p. 257, or the additional exercises on pp. 164–171 of this manual. If visual aids are required for the informative speech, discuss exercise 2, text p. 275. Use additional exercise 2 on p. 177 of this manual as a classroom activity. Show Part Two of *Introductions, Conclusions, and Visual Aids*, which accompanies *The Art of Public Speaking*. If time allows, show a full speech that uses visual aids from the DVD of student speeches that accompanies this edition. Good candidates include "Medical Robots: From Science Fiction to Science Fact," "Yoga: Uniting Mind, Body, and Spirit," and "Securing Yourself Online."	Chapters 13–14
13	**Informative Speeches**	
14	**Informative Speeches**	
15	**Informative Speeches**	

Class Meeting	Topic—Activity	Reading
16	**Introduction to Persuasive Speaking** Assign persuasive speeches. Focus class discussion on selected exercises and Using Public Speaking in Your Career, text p. 317. Show "Phony Pharmaceuticals" from the DVD of student speeches that accompanies this edition of *The Art of Public Speaking*. For commentary on the speech, see textbook pp. 318–320 and pp. 201–207 of this manual.	Chapter 16
17	**Gathering Materials** Take a library tour—see additional exercise 1 on p. 103 of this manual. Assign selected exercises from text p. 139 or from p. 103 of this manual.	Chapter 7
18	**Using Supporting Materials** Focus class discussion on exercises 1–2, text p. 163. Or select from among the additional exercises on pp. 113–115 of this manual.	Chapter 8
19	**Methods of Persuasion** Focus class discussion on selected exercises and Using Public Speaking in Your Career, text pp. 342 and 251. Use additional exercise 3 on pp. 229–230 of this manual as a classroom activity. Show "The Dangers of Cell Phones" from the DVD of student speeches that accompanies this edition of *The Art of Public Speaking*. For commentary on the speech, see textbook pp. 346–349 and pp. 226–227 of this manual.	Chapter 17
20	**Listening to Speeches** Focus class discussion on exercise 2, text p. 61. (The Listening Self-Evaluation Worksheet is available on p. 71 of this manual, or you can assign it from the assignments available on *Connect*.) Choose from additional exercises on pp. 68–70 of this manual for classroom activities.	Chapter 4
21	**Persuasive Speeches**	
22	**Persuasive Speeches**	
23	**Persuasive Speeches**	
24	**Persuasive Speeches**	

Class Meeting	Topic—Activity	Reading
25	**Midterm Examination**	
26	**Commemorative Speaking** Assign commemorative speech. Focus class discussion on exercise 3, text p. 363. Show "Elie Wiesel," "My Crazy Aunt Sue," or "The Massachusetts 54th" from the DVD of student speeches that accompanies this edition of *The Art of Public Speaking*. See pp. 234–235, 235–236, and 424–427 of this manual for commentary on these speeches.	Chapter 18, especially pp. 358–361
27	**Using Language Effectively** Focus class discussion on selections from exercises 1–3, text p. 237; Using Public Speaking in Your Career, text p. 231; and additional exercises on pp. 153–158 of this manual.	Chapter 12
28	**Using Language Effectively** Have students prepare a brief analysis of King's speech as directed in exercise 4, text p. 237. Show the video of "I Have a Dream" in class and focus discussion on King's use of language. For analysis of King's speech, see pp. 149–152 of this manual.	Martin Luther King, "I Have a Dream," pp. A2–A5
29	**Commemorative Speeches**	
30	**Commemorative Speeches**	
31	**Commemorative Speeches**	
32	**The Final Speech** Assign final speeches and begin review of elements students most need to concentrate on in preparing the final speech. Major items usually are supporting materials, organization and outlining, and delivery.	
33	**Preparing for the Final Speech: Supporting Materials** Focus class discussion on selected exercises from Chapter 8, or on analyzing speeches from pp. A1–A15 of the text or from Part Five of this manual.	Review Chapter 8

Class Meeting	Topic—Activity	Reading
34	**Preparing for the Final Speech: Organization and Outlining** Focus class discussion on selected exercises from Chapters 9–11 and additional exercises from this manual.	Review Chapters 9–11
35	**Preparing for the Final Speech: Delivery** By this point in the course, many students are ready to work on polishing their delivery skills. Choose from among the exercises in Chapter 13 of the text and the additional exercises on pp. 164–171 of this manual.	Review Chapter 13
36	**Final Speeches**	
37	**Final Speeches**	
38	**Final Speeches**	
39	**Final Speeches**	
40	**Summary and Review for Final Examination**	

Part Two

Speaking Assignments

T here are many kinds of speaking assignments that can be used in conjunction with *The Art of Public Speaking*. Most of those described below are keyed to the course outlines presented in Part One of this manual. When there are two or more options offered for a round of speeches (Option A, Option B, etc.), you should select one option, so the entire class is performing the same assignment during that round of speeches.

In addition to the formal speaking assignments presented here, the Exercises for Critical Thinking in the book and the Additional Exercises and Activities in Part Four of this manual contain a number of suggestions for speaking activities.

Introductory Speeches

Option A: A Two-Minute Speech Introducing a Classmate

The speech should be delivered extemporaneously from brief notes that occupy no more than one side of a single 4 x 6 index card. Stress that students are not to read their speeches and should use as much eye contact as possible.

In preparation for the speech, have students pair off and interview one another. The interviewing can be done in the last 15 to 20 minutes of the first class meeting. The assignment usually works better, however, if students conduct their interviews out of class. This gives them time to prepare questions for the interviews and allows for longer, more flexible interviews.

In their speeches, students will need to provide basic information such as the name of the person they are introducing, his or her home town, academic major, personal interests, hobbies, aspirations, and the like. But the speech need not be a routine recitation of biographical data. Encourage students to be creative in their interview questions and in their speeches.

Since the purpose of this speech is to give students a brief, initial exposure to speaking in front of an audience in a low-risk situation, many instructors do not affix a grade to it. Others, having found that students take the speech more seriously if they know they are being graded, weight it very lightly—in some cases, the same as a graded homework assignment, and in no circumstances more than 3 to 5 percent of the total grade for the class.

Option B: A Two-Minute Speech Introducing a Classmate

The speech should be delivered extemporaneously from brief notes that occupy no more than one side of a single 4 x 6 index card. Stress that students are not to read their speeches and should use as much eye contact as possible.

Unlike Option A above, this speech focuses specifically on the cultural background of the student being introduced to the class. Possible topics might include social customs, family traditions, holidays, clothing, food, religious traditions, sporting activities, and the like.

As in Option A, have students pair off and interview one another. The interviewing can be done in the last 15 to 20 minutes of the first class meeting. The assignment usually works better, however, if students conduct their interviews out of class. This gives them time to prepare questions for the interviews and allows for longer, more flexible interviews. If there is significant cultural diversity in your class, arrange the interview pairs so students interview someone whose cultural background is markedly different from their own.

Because this speech, like Option A, is designed to give students a brief, initial exposure to speaking in front of an audience in a low-risk situation, many instructors do not affix a grade to it. Others, having found that students take the speech more seriously if they know they are being graded, weight it very lightly—in some cases, the same as a graded homework assignment, and not more than 3 to 5 percent of the total class grade in any circumstance.

Option C: A Two-Minute Speech of Self-Introduction

The speech should be delivered extemporaneously from brief notes that occupy no more than one side of a single 4 x 6 index card. Stress that students are not to read their speeches and should use as much eye contact as possible.

In their speeches, students should begin by telling their name, home town, year in school, and academic major. They may focus the remainder of the speech however they wish—on describing an unusual or significant personal experience, on expressing an important personal belief or pet peeve, on explaining a favorite hobby or interest, on discussing someone who has been particularly influential in the speaker's life, etc. The purpose of the speech is not to persuade the audience to share the speaker's views, but to give the audience insight into the speaker's background, personality, attitudes, or aspirations.

Since the purpose of this speech is to give students a brief, initial exposure to speaking in front of an audience in a situation of minimal risk, many instructors do not affix a grade to it. Others weight it very lightly—in some cases, the same as a graded homework assignment, and in no circumstances more than 3 to 5 percent of the total grade for the class.

Option D: A Two-Minute Speech of Self-Introduction

The speech should be delivered extemporaneously from brief notes that occupy no more than one side of a single 4 x 6 index card. Stress that students are not to read their speeches and should use as much eye contact as possible.

In their speeches, students explain a significant aspect of their cultural background and how it has made a difference in their lives. Possible topics might include social customs, family traditions, holidays, clothing, food, religious traditions, sporting activities, etc. Encourage students to be creative in preparing their speeches and in finding ways to illustrate how the aspect of their culture they choose to explain relates to their personal lives.

Like the other options for introductory speeches, this speech is meant to give students a brief, initial exposure to speaking in front of an audience in a low-risk situation. Therefore, many instructors do not affix a grade to it. Others weight it very lightly—in some cases, the same as a graded homework assignment, and in no circumstances more than 3 to 5 percent of the total grade for the class. However you approach the grading of this speech, it works especially well as an ice breaker in classes with substantial cultural diversity.

**Option E: A Two-Minute Speech of Self-Introduction Based on
a Newspaper or Magazine Article**

The speech should be delivered extemporaneously from brief notes that occupy no more than one side of a single 4 x 6 index card. Stress that students are not to read their speeches and should use as much eye contact as possible.

To prepare for the speech, each student should consult a newspaper from the day they were born or a magazine such as Time or Newsweek from the week they were born. They should then select an item—article, advertisement, photograph, editorial, etc.—from the newspaper or magazine that relates to the speaker's life in some meaningful way. Using that item as a point of departure, the student should construct a speech that explains some aspect of her or his personality, background, beliefs, or aspirations.

This assignment usually produces fairly interesting and creative speeches of self-introduction. It also provides students some insight into the state of the world when they were born. Indeed, many students find this aspect of the assignment so interesting that they spend a fair amount of time just reading through the magazine or newspaper they have chosen.

A good ice-breaking assignment, this speech is designed to give students a brief, initial exposure to speaking in front of an audience in a situation of minimal risk. Many instructors do not affix a grade to it. Others, having found that students take the speech more seriously if they know they are being graded, weight it very lightly—in some cases, the same as a graded homework assignment, and not more than 3 to 5 percent of the total class grade in any circumstance.

**Option F: A Two-Minute Speech of Self-Introduction Based on
a Personal Object**

The speech should be delivered extemporaneously from brief notes that occupy no more than one side of a single 4 x 6 index card. Stress that students are not to read their speeches and should use as much eye contact as possible.

In preparation for this speech, have students select an object that represents a significant aspect of their background, personality, values, ambitions, etc. Using the chosen object as a point of departure, each student should develop a speech that explains how it relates to her or his life. For example, a journalism major might select a newspaper as a way to explain her or his professional goals. A new father might select a diaper as a vehicle for discussing his experiences as a parent. An avid tennis player might settle on a tennis racket to illustrate her passion about the sport.

If possible, students should bring the object of their speech to class on the day of their presentation. If this is not possible because the object is too large, too rare, or too valuable, the student should bring in a model, drawing, or photograph of the object. The purpose of this speech is not to explain the object in detail, but to use it as a vehicle for the speaker to introduce herself or himself to the class.

Like Option E, this assignment usually produces interesting and creative speeches of self-introduction. Since it is designed to give students a brief, initial exposure to speaking in front of an audience in a low-risk situation, many instructors do not affix a grade to it. Others weight it very lightly—in some cases, the same as a graded homework assignment, and in no circumstances more than 3 to 5 percent of the total grade for the class.

Informative Speeches

Option A: A Speech of 5 to 6 Minutes Informing the Audience About Some Object, Process, Concept, or Event

If desired, the assignment can be narrowed to concentrate specifically on a particular aspect of information-giving, such as definition, demonstration, or explanation. Encourage students to select topics that are useful and interesting. Students should turn in a complete preparation outline, but the speech itself should be delivered extemporaneously from a brief speaking outline.

Because this is the first graded speech, evaluation should focus on such basic matters as establishing eye contact, avoiding distracting mannerisms, formulating a sharp specific purpose statement, fulfilling the functions of an introduction and conclusion, limiting main points and arranging them properly, and employing connectives effectively.

Option B: A Speech of 5 to 6 Minutes Informing the Audience About Some Object, Process, Concept, or Event

Use of a visual aid is required. Students should turn in a complete preparation outline, but the speech itself should be delivered extemporaneously from a brief speaking outline.

This assignment is the same as Option A above, except for the stipulation that the speaker use a visual aid. Requiring a speech with visual aids gives students experience in a kind of speaking that is common in business and professional situations. Requiring such a speech early in the course usually increases student interest in the speeches, reduces the speakers' nervousness, and encourages them to rely less on their notes.

Urge students to be creative in selecting their visual aids and conscientious in following the guidelines for using them presented in Chapter 14.

Option C: A Speech of 5 to 6 Minutes Demonstrating the Steps of a Process or How to Perform the Steps of a Process

As in Option B above, use of a visual aid is required. Students should turn in a complete preparation outline, but the speech itself should be delivered extemporaneously from a brief speaking outline.

Students should make sure they present the steps of their process clearly and systematically, leaving out none of the essential steps along the way. In all but a few cases, these speeches will fall naturally into chronological order. Be sure students follow the guidelines for visual aids discussed in Chapter 14, and have them pay special attention to the section on speeches about processes in Chapter 15.

Option D: A Speech of 5 to 6 Minutes in Which Students Explain a Significant Aspect of a Culture Different From Their Own

Possible topics include social customs, family traditions, holidays, clothing, food, religious traditions, sporting activities, and the like. Students should turn in a preparation outline, but the speech itself should be delivered extemporaneously from a brief speaking outline.

Research is required for this speech. If students have had direct contact with a different culture, they should be encouraged to supplement their library research with their personal experience, but the speech is not to be a travelogue or a presentation on "My Summer in Europe" or "My Year as an Exchange Student in Brazil." On the other hand, a speech on how Europeans spend their summer vacations or on the educational system of Brazil would be fine.

Because students are sometimes resistant when they are required to speak about a different culture, it can be helpful to present this as the "World Travel Agency" speech. If you take this approach, tell students that the class is going to travel around the world via their speeches. They will "visit" as many different countries as there are students in the class.

To help students choose topics as quickly as possible, prepare two sets of 3 x 5 index cards. Write the name of a different country on each card in the first set. Then write two or three cultural features on each card in the second set. Put each set of cards in a separate bag and have students randomly pick a card from each bag. When they are finished, they will have a country card (for instance, Italy) and a topic card (including, for example, sports, family traditions, and politics). The student will then speak on one of those three aspects of Italian life.

However students choose their topics, they should be encouraged to be imaginative in composing their speeches. It is not enough to summarize basic information from an encyclopedia or the Internet about the country on which they are speaking. As in any informative speech, students need to explain ideas clearly and to think about ways to relate the topic to the audience. Some instructors require a visual aid for this speech. Others encourage the use of a visual aid but do not require it.

Persuasive Speeches

Option A: A Speech of 7 to 8 Minutes Designed to Persuade the Audience For or Against a Question of Policy

Speakers may seek either passive agreement or immediate action from the audience, though they should be encouraged to seek the latter if there is appropriate action for the audience to take. In either case, students should be sure to deal with all three basic issues of policy speeches—need, plan, and practicality. A complete preparation outline should be submitted. Delivery of the speech is to be extemporaneous.

This speech will require considerable research and skillful use of the methods of persuasion. Special emphasis should be given to evidence and reasoning. This is also an excellent assignment for stressing audience analysis and adaptation. You may wish to have students prepare an audience analysis questionnaire similar to that discussed in Chapter 6 to help them identify with and adapt to their target audience.

Option B: A Speech of 7 to 8 Minutes Designed to Persuade the Audience on Either a Question of Fact or a Question of Value

A complete preparation outline should be submitted. Delivery of the speech is to be extemporaneous.

As with Option A above, this speech will require considerable research and skillful handling of the methods of persuasion. Also as with Option A, this is an excellent assignment for stressing audience analysis and adaptation. Students who speak on a question of fact will need to give special attention to evidence and reasoning. Students who speak on a question of value must be sure to identify their standards for judgment and to justify their value judgment in light of those standards.

Commemorative Speech

A Speech of 4 to 5 Minutes Paying Tribute to a Person, a Group of People, an Institution, or an Idea

The subject may be historical or contemporary, famous or obscure. A preparation outline is not required. This speech should be written out and delivered from manuscript. Students should hand in their manuscripts after their speeches.

This assignment calls for a less didactic speech than the informative and persuasive speeches. It focuses particularly on the use of language, and it gives students experience in speaking from a manuscript. Encourage students to use language imaginatively and to experiment with the devices for enhancing clarity and vividness discussed in Chapter 12. Also stress that students must rehearse their speeches thoroughly, so as to present them with strong eye contact and dynamic vocal variety.

Final Speeches

Option A: A Speech of 8 to 10 Minutes That May Be Either Informative or Persuasive

A complete preparation outline should be required. Delivery of the speech is to be extemporaneous.

You can allow students to choose individually whether to give an informative speech or a persuasive speech. Usually, however, it is best to assign the entire class one or the other kind of speech. Whichever kind you assign, let students know that this speech is particularly important. Criteria for evaluation include all major aspects of speech preparation and delivery covered since the first day of class.

Option B: A Speech of 8 to 10 Minutes That Is to Be a Major Revision of an Informative or Persuasive Speech Given Earlier in the Term

A complete preparation outline should be required. Delivery of the speech is to be extemporaneous.

Because time is often cramped at the end of the term, this assignment provides for a full-length speech without requiring that students start from scratch in choosing and researching an entirely new topic. It also gives students an opportunity to learn more about the revision process, which is essential to speeches outside the classroom.

If this assignment is to succeed, you must tell each student which previous speech he or she is to revise, must be quite specific in identifying for each student the kinds of revisions that are necessary, and must make clear that major revisions—including additional research—are required if the speech is to receive a grade of B or better. Otherwise, you are likely to get little more than warmed-over rehashes of speeches you have already heard. Criteria for evaluation include all major aspects of speech preparation and delivery covered since the first day of class.

Option C: A Speech of 8 to 10 Minutes Informing the Audience About a Prominent Public Speaker

A complete preparation outline should be required. Delivery of the speech is to be extemporaneous.

Students can choose either a historical figure or a contemporary speaker for this assignment. In either case, students should deal with the following points in their speeches, though not necessarily in this order: (a) biographical background about the speaker; (b) the importance of public speaking in her or his career; (c) major ideas of her or his speeches; (d) analysis of the speaker's techniques, including organization, language, and delivery.

Complex and challenging, this speech requires substantial research and allows students to apply the principles learned in class to established public speakers. Although it usually works best in more advanced classes, it can succeed in the introductory course as well.

Make the assignment early in the course so students can work on it throughout the term. In addition, give students a list of speakers from which they can choose. One approach is to have them consult the Top 100 American Speeches of the 20th Century, which is available through AmericanRhetoric.com. You can also refer them to such books as *American Orators Before 1900* and *American Orators of the Twentieth Century*, both edited by Bernard K. Duffy and Halford R. Ryan; *Women's Voices in Our Time*, edited by Victoria L. DeFrancisco and Marvin D. Jensen; *We Shall Be Heard: Women Speakers in America*, edited by Patricia Scileppi Kennedy and Gloria Hartmann O'Shields; or *Voices of Multicultural America: Notable Speeches Delivered by African, Asian, Hispanic, and Native Americans, 1790-1995*, edited by Deborah Gillan Straub.

Encourage students to do all they can to make the speeches creative and interesting by following the guidelines for informative speaking discussed in Chapter 15. Students who choose historical speakers may be able to use photographs or slides as visual aids; those who speak on current figures might consider showing video clips of their subject in action. In either case, students should review Chapter 14 to make sure they use their visual aids properly and integrate them smoothly into the speech.

Impromptu Speech

A Two-Minute Speech to Be Delivered Impromptu

The focus of the speech may be informative, persuasive, or entertaining.

Create a set of topics such as my family, my hometown, my best friend, my favorite sport, my most embarrassing moment, my worst class, my biggest thrill, my biggest complaint, etc. Have students draw three topics and choose one to speak about. Give each speaker a few minutes to gather his or her thoughts before beginning to speak. You can do this by having the first three or four speakers choose their topics at the beginning of class. Then, as each speaker finishes, have a new student select his or her topic. Give the speakers time signals when they have one minute to go and then again when they have 30 seconds left.

This can be used as a regular, graded assignment or as an informal, non-graded speaking experience. In either case, try to keep the atmosphere low-key, since students are often particularly apprehensive about speaking impromptu.

For further discussion of approaches to impromptu speaking, see Additional Exercise/Activity 4 on pages 167–168 of this manual.

Problem-Solving Group Discussion with Symposium

Divide the class into small groups of four to six members. First, each group will be responsible for a problem-solving project in which they investigate a question of policy and recommend solutions to it. In their deliberations, the group should follow the reflective-thinking method of decision-making explained in Chapter 19. Members of the group should understand that this project will require research and group meetings outside of class.

Second, the group will be responsible for organizing and conducting a symposium in which the group presents its report to the class. One way to structure the symposium is to allow each speaker 4 to 5 minutes to explain the work of the group at each stage of the reflective-thinking process. Another approach is to have each speaker spend 4 to 5 minutes detailing some aspect of the group's recommended solutions. If time allows, follow the symposium with a question-and-answer session or general class discussion.

You can either assign topics to the groups or allow each group to choose its own topic. Students should be graded both on the quality of the group's presentation and on their individual contributions to the group.

For other approaches to this assignment, see Additional Exercises/Activities 3 and 4 on pages 248–249 of this manual.

Part Three

Evaluation and Grading

E valuating student work and assigning grades are among the most difficult tasks facing any teacher. Students take their grades very seriously, and if they believe they are being assessed unfairly, they will quickly develop a negative view of the teacher and, perhaps, of the course in general. Moreover, the self-confidence that is essential for beginning speakers can be seriously damaged if the teacher is insensitive to their need for encouragement and positive reinforcement.

Yet instructors also have an obligation to assess students objectively on the quality of the work they produce. You cannot give students higher grades than they deserve just to maintain good feelings in the class. Striking a balance between the psychological needs of the students and the integrity of the grading system is one of the most difficult challenges facing a teacher of public speaking.

There are two major considerations in meeting this challenge. The first is assessing student work fairly, objectively, and consistently. The second is explaining your assessment to students so they accept it as fair, objective, and consistent. The former revolves around your grading criteria and how you apply them. The latter depends on your ability to communicate effectively with students about your assessment of their work, and is every bit as important as the assessment itself. As this section of the manual proceeds, we shall address both of these aspects of grading and evaluation.

Criteria, Exams, and Grading Scales

When grading speeches, do all you can to let students know when and how they will be evaluated. Explain speech assignments clearly and notify students of their speaking dates well in advance. Tell students the objectives of each assignment so they will know what to concentrate on in preparing their speeches. Also, be as specific as possible about your criteria for grading speeches. You may find it helpful to give students, on the first day of class, a sheet similar to the one on page 56, listing your basic criteria for grading speeches.

Although there is no substitute for experience when it comes to grading speeches, there are some steps you can take, if you are a new instructor, to sharpen your evaluative skills. One is to talk about grading with experienced instructors who are willing to share their philosophy, methods, and criteria. Another is to view a number of student speeches—either on videotape or in other sections—and see how your assessments of them stack up against those of veteran teachers. Yet another is to have a more seasoned instructor visit your class on a day when students are giving speeches. By comparing the grades you assigned with those the other instructor would have assigned had it been his or her class, you can get a good sense of whether you need to make any adjustments in either your criteria or your methods of evaluation.

Whereas the speeches indicate how well students have mastered the skills of speechmaking, written examinations gauge how well students understand the principles underlying those skills. There are many approaches to written examinations in public speaking classes. Some instructors give one or two major examinations. Others supplement major examinations with periodic brief quizzes. Still others rely solely on a series of quizzes. Some instructors prefer objective questions;

others essay questions; others a mixture of question types. To help you construct examinations, the *Test Bank* that accompanies *The Art of Public Speaking* contains 2,600 true-false, multiple-choice, short-answer, and essay questions. In addition, it offers preconstructed true-false quizzes for each chapter of the book, as well as three complete sample final examinations that illustrate different approaches to testing and evaluation. Finally, the Test Bank includes a guest essay by Anita Vangelisti of the University of Texas on test construction and assessment.

There arc a number of ways to weight individual assignments and determine final grades. Below is one system based on the assignments in the course outlines presented in Part One of this manual. It can be adjusted easily to reflect your assignments and your approach to determining final grades.

Assignment	Proportion of Final Grade
informative speech	10 percent
persuasive speech	20 percent
commemorative speech	15 percent
final speech	20 percent
examinations	25 percent
class participation and miscellaneous assignments	10 percent

To maintain the integrity of your grading system, you will need a firm attendance policy. Public speaking is a participation course. It also runs on a very tight schedule. If students habitually skip class when they are assigned to speak, the syllabus will be thrown off very quickly. Many instructors assign an automatic grade penalty to any student who fails to deliver a speech on the specified day because of an unexcused absence. Many also limit students to a maximum of two or three unexcused absences for the entire course. Excessive absences result in a reduction of the student's final grade. Whatever policy you adopt, be sure to write it on your syllabus so students will be aware of it from the very beginning of the course.

Evaluation Forms

No matter how grades are assigned, it is important that students receive written evaluations of their speeches. Because such evaluations are usually the major channel of feedback from the instructor about the speeches, they need to be handled with great care. Evaluation forms should indicate clearly the elements of the speech on which the student is being assessed. They should also allow room for written comments.

Pages 39 to 44 of this manual contain six speech evaluation forms. The first three are suitable for almost any kind of speech. The fourth is designed for persuasive speeches on questions of policy, the fifth for speeches using Monroe's motivated sequence, and the sixth for commemorative speeches. The last three are included to suggest how evaluation forms can be adapted to the specific requirements of particular speech assignments.

In addition to varying slightly in content, each form has a somewhat different format. You may wish to use these forms as they are, or you may prefer to create your own by experimenting with formats and evaluation items. Regardless of which form you use, if you give your students a copy at the beginning of each speech assignment, they can use it as a checklist when preparing their speeches.

Strategies of Evaluation

The most difficult task when evaluating speeches is to maintain a positive, encouraging tone while at the same time being candid with students about the shortcomings of their speeches. Evaluations should be realistic in appraising the speech, but they should be offered in a kind, optimistic tone that provides hope and encouragement for future speeches.

Whether you are preparing a written evaluation, discussing speeches in class, or meeting individually with students in a post-speech conference, it is usually a good idea to adopt the "good news/bad news" strategy of evaluation. That is, focus first on what the student did well in her or his speech. Be sure to find some positive comments, even if nothing more than "Excellent choice of topic," "Nice job of meeting the time limits," or "You certainly have a strong speaking voice." In most cases, you will have a fair number of substantive positive comments to make.

Once you have provided the "good news," you can turn to the "bad news"—that is, comments about the weaknesses of the speech. There is no need, in composing these comments, to construct a high-powered rhetorical analysis. Your objective is to help students grow as speakers by letting them know exactly what they need to correct and what steps they can take to improve. Try to give each speaker a few specific items to work on in the next speech. This will focus your students' energies and give them a concrete sense of your expectations.

Evaluations by Students

It is also useful to have students fill out evaluation forms on their peers' speeches. One way to do this is to assign each student a partner who is responsible for providing a detailed, constructive evaluation of their partner's speech. Another approach is to assign a group of students as critics for each day's speeches. These students should fill out an evaluation form for each speech delivered that day. By the end of the unit, each student will have served as a critic for one day.

There are several schools of thought about dealing with student evaluations. Some instructors read the evaluations and grade them to encourage thorough, helpful, encouraging critiques. Whether or not you assign a grade to the evaluations, you should always look them over before giving them to the speaker to make sure they are sufficiently detailed and do not contain any destructive comments.

How much weight should be put on student evaluations in determining the speaker's grade? There are obvious dangers in having a student's grade hinge in any formal way on the responses of his or her classmates. In my own experience, student evaluations are most helpful as a way to encourage students to listen carefully to their classmates' speeches and to provide additional feedback to speakers.

In most cases, the students' judgments on such basic matters as organization and delivery will reflect fairly closely those of the instructor. There is always the possibility, however, that you will rate highly a speech to which students give low ratings, or vice versa. In such circumstances, you should double check your evaluation to make sure you are satisfied with it. If, after doing so, you are convinced that your original assessment is correct, you should write a note to the speaker on your evaluation form noting that her or his classmates appear to have overestimated (or underestimated) the speech and that the grade reflects your judgment rather than that of the student evaluators.

If your evaluation of the speech is higher than that of the speaker's classmates, the speaker will gladly defer to your wisdom and insight. If your evaluation is lower than that of the speaker's classmates, the speaker may challenge your wisdom and insight. In such circumstances, you should explain exactly what was wrong with the speech and how the speaker can improve next time. You should not allow students to browbeat you into changing your evaluation.

Finally, it is important to recognize that, no matter what you do, you cannot please all students when it comes to evaluation and grading. Even the most experienced, most effective teachers have students who are disgruntled over their grades. All you can do is assess your students fairly and seek to communicate that assessment clearly, concisely, and constructively. The rest is up to your students.

Criteria Used for Evaluating Speeches

The *average speech* (grade C) should meet the following criteria:

1. Conform to the kind of speech assigned—informative, persuasive, etc.

2. Be ready for presentation on the assigned date

3. Conform to the time limit

4. Fulfill any special requirements of the assignment—preparing an outline, using visual aids, conducting an interview, etc.

5. Have a clear specific purpose and central idea

6. Have an identifiable introduction, body, and conclusion

7. Show reasonable directness and competence in delivery

8. Be free of serious errors in grammar, pronunciation, and word usage

The *above average speech* (grade B) should meet the preceding criteria and also:

1. Deal with a challenging topic

2. Fulfill all major functions of a speech introduction and conclusion

3. Display clear organization of main points and supporting materials

4. Support main points with evidence that meets the tests of accuracy, relevance, objectivity, and sufficiency

5. Exhibit proficient use of connectives—transitions, internal previews, internal summaries, and signposts

6. Be delivered skillfully enough so as not to distract attention from the speaker's message

The *superior speech* (grade A) should meet all the preceding criteria and also:

1. Constitute a genuine contribution by the speaker to the knowledge or beliefs of the audience

2. Sustain positive interest, feeling, and/or commitment among the audience

3. Contain elements of vividness and special interest in the use of language

4. Be delivered in a fluent, polished manner that strengthens the impact of the speaker's message

The *below average* speech (grade D or F) is seriously deficient in the criteria required for the C speech.

Speech Evaluation Form

Speaker _____

Topic _____

Rate the speaker on each point: *E-excellent*   *G-good*   *A-average*   *F-fair*   *P-poor*

COMMENTS

INTRODUCTION

Gained attention and interest	E	G	A	F	P
Introduced topic clearly	E	G	A	F	P
Established credibility	E	G	A	F	P
Previewed body of speech	E	G	A	F	P
Related to audience	E	G	A	F	P

BODY

Main points clear	E	G	A	F	P
Main points fully supported	E	G	A	F	P
Organization well planned	E	G	A	F	P
Language accurate	E	G	A	F	P
Language clear, concise	E	G	A	F	P
Language appropriate	E	G	A	F	P
Connectives effective	E	G	A	F	P

CONCLUSION

Prepared audience for ending	E	G	A	F	P
Reinforced central idea	E	G	A	F	P

DELIVERY

Maintained eye contact	E	G	A	F	P
Used voice effectively	E	G	A	F	P
Used physical action effectively	E	G	A	F	P
Presented visual aids well	E	G	A	F	P

OVERALL EVALUATION

Topic challenging	E	G	A	F	P
Specific purpose well chosen	E	G	A	F	P
Speech adapted to audience	E	G	A	F	P
Speech completed in time limit	E	G	A	F	P

Speech Evaluation Form

Speaker _____

Topic _____

Rate the speaker on each point: *E-excellent*   *G-good*   *A-average*   *F-fair*   *P-poor*

INTRODUCTION

Gained attention and interest	E G A F P
Introduced topic clearly	E G A F P
Related to audience	E G A F P
Established credibility	E G A F P
Previewed body of speech	E G A F P

BODY

Main points clear	E G A F P
Main points fully supported	E G A F P
Organization well planned	E G A F P
Language accurate	E G A F P
Language clear	E G A F P
Language appropriate	E G A F P
Connectives effective	E G A F P

CONCLUSION

Prepared audience for ending	E G A F P
Reinforced central idea	E G A F P
Vivid ending	E G A F P

DELIVERY

Began speech without rushing	E G A F P
Maintained strong eye contact	E G A F P
Avoided distracting mannerisms	E G A F P
Articulated words clearly	E G A F P
Used pauses effectively	E G A F P
Used vocal variety to add impact	E G A F P
Prepared visual aids well	E G A F P
Presented visual aids well	E G A F P
Communicated enthusiasm for topic	E G A F P
Departed from lectern without rushing	E G A F P

OVERALL EVALUATION

Met assignment	E G A F P
Topic challenging	E G A F P
Specific purpose well chosen	E G A F P
Message adapted to audience	E G A F P
Speech completed within time limit	E G A F P
Held interest of audience	E G A F P

What did the speaker do most effectively? _____

_____

What should the speaker pay special attention to next time? _____

_____

General Comments _____

_____

_____

Speech Evaluation Form

Speaker _____

Topic _____

Rate the speaker on each point: *E-excellent*   *G-good*   *A-average*   *F-fair*   *P-poor*

What was the speaker's specific purpose?   _____

_____

Introduction gained attention	E	G	A	F	P
Introduction revealed the topic clearly	E	G	A	F	P
Introduction related topic to the audience	E	G	A	F	P
Introduction established credibility	E	G	A	F	P
Introduction previewed the body of the speech	E	G	A	F	P

List the main points of the speech. On the line at right, note the kinds of supporting materials used for each: *S-statistics*   *E-examples*   *T-testimony*

I. _____   _____

II. _____   _____

III. _____   _____

IV. _____   _____

V. _____   _____

What pattern of organization did the speaker use?   _____

_____

Conclusion reinforced the central idea	E	G	A	F	P
Conclusion ended on a strong note	E	G	A	F	P
Speaker's language was clear	E	G	A	F	P
Speaker's language was vivid	E	G	A	F	P
Speaker's language was appropriate	E	G	A	F	P
Speaker maintained strong eye contact	E	G	A	F	P
Speaker had sufficient vocal variety	E	G	A	F	P
Speaker articulated words clearly	E	G	A	F	P
Speaker seemed poised and confident	E	G	A	F	P
Speaker communicated enthusiasm for the topic	E	G	A	F	P
Overall evaluation of the speech	E	G	A	F	P

41

Policy Speech Evaluation Form

Speaker _____

Topic _____

Rate the speaker on each point: *E-excellent*   *G-good*   *A-average*   *F-fair*   *P-poor*

1. Introduction gained attention and interest	E	G	A	F	P
2. Main points clearly organized and easy to follow	E	G	A	F	P
3. Main points supported with sufficient evidence	E	G	A	F	P
4. Evidence from qualified sources	E	G	A	F	P
5. Reasoning clear and sound	E	G	A	F	P
6. Need issue dealt with convincingly	E	G	A	F	P
7. Speaker's plan clearly explained	E	G	A	F	P
8. Practicality of plan demonstrated	E	G	A	F	P
9. Connectives used effectively	E	G	A	F	P
10. Language clear and concise	E	G	A	F	P
11. Conclusion reinforced the central idea	E	G	A	F	P
12. Sufficient eye contact	E	G	A	F	P
13. Voice used to add impact	E	G	A	F	P
14. Physical action effective	E	G	A	F	P
15. Speech well adapted to the audience	E	G	A	F	P
16. Overall evaluation of the speech	E	G	A	F	P

Comments: _____

_____

_____

_____

_____

_____

Monroe's Motivated Sequence Evaluation Form

Speaker _____

Topic _____

Rate the speaker on each point:　　*E-excellent*　　*G-good*　　*A-average*　　*F-fair*　　*P-poor*

COMMENTS

ATTENTION STEP

Gained attention of listeners	E	G	A	F	P
Introduced topic clearly	E	G	A	F	P
Showed importance of topic to this audience	E	G	A	F	P

NEED STEP

Need clearly explained	E	G	A	F	P
Need demonstrated with evidence	E	G	A	F	P
Need related to audience	E	G	A	F	P

SATISFACTION STEP

Plan clearly explained	E	G	A	F	P
Plan well thought out	E	G	A	F	P

VISUALIZATION STEP

Practicality of plan shown	E	G	A	F	P
Benefits of plan related to audience	E	G	A	F	P

ACTION STEP

Call for specific action by audience	E	G	A	F	P
Vivid concluding appeal	E	G	A	F	P

DELIVERY

Maintained eye contact	E	G	A	F	P
Extemporaneous and conversational	E	G	A	F	P
Poised, confident presentation	E	G	A	F	P
Words articulated clearly	E	G	A	F	P
Physical action effective	E	G	A	F	P
Communicated enthusiasm for topic	E	G	A	F	P

OVERALL EVALUATION

Language clear, concise	E	G	A	F	P
Connectives effective	E	G	A	F	P
Completed in time limit	E	G	A	F	P

Commemorative Speech Evaluation Form

Speaker _____

Topic _____

Rate the speaker on each point: *E-excellent*   *G-good*   *A-average*   *F-fair*   *P-poor*

Introduction gained attention		E	G	A	F	P
Subject introduced clearly		E	G	A	F	P
Main ideas easily followed		E	G	A	F	P
Language clear		E	G	A	F	P
Language vivid		E	G	A	F	P
Topic dealt with creatively		E	G	A	F	P
Speech adapted to audience		E	G	A	F	P
Sufficient eye contact		E	G	A	F	P
Voice used effectively		E	G	A	F	P
Physical action effective		E	G	A	F	P
General evaluation of the speech		E	G	A	F	P

Comments

Part Four

Chapter-by-Chapter
Guide to
The Art of Public Speaking

The following pages contain guides for using each chapter of *The Art of Public Speaking*. Each chapter guide consists of a list of chapter objectives, an outline of the chapter, discussions of the Exercises for Critical Thinking and the Using Public Speaking in Your Career scenario from the textbook, and additional exercises and activities for classroom use or homework assignments. Student worksheets and surveys are also provided at the end of many of the chapter guides.

The chapter guides are all produced in Microsoft Word so you can easily combine exercises and activities to produce your own handouts and so you can revise the worksheets to adapt them to your individual needs. Headers have been removed from the worksheets so they won't need to be removed for printing. The page numbers on the worksheets have been moved to the bottom of the page.

Speaking in Public

Chapter Objectives

After reading this chapter, students should be able to:

1. Explain the value of a course in public speaking.

2. Discuss the long tradition of studying public speaking.

3. Identify the major similarities and differences between public speaking and everyday conversation.

4. Explain why a certain amount of nervousness is normal—even desirable—for a public speaker.

5. Discuss methods of controlling nervousness and of making it work for, rather than against, a speaker.

6. Identify the basic elements of the speech communication process.

7. Explain how the cultural diversity of today's world can influence public speaking situations.

8. Define ethnocentrism and explain why public speakers need to avoid it when addressing audiences of diverse racial, ethnic, or cultural background.

Chapter Outline

I.   Public speaking is a vital means of communication.

   A.   During modern times, men and women around the globe have used public speaking to spread their ideas and influence.

   B.   The need for public speaking will touch almost every person at some time in her or his life.

      1.   Public speaking helps people succeed in nearly all professions.

      2.   Public speaking is a vital means of civic engagement.

      3.   Public speaking is a form of empowerment.

II. Public speaking has been taught and studied around the globe for thousands of years.

   A.   The importance of effective public speaking has been recognized for millennia in many cultures.

   B.   In classical Greece and Rome, public speaking played a central role in education and civic life and was studied extensively.

   C.   Over the centuries, many notable thinkers have dealt with issues of rhetoric, speech, and language.

   D.   The aim of a public speaking course is to help students apply those methods and strategies.

      1.   As students read this book, they should keep in mind that the principles of public speaking are derived from a long tradition and have been confirmed by a substantial body of research.

      2.   The more students know about those principles, the more effective they will be in their own speeches, as well as in listening to the speeches of other people.

III. Public speaking and everyday conversation have a number of similarities and require similar skills.

   A.   In both, people organize their thoughts logically.

   B.   In both, people tailor their message to the audience.

   C.   In both, people tell a story for maximum impact.

   D.   In both, people adapt to feedback from listeners.

IV. There are three key differences between public speaking and everyday conversation.

   A.   Public speaking is more highly structured than ordinary conversation.

   B.   Public speaking requires more formal language than ordinary conversation.

   C.   Public speaking requires a different method of delivery from ordinary conversation.

   D.   With study and practice, most people are able to master these differences and expand their conversational skills into speechmaking.

V. One of the major concerns of students in any speech class is stage fright.

    A. It is entirely normal to feel nervous about the prospect of giving a public speech.

    B. Even experienced public speakers have stage fright before their presentations.

    C. There are six major steps students can take to control their nervousness and make it a positive force in their speeches.

        1. One is to take a speech class in which they will learn about speechmaking and gain speaking experience.

        2. Another is to be thoroughly prepared for every speech they present.

        3. It is also crucial that speakers think positively about themselves and the speech experience.

        4. Using the power of visualization is another excellent way to combat stage fright.

        5. Most speakers are also helped by knowing that their nervousness is usually not visible to the audience.

        6. It is also important not to expect perfection when delivering a speech.

    D. In addition, there are a number of specific tips that can help students deal with nervousness.

        1. Be at your physical and mental best when speaking.

        2. Quietly tighten and relax hand or leg muscles while waiting to speak.

        3. Take a few slow, deep breaths before starting to speak.

        4. Work especially hard on your introduction.

        5. Make eye contact with people in the audience.

        6. Concentrate on communicating with the audience rather than on worrying about your nervousness.

        7. Use visual aids to help occupy the attention of the audience.

VI. Public speaking helps people develop critical thinking skills.

    A. Critical thinking involves a number of skills.

        1. Critical thinking involves being able to assess the strengths and weaknesses of an argument.

        2. Critical thinking involves distinguishing fact from opinion.

        3. Critical thinking involves judging the credibility of sources.

        4. Critical thinking involves assessing the quality of evidence.

        5. Critical thinking involves discerning the relationships among ideas.

    B. These—and other—critical thinking skills are enriched by a public speaking class.

VII. There are seven elements of the speech communication process.

    A. Speech communication begins with a speaker.

    B. The message is whatever a speaker communicates to someone else.

C. The channel is the means by which a message is communicated.

D. The listener is the person who receives the communicated message.

    1. Everything a speaker says is filtered through a listener's frame of reference.

    2. Because people have different frames of reference, a public speaker must take care to adapt the message to the particular audience being addressed.

E. Feedback consists of messages sent from the listener to the speaker.

F. Interference is anything that impedes the communication of a message.

    1. Interference can be either external or internal.

    2. Successful public speakers work to hold their listeners' attention despite interference.

G. The situation is the time and place in which speech communication occurs.

VIII. Public speakers need to be aware of and responsive to today's multicultural world.

A. The United States has become the most diverse society on the face of the earth.

B. Cultural diversity is more than a U.S. phenomenon.

C. Diversity and multiculturalism are such basic facts of life in today's world that they affect many public speaking situations.

D. It is especially important for public speakers to avoid ethnocentrism.

    1. Ethnocentrism is the belief that one's own culture or group is superior to all others.

    2. Speakers can avoid ethnocentrism by respecting diverse cultural values.

    3. Speakers can also take specific steps to adapt to listeners of diverse cultural, racial, and ethnic backgrounds.

E. Listeners also need to avoid ethnocentrism.

Exercises for Critical Thinking   *(from text pages 26–27)*

1. Think back on an important conversation you had recently in which you wanted to achieve a particular result. (*Examples*: Asking your employer to change your work schedule; explaining to a friend how to change the oil and filter in a car; attempting to talk your spouse or partner into buying the computer you like rather than the one he or she prefers.) Work up a brief analysis of the conversation.

    In your analysis, explain the following: (1) your purpose in the conversation and the message strategy you chose to achieve your purpose; (2) the communication channels used during the conversation and how they affected the outcome; (3) the interference—internal or external—you encountered during the conversation; (4) the steps you took to adjust to feedback; (5) the strategic changes you would make in preparing for and carrying out the conversation if you had it to do over again.

Discussion: This exercise can be a very effective vehicle for class discussion about the basic elements of the speech communication process and how they interact. By stressing the strategic aspects of everyday conversation, this exercise also points to the similarities between conversation and public speaking. Students should find that much of the strategic thinking that goes into preparing a speech is quite similar to the strategic thinking they often put into ordinary conversation.

2. Divide a sheet of paper into two columns. Label one column "Characteristics of an Effective Public Speaker." Label the other column "Characteristics of an Ineffective Public Speaker." In the columns, list and briefly explain what you believe to be the five most important characteristics of effective and ineffective speakers. Be prepared to discuss your ideas in class.

Discussion: When this exercise is discussed in class, it provides the basis for generating a set of criteria for effective speechmaking that is agreed upon by the entire class. You, of course, should know ahead of time the criteria you want to stress, so you can direct the class discussion in that direction.

3. On the basis of the lists you developed for Exercise 2, candidly evaluate your own strengths and weaknesses as a speaker. Identify the three primary aspects of speechmaking you most want to improve.

Discussion: This exercise encourages students to set specific goals for improving their public speaking. At various times in the term, you and the student can weigh her or his progress against the goals. Some teachers have students reassess their goals every few weeks. At the end of the course, you may want students to judge how well they have met their goals and to reassess their strengths and weaknesses as speakers in light of what they have learned in the course.

Using Public Speaking in Your Career   *(from text page 17)*

It's been three years since you graduated from college. After gaining experience as an administrative assistant at a major office equipment manufacturer, you've just been promoted to marketing manager for office copiers. Though you have occasionally given brief reports to other members of your work team, you're now facing your first speech to a large audience. At your company's annual sales meeting, you will address the sales force about the company's new multifunction printer/copiers, and how to sell them to dealers such as Office Depot and OfficeMax.

You're pleased to have this opportunity and you know it shows the company's faith in your abilities. Yet the closer you get to the day of the speech, the harder it is to control the butterflies in your stomach. There will be 200 people in your audience, including all the sales managers and regional managers, in addition to the sales force. All eyes will be on you. It's important that you come across as confident and well informed, but you're afraid your stage fright will send the opposite message. What strategies will you use to control your nerves and make them work for you?

Discussion: Like the other Using Public Speaking in Your Career scenarios through-out the book, this one is intended to challenge students to apply their critical-thinking skills to a wide range of practical, career-oriented situations. Some of the scenarios have definite correct answers; others, like this one, allow for a wide range of responses and are designed to provide a spur for class discussion. In this case, you can anticipate that students will mention the major strategies discussed in the chapter for controlling stage fright—being fully prepared for the speech, thinking positively, using the power of visualization, recognizing that most nervousness is not visible to the audience, and not expecting perfection—but you should encourage them to come up with others as well.

Additional Exercises and Activities

1. On the first day of class, have students fill out and return the questionnaire on page 56 of this manual. This will give you a pretty clear early picture of the background and needs of the students enrolled in your class.

2. If your class has a fair number of international students, conduct a class discussion in which the international students compare and contrast common nonverbal signals in their countries with those in the United States.

    Discussion: Depending on the composition of your class, this can be an excellent way to generate discussion of the nonverbal dimension of intercultural communica-tion. The exercise also sensitizes U.S. students to the communication customs of students from abroad and to the adaptations international students have to make to communicate effectively in the United States. If you begin the discussion with such basic signals as those for "hello," "goodbye," "come here," "okay," and the like, it will usually move naturally to more complex signals. Given the nature of college stu-dents, the discussion will also probably turn at some point to obscene gestures un-less you declare that subject off limits.

3. Give students the following assignment: Think of a situation in which you sought to understand the message of, or to convey your own message to, someone from a different culture. The situation might have involved interpersonal communication, public speaking, or a mass media message such as a film or a television program. Write a brief analysis in which you explain (a) the participants in the communication situation, (b) the message that was meant to be communicated, (c) the difficulty you had communicating—or understanding—the message, (d) the outcome of the situation, and (e) what the situation reveals about the complexity of communicating with people of different cultural backgrounds. Be prepared to present your analysis in class.

Discussion: This exercise works best in classes in which a fair proportion of students have had personal communication with people from different cultures. It can provide an excellent vehicle for discussing ethnocentrism and the barriers it poses to intercultural communication. Because students are dealing with their own experiences, the exercise helps make the abstract concept of ethnocentrism more immediate and personal.

4. Over the years a number of metaphors have been used to describe the mix of cultures in the United States. Best known is the melting pot metaphor, which originated in 1908 with *The Melting-Pot*, a play by Israel Zangwill, an English writer of Russian-Jewish heritage. According to this metaphor, the United States is like the kind of huge container used to melt and mix steel and other metals. As immigrants come to the United States, they blend together into one assimilated culture that is stronger than the individual cultures of which it is composed.

A second metaphor compares the U.S. to a set of streams or rivers each of which is composed of many people from different cultures. The streams or rivers flow separately, maintaining their unique identity until at some point they come together to form a mighty watershed in which the individual streams and rivers are combined into one.

In a third metaphor the U.S. is compared to a garden salad in which different cultures, like the different ingredients in a salad, are combined and tossed to create the final product without losing their individual texture and flavor.

A fourth metaphor likens the U.S. to a giant quilt or tapestry in which people of different cultural backgrounds, like the individual threads and patterns of a tapestry, are woven together to produce the overall design. Like the salad metaphor, in which the various ingredients retain their own texture and flavor, the tapestry metaphor stresses the uniqueness and importance of the individual threads, patterns, and colors out of which the whole fabric is constructed.

After presenting these metaphors to the class, conduct a class discussion in which students consider the strengths and weaknesses of each metaphor for describing the cultural diversity of life in the United States.

Discussion: This exercise can be conducted in small groups or with the class as a whole. In either case, it is an excellent vehicle for prompting reflection about cultural diversity in the United States. Here are some issues to consider:

First, although the melting pot metaphor was widely employed through most of the twentieth century, it has fallen into some disfavor in recent years because it does not stress the capacity of cultural groups to maintain their individual identities as they "melt" into a single American culture. Second, the comparison of the U.S. to a set of streams or rivers that combine to form a single body of water allows for the uniqueness of individual cultures until the point at which they merge into a common current. But this metaphor also implies that the streams and rivers are inferior to or less consequential than the great body of water they form when brought together.

Third, in both the salad and tapestry metaphors, individual elements of the whole retain their identity and uniqueness even as they are combined to create a larger entity. Comparing the U.S. to a tapestry, however, suggests that at some point U.S. culture as a whole is an inert, finished product, when in fact it is constantly changing and evolving. The salad metaphor, on the other hand, captures both the dynamic quality of cultural diversity in the U.S. and the distinctiveness of individual cultural groups. For fuller analysis of these metaphors, see Myron W. Lustig and Jolene Koester, *Intercultural Competence: Interpersonal Communication Across Cultures, 5th ed*. (Boston: Pearson Education, 2005), pp. 58–60, from which this discussion is adapted.

5. Assign a two-minute speech of self-introduction in which students explain a significant aspect of their cultural background and how it has made a difference in their lives. Possible topics might include social customs, family traditions, holidays, clothing, food, religious traditions, sporting activities, and the like. Encourage students to be creative in preparing their speeches and in finding ways to illustrate how the aspect of their culture they choose to explain relates to their personal lives.

    Discussion: This assignment accomplishes three goals at once. First, it fulfills the need for an introductory, ungraded speech in which students can begin the process of feeling comfortable in front of an audience. Second, it allows everyone in the class to learn something about their fellow students, which is an important step in creating a supportive, cooperative classroom atmosphere. Third, by focusing on the different cultural backgrounds of people in the class, it creates opportunities to discuss cultural diversity and its impact on public speaking in general. For more details on this assignment, see Introductory Speech, Option D, on page 25 of this manual.

6. Assign a two-minute speech in which students introduce one of their classmates to the rest of the class. The speech should focus on some aspect of the cultural background of the person being introduced—social customs, family traditions, holidays, clothing, food, religious traditions, sporting activities, and the like. Encourage students to be creative in preparing their speeches and in talking about their classmates.

    Discussion: This assignment offers an alternative to Additional Exercise/Activity 5 above and accomplishes the same objectives. In preparation for the speech, have students pair off and interview one another. If there is great cultural diversity in your class, arrange the interview pairs so that students interview someone with a substantially different cultural background from their own. Although the interviewing can be done in the last 15 to 20 minutes of the first class meeting, the assignment usually works better if students conduct their interviews out of class. This provides time for longer interviews and gives students a better chance to get to know one another. If this assignment is used for the introductory ice breaker speech, it should not be graded. For more details, see Introductory Speech, Option B, on pages 24–25 of this manual.

7. Assign an informative speech of five to six minutes in which students explain a significant aspect of a culture different from their own—social customs, family traditions, holidays, clothing, religious traditions, music, sporting activities, educational systems, etc. Research is required for this speech. If students have had direct contact with a foreign culture, they should be encouraged to supplement their research with their personal experience, but the speech is not to be a travelogue or a presentation on "My Summer in Europe" or "My Year as an Exchange Student in Brazil." However, a speech on how Europeans spend their summer vacations, or on the educational system of Brazil, would be fine.

Discussion: Unlike Additional Exercises/Activities 5 and 6, this assignment involves a full-length, graded speech. The objectives with respect to cultural diversity, however, are much the same. Because students are sometimes resistant when they are required to speak on a different culture, it can be helpful to present this as the "World Travel Agency" speech. If you take this approach, tell students that the class is going to travel around the world via their speeches. They will "visit" as many different countries as there are students in the class.

To help students choose topics as quickly as possible, prepare two sets of 3 x 5 index cards. Write the name of a different country on each card in the first set. Then write two or three cultural features on each card in the second set (choose from the features listed at the start of this exercise, or, better yet, add some of your own devising). Put each set of cards in a separate bag and have students randomly pick a card from each bag. When they are finished, they will have a country card (for instance, Italy) and a topic card (including, for example, sports, family traditions, and politics). The student will then speak on one of those three aspects of Italian life.

However students choose their topics, they should be encouraged to be imaginative in composing their speeches. It is not enough to summarize basic information from an encyclopedia or the Internet about the country on which they are speaking. As in any informative speech, students need to explain ideas clearly and to think about ways to relate the topic to the audience. They also need to consider using visual aids. Indeed, many teachers require a visual aid for this speech. For further details on this assignment, see Informative Speech, Option D, on page 28 of this manual.

Student Introduction Questionnaire

Name _____   Year _____

Major _____

What reason(s) do you have for taking this class?

Do you have any specific goals for improving your speaking? What are they? (What would you like to learn how to do? What particular problems would you like to overcome?)

What classes in speech and related fields (such as journalism or English composition) have you had here or at other schools?

What kinds of speaking experiences have you had in your classes, jobs, religious organizations, extracurricular activities, etc.?

When did you give your last speech? What was the topic?

What are your career plans? Will public speaking be important to your career? How so?

2

Ethics and Public Speaking

Chapter Objectives

After reading this chapter, students should be able to:

1. Explain why a strong sense of ethical responsibility is vital for public speakers.

2. Discuss the five guidelines for ethical speechmaking presented in the chapter.

3. Define the differences among global plagiarism, patchwork plagiarism, and incremental plagiarism, and explain why each type of plagiarism is unethical.

4. Identify the three basic guidelines for ethical listening discussed in the chapter.

Chapter Outline

I. Questions of ethics are central to the art of public speaking.

    A. Ethics is the branch of philosophy that deals with issues of right and wrong in human affairs.

    B. Ethical issues arise when we ask whether a course of action is moral or immoral, fair or unfair, just or unjust, honest or dishonest.

    C. Questions of ethics come into play whenever a public speaker faces an audience.

II. As there are guidelines for ethical behavior in other areas of life, so are there guidelines for ethical behavior in public speaking.

   A. Public speakers should make sure their goals are ethically sound.

   B. Public speakers should be fully prepared for each speech.

   C. Public speakers should be honest in what they say.

   D. Public speakers should avoid name-calling and other forms of abusive language.

   E. Public speakers should put ethical principles into practice.

III. Plagiarism is one of the most serious ethical lapses a public speaker can commit.

   A. Plagiarism, presenting another person's language or ideas as one's own, is a serious offense.

   B. There are three types of plagiarism.

      1. Global plagiarism is taking an entire speech from a single source and passing it off as one's own.

      2. Patchwork plagiarism occurs when a speaker patches a speech together by copying verbatim from two or three sources.

      3. Incremental plagiarism occurs when a speaker fails to give credit for specific parts—increments—of the speech that are borrowed from other people.

   C. Just as one needs to credit the authors of print books and articles, so one needs to credit the authors of documents found online.

IV. Listeners, as well as speakers, have ethical obligations.

   A. Listeners should be courteous and attentive during the speech.

   B. Listeners should avoid prejudging the speaker.

   C. Listeners should maintain the free and open expression of ideas.

Exercises for Critical Thinking *(from text page 45)*

1. Look back at the story of Felicia Robinson on pages 30–31 of the textbook. Evaluate her dilemma in light of the guidelines for ethical speechmaking presented in this chapter. Explain what you believe would be the most ethical course of action in her case.

   Discussion: This exercise is designed to have students apply the guidelines for ethical public speaking discussed in the chapter. The best way to conduct the exercise is to discuss each guideline individually and then apply it to the case of Felicia Robinson. The case study approach used in this exercise is the preferred method of teaching ethics today, and it works exceedingly well in conveying the nature of ethical judgment and its application to public speakers. If students prepare this exercise before coming to class, it should generate a fruitful discussion.

2. The issue of insulting and abusive speech—especially slurs directed against people on the basis of race, religion, gender, or sexual orientation—is extremely controversial. Do you believe society should punish such speech with criminal penalties? To what degree are colleges and universities justified in trying to discipline students who engage in such speech? Do you feel it is proper to place any boundaries on free expression in order to prohibit insulting and abusive speech? Why or why not? Be prepared to explain your ideas in class.

> **Discussion:** Few issues have generated more heat on college campuses—and in American society at large—in recent years than abusive language and how to deal with it. Most controversial is the question of whether schools can justifiably impose restrictions on "hate speech" against racial or religious minorities, women, gays, lesbians, and people with physical disabilities. Defensible arguments can be made on both sides of the question. The purpose of this exercise is not to have students reach the "right" answer, but to spark intelligent discussion. For an excellent over-view of these issues, see Thomas L. Tedford and Dale A. Herbeck, *Freedom of Speech in the United States*, 6th ed. (State College, PA: Strata, 2009).

3. All the following situations could arise in your speech class. Identify the ethical issues in each and explain what, as a responsible speaker or listener, your course of action would be.

a. You are speaking on the topic of prison reform. In your research, you run across two public opinion polls. One of them, an independent survey by the Gallup Organization, shows that a majority of people in your state oppose your position. The other poll, suspect in its methods and conducted by a partisan organization, says a majority of people in your state support your position. Which poll do you cite in your speech? If you cite the second poll, do you point out its shortcomings?

> **Discussion:** Like the other two scenarios in this exercise, this one is designed to relate ethical questions directly to situations students will face in their classroom speeches. In this scenario, of course, the most ethical decision would be to use the Gallup poll rather than the partisan poll, even though the latter supports the speaker's position. It would be especially unethical to use the partisan poll without indicating its weaknesses to the audience. This would clearly violate the speaker's obligation to be honest in presenting facts and figures.

b. When listening to an informative speech by one of your classmates, you realize that much of it is plagiarized from a Web site you visited a couple weeks earlier. What do you do? Do you say something when your instructor asks for comments about the speech? Do you mention your concern to the instructor after class? Do you talk with the speaker? Do you remain silent?

Discussion: This case raises interesting questions about plagiarism and the ethical obligations of listeners. If faced with this situation in real life, most students would doubtless remain silent—not because they approved of the speaker's behavior, but because they would not want to "tell on" the speaker. Some might argue that even though plagiarism is wrong, students are under no ethical obligation to report someone who commits plagiarism in a speech. Because this is a complex issue, few classes are likely to reach agreement on it. They can, however, reach agreement on the fact that plagiarism is ethically wrong and that students who commit it should face stiff penalties if they are detected.

c. While researching your persuasive speech, you find a quotation from an article by a highly respected expert that will nail down one of your most important points. But as you read the rest of the article, you realize the author does not in fact support the policy you are advocating. Do you still include the quotation in your speech?

Discussion: This scenario gets at a fairly subtle point about ethics and public speaking. Yet it is a point worth discussing, for it shows that being an ethical speaker is not just a matter of "big" obligations such as having ethically sound goals and avoiding plagiarism. It also shows that one needs to consider the facts of a situation carefully in making ethical judgments.

In the scenario at hand, at least three defensible ethical positions can be advanced: (1) That the speaker should not quote the expert in support of any point if the expert does not support the speaker's policy; (2) That the speaker can ethically quote the expert on one aspect of the topic (the existence of a problem, for example) as long as the speaker does not state or imply that the expert supports the speaker's position in general; (3) That the speaker cannot ethically quote the expert on any aspect of the topic unless the speaker states explicitly that the expert does not support the policy advocated by the speaker. The purpose of class discussion on this scenario is not to reach unanimous agreement on one of these three positions, but to make students aware of the ethical issues involved and, in the process, to heighten their sensitivity to the wide range of ethical issues faced by public speakers.

Using Public Speaking in Your Career   *(from text page 41)*

Having graduated with a degree in public administration and hoping to pursue a career in politics, you have been fortunate to receive a staff position with one of the leading senators in your state legislature. Since your arrival two months ago, you have answered phones, ordered lunch, made copies, stapled mailings, and stuffed envelopes. Finally you have been asked to look over a speech the senator will deliver at your alma mater. Surely, you think, this will be the first of many important assignments once your value is recognized.

After reading the speech, however, your enthusiasm is dampened. You agree wholeheartedly with its support of a bill to fund scholarships for low-income students, but you're dismayed by its attack on opponents of the bill as "elitist bigots who would deny a college education to those who need it most." You haven't been asked to comment on the ethics of the speech, and you certainly don't want to jeopardize your position on the senator's staff. At the same time, you think his use of name-calling may actually arouse sympathy for the opposition.

The senator would like your comments in two hours. What will you tell him?

Discussion: Like many of the other Using Public Speaking in Your Career scenarios throughout the book, this one does not admit of an unequivocal right-or-wrong answer. Recognizing the ethical problem with the senator's speech is one thing; pointing out the problem to the senator is another. In most circumstances, a new staff member would not find it prudent to confront his or her employer on a matter of rhetorical ethics. It might be more prudent to raise the practical question of whether the senator's attack on "elitist bigots" is likely to create a backlash against the senator's position, but even this would need to be approached tactfully. On the other hand, if the senator did not want an opinion, he probably would not have asked. Apart from the ethical implications of remaining silent, there are potential practical pitfalls in this course of action as well. As your students discuss the scenario, remind them that the kinds of issues raised by it are not limited to politics and could occur in a wide range of rhetorical situations.

Additional Exercises and Activities

1. Lead a class discussion in which students develop a code of ethical speaking for their classroom. The final product of the discussion will be a list titled "Ethical Speaking for Our Speech Class." By the end of the discussion, the entire class should not only agree on the content of the list, but should pledge themselves to follow it throughout the term.

    Discussion: This exercise works extremely well in promoting dialogue about the ethics of public speaking. It also relates abstract issues of ethics to the situation in which students will be giving speeches for the next several months. By developing their own rules for ethical speechmaking, students will be more committed to following those rules.

    Don't be surprised if much of the discussion turns on questions related to plagiarism. This is probably the most pressing ethical issue facing students in a speech classroom, and many do not have a clear understanding of what constitutes plagiarism and what does not.

    As students develop their code, encourage them to be specific in their criteria. For example, rather than saying "We will not plagiarize our speeches," they should try to develop more precise statements such as "We will not copy our speeches from the work of current or previous students," or "We will always cite the sources of ideas or supporting materials that we use in our speeches."

2. Lead a class discussion in which students develop a code of ethical listening for their speech classroom. The final product of the discussion will be a list titled "Ethical Listening for Our Speech Class." By the end of the discussion, the entire class should not only agree on the content of the list, but should pledge themselves to follow it throughout the term.

    Discussion: A companion to Additional Exercise/Activity 1 above, this is an excellent way to get students thinking about the ethical obligations of listeners. Like Exercise 1, it relates ethical issues directly to the speech classroom and gives those issues more immediacy than might otherwise be the case. Also like Exercise 1, it allows students to formulate their own ethical criteria, thereby increasing the likelihood that they will feel committed to following those criteria.

    As with Exercise 1, encourage students to be specific as they develop their code. Rather than saying "We will listen courteously and attentively," for instance, they should work for statements such as "We will not do work for other classes while listening to our classmates' speeches," or "Even if we disagree with a speaker's position at the start of a speech, we will listen with an open mind to the entire speech before making a judgment about it." One way to generate criteria is to ask students what kinds of attitudes and behavior they would like to see in listeners to their own speeches.

3. Give each student the following assignment: Identify a situation in your life in which an issue related to speech ethics was involved. The issue could have affected you either as a speaker or as a listener. Work up a brief analysis in which you explain the situation and the ethical issue (or issues) involved.

    Discussion: This exercise can work very well to promote class discussion about ethical issues in public speaking. Because it deals with issues that are related to the experience of each student, the exercise often gives the discussion more immediacy than dealing with hypothetical ethical scenarios. It usually works best when given as a homework assignment so students have plenty of time to develop their analyses.

4. If your class meets during a presidential election year, ethical issues are bound to arise in relation to the candidates' campaign rhetoric. Such issues might include the use of negative campaigning, the distortion of evidence in campaign speeches and advertisements, the use of name-calling to denigrate the opposing candidate or party, and the tendency of candidates to say different things to different groups of voters. Set aside time periodically during the term to deal with such issues—especially when they achieve prominence in press coverage of the campaign.

Discussion: Because presidential campaigns usually generate fairly intense reactions, they provide an excellent vehicle for getting students interested in questions of communication ethics. They also have a tendency to provoke heated discussion—especially among students who are fiercely partisan to one candidate or another. The challenge for instructors is to keep discussion focused on ethical issues rather than on the general merits and policies of each candidate. It is important that students learn to separate their feelings for and against the candidates from their reasoned judgments about the ethics of the candidates' rhetoric.

The aims of this exercise can be achieved either through informal class discussion or through more formal assignments in which students—working individually or in groups—prepare systematic analyses for presentation in class. The same kind of exercise can also be used during local or state elections.

5. Have students create "Speech Ethics" scrapbooks in which they keep magazine, newspaper, and Internet articles that deal with ethical issues in public speaking. Articles can touch on any aspect of speech ethics, including consideration of a speaker's goals, preparation, truthfulness, evidence, reasoning, language, emotional appeal, or impact on audiences. Articles can also deal with the ethics of listening. Students should be sure to record the source and date of each article. Collect the scrapbooks near the end of the term.

Discussion: Once students start thinking about ethical issues and looking for articles that deal with them, it is astounding how many they can find. Although some instructors use this exercise as a required assignment, others use it as an extra-credit opportunity. In either case, if done properly it can be of considerable benefit for the students. Not only does it help sensitize them to the range, complexity, and importance of ethical issues in public speaking, but it often gets them reading newspapers, magazines, and substantive Web sites more regularly than they would otherwise.

6. Students often ask about ghostwriting when dealing with the issue of plagiarism. Why, they ask, is it ethical for politicians, business leaders, and other public figures to have ghostwriters and unethical for students to have someone else write their speeches? If students raise this issue, be prepared to conduct a class discussion on the relationship between plagiarism and ghostwriting.

Discussion: Scholars and popular commentators alike have spent a great deal of time on the subject of ghostwriting. Most regard it as ethically acceptable among politicians, business leaders, and other public figures as long as (1) the speaker does not deceive the audience by claiming to have written a speech when in fact it is ghostwritten, and (2) the speaker takes full responsibility for what he or she says regardless of who may have written the actual words of the speech.

Speeches given in the classroom, however, are quite different. Students are in a learning situation. They cannot learn the skills of speech preparation by having someone else compose their speeches for them. Nor can their performance in class be fairly evaluated if they do not do their own work. As noted in the chapter, when students stand up to deliver a speech, it is just like putting their name on a paper in their English class—they are declaring that the speech represents their own work, their own thinking, their own language.

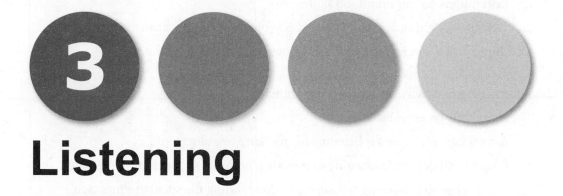

Listening

Chapter Objectives

After reading this chapter, students should be able to:

1. Explain the difference between hearing and listening.

2. Define the four different kinds of listening and explain their relationship to critical thinking.

3. Explain why good listening is important to effective speechmaking.

4. Identify the four major causes of poor listening.

5. Discuss the seven ways to become a better listener presented in the text.

Chapter Outline

I. Listening is an important skill to master.
  A. Hearing and listening are different processes.
    1. Hearing is a physiological process that involves the vibration of sound waves on the eardrums and the firing of electrochemical impulses from the inner ear to the brain.
    2. Listening is a mental process that involves paying close attention to, and making sense of, what is heard.
  B. Most people are poor listeners.

C.   In our communication-oriented age, listening is more important than ever.

1.   Listening is an important job skill.

2.   Effective listening is useful in all aspects of life, including academics.

D.   Listening is also an excellent way to improve one's speaking skills.

II.   Listening skills are closely linked to critical thinking.

A.   There are four types of listening.

1.   Appreciative listening is listening for pleasure or enjoyment.

2.   Empathic listening is listening to provide emotional support for the speaker.

3.   Comprehensive listening focuses on understanding the speaker's message.

4.   Critical listening involves evaluating a message either to accept it or reject it.

B.   Because comprehensive and critical listening are closely tied to critical thinking, they are most important for public speaking.

III.   There are four main causes of poor listening.

A.   Not concentrating is one cause of poor listening.

B.   Listening too hard can also interfere with effective listening.

C.   Jumping to conclusions also prevents listeners from hearing messages accurately.

D.   Focusing on delivery and personal appearance instead of listening to a speaker's message is another cause of poor listening.

IV.   There are seven ways to improve one's listening skills.

A.   The first step in improving listening skills is to take listening seriously.

B.   A second way to improve listening skills is to become an active listener.

C.   A third way to improve listening skills is to resist distractions.

D.   A fourth way to improve listening skills is not to be diverted by appearance or delivery.

E.   A fifth way to improve listening skills is to suspend judgment until hearing a speaker's full message.

F.   A sixth way to improve listening skills is to focus one's listening.

1.   Effective listeners focus on a speaker's main points.

2.   Effective listeners focus on the quality of a speaker's evidence.

3.   Effective listeners also focus on speaking techniques they can use in their own speeches.

G.   A seventh way to improve listening skills is to develop strong note-taking skills.

Exercises for Critical Thinking *(from text page 61)*

1. Which of the four causes of poor listening do you consider the most important? Choose a specific case of poor listening in which you were involved. Explain what went wrong.

    Discussion: This exercise is designed to have students think about the causes of poor listening in terms of their personal experience. If the students prepare this exercise before coming to class, it should generate a rich variety of examples for class discussion.

2. Using the Listening Self-Evaluation Worksheet on page 54 of the textbook, undertake a candid evaluation of your major strengths and weaknesses as a listener. Explain what steps you need to take to become a better listener.

    Discussion: This should be handled much like the third Exercise for Critical Thinking in Chapter 1. At the end of the course, students can be asked to assess their progress both as speakers and as listeners. For instructors who wish to distribute the Listening Self-Evaluation Worksheet in class, it is reprinted on page 71 of this manual.

3. Watch the lead story this week on *60 Minutes*, *Dateline*, or *20/20*. Using the key-word method of note taking, record the main ideas of the story.

    Discussion: This can be a good diagnostic tool to gauge which students take notes effectively and which do not. Because the lead story on *60 Minutes* is usually somewhat controversial, this exercise can also illustrate how a person's listening is affected by his or her attitudes on the speaker's topic. For an alternative to this exercise, see items 3 and 4 under Additional Exercises/Activities for this chapter.

4. Choose a lecture in one of your other classes. Analyze what the lecturer does most effectively. Identify three things the lecturer could do better to help students keep track of the lecture.

    Discussion: The objective of this exercise is to focus attention on things a speaker can do to help listeners gain hold of the speaker's ideas. Usually students will produce a number of excellent suggestions—such as making sure the speech is well organized, previewing main points in the introduction, using internal summaries and transitions, employing visual aids, avoiding technical language, and the like. You can then urge that students be sure to follow these suggestions in their own speeches.

Additional Exercises and Activities

1. Lead a class discussion in which students develop a code of listening behavior for their speech classroom. The final product of this discussion will be a list entitled "Listening Behavior for Our Speech Class." By the end of the discussion, the entire class should not only agree on the content of the list, but should also pledge themselves to follow it throughout the term.

    Discussion: This activity is especially helpful for relating general issues about listening directly to the classroom situation. As students create their listening code, encourage them to be specific in their criteria. For example, rather than saying "Pay attention to what the speaker is saying," they should try to develop more precise statements such as "Write down the speaker's main points," "Look attentive and interested while other students are speaking," and "Do not read the newspaper or work on other assignments during speeches."

    This exercise works well when the class is divided into groups of 4 to 5 students. Give each group 10 to 15 minutes to come up with a list of 8 to 10 items to guide listening behavior in the class. Then, working from the group lists, conduct a general discussion that eventuates in a listening code that is agreed upon by the entire class. Another approach is to have each student create her or his own list as part of a homework assignment. You can then move immediately to a general class discussion rather than first dividing the class into small groups.

2. Have one student step outside of the classroom with you. Give her or him a written copy of the following message: "To get to Lou's place, turn left at the first traffic light and go two blocks until you see a yellow house." Leaving the written copy with you, the student should return to the classroom and whisper the message to the person in the next seat. This person should then whisper the message to the person sitting next to him or her, and so on until the message has been relayed through the entire class. Have the last student to receive the message write it down on a sheet of paper and read it to the entire class. Then have the student to whom you gave the original message read that message to the class. There will almost always be an enormous variation between the original message and the message received by the last student.

    Discussion: This exercise takes only a few minutes to complete. It illustrates dramatically—and often humorously—the great distortion that can take place between what a speaker says and what a listener hears. You can, of course, substitute any message you wish for that given in the exercise.

3. Bring two short editorials to class. Read one of the editorials to your students. Have them take notes and try to identify the main points and evidence of the editorial. Check the results in the class discussion, and give pointers for listening and taking notes more effectively. Then read

the second editorial and give students a chance to apply those pointers. Again, check the results in a class discussion.

> **Discussion:** Although this exercise takes much of a class session, it can be very helpful because it prepares students for listening to speeches. Because many students do poorly on the first editorial, the exercise also serves the useful function of illustrating to students how poorly they listen and how much they need to work to improve their note taking. For an alternative, see Additional Exercise/Activity 4.

4. Show your class one of the selections from the DVD of student speeches that accompanies *The Art of Public Speaking*. Have them take notes in which they try to demarcate where the introduction of the speech ends, to list the main points and subpoints in the body, and to identify where the conclusion begins. Check the results in a class discussion and give pointers for listening and taking notes more effectively. Then play another speech and see if students do a better job of note taking. Again, check the results in a class discussion.

> **Discussion:** Because most of the student speeches on the DVD are 6 to 8 minutes long, this activity takes a whole class session, but it is extremely helpful for students. It can be made even more helpful by selecting speeches for viewing that are connected with whatever speech assignment is coming up in class. That is, if you use this exercise as students are preparing the informative speech, show two informative speeches. Not only will this help students with their listening skills, but it will give them additional exposure to the principles of informative speaking.

5. For each round of speeches, assign students specific listening tasks. For example, you might have a particular group of students (or all students) take notes on their classmates' speeches in an effort to identify the speakers' main points and evidence. After each speech, make a quick check of two or three listeners to see what they recorded.

> **Discussion:** This is one way to help students improve their listening and note-taking skills throughout the course. An added benefit of the exercise is that as students try to take notes on their classmates' speeches, they discover how helpful it is when the speaker follows a clear method of organization, previews the main points at the end of the introduction, uses connectives to help listeners keep track of main points, recaps the speech in the conclusion, avoids distracting nonverbal mannerisms, and uses her or his voice to emphasize ideas. This helps students learn what they need to do as speakers to help listeners take good notes.

6. For at least one round of speeches, have students prepare evaluations of their peers' speeches using the Speech Listening Worksheet on page 72 of this manual.

> **Discussion:** This is an excellent alternative to Additional Exercise/Activity 5 above. In addition to including the usual items for speech evaluation, the worksheet on page 72 is designed to gauge students' listening skills by requiring them to state the speaker's specific purpose, main points, pattern of organization, and types of supporting materials. Some teachers use the worksheet for every speech, and they report that it helps considerably to improve students' listening skills by the end of the term.

7. Have students keep a personal journal of their listening activities for a full day. The journal should include brief descriptions of all the listening situations each student experienced during that day. It should also include the student's analysis of how well he or she listened in each situation and of why he or she did (or did not) listen effectively in each situation. At the end of the day, the student should fill out the Listening Self-Evaluation Worksheet, which is available on page 71 of this manual, or you can assign the worksheet from the assignments available in *Connect*. Finally, the journal should conclude with the student's honest assessment of her or his strengths and weaknesses as a listener and an explanation of what specific steps the student should take to become a better listener.

> **Discussion:** This is a useful alternative to the second Exercise for Critical Thinking on page 61 of the textbook. Like that exercise, it is a way to get students to think about their personal listening habits and how to improve them. Some teachers have students complete a listening journal two or three times during the course, as a way for students to keep track of their progress (or lack of progress) in strengthening their listening skills.

Listening Self-Evaluation Worksheet

How often do you indulge in the following 10 bad listening habits? Check yourself carefully on each one:

HABIT	FREQUENCY					SCORE
	Almost always	Usually	Some-times	Seldom	Almost never	
1. Giving in to mental distractions	_____	_____	_____	_____	_____	_____
2. Giving in to physical distractions	_____	_____	_____	_____	_____	_____
3. Trying to recall everything a speaker says	_____	_____	_____	_____	_____	_____
4. Rejecting a topic as uninteresting before hearing the speaker	_____	_____	_____	_____	_____	_____
5. Faking paying attention	_____	_____	_____	_____	_____	_____
6. Jumping to conclusions about a speaker's meaning	_____	_____	_____	_____	_____	_____
7. Deciding a speaker is wrong before hearing everything she or he has to say	_____	_____	_____	_____	_____	_____
8. Judging a speaker on personal appearance	_____	_____	_____	_____	_____	_____
9. Not paying attention to a speaker's evidence	_____	_____	_____	_____	_____	_____
10. Focusing on delivery rather than on what the speaker says	_____	_____	_____	_____	_____	_____
					TOTAL	_____

How to score:

For every "almost always" checked, give yourself a score of   2
For every "usually" checked, give yourself a score of   4
For every "sometimes" checked, give yourself a score of   6
For every "seldom" checked, give yourself a score of   8
For every "almost never" checked, give yourself a score of   10

Total score interpretation:

Below 70	You need lots of training in listening.
From 71 to 90	You listen well.
Above 90	You listen exceptionally well.

Speech Listening Worksheet

Practice your listening skills by completing this form as you listen to a classroom speech, a speech on video, or a speech outside the classroom.

1. What is the topic of the speech?

2. What is the speaker's specific purpose?

3. Which of the following methods of gaining interest and attention does the speaker use in the introduction?

    ❑ Relate the topic to the audience   ❑ State the importance of the topic
    ❑ Startle the audience   ❑ Arouse the curiosity of the audience
    ❑ Question the audience   ❑ Begin with a quotation
    ❑ Tell a story   ❑ Refer to the occasion
    ❑ Invite audience participation   ❑ Use visual or audio aids
    ❑ Refer to a previous speaker   ❑ Begin with humor

4. Does the speaker preview the main points of the speech in the introduction?

5. List the main points developed in the body of the speech.

6. What pattern of organization does the speaker use?

7. Are the speaker's main points clear and easy to follow? Why or why not?

8. Does the speaker use a transition or other connective between each main point of the speech?

9. Which of the following methods of referring to the central idea does the speaker use in the conclusion?

    ❑ Restate the main points   ❑ End with a quotation
    ❑ Make a dramatic statement   ❑ Refer to the introduction
    ❑ Challenge the audience   ❑ Call for action

Giving Your First Speech

Chapter Objectives

After reading this chapter, students should be able to:

1. Explain the major factors involved in developing and organizing their first classroom speech.

2. Explain the nature of extemporaneous delivery and how they can work on speaking extemporaneously as they rehearse their first classroom speech.

3. Explain the elements discussed in the textbook with regard to delivering the first classroom speech.

Chapter Outline

I. The first speech assignment is often called an ice breaker speech because it is designed to "break the ice" by getting students up in front of the class as soon as possible.
   A. There are many options for this assignment.
   B. Whatever the assignment, the speech is usually brief and is often ungraded.

II. The initial step in giving the first speech is deciding on a topic, identifying main points, and developing those points creatively.
   A. Students should make sure their topic is appropriate for the time limit.
   B. Once students have a speech topic, they should be creative in developing it.
      1. They can structure the speech to make it interesting.

2. They can think of ways to make the speech mysterious or suspenseful.

3. They can talk about dangerous situations, adventure, or drama.

4. They can use colorful, descriptive language.

5. They can use humor as long as it is in good taste and grows naturally out of the speech content.

III. The second step in giving the first speech is organizing the content.

A. The introduction should get the audience's attention and reveal the topic of the speech.

B. The body can be organized in a number of ways, including chronological order and topical order.

C. The conclusion should signal the end of the speech, reinforce the major theme, and, if possible, end on a dramatic or thought-provoking note.

IV. The third step in giving the first speech is working on delivery.

A. Most experts recommend speaking extemporaneously, which involves planning main points and supporting materials but not memorizing the speech.

B. Effective extemporaneous delivery requires a great deal of rehearsal.

C. There are several things to concentrate on when presenting the speech in class.

1. Before beginning, speakers should take a moment to arrange their notes, set their body in an upright but relaxed posture, and smile at the audience.

2. During the speech, they should gesture naturally.

3. They should also maintain eye contact with the audience.

4. Speaking expressively is important for an effective presentation.

5. Speakers should also remember that nervousness is natural and that the anxiety they feel inside is usually not visible to the audience.

Exercises for Critical Thinking *(from text page 75)*

1. Examine the two sample speeches with commentary on pages 72–73 of the textbook. Choose one, and answer the following questions about it.

   a. How does the opening paragraph gain the attention of the audience, introduce the subject of the speech, and preview the main points to be discussed in the body?

   b. How clearly is the body of the speech organized? What does the speaker do to help listeners follow the progression of ideas?

   c. How does the speaker conclude? Does the conclusion reinforce the central theme of the speech?

Discussion: By analyzing introductory speeches, students will get a better idea of how to construct their own speeches. This exercise will help them focus in particular on what makes for an effective introduction, body, and conclusion. Given that students are asked to analyze only one of the introductory speeches—either "There's an App for That," a speech of self-introduction, or "Fork in the Road," a speech introducing a classmate—they will likely select the speech that is closest to their classroom assignment. If you don't want students choosing which speech to analyze, you can specify one (or both) ahead of time.

The texts of "There's an App for That" and "Fork in the Road" appear on pages 72–73 of the textbook. Videos of both are available online and on the DVD of student speeches that accompanies this edition of *The Art of Public Speaking*. Below are examples of what students might say about each speech.

"There's an App for That"

Introduction: The introduction gains the audience's attention by asking brief questions and answering them with the familiar tagline "There's an App for That." This widely recognized phrase not only pulls the audience into the speech but establishes the theme that will run from beginning to end. By turning the question "Is there an app for that" on himself, the speaker reveals the subject of his speech. He then previews his main points by identifying the Photobucket, ESPN, and Pandora apps on his iPhone.

Body: Each main point in the body of the speech is organized around a different app. Notice, however, that the purpose of the main points is not to discuss the apps, but to use them to reveal different aspects of the speaker's life. The first main point uses the Photobucket app to discuss the speaker's family. The second main point uses the ESPN ScoreCenter app to discuss the speaker's athletic interests. The third main point uses the Pandora app to discuss the speaker's musical talents. The speaker helps the audience follow along by stating the name of the app at the beginning of each paragraph and then discussing specific aspects of his life. Signposts like "First" and "Finally" help the audience know where they are in the speech.

Conclusion: The speaker concludes by restating the apps and by returning to the question with which the speech began. In addition to reinforcing the central idea, this gives the speech a sense of psychological unity.

"Fork in the Road"

Introduction: This speaker uses a quotation to gain the audience's attention and to establish the speech's central theme of coming to a fork in the road of life. By relating the quotation to Bethany and her passion for art and medicine, the speaker reveals the subject of the speech and previews the points she will discuss in the body.

Body: The body of the speech consists of two main points—one devoted to Bethany's passion for art, the other to Bethany's passion for medicine. In each main point, the speaker illustrates Bethany's passions with specific examples, which are necessary for helping the audience understand and visualize important aspects of their classmate's life. The speaker states each main point clearly, and she provides a transition statement as she moves from main point one to main point two. All in all, the speech provides a model of exemplary organization in an introductory presentation.

Conclusion: In the final paragraph, the speaker returns to the central theme of coming to a fork in the road. Doing so ties the speech together and signals that the speech is coming to an end. The speaker's rhetorical questions in the final paragraph reiterate the main points. The speech concludes adroitly by turning the theme of a "fork in the road" into the idea of a "road to success."

2. Are there occasions outside the classroom on which you might give a speech of self-introduction? Identify such an occasion and explain how you might apply the principles of introductory speeches discussed in this chapter.

Discussion: This is a good exercise to assign for homework or to use for a classroom discussion. Either way, the goal is to get students thinking about how introductory speeches are more than just ice breakers. By learning how to deliver effective speeches of self-introduction in the classroom, students will be better prepared for a variety of occasions later in life. One such occasion is the job interview. Nowadays, employers often ask prospective employees to give a brief presentation about themselves and the reasons they are applying for a position. In addition to directing students toward their careers, however, having them think through possible scenarios for speeches of self-introduction can ease some of their anxiety about delivering their first speech.

Additional Exercises and Activities

1. Show the class one or more of the speeches of self introduction from the DVD of student speeches that accompanies this edition of *The Art of Public Speaking*. Use the DVD to illustrate points about how students can prepare and deliver effective introductory speeches.

Discussion: The DVD of student speeches that accompanies this edition of *The Art of Public Speaking* contains four excellent speeches of self introduction as well as a "needs improvement" version of one of the speeches. In addition to "There's an App for That," which is discussed in Exercise for Critical Thinking 1 on pages 74–75 of this manual, the DVD contains "New Game, New Life," "A Heart Worn on My Hand," and "Pot, Soil, Water." For the text and discussion of "New Game, New Life," see pages

260–261 of this manual. For the text and discussion of "A Heart Worn on My Hand," see pages 262–263 of this manual. For the text and discussion of the final and needs-improvement versions of "Pot, Soil, Water," see pages 264–268 of this manual.

2. Show the class one or more of the speeches introducing a classmate from the DVD of student speeches that accompanies this edition of *The Art of Public Speaking*. Use the DVD to illustrate points about how students can prepare and deliver effective introductory speeches.

 Discussion: The DVD of student speeches accompanying this edition of *The Art of Public Speaking* contains three speeches introducing a classmate. "Fork in the Road" is discussed in Exercise for Critical Thinking 1 on pages 74–76 of this manual. You'll find the text and discussion of "Brooklyn Roads" on pages 279–280 of this manual. The text and discussion of "Rhymes with Orange" appears on pages 281–282 of this manual.

5

Selecting a Topic and a Purpose

Chapter Objectives

After reading this chapter, students should be able to:

1. Explain four methods they can use to brainstorm for a speech topic.

2. Identify the difference between a general and a specific purpose.

3. Distinguish between the specific purpose and the central idea of a speech.

4. Formulate a specific purpose statement and a central idea in accordance with the guidelines presented in the text.

Chapter Outline

I. The first step in speechmaking is choosing a topic.

   A. Topics for speeches outside the classroom are usually determined by the occasion, the audience, and the speaker's qualifications.

   B. There are several sources for topics for classroom speeches.

      1. Topics for classroom speeches can come from subjects about which students already know a great deal.

      2. Topics for classroom speeches can come from subjects about which a student is interested and wants to learn more.

3. Topics for classroom speeches can come from issues about which students hold strong opinions and beliefs.

4. Students can use several brainstorming procedures to help select a topic.

5. Whatever method students use, they should settle on a topic as early as possible.

II. After choosing a topic, speakers need to determine the general purpose of the speech.

   A. There are usually two general purposes for classroom speeches—to inform or to persuade.

   B. When the general purpose is to inform, speakers act as teachers.

   C. When the general purpose is to persuade, speakers act as advocates.

III. Once the general purpose is clear, the next step is narrowing to the specific purpose.

   A. The specific purpose should indicate precisely what the speaker wants the audience to know or believe after the speech.

   B. There are five tips for forming a good specific purpose statement.

      1. It should be a full infinitive phrase, not a fragment.

      2. It should be phrased as a statement, not a question.

      3. It should avoid figurative language.

      4. It should be limited to one distinct idea.

      5. It should not be too vague or general.

   C. Once students have a specific purpose statement, they should ask themselves the following questions:

      1. Does the specific purpose meet the assignment?

      2. Can this specific purpose be accomplished effectively in the time allotted?

      3. Is the specific purpose relevant to the audience?

      4. Is the specific purpose too trivial for the audience?

      5. Is the specific purpose too technical for the audience?

IV. The central idea further refines and sharpens the specific purpose statement.

   A. The central idea is a concise statement of what the speaker expects to say in the speech.

   B. Often called a thesis statement, the central idea encapsulates the main points to be developed in the body of the speech.

   C. Unlike the specific purpose statement, the central idea usually crystallizes late in the process of preparing a speech.

   D. A well-worded central idea should meet four criteria.

      1. It should be expressed in a full sentence.

      2. It should not be in the form of a question.

      3. It should avoid figurative language.

      4. It should not be too vague or general.

Exercises for Critical Thinking   *(from text pages 94–95)*

1. Using one of the four brainstorming methods described in this chapter, come up with three topics you might like to deal with in your next classroom speech. For each topic, devise a specific purpose statement suitable for the speech assignment. Make sure your specific purpose statements fit the guidelines discussed in the chapter.

    Discussion: This exercise gives students an opportunity to practice brainstorming, to begin the process of selecting a topic for their next speech, and to work on framing specific purpose statements. In class discussion, you can assess not only the suitability of the students' topics, but also how effectively the students have phrased their specific purposes.

2. Here are several specific purpose statements for classroom speeches. Identify the problem with each, and rewrite the statement to correct the problem.

    a. To inform my audience how to sign up for Facebook.

    Discussion: Given that many students already have a Facebook account, or could figure out how to sign up for one on their own, this specific purpose is too trivial for most classroom speeches.

    b. To persuade my audience that the U.S. government should increase funding for stem cell research and support the development of hydrogen-fuel vehicles.

    Discussion: This specific purpose statement contains two separate ideas. A more effective statement would be "To persuade my audience that the U.S. government should increase funding for stem cell research." Or "To persuade my audience to support the development of hydrogen-fuel vehicles."

    c. What is an Individual Retirement Account?

    Discussion: This specific purpose statement is phrased as a question. A more effective statement would be "To inform my audience about the types and benefits of Individual Retirement Accounts."

    d. To inform my audience why square grooves are superior to U-shaped grooves on golf clubs.

    Discussion: This specific purpose statement is too technical—and perhaps too trivial—for an audience not composed of golf enthusiasts. A more effective specific purpose statement for a classroom speech on golf might be "To inform my audience about the development of golf as a popular sport." Or "To inform my audience about the different kinds of clubs used in playing golf."

e. To inform my audience about New Zealand.

   Discussion: This specific purpose statement is too broad. A more effective statement would be "To inform my audience about the major tourist attractions in New Zealand."

f. Donate blood.

   Discussion: This specific purpose statement is written as a fragment. A more effective statement would be "To persuade my audience to contribute to the next campus blood drive."

g. To persuade my audience that something has to be done about the problem of antibiotic-resistant bacteria.

   Discussion: This specific purpose statement is too broad; it does not specify what should be done about the problem of antibiotic-resistant bacteria. A more effective specific purpose statement would be "To persuade my audience that the federal government should increase research to deal with the alarming growth of antibiotic-resistant bacteria."

3. Below are three sets of main points for speeches. For each set, supply the general purpose, specific purpose, and central idea.

   General Purpose: To persuade

   Specific Purpose: To persuade my audience to study abroad during their college career.

   Central Idea: You should study abroad because it will enhance your personal development, your academic development, and your career development.

   Main Points: I. You should study abroad because it will enhance your personal development.

                       II. You should study abroad because it will enhance your academic development.

                      III. You should study abroad because it will enhance your career development.

General Purpose: To inform

Specific Purpose: To inform my audience about the three events in a triathlon.

Central Idea: The three events in a triathlon are swimming, cycling, and running.

Main Points:
    I. The first event in a triathlon is swimming.

    II. The second event in a triathlon is cycling.

    III. The third event in a triathlon is running.

General Purpose: To inform

Specific Purpose: To inform my audience about the accomplishments of Thomas Jefferson.

Central Idea: Thomas Jefferson was an accomplished writer, president, and architect.

Main Points:
    I. As a writer, Thomas Jefferson penned the Declaration of Independence and *Notes on the State of Virginia.*

    II. As President, Thomas Jefferson negotiated the Louisiana Purchase and approved the Lewis and Clark expedition.

    III. As an architect, Jefferson designed Monticello and the University of Virginia.

Discussion: The virtue of this exercise is that it clarifies the relationships among the specific purpose, the central idea, and the main points. It looks easy, but quite a few students have trouble with it. (For variations, see Additional Exercises/Activities 1 and 2 on pages 83–86 of this manual.)

Using Public Speaking in Your Career *(from text page 83)*

Your communication degree has helped you land a job as spokesperson for the mayor of a medium-sized city on the West Coast. A year after starting the job, you are selected to organize an information campaign explaining the benefits of a new youth center proposed by the mayor.

To launch this campaign, you've decided to hold a news briefing at the end of the week. To open the briefing, you will present a short set of comments on the mayor's initiative. You decide to focus on four benefits of the youth center: (1) It will offer a range of activities—from sports to the arts—in a safe environment; (2) It will provide social networks for youths from all walks of life; (3) It will operate most hours of the day and night; (4) It will be free and open to everyone.

Following the format used in this chapter, state the general purpose, specific purpose, central idea, and main points of your comments.

Discussion: As with the other Using Public Speaking in Your Career scenarios throughout the book, this one is intended to illustrate how one might apply the principles discussed in the book to situations outside the classroom. The purpose is less to have students come up with the "right" answer than to get them thinking about the practical applications of what they are reading and studying in class. Here is what a reasonable answer to the questions posed in this scenario might look like:

General Purpose: To inform

Specific Purpose: To inform my audience of the benefits of the proposed youth center.

Central Idea: The youth center will offer teenagers a safe, social, flexible, and free place to spend their time.

Main Points:
    I. The youth center will offer a range of activities in a safe environment.

    II. The youth center will provide social networks for youths from all walks of life.

    III. The youth center will operate most hours of the day and night.

    IV. The youth center will be free and open to everyone.

Additional Exercises and Activities

1. Below are two central ideas for speeches. For each central idea provide the general purpose, specific purpose, and main points of the speech.

General Purpose:

Specific Purpose:

Central Idea: The four stages of alcoholism are the warning stage, the danger stage, the crucial stage, and the chronic stage.

Main Points:
    I.

    II.

    III. ____

    IV.

General Purpose:

Specific Purpose:

Central Idea: You should join a sorority or fraternity because of the social, academic, and economic benefits.

Main Points: I.

    II.

    III.

Discussion: This complements Exercise 3 on pages 94–95 of the textbook and gives students additional work in understanding the relationships among the general purpose, specific purpose, central idea, and main points of the speech. For another exercise along these lines, see Additional Exercise/Activity 2 on pages 85–86 of this manual. Here are the answers to the present exercise.

General Purpose: To inform

Specific Purpose: To inform my audience of the four stages of alcoholism.

Central Idea: The four stages of alcoholism are the warning stage, the danger stage, the crucial stage, and the chronic stage.

Main Points: I. The first stage of alcoholism is the warning stage.

    II. The second stage of alcoholism is the danger stage.

    III. The third stage of alcoholism is the crucial stage.

    IV. The fourth stage of alcoholism is the chronic stage.

General Purpose: To persuade

Specific Purpose: To persuade my audience to join a sorority or a fraternity.

Central Idea: You should join a sorority or fraternity because of the social, academic, and economic benefits.

Main Points: I. You should join a sorority or fraternity because of the social benefits.

    II. You should join a sorority or fraternity because of the academic benefits.

    III. You should join a sorority or fraternity because of the economic benefits.

2. Below are two central ideas for speeches. For each central idea provide the general purpose, specific purpose, and main points of the speech.

General Purpose:

Specific Purpose:

Central Idea: The pyramids of ancient Egypt had three major uses—as tombs for the burial of monarchs, as temples for worshipping the gods, and as observatories for studying the stars.

Main Points:

General Purpose:

Specific Purpose:

Central Idea: Handwriting analysts try to determine personality traits by examining the consistency, angularity, and size of a person's writing.

Main Points:

Discussion: By not providing the number of main points, this exercise is somewhat more difficult than the previous one. It provides additional work for students who are having trouble with the relationships among the general purpose, specific purpose, central idea, and main points. Here is what the exercise should look like when all the blanks are filled in.

General Purpose: To inform

Specific Purpose: To inform my audience of the three major uses of the pyramids of ancient Egypt.

Central Idea: The pyramids of ancient Egypt had three major uses—as tombs for the burial of monarchs, as temples for worshipping the gods, and as observatories for studying the stars and the planets.

Main Points: I. The first major use of the pyramids of ancient Egypt was as tombs for the burial of monarchs.

II. The second major use of the pyramids of ancient Egypt was as temples for worshipping the gods.

III. The third major use of the pyramids of ancient Egypt was as observatories for studying the stars and the planets.

General Purpose:	To inform
Specific Purpose:	To inform my audience how handwriting analysts try to determine personality traits by examining a person's handwriting.
Central Idea:	Handwriting analysts try to determine personality traits by examining the consistency, angularity, and size of a person's handwriting.
Main Points:	I. Handwriting analysts try to determine personality traits by examining the consistency of a person's handwriting.
	II. Handwriting analysts try to determine personality traits by examining the angularity of a person's handwriting.
	III. Handwriting analysts try to determine personality traits by examining the size of a person's handwriting.

3. Once students start to work on each speech assignment, set aside part of a class session to discuss the students' topics. Ask each student to reveal her or his topic and specific purpose. Ask other classmates to indicate whether they find the topic interesting and what suggestions they have for the speaker's approach to it.

Discussion: In some classes this works very well. In other classes—when the students are not well prepared or are reluctant to share their opinions—it is less effective. Some teachers use this activity quite successfully to help students focus their topics and adjust them to their classmates.

4. Divide the class into groups of 5 to 6 students each. Assign each group one of the following resources to investigate for possible speech topics: (a) an issue of a magazine such as *Time, Newsweek,* or *U.S. News and World Report*; (b) the Sunday edition of the leading local newspaper; (c) any issue of a major national newspaper—*New York Times, Los Angeles Times, Washington Post, Christian Science Monitor*; (d) an hour of news broadcasting on CNN; (e) two nights of the evening news telecast on ABC, NBC, or CBS. On the basis of these resources, each group is responsible for bringing into class five speech topics and specific purpose statements for each of those topics. Conduct a class discussion on the kinds and quality of topics and specific purpose statements generated by each group.

Discussion: This exercise requires a fair amount of time outside of class and works especially well in courses that include a unit on group discussion. An added benefit of the exercise is that it often leads several students to topics that they eventually use in one or more of their speeches during the term.

6

Analyzing the Audience

Chapter Objectives

After reading this chapter, students should be able to:

1. Explain why public speakers must be audience centered.

2. Explain what it means to say that audiences are egocentric.

3. Identify the major demographic traits of audiences.

4. Identify the major situational traits of audiences.

5. Use a questionnaire as a method of audience analysis for classroom speeches.

6. Explain how a speaker can adapt to the audience while preparing the speech and while delivering the speech.

Chapter Outline

I. Good speakers are audience-centered.
    A. They understand that the primary purpose of public speaking is to gain a desired response from their listeners.
    B. They keep three questions in mind as they prepare their speeches:
        1. To whom am I speaking?

2. What do I want the audience to know, believe, or do as a result of my speech?

3. How can I most effectively compose and present my speech to accomplish that aim?

C. They seek to create a bond—what communication scholars call identification—with listeners by emphasizing common values, goals, and experiences.

II. It is important for student speakers to approach their classmates as a real audience.

A. Because the classroom seems like an artificial speaking situation, it is easy for students to lose sight of their classmates as an authentic audience.

B. The best student speakers take their audience seriously and treat their classmates as worthy of their best effort.

III. Good speakers understand the psychology of audiences.

A. A speaker's task is to make the audience want to pay attention to her or his message.

B. The auditory perception of audiences is always selective.

1. Everything a speaker says is filtered through a listener's frame of reference.

2. Every speech contains two messages—that sent by the speaker and that received by the audience.

C. Audiences are egocentric, paying closest attention to the messages that affect them directly.

D. These psychological principles have two important implications for speakers.

1. Listeners will judge a speech on the basis of what they already know and believe.

2. Speakers must take care to relate their messages to an audience's existing knowledge and beliefs.

IV. The first stage of audience analysis is examining demographic traits of the audience and how they might affect reception of the speech.

A. Demographic audience analysis is a useful tool in understanding audiences, but it needs to be used properly.

1. When analyzing demographic information about the audience, it is essential to avoid stereotyping.

2. Demographic audience analysis should always be combined with situational audience analysis.

B. Few things affect a person's outlook more than her or his age.

C. Gender issues can have a strong impact on how an audience responds to a speech.

D. The religious views of the audience need to be considered.

E. It is important to adapt to the audience on the basis of sexual orientation.

F. It is also important to consider the racial, ethnic, or cultural background of audience members.

    G. The group membership of an audience is another important factor to consider.

    H. There are also a number of other potentially important demographic variables, including occupation, economic position, education, and place of residence.

V. Another stage of audience analysis is examining features of the audience unique to the speaking situation at hand.

    A. The first factor to consider is the size of the audience.

    B. The second factor to consider is the physical setting of the speech.

    C. The third factor to consider is the audience's disposition toward the topic.

        1. A speaker needs to assess the audience's interest in the topic.

        2. A speaker needs to assess the audience's knowledge about the topic.

        3. A speaker needs to assess the audience's attitude toward the topic.

    D. The fourth factor to consider is the audience's disposition toward the speaker.

    E. The fifth factor to consider is the audience's disposition toward the occasion.

VI. There are several ways to get demographic and situational information about the audience.

    A. For speeches outside the classroom, speakers often make informal inquiries about their audience.

    B. For classroom speeches, students often use audience-analysis questionnaires.

        1. There are three basic types of questions for such questionnaires.

            a. Fixed-alternative questions offer a choice between two or more specific responses.

            b. Scale questions allow for a continuum of answers.

            c. Open-ended questions give maximum leeway in responding.

        2. There are four guidelines for effective audience-analysis questionnaires.

            a. They should be carefully planned to elicit the necessary information.

            b. They should use all three types of questions to get specific and detailed information.

            c. They should be clear and unambiguous.

            d. They should be relatively brief.

VII. Once speakers complete their audience analysis, they use that analysis to adapt their speech to their listeners.

    A. Most of the work of audience adaptation takes place before the speech as part of the preparation process.

        1. A speaker should keep the audience in mind at every stage of speech preparation.

2. A speaker should keep the following questions constantly in mind while preparing the speech.

    a. How is the audience likely to respond to what I will say?

    b. How can I adjust my message to make it as clear and convincing as possible?

3. Adjusting the message to the audience requires that speakers anticipate how listeners will respond and be creative in thinking of ways to adapt.

B. Audience adaptation also takes place during the presentation of the speech.

1. No matter how hard a speaker works ahead of time, things do not always go smoothly on the day of the speech.

2. Skillful speakers learn to adapt to these kinds of changes.

Exercises for Critical Thinking   *(from text page 117)*

1. Advertisers are usually very conscious of their audience. Choose an issue of a popular magazine such as *Time, Newsweek, Sports Illustrated, Vanity Fair, Rolling Stone,* or the like. From that issue select three advertisements to analyze. Try to determine the audience being appealed to in each advertisement, and analyze the appeals (verbal and visual) used to persuade buyers. How might the appeals differ if the ads were designed to persuade a different audience?

    Discussion: Because the audience appeal of most magazine advertisements is quite obvious, this exercise usually promotes vigorous class discussion on the principles of audience analysis and adaptation. In addition, it almost always provokes questions about the ethics of audience adaptation. If you use this exercise, be sure to have students bring a copy of their advertisements to class.

2. Below are three general speech topics and, for each, two hypothetical audiences to which a speech might be delivered. For each topic, write a brief paragraph explaining how you might adjust your specific purpose and message according to the demographic characteristics of the audience.

    a. *Topic:*   "Data Encryption"

       Audience #1:   50% computer science majors, 30% physics majors, 20% fine arts majors

       Audience #2:   40% business majors, 40% history majors, 20% computer science majors

    Discussion: Audience #1 will likely be more interested in and knowledgeable about the topic than will audience #2. The speaker addressing audience #2 will have to give special attention to gaining attention, to relating the topic to the audience, and to avoiding technical language.

b. *Topic:*   "Sexual Assault: The Biggest Campus Crime"

   Audience #1:   80% female, 20% male

   Audience #2:   80% male, 20% female

Discussion: Although sexual assault is a topic of great interest to both male and female students, the orientations of each toward the topic are usually different. Because women face the threat of sexual assault on a daily basis, a speech to audience #1 might stress steps that women can take to avoid becoming victims of sexual assault. Because men do not face the same personal threat of sexual assault, a speech to audience #2 might seek to sensitize male listeners to the seriousness of the problem, demonstrate that men are not immune from the problem because their wives, sisters, mothers or girlfriends could become victims of sexual assault, and explain steps men can take to make campus a safer place for women students.

c. *Topic:*   "The Fall of the Berlin Wall"

   Audience #1:   Day class: 70% age 18 to 22, 30% age 23 and over

   Audience #2:   Evening class: 50% age 35 and over, 30% age 23 to 34, 20% age 18 to 22

Discussion: The Berlin Wall fell in November 1989, an event that was watched on television by people around the globe. Although most members of audience #1 have probably seen video of this historic occurrence, they are too young to have a firsthand recollection of it or of its emotional impact. A speech to this group would have to provide substantial historical information about the wall, its role in the Cold War, and the events that led to its destruction. Nor can a speaker addressing audience #1 assume that most of his or her listeners will necessarily be interested in the topic.

On the other hand, a speaker addressing audience #2 can assume that most listeners have a fair stock of knowledge about the fall of the Berlin Wall. Much of the audience lived through at least part of the Cold War and may recall the destruction of the wall rather vividly. They are more likely to be interested in the subject than audience #1, and they probably will not need a great deal of historical background about it. Finally, the speaker will have to take some account of the 20 percent of this audience who are too young to know much about the wall or the events of November 1989.

3. For your next speech, design and circulate among your classmates an audience-analysis questionnaire like that discussed on pages 111–113 of the textbook. Use all three kinds of questions explained in the text: fixed-alternative, scale, and open-ended. After you have tabulated the results of the questionnaire, write an analysis explaining what the questionnaire

reveals about your audience and what steps you must take to adapt your speech to the audience.

Discussion: Although speakers outside the classroom seldom use questionnaires, this exercise is extremely useful because it requires students to engage in systematic audience analysis. It also requires them to conceive of their classmates as a genuine audience.

This exercise works best in conjunction with the first persuasive speech. You can set aside 5 to 10 minutes at the start of several class meetings to allow students to respond to questionnaires, or you can have students fill in the questionnaires at home and return them at the next class meeting. Finally, I would recommend having students turn in the analyses of their questionnaires at the time they turn in their preparation outlines.

Using Public Speaking in Your Career   *(from text page 110)*

As an economics professor, your research, writing, and teaching on the Social Security system has attracted media attention. Aware of your expertise, the local Rotary club has invited you to speak on the subject at the club's weekly meeting.

Having taken a public speaking class in college, you know how important it is to analyze the audience you will be addressing. To prepare for your speech, you have arranged a telephone interview with the club's president to find out more about your audience. List (1) the two most important questions you want to ask the president about the demographics of your audience, and (2) the two most important questions you want to ask about the situational traits of your audience. Be specific in your questions and be prepared, if necessary, to explain your choice of questions.

Discussion: There is no right or wrong answer to this scenario. Its purpose is to have students see how the principles of audience analysis discussed in the chapter can be applied in real-life situations outside the classroom. As far as demographic audience analysis is concerned, most people would agree that age is the paramount factor in this scenario. An audience of older people will have a different perspective on the subject of Social Security than will younger people. Students may also identify group membership as an important demographic variable. Members of the Democratic Party are more likely to oppose changes in the Social Security system than are members of the Republican Party.

Although all the situational factors discussed in the chapter could conceivably come into play in the scenario, the most important is probably the attitude of the audience toward the topic. Audience members who have a negative attitude toward proposals that would allow workers to invest part of their Social Security contributions in personal retirement accounts will be much less receptive to the speaker's ideas. The speaker will need to find ways to allay their opposition and to establish common ground with them.

The knowledge of the audience about the topic is another important situational variable. If the audience is already well-versed on the debates over Social Security and the details of plans that would allow workers to invest a portion of their contributions in individual retirement accounts, then the speaker will be able to discuss the topic at a more advanced level. On the other hand, if the audience has a lower level of knowledge, the speaker will need to spend much of his or her time explaining the basic issues before going on to more complex aspects of the topic.

In addition, it would be very helpful to know the size of the audience and the physical setting for the speech. With a small audience, it would be possible to take an informal, interactive approach that would make it easier to communicate with audience members on a personal basis. Physical setting is always something a speaker should inquire about regardless of the other situational or demographic variables. The time of day, the size and configuration of the room, the kinds of facilities for visual aids, and the like will have an impact on almost any speech.

Additional Exercises and Activities

1. Below are five specific purpose statements for classroom speeches. For each specific purpose statement, lead a class discussion that seeks to answer the question: "What steps would a speaker with this specific purpose statement need to take to adapt her or his speech to the interests, knowledge, and attitudes of this class?"

    a. To inform my audience how they can protect their apartment or dorm room against burglaries.

    b. To inform my audience about the principles of aerodynamics that allow an airplane to fly.

    c. To inform my audience about the causes, symptoms, and treatment of eating disorders.

    d. To persuade my audience that capital punishment should be abolished in all parts of the United States.

    e. To persuade my audience to participate in intramural sports.

    Discussion: This is an excellent alternative (or supplement) to Exercise 2 on page 117 of the textbook. While that exercise asks students to generalize about hypothetical listeners, this exercise gets them thinking about a specific real audience—their speech class. As a result, it has two benefits. One, of course, is to expand their understanding of the factors involved in audience analysis and adaptation in general. The second is to give them insight into the audience they will be addressing in their classroom speeches.

This exercise can be conducted entirely in class or, to save time, it can be given to students as a homework assignment.

2. You may wish to have your students prepare a formal demographic analysis of the class. One method is to lead a class discussion in which students create the items for a demographic audience analysis questionnaire. Another method is to give students a questionnaire format such as that on page 96 of this manual.

Discussion: Although the demographic questionnaire is not as useful for students as creating a situational audience analysis questionnaire, it is a good way to begin to get them attuned to the process of audience analysis. You should be aware, however, that some schools have deemed demographic questionnaires to be an invasion of students' privacy. If you have any doubts about the situation at your school, be sure to check before distributing the questionnaire.

3. Have students prepare an Audience Analysis and Adaptation Worksheet (see pages 97–98 of this manual) in conjunction with one or more of their speeches. Hand out the worksheets early, so students can use them throughout the speech preparation process. You can have the students turn in their worksheets at the same time as their initial preparation outlines, or you can require that they be turned in on the day of each student's speech.

Discussion: This is a relatively detailed worksheet, but if students use it conscientiously, it will help them become much more aware of the factors involved in audience analysis and adaptation. To help ensure that students take the worksheet seriously, you should probably make it a graded assignment. Some teachers simply include the worksheet as part of the overall grade for the speech; others assign a separate grade for the worksheet.

4. Distribute Barbara Bush's "Choices and Changes" from pages 419–421 of this manual. Have students analyze the speech in light of how Bush adapts her message to the audience, situation, and occasion.

Discussion: Barbara Bush's commencement speech at Wellesley College is an excellent study in audience analysis and adaptation. As the discussion on pages 422–423 of this manual explains, the choice of Bush as speaker touched off a protest among roughly one-quarter of Wellesley's graduating seniors. The protest in turn sparked a national controversy involving students, educators, politicians, and newspaper editorialists. When Bush rose to speak, she faced an immediate audience that had been polarized by the controversy and many members of which were skeptical, some even hostile, to her appearance at Wellesley.

This exercise usually works best if you have students prepare their analyses as a homework assignment, so they will be fully prepared to deal with the speech in class. See pages 422–423 for commentary on the speech that you can use to help guide class discussion.

Questionnaire for Demographic Audience Analysis

1. Age _____

2. Sex: Male _____   Female _____

3. Relationship status: Married _____   Single _____

   Divorced _____   Engaged _____

   Widowed _____   Partnered _____

4. Religion _____

5. Race/Ethnic Background _____

6. Year in school: Freshman _____   Sophomore _____

   Junior _____   Senior _____

7. Major (declared or anticipated) _____

8. Home town _____

   Population _____

9. Campus organizations to which you belong _____

   _____

10. Off-campus organizations to which you belong _____

   _____

11. Jobs you have held _____

   _____

   _____

   _____

Audience Analysis and Adaptation Worksheet
Part I

Speaker _____   **Topic** _____

What is the audience for this speech? _____

_____

What is the specific purpose of this speech? _____

_____

In choosing a specific purpose, how can you narrow the topic so it will be appropriate to this audience?

_____

_____

Demographic audience analysis: What special adaptation is necessary in the speech because of the audience's

age _____

gender _____

sexual orientation _____

religion _____

racial, ethnic, and cultural background _____

group membership _____

other (specify) _____

Situational audience analysis: What special adaptation is necessary in the speech because of the audience's

size _____

response to the physical setting _____

knowledge about the topic _____

interest level in the topic _____

attitude toward the topic _____

disposition toward the speaker _____

disposition toward the occasion _____

(continued in Part II)

Audience Analysis and Adaptation Worksheet
Part II

Speaker _____   **Topic** _____

Adaptation in the speech: Answer each of the following questions.

What device(s) did you use in the introduction to gain attention from this audience?

_____

_____

What steps did you take to relate the topic directly to this audience in the introduction?

_____

_____

_____

What are the main points of the speech? Why did you develop these particular main points for this audience?

_____

_____

_____

What decisions did you make in choosing supporting materials for this audience?

_____

_____

What steps did you take to make your language clear and appropriate to this audience?

_____

_____

What adjustments did you make in delivery—rate of speech, volume, tone of voice, gestures, and the like—to communicate your ideas to this audience?

_____

_____

_____

7 Gathering Materials

Chapter Objectives

After reading this chapter, students should be able to:

1. Explain how drawing on their own knowledge and experience can enrich their speeches.

2. Explain the major resources available for researching speeches in the library.

3. Explain how to use the Internet for speech research efficiently and responsibly.

4. Delineate the three stages of interviewing and explain the responsibilities of the interviewer at each stage.

5. Follow the four tips for doing research discussed in the chapter.

Chapter Outline

I.   A speaker's own knowledge and experience can be a valuable resource for information on a speech topic.

   A. We usually speak best about topics with which we are familiar.

   B. Supplementing facts and figures from books with personal experience can add color and emotion to a speech.

II. Library research is an important source of material for speeches.

   A. Librarians are an excellent resource.

    B.   The catalog lists all the books, periodicals, and other resources owned by the library.

    C.   Reference works contain a wealth of information about almost any topic.

        1.   Encyclopedias provide accurate, objective information on a wide range of subjects.

        2.   Yearbooks are annual publications that are invaluable for current information.

        3.   Quotation books can be useful, especially for introductions and conclusions.

        4.   Biographical aids provide information about people in the news.

    D.   Newspaper and periodical databases are invaluable for research on many topics.

    E.   Academic databases are the best way to find scholarly research.

III.   When used responsibly and efficiently, the Internet can be a powerful tool for speech research.

    A.   Search engines are the key to finding materials on the Internet.

    B.   In addition to search engines, there are specialized resources for finding materials on the Internet.

        1.   Virtual libraries combine Internet technology with traditional library methods of assessing data.

        2.   Government resources allow instant access to an endless number of government documents and publications.

        3.   Wikipedia can be a valuable online resource when it is used critically and in conjunction with other research materials.

    C.   There are three primary criteria for evaluating the quality of documents found on the Internet.

        1.   If possible, one should assess the objectivity and expertise of a document's author.

        2.   If there is no identifiable author, one should assess the sponsoring organization that produced the document.

        3.   Regardless of authorship or sponsorship, it is important to check the recency of the document.

IV.   Interviewing people with specialized knowledge is another way to gather materials for a speech.

    A.   The first stage in the interviewing process takes place before the interview.

        1.   The interview process begins when a speaker formulates a purpose for the interview.

        2.   Once the purpose of the interview is clear, a speaker must decide whom to interview and set up an appointment with that person.

        3.   Next the speaker needs to decide whether or not to record the interview.

        4.   The most important task before the interview is preparing the questions to be asked.

B. The second stage of the interview process takes place during the interview itself.

    1. It is important to dress appropriately and to show up on time.

    2. It is a good idea at the outset to restate the purpose of the interview so as to refresh the interviewee's memory.

    3. If the interviewee consents to having the interview recorded, the equipment should be set up quickly and inconspicuously.

    4. The most important part of the interview is asking the questions.

    5. In addition to asking good questions, the interviewer must listen carefully to the answers.

    6. Finally, the interviewer should try not to exceed the stipulated time period for the interview.

C. The third stage of the interview process takes place after the interview.

    1. While the interview is still fresh, the researcher should review her or his notes.

    2. As soon as possible after the interview, the researcher should transcribe ideas and information from the interview into the same format as the rest of her or his research notes.

V. Regardless of which resources speakers rely on in gathering speech materials, there are several ways to make their research more productive.

A. It is imperative that speakers begin their research early.

B. Speakers should create a preliminary bibliography of research sources.

C. Speakers can save time and energy by taking research notes efficiently.

    1. They should take plenty of notes.

    2. They should record notes in a consistent format and make a subject heading for each note.

    3. They should make a separate entry for each note.

    4. They should distinguish among direct quotations, paraphrases, and their own ideas.

D. The research process is most productive when speakers think about their materials as they research.

Exercises for Critical Thinking *(from text page 139)*

1. Using one of the periodical and newspaper databases discussed on pages 122–123 of the textbook, find three magazine or newspaper articles on the topic of your next speech. Prepare a preliminary bibliography entry for each article. Read the full text of the articles and assess their value for your speech.

Discussion: It is astounding how many college students have never used a periodical and newspaper database such as *ProQuest*, *LexisNexis Academic*, or *World News Connection*. This exercise is meant to remedy that situation and to help students get started on researching their next speech. For an alternative to this exercise, see the second Additional Exercise/Activity on page 103.

2. Using Google or another search engine, find three high-quality documents on the topic of your next speech. Prepare a preliminary bibliography entry for each article. Read the full text of the documents and assess them in light of the criteria for evaluating Internet documents discussed on pages 127–129 of the textbook.

Discussion: It is vital that students think critically about their research materials, especially when found on the Internet. As explained on pages 127–129 of the textbook, students need to evaluate the authorship, sponsorship, and recency of Web documents. If you assign this exercise as homework, you can use the class discussion to clarify how to conduct research on the Web effectively. For an alternative to this exercise, see the third Additional Exercise/Activity on page 103.

3. Plan to conduct an interview for one of your classroom speeches. Be sure to follow the guidelines presented in this chapter for effective interviewing. Afterward, evaluate the interview. Did you prepare for it adequately? Did you get the information you needed? What would you do differently if you could conduct the interview again?

Discussion: This exercise is most applicable if you assign students to conduct a research interview for one of their speeches. Having students write evaluations of their interviews requires them to think systematically about the interview process.

Using Public Speaking in Your Career *(from text page 129)*

After receiving your master's degree in education administration, you took a job at the state department of education. At the request of the governor, your section of the department has developed a new early childhood intervention program for children from impoverished households. Now you have been asked to help publicize the program and to build support for it. You will be speaking to church groups, teachers' associations, family advocacy groups, and others with an interest in children's welfare. You want to prepare a talk that makes good use of statistics and expert testimony to demonstrate the value of early childhood education programs, especially for poor children.

As part of your research, you decide to look on the Web for supporting materials. List three reputable Web sites that provide useful statistics or testimony on the value of early childhood education. Explain why each Web site is reputable and list one statistic or expert quotation you obtain from each source.

Discussion: The purpose of this scenario is to help students see how the skills of Internet research discussed in this chapter can be applied in real-life situations outside the classroom. When you assign this scenario, be sure to emphasize the final sentence, which instructs students to explain why each of their three Web sites is reputable and to list one statistic or expert quotation obtained from each site. If you have time, ask some students to share their research results with the class. Use the ensuing discussion to explore the criteria for credible, high-quality sources of statistics and testimony.

Additional Exercises and Activities

1. Arrange for your students to take a tour of the campus library. Students should read Chapter 7 before the tour, and they should be assigned application exercises from the chapter after the tour.

     Discussion: Because so many students do not know how to use the library efficiently, this activity is extremely beneficial. Not only are most libraries pleased to conduct such a tour, but they are quite adept at orienting it to the specific needs of individual classes. Arrange the tour two or three weeks in advance. Then contact the library a few days before the tour to indicate whether your students are mostly freshmen, sophomores, juniors, or seniors; what research tasks they will face in preparing their speeches; and any special features of the library you wish to have stressed on the tour. Students usually find the tour so helpful that, at the end of the term, they often rank it—and the development of their research skills—among the most valuable aspects of their speech class.

2. Using the Library Research Worksheet on page 104 of this manual, have students find three articles on the topic of their next speech. The articles can be from periodicals or newspapers. In addition to finding the articles, students should provide proper bibliographic citations and answer the questions listed on the worksheet.

     Discussion: This assignment offers an alternative to Exercise for Critical Thinking 1 and accomplishes the same objectives. The Library Research Worksheet gives students a convenient form to fill out in completing their research.

3. Using the Internet Research Worksheet on page 105 of this manual, have students find two Internet documents on the topic of their next speech. In addition to finding the documents, students should provide proper bibliographic citations and answer the questions listed on the worksheet.

     Discussion: This assignment offers an alternative to Exercise for Critical Thinking 2 and accomplishes the same objectives. The Internet Research Worksheet gives students a convenient form to fill out in completing their research.

Library Research Worksheet

Name _____ **Section** _____

Topic _____

Find three articles in the library on the subject of your next speech. The articles can be from periodicals or newspapers. Provide a complete citation for each article following the bibliography format required by your instructor and answer the questions about each article.

1. Article: _____

_____

Did you locate this article through a periodical and newspaper database?   Yes ❏ No ❏

If you answered yes, what is the name of the database? _____

If you answered no, how did you locate the article? _____

Why will the article be useful for your speech? Be specific. _____

_____

_____

2. Article: _____

_____

Did you locate this article through a periodical and newspaper database?   Yes ❏ No ❏

If you answered yes, what is the name of the database? _____

If you answered no, how did you locate the article? _____

Why will the article be useful for your speech? Be specific. _____

_____

_____

3. Article: _____

_____

Did you locate this article through a periodical and newspaper database?   Yes ❏ No ❏

If you answered yes, what is the name of the database? _____

If you answered no, how did you locate the article? _____

Why will the article be useful for your speech? Be specific. _____

_____

_____

Internet Research Worksheet

Name _____   **Section** _____

Topic _____

Find two documents from the Internet on the subject of your next speech. Provide a complete citation for each article following the bibliography format required by your instructor and answer the questions about each document.

1. Document: _____

    _____

    Did you locate this document through a search engine?   Yes ❑   No ❑

    If you answered yes, what is the name of the search engine? _____

    If you answered no, how did you locate the document? _____

    Why will the document be useful for your speech? Be specific. _____

    _____

    _____

    Explain why the author or sponsoring organization for this document should be accepted as a credible source on your speech topic.

    _____

    _____

2. Document: _____

    _____

    Did you locate this document through a search engine?   Yes ❑   No ❑

    If you answered yes, what is the name of the search engine? _____

    If you answered no, how did you locate the document? _____

    Why will the document be useful for your speech? Be specific. _____

    _____

    _____

    Explain why the author or sponsoring organization for this document should be accepted as a credible source on your speech topic.

    _____

    _____

8 Supporting Your Ideas

Chapter Objectives

After reading this chapter, students should be able to:

1. Explain why speakers need strong supporting materials for their ideas.

2. Distinguish among extended examples, brief examples, and hypothetical examples.

3. Explain how to use examples effectively in a speech.

4. Identify three questions for judging the reliability of statistics.

5. Discuss how to use statistics effectively in a speech.

6. Distinguish between peer testimony and expert testimony and explain the proper use of testimony in a speech.

Chapter Outline

I. Speeches need strong supporting materials to bolster the speaker's point of view.
   - A. A speech composed of unsupported assertions may leave an audience skeptical and unconvinced.
   - B. Specific and credible details are more convincing than are unsupported generalizations.

II. Examples are the first major kind of supporting material.

   A. Examples are an excellent way to get an audience involved with a speech.

   B. There are three types of examples—brief, extended, and hypothetical.

      1. Brief examples are specific instances that a speaker refers to in passing.

      2. Extended examples are longer and more detailed than brief examples.

      3. Hypothetical examples describe an imaginary situation.

   C. There are several tips for using examples effectively.

      1. A speaker should use examples to clarify ideas.

      2. A speaker should use examples to reinforce ideas.

      3. A speaker should use examples to personalize ideas.

      4. A speaker should use extended examples that are vivid and richly textured.

      5. A speaker should practice delivery to enhance the impact of extended examples.

III. Statistics are the second major kind of supporting material.

   A. When used properly, statistics are an effective way to support a speaker's ideas.

   B. Because statistics can be easily manipulated and distorted, speakers should evaluate their statistics carefully.

      1. Speakers need to make sure their statistics are representative of what they claim to measure.

      2. Speakers need to understand the differences among basic statistical measures such as the mean, the median, and the mode.

      3. Speakers need to determine whether their statistics come from reliable sources.

   C. There are several tips for using statistics effectively.

      1. Statistics should be used to quantify ideas.

      2. Statistics should be used sparingly.

      3. The source of statistics should be identified in the speech.

      4. Statistics should be explained and made meaningful to the audience.

      5. Complicated statistics should be rounded off.

      6. Statistical trends should be clarified with visual aids.

IV. Testimony is the third basic kind of supporting material.

   A. Testimony can be highly effective when used in a speech.

   B. There are two kinds of testimony—expert testimony and peer testimony.

      1. Expert testimony comes from people who are acknowledged authorities in their fields.

      2. Peer testimony comes from ordinary people who have firsthand experience with a topic.

   C. Testimony can be presented by quoting or by paraphrasing.

D. There are several tips for using testimony effectively.

1. Speakers should quote or paraphrase accurately.

2. Speakers should use testimony from qualified sources.

3. Speakers should use testimony from unbiased sources.

4. Speakers should identify the people being quoted or paraphrased.

V. Speakers need to identify orally the sources of their supporting materials.

A. Unlike written citations, oral citations do not follow a standard format.

1. The content of an oral citation depends on the topic, the audience, the speaker's claim, and the kind of supporting material being used.

2. Most citations will include some combination of the document title, the author or sponsoring organization, the author's qualifications, and the date on which the document was published.

B. Regardless of which elements are included, oral citations should be integrated smoothly into the speech.

Exercises for Critical Thinking *(from text page 163)*

1. Each of the following statements violates at least one of the criteria for effective supporting materials discussed in this chapter. Identify the flaw (or flaws) in each statement.

a. As Taylor Swift stated in a recent interview, U.S. policy toward North Korea should put more emphasis on bilateral negotiations.

Discussion: Although a concerned citizen, Taylor Swift is not a highly qualified source on foreign policy toward North Korea. The speaker would be better off citing someone who is an authority in the area.

b. According to *The New York Times Almanac*, California has the largest Native-American population of any state in the union—421,346. Arizona is second with 294,118 and Oklahoma is third with 287,124.

Discussion: This is an instructive set of statistics from a reliable source, but the speaker should round off the numbers. There is no reason to give exact figures down to the individual Native-American. In fact, by not rounding off, the speaker actually dilutes the impact of the figures. It would be more effective to say that California has the largest Native-American population in the United States with "more than 420,000," that Arizona has the second largest Native-American population with "almost 295,000," and that Oklahoma is third with "more than 287,000."

c. I don't know why rental car companies don't like to rent to people under the age of 25. My friends and I drive a lot, and none of us has been in an accident.

Discussion: The example cited here cannot be taken as representative of drivers under the age of 25. The experience of the speaker and his or her friends is not a sufficient basis for reaching a sweeping conclusion about the accident rates for people under the age of 25 in general.

d. In a random survey conducted last month among people visiting Las Vegas casinos, 96 percent of respondents opposed limitations on gambling in the United States. Clearly, then, the American people oppose such limitations.

Discussion: People visiting Las Vegas casinos are likely biased when it comes to limitations on gambling. Also, the sample is too restricted to be considered representative of the opinion of "the American people."

e. In the words of one expert, "The state education budget has been cut so much in recent years that any further cuts will do irreparable harm to our schools and the children they serve."

Discussion: The speaker does not identify "one expert" or present the expert's credentials as an authority on the topic.

f. Figures compiled by the Bureau of Labor Statistics show that the median salary for petroleum engineers in the U.S. is $108,910. This shows that petroleum engineers average almost $109,000 a year in salary.

Discussion: The speaker is confusing the median salary with the mean, which is popularly called the average. The median is the middle figure in a group once the numbers are arranged from highest to lowest and may differ considerably from the average.

g. According to a study by American Airlines, passenger satisfaction among frequent fliers is growing each year.

Discussion: Because American Airlines is an airline company, it can hardly be considered an objective source on the feelings of passengers. Although it is possible that the airline could hire a research firm that would conduct a scientifically valid study, a study from an independent consumer group would be a more credible source in this case.

2. Analyze "Bursting the Antibacterial Bubble" in the appendix of sample speeches following Chapter 19. Identify the main points of the speech and the supporting materials used for each. Evaluate the speaker's use of supporting materials in light of the criteria discussed in this chapter.

> **Discussion:** By analyzing the use of supporting materials in a speech, students often get a better idea of how to use them in their own speeches. "Bursting the Antibacterial Bubble" has a variety of supporting materials and illustrates how they can be employed to clarify and bolster a speaker's ideas. It also provides an opportunity for students to discuss how the speaker could have employed supporting materials more effectively. In addition to having students read the speech, you may want to show the video of it, which is available as part of the DVD of student speeches that accompanies this edition of *The Art of Public Speaking*. The video is also available in the online Media Library for this chapter at *Connect*. Here is a synopsis of the speech, paying close attention to its main points and use of supporting materials:

> Specific Purpose: To persuade my audience that action must be taken to deal with the problems created by the use of antibacterial household products.

> Central Idea: The use of antibacterial household products is creating health and environmental problems that require action by government and consumers alike.

> Method of Organization: Problem-Solution

> Introduction: The introduction consists of paragraphs 1–4. Paragraphs 1–2 gain attention by comparing the plotline of the film The Boy in the Plastic Bubble with the overuse of antibacterial products in contemporary society. In paragraphs 3–4 the speaker builds her credibility and relates the topic directly to her classmates by citing the results of her audience-analysis questionnaire. Paragraph 4 also states the speaker's central idea and previews the main points she will develop in the body of the speech.

> Body: There are two main points in the body of this speech. The first outlines the problem and is developed in paragraphs 5–14. The speaker documents the wide use of antibacterial products (paragraphs 5–7), explaining that they are not effective in stopping the spread of germs or diseases such as colds and flus (paragraphs 8–7), that they can actually increase a person's chances of getting sick (paragraphs 10–12), and that they appear to harm the environment (paragraphs 13–14). Because most of the speaker's classmates were not aware of the problems caused by antibacterial products, it was imperative that she present a convincing explanation of the extent and seriousness of the problem, which is why she devotes so much attention to this aspect of her speech.

After a transition in paragraph 15, the speaker presents her solution in the second main point (paragraphs 16–19). The first part of the solution is for the federal government to regulate the use of antibacterial chemicals in household products; the second part is for consumers to avoid purchasing such products.

Conclusion: The conclusion consists of paragraphs 20–21. In paragraph 20 the speaker provides an excellent summary of both her main points. In paragraph 21 she returns to her opening image of trying to create a bubble around ourselves to keep out germs and disease. But, she concludes, what we really have is a false bubble created by advertisers. The time has come to burst that bubble and "wash our hands of the whole mess." Although this might appear to be a mixed metaphor, it works well in this case because of its continuity with the bubble imagery that runs throughout the speech and with the notion that we can keep ourselves more healthy by washing our hands with ordinary soap and water than by wasting money on antibacterial products.

Supporting Materials: Because this speech deals with a controversial topic and because most people are not aware of the potential dangers of antibacterial household products, it is imperative that the speaker back up her claims with strong evidence. For the most part, she does this quite effectively, citing a wide range of studies and experts in support of her position.

She begins the body of her speech with a series of brief examples showing the wide range of antibacterial household products currently on the market (paragraphs 5–7). These include soaps, cotton swabs, shampoos, cutting boards, socks, toothpaste, mouthwash, toothbrushes, mattresses, countertops, and even children's toys. As you can see from the video of the speech, the speaker holds up several of these products for her audience to see as she discusses them. Although the audience did not need to see these products to understand the speaker's meaning, using the products as visual aids makes the speaker's ideas more vivid and more memorable.

The speaker does not present any extended examples, but this should not be considered a weakness in her speech. While one or two extended examples might have helped reinforce her argument, it is difficult to identify anything currently in the speech that she should have removed to make room for extended examples. The key to using supporting materials effectively is choosing those that will best buttress the speaker's ideas given the topic, audience, and length of the speech. In this case, once the speaker gets past the brief examples of antibacterial products in paragraphs 5–7, she turns to statistics and expert testimony as the most effective means of supporting her claims.

The speaker employs statistics in paragraphs 5, 6, 8, and 13. In paragraph 5 she cites the Alliance for the Prudent Use of Antibiotics to show that

75 percent of liquid soaps and 33 percent of bar soaps contain antibacterial ingredients. In paragraph 6 she states that there are more than 1,000 anti-bacterial household products currently on the market. In paragraph 8 she refers to a study by the Columbia University School of Nursing showing that 238 families who used antibacterial products were just as prone to fevers, sore throats, stomach problems, and the like as families who used non-antibacterial products. In paragraph 13 she presents statistics from Rolf Haden of the Johns Hopkins University School of Public Health showing that each year the U.S. releases into the water supply more than 2 million pounds of the active chemicals in antibacterial products. These statistics quantify the speaker's claims, and they come from credible sources.

Especially noteworthy is the speaker's use of testimony, which runs throughout both the problem and solution sections of the speech. In para-graph 7 she paraphrases the Boston Globe on some of the larger household items that have been coated with antibacterial chemicals. She follows this with a striking quotation from the New York Times stating that the antibacte-rial craze is "the biggest coup since bottled water."

In paragraph 8 the speaker combines statistics from the Columbia Univer-sity School of Nursing with a quotation from Erik Kupferberg, associate direc-tor of the Harvard School of Public Health, stating that "antimicrobial products don't significantly eliminate the number of germs you encounter on a daily basis." She then adds a quotation in paragraph 9 from Dr. Elaine Larson of Columbia University to support the point that most of the infections healthy people get are from viruses, which, unlike bacteria, cannot be killed by anti-bacterial products. In all three cases, the speaker relies on authoritative sources and identifies them clearly.

The same is true of the testimony used in paragraphs 10–12 to support the claim that antibacterial products actually increase a person's chances of getting sick. In paragraph 10 the speaker paraphrases microbiology professor Stuart Levy. In paragraph 10 she quotes research scientist Dr. James Chin, and in paragraph 11 she quotes Dr. Myron Genel, chairman of the American Medical Association's council on scientific affairs. She caps off the problem section of her speech in paragraph 14 by citing a report from the U.S. Geolog-ical Survey about the environmental hazards of the chemicals used in antibac-terial products. Using highly qualified sources of testimony is important in any speech, but it is especially important in this case because so many of the speaker's classmates were skeptical about her claims before the speech.

The speaker also uses testimony in paragraphs 18–19, which are part of the solution section. Paragraph 18 cites the Centers for Disease Control (CDC) to show that washing one's hands with plain soap and water is the best way to avoid germs, while paragraph 19 draws upon a study from the

University of North Carolina and quotes its co-author, epidemiologist Emily Sickbert-Bennett.

Some students may identify the material from the Centers for Disease Control as a statistic because it includes the statement that one should wash one's hands for 15–20 seconds. This is one of those instances in which a piece of evidence can be categorized in more than one fashion. To my mind, the most important thing is not whether one labels the information from the CDC as a statistic or a piece of testimony, but whether students understand the importance of strong supporting materials and are able to assess their use in the speech as a whole.

The only point that is not explicitly supported with evidence is the speaker's call in paragraphs 16–17 for federal legislation regulating the use of household antibacterial products. She does support her argument with analogical reasoning, but it is possible to argue in opposition that antibiotics and antibacterial household products are not essentially alike—that just because the former are regulated by the FDA, it does not necessarily follow that the latter should also be regulated. The speaker's position on this point would be more persuasive if she backed it up with expert testimony. With that exception, however, the speech provides an excellent example of how to use supporting materials—especially in a situation where the subject is controversial and the audience is not initially inclined to accept the speaker's position.

Additional Exercises and Activities

1. Have students prepare and present a one-point speech in which they state their point, support it with three pieces of supporting material, and then summarize the point. The speech should be 1 to 2 minutes in length and should be accorded the same weight in grading as a homework assignment.

    Discussion: If done properly, this can be an excellent way to give students an extra oral performance while at the same time helping them learn to use supporting materials effectively. Students should be allowed—indeed, encouraged—to use materials from the major speech assignment on which they are currently working. For example, if you deal with Chapter 8 during the unit on persuasive speaking, urge students to develop their one-point speech using materials that will appear in their persuasive speech. Some teachers require that students use all three kinds of supporting materials in the speech; others require that they use at least two. In most cases, the entire class will be able to present their speeches in a single session.

2. Evaluate the use of supporting materials in the following speech excerpt. Be sure to deal with all the supporting materials in each paragraph, and be specific in assessing their strengths and weaknesses.

> According to emergency medicine specialist Dr. Randall Sword, emergency rooms will handle more than 160 million cases this year alone. This means that one out of every 16 Americans will spend time in an emergency room this year. Unfortunately, the National Academy of Sciences states that "emergency medical care is one of the weakest links in the delivery of health care in the nation." In fact, medical researchers estimate that 5,000 deaths annually from poisoning, drowning, and drug overdoses, as well as 20 percent of all deaths from automobile accidents, would not have happened if the victims had received prompt and proper emergency room care.
>
> One cause of this problem is that many doctors are not properly trained in emergency care. According to *U.S. News and World Report*, fewer than 50 percent of emergency room physicians have completed special emergency training courses. A survey by Frey and Mangold found that untrained emergency room physicians felt they were unsure how to diagnose or treat many of the extreme abdomen, chest, and cardiac disorders that often appear in hospital emergency rooms.
>
> Another cause of the problem is that precious time is often wasted on useless paperwork before vital emergency treatment begins. Several years ago, a man driving by an elementary school in my hometown had a heart attack and crashed into a schoolyard. Seven children were taken to the emergency room three blocks away, but the real tragedy had not yet begun. Once in the emergency room, the children were denied treatment until their parents were contacted and the admitting forms were filled out. By the time the forms were completed, two of the children had died.

Discussion: This speech excerpt is brief enough to be used as a classroom activity. One approach is to divide the class into groups of four to five students each. Give each group ten minutes to read and analyze the excerpt, and then have each group make a two-minute report to the class assessing the strengths and weaknesses of the supporting materials in the excerpt. Another approach, of course, is to give the excerpt to each student individually. In either case, you should be able to generate an effective class discussion. Here is a brief analysis of the excerpt:

Paragraph One: The statistic in sentence 1 comes from a credible source. In sentence 2 the speaker does a nice job of showing what the statistic means for the U.S. public in general, though she might also have related it directly to her audience by stating how many of them would probably require emergency care during the year. The quotation from the National Academy of Sciences is excellent, and it is followed by statistics showing the seriousness of the problem. The statistics, however, should have been attributed to a specific source, rather than to unidentified "medical researchers."

Paragraph Two: The supporting materials in this paragraph are certainly relevant to the speaker's claim that doctors are not properly trained in emergency care. The statistics in sentence 2 are from a credible source, and the source is clearly identified. Unfortunately, in sentence 3 the speaker does not identify Frey and Mangold or their qualifications with respect to the topic.

Paragraph Three: While the extended example in this paragraph is dramatic, vivid, and relevant to the speaker's point, the speaker should have provided statistics or testimony to show that the example is not atypical.

3. Have students analyze one of the persuasive speeches from Part Five of this manual. Have students focus their analysis on the speaker's use of supporting materials.

Discussion: Every persuasive speech in Part Five deals with a question of policy and provides an excellent vehicle for giving students additional work analyzing the use—and occasional misuse—of supporting materials. For texts and discussions of the persuasive speeches, see pages 345–418 of this manual.

9 Organizing the Body of the Speech

Chapter Objectives

After reading this chapter, students should be able to:

1. Explain why it is important to organize speeches clearly and coherently.

2. Identify the five major patterns of organizing main points in a speech.

3. Discuss the guidelines given in the text for organizing main points.

4. Explain the four kinds of speech connectives and their roles in a speech.

Chapter Outline

I. The ability to organize one's ideas clearly and coherently is a vital skill.
    A. Clear organization is essential to effective public speaking.
    B. Clear organization is also connected to critical thinking.
        1. Organizing speeches helps students understand the relationships between ideas.
        2. The skills of critical thinking used in organizing speeches will benefit students in many aspects of their lives.

II. The main points are the most important element in organizing the body of a speech.

    A. Because main points are the central features in the body of a speech, they should be selected carefully.

    B. Speeches should have a limited number of main points.

        1. Most speeches contain from two to five main points.

        2. If a speaker discovers that she or he has too many main points, the points should be condensed into a few broad categories.

    C. Main points should be organized strategically to achieve the speaker's purpose.

        1. When arranged chronologically, main points follow a time sequence.

        2. When arranged spatially, main points follow a directional pattern.

        3. When arranged causally, main points show a cause-and-effect relationship.

        4. Main points can also be organized in problem-solution order.

        5. Main points are most often arranged in topical order.

    D. There are three tips for preparing effective main points.

        1. Speakers should keep their main points separate and distinct.

        2. Speakers should try to use parallel wording in their main points.

        3. Speakers should balance the amount of time devoted to each main point.

III. Once the main points of a speech are in strategic order, a speaker must make sure that the supporting materials are effectively organized.

    A. It is crucial that supporting materials be well organized because misplaced supporting materials are confusing to listeners.

    B. Details and evidence need to be directly relevant to the main points they support.

IV. Speakers should use connectives to strengthen their organization in the body of the speech.

    A. Connectives are words or phrases that join one thought to another and indicate the relationship between them.

    B. There are four types of connectives.

        1. Transitions indicate when a speaker has completed one thought and is moving on to another.

        2. Internal previews let the audience know what the speaker will take up next.

        3. Internal summaries remind listeners of what they have just heard.

        4. Signposts are brief statements that indicate exactly where a speaker is in the speech or that focus attention on key ideas.

Exercises for Critical Thinking   *(from text pages 181–182)*

1. What organizational method (or methods) might you use to arrange main points for speeches with the following specific purpose statements?

    To inform my audience of the causes and effects of Parkinson's disease.

    > **Discussion:** A speech with this specific purpose would probably be structured in causal order.

    To inform my audience about the major kinds of symbols used in Native American art.

    > **Discussion:** Although a speech with this specific purpose would probably be arranged in topical order, it might be organized chronologically if the speaker were to deal with the changes in Native American art symbols over the years.

    To persuade my audience that the state legislature should enact tougher laws to curb the problem of predatory lending to college students.

    > **Discussion:** Based on the methods of organization discussed in this chapter, a speech with this specific purpose would most likely be arranged in problem-solution order. In Chapter 16, we shall discuss more specialized methods for organizing persuasive speeches.

    To inform my audience about the major stages of the civil rights movement from 1955 to 1970.

    > **Discussion:** The most obvious choice for a speech with this specific purpose would be chronological order, but it could also be arranged topically.

    To inform my audience about the educational philosophy of Jean Piaget.

    > **Discussion:** A speech with this specific purpose would most likely be organized topically, with each main point dealing with a different aspect of Piaget's philosophy of education.

    To inform my audience about the geographical regions of Brazil.

    > **Discussion:** A speech with this specific purpose would probably be organized spatially, though it could also be structured topically.

2. Turn to the outline of main points and supporting materials for the speech about hypnosis on page 167 of the textbook. Create appropriate transitions, internal previews, internal summaries, and signposts for the speech.

Discussion: The purpose of this exercise is to give students practice in thinking about where connectives are needed in a speech and in creating the appropriate connectives. The exercise seems to work best when used as an in-class activity. Divide the class into groups, and have each group perform the exercise. Follow this with a class discussion in which each group presents its handiwork.

3. Identify the organizational method used in each of the following sets of main points.

   I. Fraudulent charity fund-raising is a widespread national problem.

   II. The problem can be solved by a combination of government regulation and individual awareness.

   (problem-solution)

   I. At the top of the rain forest is the emergent layer, where trees can be 200 feet tall.

   II. Below the emergent layer is the canopy, where vegetation is so dense that it filters out 80 percent of the sunlight.

   III. Beneath the canopy is the understory, where trees are less than 12 feet tall and grow large leaves to collect the small amount of sunlight.

   IV. At the bottom is the forest floor, where there are almost no plants because of the lack of sunlight.

   (spatial)

   I. Sonia Sotomayor is best known as the first Hispanic justice of the U.S. Supreme Court.

   II. Sonia Sotomayor is also an accomplished communicator who has given hundreds of public speeches.

   (topical)

   I. Founded in 1948, NASCAR was limited primarily to the South through the 1950s and 1960s.

   II. The modern era of NASCAR began in the 1970s with the development of the points system to crown a yearly champion.

   III. Today NASCAR is one of the most popular spectator sports in America.

   (chronological)

   I. Caused by an antibiotic-resistant strain of staphylococcus bacteria, MRSA has become increasingly prevalent among college students.

   II. The effects of MRSA include skin infections, damage to internal organs, pneumonia, and, in some cases, death.

   (causal)

Using Public Speaking in Your Career   *(from text page 173)*

You are the purchasing manager for a large jewelry manufacturer. The company's president sent you abroad to find new suppliers of base metals, including brass, copper, nickel, and aluminum. You were asked to evaluate each supplier based on the quality, availability, and cost of its products.

You have just returned from a 12-day trip to suppliers in Cambodia, China, South Korea, and the United Arab Emirates. You will present your findings and recommendations to the company's senior executives, but you're not sure how best to organize your speech.

Your major choices are chronological order, problem-solution order, and topical order. What might be the main points of your speech with each of these methods of organization? Explain which method you think would be most effective for your presentation.

Discussion: The purpose of this scenario is to have students see how the principles of speech organization discussed in the chapter can arise in real-life situations outside the classroom. Begin class discussion by focusing on the first question posed at the end of the scenario. Students should have little difficulty understanding that chronological order would result in a speech that narrates the events of the trip in the order they occurred. Students should also pick up quickly on the fact that spatial order would discuss the sites by starting in, say, China, and working one's way west through South Korea and Cambodia before ending with the base-metal supplier in the United Arab Emirates.

The most difficult method of organization for students to grasp is topical order. One option, if the speech were arranged topically, would be to devote each main point to a different company without regard to its geographical location or to where it fell in the time sequence of the trip. Another option would be to focus each main point on one of the three major criteria for the base metals you inquired about during your trip—quality, availability, and cost. In this case, information about the specific companies would appear, where relevant, as subpoints under each of the main points.

Once students understand the different methods of organization, you can turn to the question of which method would be most effective for the presentation to the senior executives. There is no right or wrong answer to this question, since any of the three methods could work effectively depending on the specific ideas the speaker wanted to communicate in her or his presentation. The important thing is to explore the strategic factors that might go into a decision to use one or another method of organization—both in this scenario and in general.

Additional Exercises and Activities

1. Have students read "The Horrors of Puppy Mills" in the appendix of sample speeches that follows Chapter 19 in the textbook. Assign students three tasks: (1) Pick out the main points of the speech; (2) Locate places where it uses connectives; (3) In each case, identify the kind of connective used—transition, internal preview, internal summary, or signpost.

    > **Discussion:** This exercise can be done with almost any of the speeches in the appendix of the book or in Part Five of this manual. I recommend "The Horrors of Puppy Mills" because it is rich in its use of connectives, especially signposts. Other excellent choices are "Ramadan," which appears in the appendix of the textbook, and "Securing Yourself Online," which appears in Part Five of this manual and can readily be copied for distribution to students.
    >
    > Regardless of the speech you assign, this exercise usually works best when it is given as a homework assignment followed by a class discussion. Be sure, in the discussion, to ask students to assess how well the speaker uses connectives and to identify places where additional connectives would have enhanced the clarity or coherence of the speech.

2. Below is a speech outline with 12 main points. Reorganize the outline so as to reduce the original 12 main points to three main points, each with three subpoints. Use the new main points and subpoints to fill in the blank outline that follows. Be sure to use parallel wording when stating the main points.

    I.   The first part of preparing for a backpacking trip is plotting the course.

    II. Choose a course that is suitable for everyone in the hiking group.

    III. Check detailed maps so you can identify obstacles on your course.

    IV. Consider the climate of the hiking area when plotting your course.

    V.   Preparing your food is also important.

    VI. Work out a menu that covers all meals you will eat on the trip.

    VII. Shop for the food you will need.

    VIII. Carefully pack the food in waterproof bags.

    IX. Good equipment is a necessity as well.

    X.   You will need a tent that is lightweight yet spacious.

    XI. You will need strong, comfortable hiking boots.

    XII. You will need proper clothing for the terrain and climate.

I.

    A.

    B.

    C.

II.

    A.

    B.

    C.

III.

    A.

    B.

    C.

Discussion: When reorganized, the outline should look similar to the one printed below. Although the main points need not be stated exactly as written here, they should use parallel wording. The most important matter, however, is that students see how the 12 original points can be regrouped into three main points with three subpoints each.

I. The first part of preparing for a backpacking trip is plotting the course.

    A. Choose a course that is suitable for everyone in the hiking group.

    B. Check up-to-date maps so you can identify obstacles on your course.

    C. Consider the climate of the hiking area when plotting your course.

II. The second part of preparing for a backpacking trip is getting the food.

    A. Work out a menu that covers all meals you will eat on the trip.

    B. Shop for the food you will need.

    C. Pack the food in waterproof bags.

III. The third part of planning a backpacking trip is choosing the equipment.

    A. Pick a tent that is lightweight yet spacious.

    B. Look for strong, comfortable hiking boots.

    C. Get proper clothing for the terrain and climate.

3. Identify the organizational method used in each of the following sets of main points.

    I.   Early people did not have money, but used a system of exchange based on the barter of goods and services.

    II. Coin money was invented in ancient Turkey, China, and India before the birth of Christ.

    III. Paper money began in China about 600 A.D. but did not become popular in the West until the 1600s.

    IV. Today almost every country has an official currency tied to the international rate of exchange.

    I.   Genetic engineering is producing new plant hybrids that will vastly increase world agricultural production.

    II. Genetic engineering is producing breakthroughs in medicine that will allow people to live healthier lives.

    III. Genetic engineering is producing bacteria that will help clean up industrial pollutants.

    I.   Gambling addiction is an increasingly serious problem throughout the United States.

    II. The problem of gambling addiction can best be solved by a combination of education and rehabilitation.

    I.   There are several causes for the destruction of the rain forests in South America.

    II. If the destruction of the rain forests continues, the effects will have global impact.

    I.   The top layer of the earth is a rocky "skin" called the crust.

    II. Beneath the crust is a thick layer of rock called the mantle.

    III. The next lower section is a mass of melted rock called the outer core.

    IV. At the center of the earth is a solid mass called the inner core.

Discussion: This complements Exercise 3 on page 182 of the textbook and gives students additional work in understanding the methods of organization discussed in this chapter. Alternatively, you can assign the worksheet to students from the assignments available in *Connect*.

    I.   Early people did not have money, but used a system of exchange based on the barter of goods and services.

    II. Coin money was invented in ancient Turkey, China, and India before the birth of Christ.

III. Paper money began in China about 600 A.D. but did not become popular in the West until the 1600s.

IV. Today almost every country has an official currency tied to the international rate of exchange.

(chronological)

I. Genetic engineering is producing new plant hybrids that will vastly increase world agricultural production.

II. Genetic engineering is producing breakthroughs in medicine that will allow people to live healthier lives.

III. Genetic engineering is producing bacteria that will help clean up industrial pollutants.

(topical)

I. Gambling addiction is an increasingly serious problem throughout the United States.

II. The problem of gambling addiction can best be solved by a combination of education and rehabilitation.

(problem-solution)

I. There are several causes for the destruction of the rain forests in South America.

II. If the destruction of the rain forests continues, the effects will have global impact.

(causal)

I. The top layer of the earth is a rocky "skin" called the crust.

II. Beneath the crust is a thick layer of rock called the mantle.

III. The next lower section is a mass of melted rock called the outer core.

IV. At the center of the earth is a solid mass called the inner core.

(spatial)

4. Have students complete the Connectives Worksheet, which is on page 125 of this manual.

Discussion: Easily copied and distributed, the Connectives Worksheet works best when assigned as homework. It familiarizes students with the basic functions of connectives and requires them to write a transition, an internal summary, and a combination transition-internal preview.

Connectives Worksheet

As discussed on pages 177–180 of your textbook, connectives are words or phrases that connect the ideas of a speech and indicate the relationships among them. Below are excerpts from two speech outlines—one on immigration, the other on the shortage of nurses in U.S. hospitals. For each outline, provide the connective(s) indicated in the space provided.

***

I.   Over the years, millions of people have immigrated to the United States.
   A.   Since the American Revolution, more than 90 million people have immigrated to the U.S.
   B.   Today there are over 38 million Americans who were born in other countries.

Transition: _____

_____

_____

II.   There are several reasons why people immigrate to the United States.
   A.   Many people immigrate in search of economic opportunity.
   B.   Others immigrate to attain political freedom.
   C.   Still others immigrate to escape religious persecution.

Internal Summary: _____

_____

_____

***

I.   The shortage of nurses has become a serious national problem.
   A.   More than 60 percent of U.S. hospitals have nurse shortages severe enough to threaten the quality of health care.
   B.   Experts warn that the shortage will become even worse in the years ahead unless steps are taken to solve it.

Transition and Internal Preview: _____

_____

_____

II.   The problem can be solved by offering nurses better salaries and better working conditions.
   A.   Better salaries will attract more people to nursing as a profession.
   B.   Better working conditions will improve morale and reduce burnout among nurses.

10
Beginning and Ending the Speech

Chapter Objectives

After reading this chapter, students should be able to:

1. Identify the four objectives of a speech introduction.

2. Explain seven methods that can be used to gain attention in an introduction.

3. Identify the major functions of a speech conclusion.

4. Explain the methods a speaker can use to fulfill the functions of a conclusion.

Chapter Outline

I.   Speeches need effective introductions and conclusions.
     A. An effective introduction gets the speaker off on the right foot.
     B. An effective conclusion ends the speech on a strong note.

II. There are four objectives of a speech introduction.
     A. The first objective is to gain the attention and interest of the audience.
         1. One method of gaining attention is to relate the topic to the audience.

    2.   A second method is to state the importance of the topic.

    3.   A third method is to startle the audience.

    4.   A fourth method is to arouse the curiosity of the audience.

    5.   A fifth method is to question the audience.

    6.   A sixth method is to begin with a quotation.

    7.   A seventh method is to tell a story.

    8.   Other methods of gaining attention include referring to the occasion, inviting audience participation, using audio equipment or visual aids, relating to a previous speaker, and beginning with humor.

  B. The second objective of a speech introduction is to reveal the topic of the speech.

  C. The third objective of a speech introduction is to establish the credibility and goodwill of the speaker.

    1.   Credibility is a matter of being perceived by the audience as qualified to speak on a particular topic.

    2.   Establishing goodwill is a matter of showing that the speaker has the audience's best interests in mind.

  D. The fourth objective of a speech introduction is to preview the body of the speech.

III. There are five tips for preparing an effective introduction.

  A. The introduction should usually be relatively brief.

  B. Speakers should keep an eye out for potential introductory material as they research the speech.

  C. Speakers should be creative when devising their introductions.

  D. Speakers should not be concerned with the exact wording of the introduction until the body of the speech is finished.

  E. The introduction should be worked out in detail so it can be delivered effectively.

IV. A speech conclusion has two primary functions.

  A. The first function is to signal the end of the speech.

    1.   One way to signal the end of a speech is with a brief verbal cue such as "In conclusion" or "One last thought."

    2.   Another way to signal the end is by the speaker's manner of delivery.

  B. The second function of a conclusion is to reinforce the audience's understanding of or commitment to the central idea of the speech.

    1.   There are four methods of accomplishing this.

       a.   One method is to summarize the main points of the speech.

       b.   A second method is to conclude with a quotation.

       c.   A third method is to end with a dramatic statement.

       d.   A fourth method is to refer back to the introduction of the speech.

    2.   These methods can be used separately or in combination to create an effective conclusion.

V.   There are four tips for preparing an effective conclusion.

    A.   Speakers should keep an eye out for potential concluding materials as they research the speech.

    B.   Speakers should conclude with a bang instead of a whimper.

    C.   Speakers should not be long-winded in the conclusion.

    D.   Speakers should prepare the content and delivery of their conclusions with special care.

Exercises for Critical Thinking *(from text page 203)*

1.   Here are six speech topics. Explain how you might relate each to your classmates in the introduction of a speech.

Social Security	laughter
coffee	steroids
illiteracy	blood donation

Discussion: Students often have great difficulty deciding how to relate their speech topics directly to their classmates. This exercise is designed to give them some practice, and it works equally well as a homework assignment, as a group activity in class, or simply as the basis for a general class discussion. After the class deals with each item, you may want to read your students the following excerpts from the introductions of student speeches on each of the six topics.

Social Security:

> Many of you may think, "What does Social Security have to do with me? I'm young, healthy, and nowhere near retirement age."

> But Social Security has a lot to do with you. If you don't have a job today, you will in a couple of years. And when you do, you will pay Social Security taxes. How much will you pay? That depends on how much you earn. If you earn $40,000, you will pay more than $3,000 a year in Social Security taxes. At present tax rates, that comes to more than $125,000 in the course of your working career. You should know where your money goes and whether you will ever benefit from it.

coffee:

> Are you an addict? Do you need a daily fix to keep going? Are you hooked on one of the most popular beverages on the planet, a beverage that is a way of life for sleep-deprived college students?
>
> I'm talking, of course, about coffee. According to *Newsweek* magazine, we are drinking record quantities of coffee these days. I don't know about you, but in my experience, I can't get to class—whether it's at 8 a.m. or 4 p.m.— without first downing cup after cup of coffee.

illiteracy:

> Imagine that you are in France visiting some friends. Because your friends are busy, you offer to go to the grocery store—even though you don't know a word of French. At the store, you look for what you need, but none of the cans or boxes have pictures on them. You come out of the store thinking you have bought a box of cereal and a can of soup, but when you get to your friends' house, you discover that you have a box of laundry detergent and a can of dog food.
>
> Although this scenario is admittedly far-fetched, it should give you some idea of how frustrating it is to look at a bunch of letters and not know what they mean. This is the same frustration that millions of adults in the United States experience every day because they are functionally illiterate.

laughter:

> The neural circuits in your brain begin to reverberate. Chemical and electrical impulses start flowing rapidly through your body. Your pituitary gland is stimulated. Hormones and endorphins race through your blood.
>
> Your body temperature rises by half a degree. Your pulse and blood pressure increase. Your arteries and chest muscles contract, your vocal chords quiver, and your face contorts. Pressure builds in your lungs. Your lower jaw suddenly becomes uncontrollable and breath bursts from your mouth at seventy miles per hour.
>
> This is surely no laughing matter. Or is it? It is! This is a medical description of what happens in your body during a burst of laughter. It sounds dreadful, but we all know it feels great.

steroids:

> Imagine that you're one of an elite group of students fighting for a spot at the top of your class. You're fully aware of the implications of an upcoming exam. If you blow it, you lose your rank. However, a good grade virtually assures you of prestige and a comfortable job.

So you look for that extra edge—a little something to push your already strained mind further. If there were a pill that would increase your mental sharpness for a short period of time and ensure you a high score on the exam, chances are many of you would consider taking it.

Amateur and professional athletes are faced with a similar dilemma every day of their competitive lives. In the never-ending search for the extra edge in sports, many athletes have given in to the lure of anabolic steroids.

blood donation:

Picture this: You're walking home from class with your best friend. You begin to cross College Avenue. All of a sudden, out of nowhere comes a car that doesn't stop for the red light. Your friend is hit. It happened so fast that all you know is your friend is down and can't move.

The ambulance arrives and takes your friend to the hospital. At the hospital you find out your friend has serious internal bleeding and desperately needs blood. One major problem—at this time there is no blood available in your friend's blood type. Your throat tightens up. You naturally thought there was always enough blood. Now you find out there isn't.

Even though this situation is hypothetical, it is far from impossible. A poster from the Red Cross sums this up well: "Blood is like a parachute. If it's not there when you need it, chances are you'll never need it again."

2. Think of a speech topic (preferably one for your next speech in class). Create an introduction for a speech dealing with any aspect of the topic you wish. In your introduction, be sure to gain the attention of the audience, to reveal the topic and relate it to the audience, to establish your credibility, and to preview the body of the speech.

Discussion: This exercise is designed to give students practice developing a complete introduction. For an alternative activity, see the first entry under Additional Exercises/Activities in this chapter.

3. Using the same topic as in Exercise 2, create a speech conclusion. Be sure to let your audience know the speech is ending, to reinforce the central idea, and to make the conclusion vivid and memorable.

Discussion: This exercise is designed to give students practice in developing a complete conclusion. For an alternative activity, see the first entry under Additional Exercises/Activities in this chapter.

Using Public Speaking in Your Career   *(from text page 198)*

Your degree in civil engineering has served you well and you are now the chief city planner for a major metropolis. After studying the issue for more than a year, you and the planning commission have decided that the best way to relieve the city's growing traffic congestion is to build a new downtown freeway. Unfortunately, there is no way to build the freeway without knocking down a number of houses and businesses.

Not surprisingly, the neighborhood association that represents the area through which the new freeway will run has expressed a number of concerns about the proposal. Because of your excellent public speaking skills, you have been chosen to represent the city at a meeting of the neighborhood association. You know that if your speech is to be persuasive, you must use the introduction to establish your credibility and goodwill so your listeners will be willing to listen receptively to what you say in the body.

Write a draft of your introduction. Be sure to address all four functions of a speech introduction discussed in this chapter.

> **Discussion:** As with most of the other Using Public Speaking in Your Career scenarios throughout the book, there is no single correct answer to this one. Its purpose is to get students thinking about the functions of speech introductions and to illustrate how those functions are just as important for speeches outside the classroom as for those in the classroom. The best way to handle this exercise is to divide the class into groups and give each 15 to 20 minutes of class time to compose an introduction. Have one member from each group present its introduction to the class, and follow with a general discussion about all of the groups' introductions.

Additional Exercises and Activities

1. Divide the class into groups of 3 to 5 students. Assign each group a topic on which it must prepare a complete introduction and conclusion. Give the groups 20 minutes to work on their introductions and conclusions. Each group should pick one of its members to deliver its introduction and conclusion to the class.

    > **Discussion:** This is an effective alternative to Exercises 2 and 3 on page 203 of the textbook. By working in groups, students can use brainstorming to devise more creative introductions and conclusions. Presenting the introductions and conclusions orally allows the whole class to participate in a discussion about the strengths and weaknesses of each group's results.

2.   Here are four complete introductions from classroom speeches. Each has at least one flaw that keeps it from fulfilling all the functions of a good introduction. In each case identify the flaw (or flaws) and make specific suggestions for improving the introduction.

a.   What tiny crystal fortified the coffers of many ancient empires and laid waste to others? What mineral has the power to create and the power to destroy? What is "good as gold" when scarce and "cheap as dirt" when abundant?

The answer to all of these questions is salt, the spice of life. Today I would like to look at the importance of salt in history, at how we spice up our lives with salt today, and at the role salt will probably play in the future.

b.   We have so much unused human potential. By improving the use of your time, you can have much more time for social activities. You can use your mental processes more fully, thereby improving your grades. You can also increase your physical stamina and improve your health. We must learn to know our bodies.

c.   A six-year-old collie lay battered and helpless by the side of the road. The car that hit her had broken her pelvis, dislocated her hip, and smashed her jaw. It had also blinded her, and she whimpered in pain and fear.

Unfortunately, this true story happens much too frequently because of the growing problem of pet overpopulation. Having grown up on a farm with animals of all kinds, I care deeply about their welfare, and I have become aware through my veterinary courses of how serious the problem of pet overpopulation is.

d.   Every problem has at least two sides. When one side is right, and the other side is wrong, the problem is easy to solve. But what if both sides have merit in their arguments? How do you solve these problems?

Balancing the rights of everyone in an adoption is one of these problems. The parents who give up the child have a right that all the information they disclose be kept confidential, while the adopted child has a right to know about the identity of his or her natural parents.

Today I'd like to explore this problem with you and look at one approach to solving it.

Discussion: This is an excellent exercise because it gets students to focus on all four objectives of a speech introduction. You can also assign the exercise to students from the assignments available in *Connect*. Here is a brief analysis of each of the introductions in the exercise.

a.   This introduction uses a series of questions to get attention, introduces the topic clearly, and has a concise preview statement. Its most obvious flaw is a lack of material establishing the speaker's credibility. It might also be improved by relating the topic of salt directly to the audience at the outset.

b. By relating to the audience, this introduction does a fair job of capturing attention—but that is all. It does not reveal the topic of the speech, establish the credibility of the speaker, or preview the main points of the speech.

c. This introduction does an excellent job of gaining attention, of introducing the topic of pet overpopulation, and of establishing the speaker's credibility. It is flawed, however, by its lack of a preview statement. As with the introduction on salt, it also could be strengthened if it related the topic directly to the audience.

d. This introduction does a good job of revealing the topic and previewing the main points of the speech. It does nothing to establish the speaker's credibility, and it is weak as an attention-getter.

3. Have the class pay special attention to their classmates' introductions and conclusions during the next round of speeches. Afterward, have the class select the three most effective introductions and the three most effective conclusions.

Discussion: This is a good way to review the principles of effective introductions and conclusions. Surprisingly, students usually tend to agree about the most effective introductions and conclusions. To avoid hurt feelings, though, it is a good idea not to rank-order the three top choices.

4. Show students Part One of *Introductions, Conclusions, and Visual Aids*, which accompanies *The Art of Public Speaking*.

Discussion: *Introductions, Conclusions, and Visual Aids* is a 30-minute DVD produced exclusively to accompany *The Art of Public Speaking*. Part One deals with the principles of effective introductions and conclusions and is illustrated with selections from a wide range of speeches. Use the DVD as a springboard for class discussion about the criteria for introductions and conclusions discussed in this chapter of the book.

Outlining the Speech

Chapter Objectives

After reading this chapter, students should be able to:

1. Explain why it is important to outline speeches.

2. Explain the differences between a preparation outline and a speaking outline.

3. Construct a preparation outline following the guidelines presented in the book.

4. Construct a speaking outline following the guidelines presented in the book.

Chapter Outline

I. Outlines are essential to effective speeches.

   A. An outline helps a speaker see the full scope and content of the speech at a glance.

   B. An outline helps a speaker judge whether each part of the speech is fully developed.

   C. An outline helps create a coherent structure for the speech.

II. Creating a preparation outline is a vital step in putting a speech together.

   A. A preparation outline is a detailed outline used to plan a speech.

   B. The process of writing a preparation outline requires that a speaker bring together all the major elements of the speech.

    C. There are eight guidelines for effective preparation outlines.

        1. The preparation outline should include the speaker's specific purpose statement.

        2. The preparation outline should include the speaker's central idea.

        3. The preparation outline should clearly label the introduction, body, and conclusion of the speech.

        4. The preparation outline should have a consistent pattern of symbolization and indentation.

        5. The preparation outline should state main points and subpoints in full sentences.

        6. The preparation outline should label transitions, internal summaries, and internal previews.

        7. The preparation outline should include a bibliography.

        8. The preparation outline may also include a title for the speech.

III. Once the preparation outline is completed, a speaking outline can be drawn up.

    A. A speaking outline is a brief outline used to deliver a speech.

    B. The primary purpose of a speaking outline is to help a speaker remember what to say.

        1. It includes key words and phrases from the preparation outline.

        2. It includes essential statistics and quotations the speaker does not want to forget.

        3. It includes cues to direct and sharpen a speaker's delivery.

    C. Speaking outlines are especially effective for extemporaneous speeches.

    D. There are four guidelines for effective speaking outlines.

        1. The speaking outline should follow the same visual framework used in the preparation outline.

        2. The speaking outline should be plainly legible.

        3. The speaking outline should be as brief as possible.

        4. The speaking outline should include cues for delivering the speech.

Exercises for Critical Thinking *(from text pages 218–219)*

1.   In the left-hand column below is a partially blank outline from a speech about the Golden Gate Bridge. In the right-hand column, arranged in random order, are the subpoints to fill in the outline. Choose the appropriate subpoint for each blank in the outline.

To complete this exercise online, go to the interactive Outline Exercises in the Study Aids for this chapter. You will also find several additional scrambled outlines that you can use to hone your outlining skills.

Outline	Subpoints
I. More than 20 years passed from the time the Golden Gate Bridge was proposed to the time it opened.	Today, those towers make it the world's third tallest suspension bridge.
A.	Construction finally began in 1933 and ended in 1937.
B.	The span between its towers is 4,200 feet.
C.	At the time it was built, the Golden Gate was also the longest suspension bridge in the world.
D.	In 1923, the State of California passed legislation authorizing construction of the bridge.
II. Now 75 years old, the Golden Gate Bridge remains a marvel of modern engineering.	Its two towers rise almost 750 feet above the waters of the Pacific Ocean.
A.	Once construction of the bridge was authorized, it took ten years to approve the design and financing.
1.	That span makes it the ninth longest suspension bridge in the world today.
2.	At the time it was built, the Golden Gate was the tallest suspension bridge in the world.
B.	The bridge was originally proposed in 1916 but faced years of legal hurdles.
1.	
2.	

Discussion: This is an excellent exercise to help students develop outlining skills. You can do the exercise in class, or you can have students use the interactive outlining feature in the online Study Aids for this chapter at *Connect*. In case you wish to assign more than one such exercise, there are four additional scrambled outlines among the online Study Aids, three among the Additional Exercises/Activities in this manual (pages 139–145), and two more among the essay exam questions in Chapter 11 of the *Test Bank*.

   When filled in, the outline on the Golden Gate Bridge should look like the following.

   I.   More than 20 years passed from the time the Golden Gate Bridge was proposed to the time it opened.

     A.   The bridge was originally proposed in 1916 but faced years of legal hurdles.

     B.   In 1923, the State of California passed legislation authorizing construction of the bridge.

     C.   Once construction of the bridge was authorized, it took ten years to approve the design and financing.

     D.   Construction finally began in 1933 and ended in 1937.

  II.   Now 75 years old, the Golden Gate Bridge remains a marvel of modern engineering.

     A.   At the time it was built, the Golden Gate was the tallest suspension bridge in the world.

        1.   Its two towers rise almost 750 feet above the waters of the Pacific Ocean.

        2.   Today, those towers make it the world's third tallest suspension bridge.

     B.   At the time it was built, the Golden Gate was also the longest suspension bridge in the world.

        1.   The span between its towers is 4,200 feet.

        2.   That span makes it the ninth longest suspension bridge in the world today.

2.   From the preparation outline on the Golden Gate Bridge you constructed in Exercise 1, create a speaking outline that you might use in delivering the speech. Follow the guidelines for a speaking outline discussed in this chapter.

> **Discussion:** This exercise helps clarify the differences between a preparation outline and a speaking outline and gives students practice in creating a speaking outline. Whether or not you have students complete this exercise at home, you can direct class discussion toward the elements of effective preparation and speaking outlines.

Using Public Speaking in Your Career   *(from text page 215)*

As the defense attorney in a car theft case, you need to prepare your closing argument to the jury before it begins its deliberations. After reviewing evidence from the trial, you decide to stress the following points to demonstrate the innocence of your client:

a.   The stolen car was found abandoned three hours after the theft with the engine still warm; at the time the car was found, your client was at the airport to meet the flight of a friend who was flying into town.

b.   Lab analysis of muddy shoe prints on the floor mat of the car indicates that the prints came from a size 13 shoe; your client wears a size 10.

c.   Lab analysis shows the presence of cigarette smoke in the car, but your client does not smoke.

d.   The only eyewitness to the crime, who was 50 feet from the car, said the thief "looked like" your client; yet the eyewitness admitted that at the time of the theft she was not wearing her glasses, which had been prescribed for improving distance vision.

e.   The car was stolen at about 1 p.m.; your client testified that he was in a small town 250 miles away at 11 a.m.

f.   In a statement to police, the eyewitness described the thief as blond; your client has red hair.

As you work on the outline of your speech, you see that these points can be organized into three main points, each with two supporting points. Compose an outline that organizes the points in this manner.

Discussion: As with the other Using Public Speaking in Your Career scenarios throughout the book, this one is meant to illustrate that the principles of effective speechmaking are applied in a wide range of situations outside the classroom. In dealing with this scenario, students should construct an outline whose three main points deal with lab analysis, with the timeline of events, and with eyewitness testimony. Once the six points stated in the scenario are reorganized as subpoints under the lab analysis, timeline, and eyewitness main points, the outline will look as follows (allowing, of course, for differences in the exact wording of main points and in the order of some subpoints).

   I. Lab analysis does not support a guilty verdict.

      A. Lab analysis of muddy shoe prints on the floor mat of the car indicates that the prints came from a size 13 shoe; the defendant wears a size 10.

      B. Lab analysis also shows the presence of cigarette smoke in the car, but the defendant does not smoke.

  II. The timeline of events in the case does not support a guilty verdict.

      A. The stolen car was found abandoned three hours after the theft with the engine still warm; at the time the car was found, the defendant was at the airport to meet the flight of a friend who was flying into town.

      B. The car was stolen at about 1 p.m.; the defendant testified that he was in a small town 250 miles away at 11 a.m.

 III. Eyewitness testimony does not support a guilty verdict.

      A. The only eyewitness to the crime, who was fifty feet from the car, said the thief "looked like" the defendant; yet the eyewitness admitted that at the time of the theft she was not wearing her glasses, which had been prescribed for improving distance vision.

      B. In a statement to police, the eyewitness described the thief as blond; the defendant has red hair.

Additional Exercises and Activities

1. In the left-hand column below is a partially blank outline from a speech about suicide among college students. In the right-hand column, arranged in random order, are the subpoints to fill in the outline. Choose the appropriate subpoint for each blank in the outline.

Outline	**Subpoints**
I. Suicide among college students is a serious problem.	Even on our campus the rate of suicide and attempted suicide is quite high.
A.	There are also more subtle warning signs that a person may try to commit suicide.
B.	There are excellent services available on campus and in the community to help potential suicide victims.
C.	In town students can go to the Suicide Prevention Center.
1.	One warning sign is loss of appetite.
2.	Identifying potential suicide victims is easier than you think.
II. We can help solve the problem by knowing how to identify potential suicide victims and whom to contact about helping them.	Dean Howard also said that for every known suicide attempt, two or three more go unnoticed.
A.	According to the National Institute of Mental Health, suicide is the fastest growing cause of death for people aged 17 to 24 nationwide.
1.	In an interview with Roger Howard, associate dean of students, I learned that last year there were over 60 known suicide attempts on our campus.
2.	A second warning sign is prolonged depression.
a.	The National Institute of Mental Health says 80 percent of the people who commit suicide tell someone ahead of time that they are going to kill themselves.
b.	
c.	A third warning sign is giving away one's possessions.
B.	Last year 10,000 young Americans committed suicide.
1.	
2.	On campus students can go to the University Counseling Service.

Discussion: When filled in, the outline should look like the one below. (The order of points IA and IB can be reversed without damaging the students' answers.)

I. Suicide among college students is a serious problem.

    A. According to the National Institute of Mental Health, suicide is the fastest growing cause of death for people aged 17 to 24 nationwide.

    B. Last year 10,000 young Americans committed suicide.

    C. Even on our campus the rate of suicide and attempted suicide is quite high.

        1. In an interview with Roger Howard, associate dean of students, I learned that last year there were over 60 known suicide attempts on our campus.

        2. Dean Howard also said that for every known suicide attempt, two or three more go unnoticed.

II. We can help to solve the problem by knowing how to identify potential suicide victims and whom to contact about helping them.

    A. Identifying potential suicide victims is easier than you might think.

        1. The National Institute of Mental Health says that 80 percent of the people who commit suicide tell someone ahead of time that they are going to kill themselves.

        2. There are also more subtle warning signs that a person may try to commit suicide.

            a. One warning sign is loss of appetite.

            b. A second warning sign is prolonged depression.

            c. A third warning sign is giving away one's possessions.

    B. There are excellent services on campus and in the community to help potential suicide victims.

        1. On campus students can go to the University Counseling Service.

        2. In town students can go to the Suicide Prevention Center.

2. In the left-hand column below is a blank outline from a speech about the achievements of Booker T. Washington. In the right-hand column, arranged in random order, are the main points and subpoints to fill in the outline. Choose the appropriate main point or subpoint for each blank in the outline.

Outline	Main Points and Subpoints
I.	All told, Washington delivered some 4,000 public speeches during his 30-year career as an orator.
A.	Some people praise the speech as a brilliant example of audience adaptation in a very difficult situation.
1.	Washington is also known as one of the ablest speakers in American history.
2.	When Washington founded Tuskegee Institute in 1881, the school had only one dilapidated building and an enrollment of 40 students.
B.	Today, Tuskegee Institute remains a leader in applied research and practical education.
II.	Washington's most famous speech is his "Atlanta Exposition Address" of 1895.
A.	The growth of Tuskegee Institute under Washington's guidance was nothing short of phenomenal.
B.	To this day, Washington's speech at Atlanta remains highly controversial.
1.	Booker T. Washington is best known for founding Tuskegee Institute in Alabama.
2.	By the time Washington died in 1915, Tuskegee Institute occupied 2,000 acres of land, enrolled 1,500 students, and boasted a faculty of 200 instructors.
a.	Other people condemn the speech for failing to denounce racial segregation and inequality.
b.	In the "Atlanta Exposition Address" Washington urged blacks to strive for economic advancement rather than to agitate for immediate social equality.

Discussion: When filled in, the outline should look like the one below.

I. Booker T. Washington is best known for founding Tuskegee Institute in Alabama.

    A. The growth of Tuskegee Institute under Washington's guidance was nothing short of phenomenal.

        1. When Washington founded Tuskegee Institute in 1881, the school had only one dilapidated building and an enrollment of 40 students.

        2. By the time Washington died in 1915, Tuskegee Institute occupied 2,000 acres of land, enrolled 1,500 students, and boasted a faculty of 200 instructors.

    B. Today, Tuskegee Institute remains a leader in applied research and practical education.

II. Booker T. Washington is also known as one of the ablest speakers in American history.

    A. All told, Washington delivered some 4,000 public speeches during his 30-year career as an orator.

    B. Washington's most famous speech is his "Atlanta Exposition Address" of 1895.

        1. In the "Atlanta Exposition Address" Washington urged blacks to strive for economic advancement rather than to agitate for immediate social equality.

        2. To this day, Washington's speech at Atlanta remains highly controversial.

            a. Some people praise the speech as a brilliant example of audience adaptation in a very difficult situation.

            b. Other people condemn the speech for failing to denounce racial segregation and inequality.

3. In the left-hand column below is a partially blank outline from a speech about robots. In the right-hand column, arranged in random order, are the subpoints to fill in the outline. Choose the appropriate subpoint for each blank in the outline.

Outline	**Subpoints**
I. Robots have captured the human imagination for centuries.	Astronauts use robots to perform maintenance on the International Space Station.
A.	In 1937, Westinghouse created a seven-foot robot that could walk, talk, blow up balloons, and smoke cigarettes.
B.	They also allow surgeons to operate on patients from thousands of miles away.
C.	Robots have become indispensable to space exploration.
II. Today robots are used in many fields, including space exploration and medicine.	In 1497, Leonardo da Vinci designed a mechanical suit of armor that could sit up and move its arms, neck, and jaw.
A.	They can navigate hospital corridors to deliver pharmaceuticals, X-rays, and bandages.
1.	In addition, NASA sends robotic spacecraft to explore distant planets.
2.	Robots are becoming more and more important in medicine.
B.	
1.	In 1773, Pierre and Henry Louis Jaquet-Droz built dolls that could write, play music, and draw pictures.
2.	

Discussion: When filled in, the outline should look like the one below.

I. Robots have captured the human imagination for centuries.

    A. In 1497, Leonardo da Vinci designed a mechanical suit of armor that could sit up and move its arms, neck, and jaw.

    B. In 1773, Pierre and Henry Louis Jaquet-Droz built dolls that could write, play music, and draw pictures.

    C. In 1937, Westinghouse created a seven-foot robot that could walk, talk, blow up balloons, and smoke cigarettes.

II. Today robots are used in many fields, including space exploration and medicine.

    A. Robots have become indispensable to space exploration.

        1. Astronauts use robots to perform maintenance on the International Space Station.

        2. In addition, NASA sends robotic spacecraft to explore distant planets.

    B. Robots are becoming more and more important in medicine.

        1. They can navigate hospital corridors to deliver pharmaceuticals, X-rays, and bandages.

        2. They also allow surgeons to operate on patients from thousands of miles away.

Using Language

Chapter Objectives

After reading this chapter, students should be able to:

1. Explain why the effective use of language is vital to a public speaker.

2. Explain the differences between denotative and connotative meaning.

3. Explain the importance of using language accurately in public speeches.

4. Identify three methods public speakers can use to help ensure that their language will be clear to listeners.

5. Explain how public speakers can use imagery and rhythm to help bring their ideas to life.

6. Explain why public speakers need to use inclusive language and identify four ways they can do so.

Chapter Outline

   I. Language is important.
      A. Contrary to popular belief, language does not simply mirror reality.
      B. Language helps create our sense of reality by giving meaning to events.
      C. Words are vital to thinking itself.
      D. Words are the tools of a speaker's craft.

II. Words have two kinds of meaning—denotative and connotative.

  A. Denotative meaning is precise, literal, and objective.

  B. Connotative meaning is more variable, figurative, and subjective.

  C. Choosing words skillfully for their denotative and connotative meanings is a crucial part of the speaker's art.

III. Public speakers need to use language accurately.

  A. Using language accurately is as vital to a speaker as using numbers accurately is to an accountant.

  B. Speakers who have serious aspirations should develop a systematic plan for improving their vocabulary.

IV. Public speakers need to use language clearly.

  A. Because listeners cannot turn to a dictionary or reread a speaker's words to discover their meaning, a speaker's meaning must be immediately comprehensible.

  B. One way to ensure that a speaker's meaning is clear is to use familiar words.

  C. A second way to ensure that a speaker's meaning is clear is to use concrete words.

  D. A third way to ensure that a speaker's meaning is clear is to eliminate linguistic clutter.

V. Public speakers need to use language vividly.

  A. Effective speakers use imagery to express their ideas vividly.

    1. One way to generate imagery is to use concrete words.

    2. A second way to generate imagery is through the use of simile.

    3. A third way to generate imagery is through the use of metaphor.

  B. Effective speakers use rhythm to enhance the vividness of their discourse.

    1. Language has a rhythm created by the choice and arrangement of words.

    2. There are four basic stylistic devices for enhancing the rhythm of a speech.

      a. The first device is parallelism—the similar arrangement of a pair or series of related words, phrases, or sentences.

      b. The second device is repetition—repeating the same word or set of words at the beginning or end of successive clauses or sentences.

      c. The third device is alliteration—repeating the initial consonant sound in close or adjoining words.

      d. The fourth device is antithesis—juxtaposing contrasting ideas, usually in parallel structure.

VI. Public speakers need to use language appropriately.

  A. A speaker's language should be appropriate to the occasion.

  B. A speaker's language should be appropriate to the audience.

      C. A speaker's language should be appropriate to the topic.

      D. A speaker's language should be appropriate to the speaker himself or herself.

VII. Public speakers are more effective when they use inclusive language.

      A. Audiences today expect public speakers to use inclusive language that is respectful of the different groups that make up American society.

      B. There are four principles for inclusive language that have become so widespread that no aspiring speaker can afford to ignore them.

          1. The first principle is to avoid the generic "he."

          2. The second principle is to avoid the use of "man" when referring to both men and women.

          3. The third principle is to avoid stereotyping jobs and social roles by gender.

          4. The fourth principle is to use names that groups use to identify themselves.

      C. If speakers have questions about inclusive language, they should consult one of the many guidebooks or up-to-date information on the Internet on this subject.

Exercises for Critical Thinking *(from text page 237)*

1. Arrange each of the sequences below in order, from the most abstract word to the most concrete word.

    a. housing complex, building, dining room, structure, apartment

       (structure, building, housing complex, apartment, dining room)

    b. *Mona Lisa*, art, painting, creative activity, portrait

       (creative activity, art, painting, portrait, *Mona Lisa*)

    c. automobile, vehicle, Ferrari, transportation, sports car

       (transportation, vehicle, automobile, sports car, Ferrari)

2. Rewrite each of the following sentences using clear, familiar words.

    a. My employment objective is to attain a position of maximum financial reward.

       (I want a job that pays well.)

    b. All professors at this school are expected to achieve high standards of excellence in their instructional duties.

       (All professors here are expected to be good teachers.)

    c. In the eventuality of a fire, it is imperative that all persons evacuate the building without undue delay.

       (In case of fire, get out of the building as quickly as possible.)

3. Each of the statements below uses one or more of the following stylistic devices: metaphor, simile, parallelism, repetition, alliteration, antithesis. Identify the device (or devices) used in each statement.

    a. "We are a people in a quandary about the present. We are a people in search of our future. We are a people in search of a national community." (Barbara Jordan)

        (repetition and parallelism)

    b. "The vice presidency is the sand trap of American politics. It's near the prize, and designed to be limiting." (Howard Fineman)

        (metaphor)

    c. "People the world over have always been more impressed by the power of our example than by the example of our power." (Bill Clinton)

        (antithesis)

    d. "America is not like a blanket—one piece of unbroken cloth, the same color, the same texture, the same size. America is more like a quilt—many patches, many sizes, and woven and held together by a common thread." (Jesse Jackson)

        (simile, repetition, parallelism)

4. Analyze Martin Luther King's "I Have a Dream" in the appendix of sample speeches that follows Chapter 19 in the textbook. Identify the methods King uses to make his language clear, vivid, and appropriate. Look particularly at King's use of familiar words, concrete words, imagery, and rhythm.

    Discussion: King's speech usually works quite well for study in the classroom. Because it is so famous, students look forward to reading it; yet it is short enough for them to do a thorough job of analysis. Also, the speech is so rich in its use of language that students can readily identify the major techniques King uses to make his ideas clear and compelling.

    Have students prepare their analysis as a homework assignment based on the transcript of the speech in the textbook. Then, before discussing the speech in class, show students the video of the speech from Volume I of the Great Speeches series that accompanies *The Art of Public Speaking*. If you show the video, take advantage of the opportunity to discuss how King's masterful delivery reinforces the impact of his words. Here is a synopsis of the speech.

    Specific Purpose: To reinforce the commitment of the audience to the principles of the nonviolent civil rights movement.

    Central Idea: By continued nonviolent protest, African Americans will achieve their full citizenship rights.

Method of Organization: Topical

Introduction: The opening sentence constitutes the introduction of King's speech. Such a perfunctory introduction is unusual, but it was appropriate in King's situation. The audience had been waiting all afternoon to hear King speak. He did not need any special devices to secure their attention or to build his credibility. The speech might have been improved by an explicit preview statement, but the opening paragraph implies that King will focus on the meaning and importance of "the greatest demonstration for freedom in the history of our nation."

Body: There are four main sections in the body of the speech. The first runs from paragraph 2 through paragraph 8. In this section King addresses the nation at large and develops two subpoints. In paragraphs 3–6 he bemoans the "shameful condition" of American blacks, who still face poverty, segregation, and discrimination 100 years after the Emancipation Proclamation. In paragraphs 7–8 King reminds the nation of "the fierce urgency of now" and warns that continued protest will "shake the foundations of our nation until the bright day of justice emerges."

The second section of the body consists of paragraphs 9–14, in which King speaks primarily to his followers. He develops four subpoints: (1) In paragraphs 9–10 he urges black Americans to maintain their commitment to nonviolent methods of protest. (2) In paragraph 11, which received more applause than any other part of the speech, King reaffirms the need for blacks and whites to work together for freedom and equality. (3) In paragraph 12 King again stresses that African Americans cannot be satisfied until their grievances are resolved. (4) In paragraphs 13–14 King acknowledges that many African Americans have suffered "trials and tribulations" in their quest for freedom, but he urges them to keep the faith that their situation "can and will be changed."

The third section of the body consists of paragraphs 15–21, in which King dramatizes his "dream" of all Americans living in freedom and brotherhood. This is the most famous section of the speech, but the ideas were not new. King had said much the same thing, including repetition of the phrase "I Have a Dream," in a speech at Detroit two months earlier.

The fourth section of the body consists of paragraphs 22–29. Here King reaffirms his belief that "we will be free one day." He recites the first verse of "My Country 'Tis of Thee," builds into the series of sentences beginning with "Let freedom ring," and then moves into the emotionally charged final paragraph.

Conclusion: "I Have a Dream" is one of those speeches in which it is almost impossible to identify a discrete conclusion. The speech builds steadily to the powerful closing lines without a discernible shift from body to conclusion. The important question when judging a speech is not "Does the speech have a conclusion?" but "Does the speech conclude effectively?" In King's case the answer to the latter question is unequivocally yes.

Language: The most important feature of King's language is his use of familiar, concrete words. From beginning to end, he relies on words and phrases that create sharp, vivid images—"flames of withering injustice," "manacles of segregation and chains of discrimination," "sunlit path of racial justice," "whirlwinds of revolt," "heightening Alleghenies of Pennsylvania." This kind of language helps King make tangible the abstract principles of liberty and equality.

This is best seen in the "dream" section (paragraphs 15–21). Dreams are visual phenomena, and King's "dream" is strikingly visual. Instead of talking in vague terms about the ideals of freedom and justice, he makes those ideals concrete. Listening to him, we can almost see the sons of former slaves and the sons of former slave owners sitting down together on the red hills of Georgia. We can feel the sweltering heat of Mississippi and the cool breezes of the oasis of freedom and justice it will become. We can picture little black boys and black girls joining hands in Alabama with little white boys and white girls. By making his "dream" so vivid, King communicates it much more effectively than he could have through abstract language.

King's speech is also notable for its heavy use of metaphor. Most obvious is the extended metaphor of the "promissory note" or "bad check" in paragraphs 4–6, but there are also a number of brief metaphors scattered throughout the speech (see especially paragraphs 2–3, 7–9, 13, and 22) as well as a brace of similes in paragraph 2.

It is important to note that most of the metaphors and similes occur in pairs and are arranged to emphasize progress from a negative condition to a positive condition. For example: "It came as a joyous daybreak to end the long night of their captivity" (paragraph 2); ". . . to rise from the dark and desolate valley of segregation to the sunlit path of racial justice" (paragraph 7); ". . . to lift our nation from the quicksands of racial injustice to the solid rock of brotherhood" (paragraph 7); "The whirlwinds of revolt will continue to shake the foundations of our nation until the bright day of justice emerges" (paragraph 8); ". . . transform the jangling discords of our nation into a beautiful symphony of brotherhood" (paragraph 22). These metaphors strengthen King's message that continued protest will change things for the better.

King also relies heavily on repetition and parallelism to reinforce his ideas and accent the cadence of his speech. There are eight major units of repetition and parallelism: (1) The "One hundred years later . . ." series in paragraph 3; (2) The "Now is the time . . ." series in paragraph 7; (3) The "We must . . ." and "We must not . . ." series in paragraphs 9 and 10; (4) The "We can never be satisfied . . ." and "We cannot be satisfied . . ." series in paragraph 12; (5) The "Go back to . . ." series in paragraph 14; (6) The "I have a dream . . ." series in paragraphs 15–21; (7) The "to . . . together" series in paragraph 22; (8) The "Let freedom ring . . ." series in paragraphs 24–28.

Finally, one can observe the heavy religious tone of King's speech. Not only are there a number of explicit religious references, but many of King's words and images are biblical in origin. For example, "It came as a joyous daybreak to end the long night of their captivity" (paragraph 2) brings forth images of the exodus of the Jews from ancient Egypt. The phrase "until justice rolls down like waters and righteousness like a mighty stream" (paragraph 12) echoes the words of the prophet Amos. Similarly, King's statement in paragraph 21 that "every valley shall be exalted, every hill and mountain shall be made low, the rough places will be made plane and the crooked places will be made straight, and the glory of the Lord shall be revealed, and all flesh shall see it together" is repeated almost verbatim from the Old Testament book of Isaiah.

Using Public Speaking in Your Career   *(from text page 231)*

Since graduating from college, you have developed a successful business that is located near the campus. As part of its plan to involve more alumni and community members in college affairs, the school has asked you to speak with new students during registration week for the fall term. In the opening section of your speech, you want the audience to feel what you felt the first few days you were on campus as a new student. The best strategy, you decide, is to present two or three similes that complete the sentence "Beginning college is like. . . ." Write your similes.

Discussion: As with the other Using Public Speaking in Your Career scenarios throughout the book, this one is designed to demonstrate how the skills of public speaking discussed in the chapter apply to situations outside the classroom. An excellent way to use this scenario is to divide the class into groups and give each group five minutes to come up with several similes that complete the sentence, "Beginning college is like. . . ." Have one member from each group present its similes to the class, and follow with a general discussion about similes and other figures of speech.

Additional Exercises and Activities

1. In each of the following sentences, select the most appropriate word to complete the statement:

    a. insisted, persisted, urged, persevered

        I _____ her to treat her roommates more kindly.

        Though he tried to prove his innocence, the district attorney _____ in believing him guilty.

        Despite the difficulty of the job, she _____ until she completed it.

        He _____ that gun control legislation will do little to reduce crimes of violence.

    b. guess, prediction, estimate, forecast

        I just read the *Wall Street Journal*'s _____ for the economy next year.

        Will you turn on the television and get the weather _____ for to-morrow?

        It's always a good idea to get a written _____ before taking your car in for repairs.

        Chien doesn't have the foggiest idea how many jelly beans are in the jar. He's just making a _____.

    c. snap, tap, clap, slap

        I knew someone was following me through the woods when I heard a twig _____ behind me.

        The insistent _____ of the flag against the pole increased the drama of the military funeral.

        Sheila walked with so much spring in her step you could hear her feet _____ on the sidewalk.

        All at once we heard a tremendous _____ of thunder.

Discussion: This is an enjoyable exercise that increases students' awareness of the importance of careful, accurate word choice. The correct answers follow.

a.   insisted, persisted, urged, persevered

I ____urged____ her to treat her roommates more kindly.

Though he tried to prove his innocence, the district attorney ____persisted____ in believing him guilty.

Despite the difficulty of the job, she ____persevered____ until she completed it.

He ____insisted____ that gun control legislation will do little to reduce crimes of violence.

b.   guess, prediction, estimate, forecast

I just read the Wall Street Journal's ____prediction____ for the economy next year.

Will you turn on the television and get the weather ____forecast____ for tomorrow?

It's always a good idea to get a written ____estimate____ before taking your car in for repairs.

Chien doesn't have the foggiest idea how many jelly beans are in the jar. He's just making a ____guess____ .

c.   snap, tap, clap, slap

I knew someone was following me through the woods when I heard a twig ____snap____ behind me.

The insistent ____slap____ of the flag against the pole increased the drama of the military funeral.

Sheila walked with so much spring in her step you could hear her feet ____tap____ on the sidewalk.

All at once we heard a tremendous ____clap____ of thunder.

2. Have students analyze "The Massachusetts 54th," which appears on pages 424–427 of this manual. Students should focus their analysis on how the speaker utilizes imagery, parallelism, repetition, and other resources of language to enhance the impact of his ideas.

> **Discussion:** "The Massachusetts 54th" is an excellent speech to study in conjunction with Chapter 12—especially if you do not deal with it as part of the section on commemorative speaking in Chapter 18. It is particularly valuable as a complement to Exercise 4 on page 237 of the textbook, in which students analyze Martin Luther King's "I Have a Dream."
>
> Although most students are fascinated by the stylistic brilliance of King's masterpiece, they are often so overwhelmed by it that they cannot envision themselves emulating King's use of language in their own speeches. "The Massachusetts 54th," however, is a classroom speech, and it shows how students can use the same devices as King to elevate and enliven their discourse. For analysis of "The Massachusetts 54th," see pages 426–427 of this manual. If you discuss the speech in class, you may also want to show the video of it, which is available on the DVD of student speeches that accompanies this edition of *The Art of Public Speaking*.

3. Have students compose one page of prose in which they use all the resources of language discussed in the textbook—imagery, simile, metaphor, antithesis, alliteration, etc.—to describe a scene or to capture an emotion. Possible topics include:

the beach at sunset	my happiest moment
walking in the forest	my most fearful experience
a rainy night	my favorite person
life in the city	my most embarrassing moment
a boisterous party	my worst experience
any special location	my favorite childhood memory

> **Discussion:** Encourage students to be as "literary" or "poetic" as they wish in this exercise. Some will go overboard and become excessively maudlin or melodramatic, but some will create surprisingly effective and moving prose. If you have students present orally what they have written, this exercise can also provide an additional brief speaking opportunity in class.

4. The following paragraph is filled with verbal clutter. Following the model on pages 226–227 of the textbook, edit the paragraph so as to eliminate the unnecessary words. You should be able to find 25 to 30 such words. If you don't find that many, go back to the paragraph and edit it again.

Imagine the thought of burning up a priceless painting by Rembrandt just in order to stay warm for ten minutes. Sounds really crazy, doesn't it? But that is comparable to just what is happening right now in the Amazon rain forest of Brazil. The president of Brazil authorized a 14,000-mile network of highways to open up the vast area of the rain forest to settlement. Unfortunately, the project has been nothing but a disaster from the very beginning. Working in the hot, torrid, steamy jungle caused many fatal deaths among the workers. Soon a whole lot of foreign businesses began to get themselves involved in the project. Today there is a very real danger that the rain forest will be irrevocably destroyed completely and altogether.

Discussion: This exercise is especially helpful if you have students prepare a manuscript speech. It works well as an in-class exercise, since it can be completed fairly quickly. To give students additional practice in clearing the underbrush out of their prose, this exercise can be supplemented with Additional Exercise/Activity 5 below. Here is what the paragraph looks like when it has been edited to eliminate the clutter.

Imagine ~~the thought of~~ burning up a priceless painting by Rembrandt just ~~in order~~ to stay warm for ten minutes. Sounds ~~really~~ crazy, doesn't it? But that is comparable to ~~just~~ what is happening ~~right now~~ in the Amazon rain forest of Brazil. The president of Brazil authorized a 14,000-mile network of highways to open up the vast ~~area of the~~

~~rain forest~~ to settlement. Unfortunately, the project has been ~~nothing but~~ a disaster from the ~~very~~ beginning. Working in the ~~hot, torrid, steamy~~ jungle caused many ~~fatal~~ deaths among the workers. Soon ~~a whole lot of~~ foreign businesses began to get ~~themselves~~ involved in the project. Today there is a ~~very real~~ danger that the rain forest will be irrevocably destroyed ~~completely and altogether~~.

5. The following paragraph is filled with verbal clutter. Following the model on pages 226–227 of the textbook, edit the paragraph so as to eliminate the unnecessary words. You should be able to find 30 to 35 such words. If you don't find that many, go back to the paragraph and edit it again.

Rock music is such a big and important part of our lives today that it is extremely difficult to imagine a time when people lived without it. But there was once such a time. The early 1950s were a time of bubble gum and soda pop—a pure and simple age. Then a new kind of music started coming on the scene like a huge tidal wave on a calm and quiet beach. A whole lot of young performers were appearing who were revolutionizing the shape of American popular music. Bill Haley, Chuck Berry, Elvis Presley, Fats Domino, Little Richard, Jerry Lee Lewis—the list is a long one that goes on and on. But one rock and roll performer stands out above the rest as the most original and innovative of them all. His name? Buddy Holly.

Discussion: Like the previous Additional Exercise/Activity, this works well as an in-class activity and is especially helpful if you have students prepare a manuscript speech. Here is what the paragraph looks like when it has been edited to eliminate the clutter.

Rock music is such a big ~~and important~~ part of our lives ~~today~~ that it is ~~extremely~~ difficult to imagine a time when people lived without it. But there was ~~once~~ such a time. The early 1950s were a time of bubble gum and soda pop—a pure and simple age. Then a new kind of music started ~~coming on the scene~~ like a ~~huge~~ tidal wave on a ~~calm and~~ quiet beach. A ~~whole~~ lot of young performers ~~were appearing who~~ were revolutionizing ~~the shape of~~ American popular music. Bill Haley, Chuck Berry, Elvis Presley, Fats Domino, Little Richard, Jerry Lee Lewis—the list ~~is a long one that~~ goes on and on. But one ~~rock and roll~~ performer stands out ~~above the rest~~ as the most ~~original and~~ innovative of ~~them~~ all. His name? Buddy Holly.

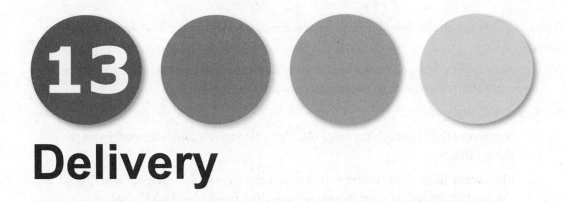

13

Delivery

Chapter Objectives

After reading this chapter, students should be able to:

1. Explain why good delivery is important to successful speaking.

2. Explain the major characteristics of effective speech delivery.

3. Identify the four methods of delivering a speech.

4. Explain the eight aspects of voice usage that are crucial to public speaking.

5. Discuss the four aspects of physical action that are most important to a public speaker.

6. Explain the five-step method presented in the chapter for practicing extemporaneous speech delivery.

7. Identify the two stages in preparing for a question-and-answer session and explain six things a speaker should keep in mind when responding to questions during the session itself.

Chapter Outline

I. Good delivery can make the difference between a successful speech and an unsuccessful speech.

   A. Speech delivery is based on nonverbal communication: the speaker's use of voice and body to convey the message expressed by words.

   B. Good delivery is an art.

   1. It conveys the speaker's message clearly, interestingly, and without distracting the audience.

   2. Most audiences prefer delivery that combines a certain degree of formality with the best attributes of good conversation—directness, vocal and facial expressiveness, and a lively sense of communication.

II. There are four basic methods of delivering a speech.

   A. Some speeches are read verbatim from a manuscript.

   1. Manuscript speeches are often used in situations that require absolute accuracy of wording or that impose strict time limits upon the speaker.

   2. When speaking from manuscript, speakers should rehearse the speech aloud to make sure it sounds natural, to work on establishing eye contact with listeners, and to concentrate on talking with the audience rather than reading to them.

   B. Some speeches are recited from memory.

   1. Nowadays it is customary to deliver only the shortest speeches from memory.

   2. When delivering a speech from memory, the speaker should learn it so thoroughly that she or he can concentrate on communicating with the audience rather than on remembering specific words.

   C. Some speeches are delivered impromptu.

   1. Impromptu speeches are presented with little or no immediate preparation.

   2. When speakers find themselves faced with an impromptu speaking situation, they should follow four simple steps to organize their thoughts quickly.

   a. First, they should state the point to which they are responding.

   b. Second, they should state the point they want to make.

   c. Third, they should use whatever support they have—examples, statistics, or testimony—to prove their point.

   d. Fourth, they should summarize their point.

   3. In addition, an impromptu speaker should try to remain calm, to maintain strong eye contact, to speak at a clear, deliberate pace, and to use signposts to help the audience keep track of the main ideas.

D. Some speeches are delivered extemporaneously.

    1. Extemporaneous speeches are carefully prepared and practiced in advance.

    2. They are presented from a set of notes, but the exact wording is chosen at the moment of delivery.

    3. There are several advantages to extemporaneous delivery.

        a. It gives greater control over ideas and language than impromptu delivery.

        b. It allows for greater spontaneity and directness than memorized or manuscript delivery.

        c. It encourages conversational vocal qualities, natural gestures, and strong eye contact.

III. Effective speakers learn to control their voices to enhance the impact of their message.

    A. The volume of a speaker's voice is basic to effective delivery.

    B. The pitch of a speaker's voice has an impact on delivery.

    C. The rate of a speaker's voice will affect the outcome of a speech.

    D. Effective pauses can contribute greatly to a speaker's impact.

    E. Vocal variety is one of the most important elements in effective delivery.

        1. Vocal variety refers to modulations in the rate, pitch, volume, and timing of a speaker's voice.

        2. Speakers who possess strong vocal variety come across as lively, dynamic, and communicative.

    F. Pronunciation is another vocal feature that influences the outcome of a speech.

    G. Articulation also has an impact on how a speech is received.

    H. A speaker's dialect can influence how the speech is received.

IV. Effective speakers learn to use their body to enhance the impact of their message.

    A. Physical actions can play a major role in the outcome of a speech.

    B. Four aspects of physical action are especially important for public speakers.

        1. The first aspect is personal appearance.

        2. The second aspect is movement.

        3. The third aspect is gestures.

        4. The fourth aspect is eye contact.

V. Speakers can improve their speech delivery by following a five-step method.

    A. First, the speaker should go over her or his preparation outline aloud.

    B. Second, the speaker should prepare a speaking outline.

C. Third, the speaker should practice the speech aloud several times using only the speaking outline.

D. Fourth, the speaker should polish and refine the delivery.

E. Fifth, the speaker should give the speech a dress rehearsal under conditions as close as possible to those he or she will face during the actual speech.

F. In order for this method to be effective, speakers must start early.

VI. Answering audience questions is often an important part of public speaking.

A. Many speeches include a question-and-answer session with the audience.

B. Thorough preparation is essential for a successful question-and-answer session.

1. The first step in preparing is to formulate answers to possible questions.

2. The second step in preparing is to practice delivering the answers.

C. Managing the question-and-answer session is an important skill in its own right.

1. It is vital to approach questions with a positive attitude.

2. Listening carefully to questions is vital to a successful question-and-answer session.

3. Answers should be directed to the entire audience, not just to the questioner.

4. Questions should be answered honestly and straightforwardly.

5. Unless there is a moderator for the question period, the speaker is responsible for keeping it on track.

Exercises for Critical Thinking   *(from text page 257)*

1. An excellent way to improve your vocal variety is to read aloud selections from poetry that require emphasis and feeling. Choose one of your favorite poems that falls into this category, or find one by leafing through a poetry anthology.

Practice reading the selection aloud. As you read, use your voice to make the poem come alive. Vary your volume, rate, and pitch. Find the appropriate places for pauses. Underline the key words or phrases you think should be stressed. Modulate your tone of voice; use inflections for emphasis and meaning.

For this to work, you must overcome your fear of sounding affected or "dramatic." Most beginning speakers do better if they exaggerate changes in volume, rate, pitch, and expression. This will make you more aware of the ways you can use your voice to express a wide range of moods and meanings. Besides, what sounds overly "dramatic" to you usually does not sound that way to an audience. By adding luster, warmth, and enthusiasm to your voice, you will go a long way toward capturing and keeping the interest of your listeners.

If possible, practice reading the selection into a digital recorder. Listen to the playback. If you are not satisfied with what you hear, practice the selection some more and record it again.

Discussion: Beginning speakers are often much less animated delivering a speech than in ordinary conversation. This is due partly to inexperience, partly to nervousness, partly to fear of sounding affected. But whatever the cause, the result is dull and lifeless delivery.

This exercise is designed to help students over this barrier. At the start of the course they are likely to feel more comfortable using their voices expressively when reciting poetry than when delivering a speech. As they work with their poems, they often become more accustomed to modulating their voices to enhance the meaning of the words. As a capstone to the exercise, have students present their poems orally in class.

2. Watch a 10-minute segment of a television drama with the sound turned off. What do the characters say with their dress, gestures, facial expressions, and the like? Do the same with a television comedy. How do the nonverbal messages in the two shows differ? Be prepared to report your observations in class.

Discussion: This exercise attunes students to the dimensions and effects of nonverbal communication, and it usually generates a lively class discussion. It works best if you assign particular programs for the entire class to watch.

3. Attend a speech on campus. You may choose either a presentation by a guest speaker from outside the college or a class session by a professor who has a reputation as a good lecturer. Prepare a brief report on the speaker's delivery.

In your report, first analyze the speaker's volume, pitch, rate, pauses, vocal variety, pronunciation, and articulation. Then evaluate the speaker's personal appearance, bodily action, gestures, and eye contact. Explain how the speaker's delivery added to or detracted from what the speaker said. Finally, note at least two techniques of delivery used by the speaker that you might want to try in your next speech.

Discussion: This exercise provides for an out-of-class speech observation. You may want to have students write a brief paper reporting their observations; you may prefer that they use an observation worksheet such as the one provided on page 172.

Using Public Speaking in Your Career *(from text page 253)*

Utilizing your business degree and computer savvy, you have made a success of the online marketing company you started after graduating from college. Now in its third year, the company has prepared a proposal to design the e-commerce site for a major sporting goods retailer. In your 30-minute presentation to the retailer's management team, you will review the home-page designs, site maps, and security protocols.

You notice on the agenda that another 30 minutes have been allotted after your presentation for questions and answers. Knowing from your previous experience with clients how important the Q&A session can be, you want to be sure you are ready for it. What steps will you take to prepare?

Discussion: Like the Using Public Speaking in Your Career scenarios in other chapters, this one is designed to show how the principles of public speaking discussed in the textbook are used in everyday life. In this case, you can anticipate that students will mention what the chapter identifies as the major steps in preparing for a question-and-answer session: formulating answers to possible questions and practicing the delivery of those answers. In class discussion, encourage students to be specific about the processes involved in both of these steps, and use the discussion as a springboard to exploring how to manage the question-and-answer session itself.

Additional Exercises and Activities

1.   Lead a class discussion in which students develop a set of criteria for effective speech delivery. After the discussion, codify the criteria into an evaluation worksheet that can be used by the class for the remainder of the term.

Discussion: Although this exercise takes most of a class period, it can be quite helpful. At the start of the discussion, tell students that they should draw their criteria not only from the textbook, but also from their own experience. Although most of the class may not have much background as public speakers, they all have considerable experience as consumers of speeches (in classroom lectures, if nowhere else). As a result, they are already fairly expert in detecting delivery behaviors that enhance or inhibit effective communication.

By combining what they have read in the textbook with what they have learned from experience, most classes put together an excellent set of criteria for speech delivery. Moreover, because they have generated the evaluation worksheet themselves, students are more committed to it.

2.   Show students one or more selections from the DVD of student speeches that accompanies this edition of *The Art of Public Speaking*. Use the DVD to illustrate points about effective and ineffective speech delivery.

Discussion: It is extremely difficult to teach delivery from a textbook. Perhaps the greatest benefit of using videos in the speech classroom is that they help students see in action the principles of delivery discussed in the textbook. Any of the speeches on the DVD of student speeches that accompanies *The Art of Public Speaking* can be used for this purpose, and you will want to choose speeches that illustrate most clearly the points you emphasize in your classes.

Of all the speeches available on the DVD, the most remarkable in terms of delivery is Sajjid Zahir Chinoy's "Questions of Culture." Presented at the University of Richmond's commencement ceremonies in May 1996, Chinoy's address was given extemporaneously, without notes, to an audience of several thousand people. The text of the speech appears on pages A13–A15 of the textbook. What follows is a synopsis.

Introduction: As in many commemorative speeches, the introduction of Chinoy's speech is very brief. It comprises only the first paragraph and consists of his salutation. Although the speech could have profited from a brief reference to the occasion or a statement by Chinoy that he was privileged to be chosen as the student commencement speaker, the lack of further introductory remarks proved not to be a serious problem.

Body: The body of Chinoy's speech runs from paragraph 2 through paragraph 23 and is divided into three main sections. The first section deals with Chinoy's departure from Bombay, India, and the questions of culture he contemplated during his flight to the United States (paragraphs 2–8). In paragraphs 2–6 he deals with his personal questions of culture and whether he would fit in as one of only three Indian students at the University of Richmond. In paragraphs 7–8 he shifts to global questions of culture and ethnicity, noting that countries, like individuals, face the problem of bringing different cultures together in peace and harmony.

The second major section of the body runs from paragraph 9 through paragraph 17. In these paragraphs Chinoy explains how his personal questions of culture were answered in the affirmative by his experiences at the University of Richmond. Referring to his time at the university as "the four most spectacular years of his life," Chinoy focuses on four special moments of human interaction—his first Thanksgiving in America (paragraph 11), his first Christmas eve (paragraph 12), his talk with a friend before a calculus exam (paragraph 13), and his roommate's support when India was undergoing communal riots in Chinoy's home town (paragraph 14). As a result of these and other experiences, Chinoy says, he discovered that the commonality of the human experience far transcends superficial differences of culture, language, and background.

In the third section of the body Chinoy compares his positive experiences at the University of Richmond with the cultural conflicts ravaging people and countries around the world (paragraphs 18–23). After looking at tragic events in Bosnia, India, and Africa (paragraphs 19–21), he laments all the "madness" that has occurred because people have stressed their differences rather than their "inherent similarities." He ends the body in paragraph 23 with the statement: "Two similar questions of culture in 1992. Two diametrically opposite results in 1996."

Conclusion: The conclusion consists of paragraphs 24–26. After encouraging the graduating class to distinguish itself, Chinoy returns to his central theme in paragraph 25 by urging his listeners to remember that it is cultural understanding—or the lack of it—that "can mean the difference between complete despair for one young boy in Bosnia and remarkable hope for another young boy at Richmond." With these words, Chinoy brings the entire speech together and reinforces the connections between his personal questions of culture and the global questions of culture broached in the first section of the body.

Chinoy closes the speech in paragraph 26 with the simple words, "Thank you." Although a case can be made that a speaker should not, in normal circumstances, dilute the impact of his or her conclusion by adding "Thank you" at the end, in this case the words are entirely appropriate because they can be read not just as thanking the audience for listening, but also as thanking it for providing the positive cultural experience that made Chinoy's years at Richmond so rewarding.

All in all, this is an exceptional speech. Not only is it perfectly suited to the audience and occasion, but it is superbly developed, written, and structured. Chinoy moves with great skill between his personal experiences and the larger questions of culture confronting the world. Although one might cavil that Chinoy's solution to those questions is oversimplified, it is hard to dispute his point that the world needs much more cultural understanding if it is to avoid the "madness" that Chinoy so eloquently laments.

This speech is also noteworthy for its delivery. Although Chinoy had a written manuscript, he delivered the speech extemporaneously and without notes—an especially remarkable feat given the size of his audience and the importance of the occasion. The moral to be stressed for students, however, is not that they must give all their speeches without notes—after all, Chinoy was an accomplished speaker with a great deal of experience in competitive debate and forensics—but how important it is to speak fluently, sincerely, dynamically, and with strong eye contact, regardless of the amount of notes one uses.

3.   Show students a video of a speech. After a couple of minutes turn off the sound and have students concentrate on the cues sent by the speaker's appearance, bodily movement, gestures, and eye contact. After a couple of minutes turn the sound back on so students can concentrate on the interaction of the speaker's vocal and physical communication.

Discussion: This is an easy way to illustrate the wide range of nonverbal cues sent by a speaker. To their surprise, students can usually tell from physical action alone whether the speaker is intent on communicating with the audience or is simply going through the motions. To save time, try combining this activity with the preceding exercise.

4. Assign one or more rounds of impromptu speeches. Speeches should be one and a half minutes to two minutes in length. Encourage students to follow the guidelines for impromptu speaking discussed on pages 241–242 of the textbook.

> **Discussion:** When you announce this assignment, most students will act as if you had condemned them to a fate worse than death. Yet for most students, impromptu speeches, if handled properly by the instructor, can be an enormously valuable confidence builder.
>
> One way to approach impromptu speeches is to assign two or three at various intervals throughout the term. Another approach is to devote as many as three consecutive days to impromptu speeches, with each student in the class giving a speech on each day. The latter approach works particularly well because it gives students a chance to become comfortable with the impromptu situation. With each succeeding day, students gain poise and confidence. By the third day, many are so relaxed—and are giving such good speeches—that they ask to do more impromptu presentations. Another benefit of this approach is that students get so used to speaking without notes that their skills of extemporaneous speaking also improve dramatically—especially with respect to eye contact, gestures, and vocal variety.
>
> If you assign two or more consecutive days of impromptu speaking, try to schedule them about two-thirds of the way through the term. If you assign them too early, students will not have learned enough about speechmaking in general to have a solid foundation for giving impromptu speeches. In addition, impromptu speaking involves considerable psychological risk on the part of students. The more comfortable students are with their classmates, the more willing they are to take the necessary risk. If you assign a series of impromptu speeches too early in the semester, students may recoil from the assignment rather then benefiting from it.
>
> Although impromptu speeches can be used as a graded assignment, most teachers use them as an informal, non-graded speaking experience. Because students are usually apprehensive about speaking impromptu—especially initially—you should do all you can to maintain a low-key, supportive atmosphere.
>
> One of the major questions with respect to impromptu speaking is how to select topics. When faced with impromptu speaking situations outside the classroom, students will speak about issues of immediate concern to their job, their church, their community, and the like. One way to approximate this experience is to develop a topic for each student based on one of her or his previous classroom speeches.

For example, if a student has given an informative speech on the benefits of learning CPR, you might assign him or her the following topic: "Doesn't learning CPR take a lot of time and money? Besides, I have never come across a person having a heart attack or drowning. It all seems like a lot of bother for something most people will never use. Is it really that important to know CPR?"

Or if a student has given a persuasive speech urging the audience to help save the world's rain forests, you might give her or him this topic: "Of course, it would be nice to save the rain forests in South America, but who are we to tell South Americans what to do with their land? After all, the United States uses more natural resources per capita than any other country in the world. Aren't we being hypocritical in asking other people to save the rain forests while we continue our dependence on foreign oil?"

Now you have created a situation analogous to one people often face in real life—defending their position on a subject with which they are already familiar. Students should feel free to use material from their previous speech in the impromptu speech—indeed, they should be encouraged to do so.

If you conduct a second round of impromptu speeches, again give students a choice of topics that will allow them to draw on familiar ideas and experiences. Some possibilities include: (1) What is your favorite—or least favorite—hobby, academic subject, sport, time of year, etc.? Why? (2) What are two or three things that really annoy you? (3) What is the most—or least—favorite aspect of your college experience so far? (4) If you could change any single aspect of college life at this school, what would it be? (5) What do you think it means to be successful in life? (6) What is the most fulfilling or rewarding aspect of your life to date? These topics are so universal that students will have no difficulty finding one on which to speak.

If you hold a third round of speeches, you can use the same set of topics—just make sure each student chooses a different individual topic from the one he or she chose in the second round. You can also devise new topics of a similar nature for the third round. You might even require that each student supply one or two topics that can go into the pool of possible topics for the entire class. This works especially well when students have responded positively to the first two days of impromptu speeches.

Regardless of the kinds of topics you use, give each student a few minutes to prepare the speech. You can do this by having the first 3 to 4 speakers choose their topics at the beginning of class. Then, as each speaker finishes, have a new student select his or her topic. If the speeches are to be two minutes in length, give the speakers time signals when they have one minute to go and then again when they have 30 seconds left. If you have an especially large class, you may have to reduce the length of the speeches to ensure that all students have an opportunity to perform on each day of impromptu speeches.

5. Divide the class into groups of 3 to 5 students. Assign each group a short children's story to present at the next class session. In presenting the story, each group is to act as if its audience were a ward of small children at a local hospital. Tell the students they must exaggerate their voice, their gestures, their facial expressions, and their bodily actions just as they would if they were actually telling the story to a group of children. Presentations should be 5 to 7 minutes in length, and each group should get together for an hour or so the evening before the assignment is due to assign speaking parts and to rehearse its presentation.

> **Discussion:** This exercise can work very well to help students use their voices and bodies expressively to communicate with an audience. By role playing as if they were addressing an audience of small children, many students feel less inhibited than if they were "actually" addressing their peers. They also tend to feel less intimidated speaking as members of groups. Indeed, a side benefit of this exercise is that it can help break down barriers among members of the class—especially if it is assigned fairly early in the quarter or semester.

> Good candidates for children's stories include such time-honored classics as "The Three Little Pigs," "Little Red Riding Hood," "Goldilocks," and "The Gingerbread Man"—all of which contain vivid action and dramatic dialogue. There are also a number of more contemporary stories that work quite well, including Maurice Sendak's "Where the Wild Things Are," Dr. Seuss's "The Cat in the Hat" and "Green Eggs and Ham," Bill Martin Jr.'s "Chicka Chicka Boom Boom," and Eric Carle's "The Very Hungry Caterpillar."

> To help ensure that all students participate fully in this exercise, many teachers assign some sort of minor grade to each group's presentation.

6. Arrange to record at least one round of informative or persuasive speeches. Meet individually with each student to review her or his video. Stop the video periodically to point out what the speaker does particularly well and to indicate where improvement is needed.

> **Discussion:** This can be extraordinarily valuable for students because it gives them a chance to hear and see themselves as others hear and see them. It also gives you a chance to give each student a constructive "blow-by-blow" critique of his or her speech. At first students are somewhat apprehensive about being recorded. But once they see how valuable it is, they often request to have the next speech recorded as well.

7. As an alternative to the preceding exercise, have students use their videos to prepare written self-assessments of their speeches.

> **Discussion:** Given the size of many classes, it is often impractical for instructors to meet with each student individually to review her or his video. Another option is to have students review their own videos and prepare self-assessments of them. Some instructors provide students a detailed evaluation worksheet for this purpose. Others require students to answer a set of questions covering each major aspect of the speech from topic selection and audience adaptation to supporting materials, delivery, and visual aids. Still others make the assignment open-ended and ask students to produce a two-page typed self-assessment. If you choose this last option, make sure students understand that the self-assessment is to be thoughtfully composed and carefully proofread. Tell them to focus both on the major strengths of the speech and on areas they wish to improve upon in the next speech.
>
> In my experience, most students take this assignment seriously and do a fine job of assessing their performance. Nonetheless, I recommend making it a graded assignment, if for no other reason than to reward students who do an especially thorough job with it. I have also found an interesting dynamic in the assessments. On the one hand, students can be rather hard on themselves—especially with regard to small matters of delivery. On the other hand, they recognize the fact that they look much more confident on tape than they felt internally while they were presenting the speech.
>
> Regardless of the approach you take to the self-assessment, it can be exceptionally effective, for it is founded on the principles of self-teaching. It should not be used, however, as a replacement for a thorough assessment from the instructor. Usually, the two assessments will be remarkably close in their judgments. If there are major discrepancies in some cases, you might wish to schedule individual conferences to clarify your judgments about the speech and to make sure students have a clear sense of what they need to concentrate on in their next presentation.
>
> For sample assignments, see the Informative Speech Self-Assessment on page 193 of this manual, and the Persuasive Speech Self-Assessment on page 214. Both are also available in the online assignments for Chapters 15–17 at *Connect*.

8. Radio and television announcers must have outstanding articulation. One way they develop it is by practicing tongue twisters such as those listed below. Give students the list so they can work on their articulation. Tell students to begin by saying the tongue twisters slowly and firmly, so that each sound is clearly formed. Once they have the sounds correct, they can gradually increase to a normal rate of speech.

   a.   Pure food for four pure mules.

   b.   Which wily wizard wished wicked wishes for Willy?

   c.   The sixth sick Sheik's sheep is sick.

   d.   Fetch me the finest French-fried freshest fish that Finney fries.

   e.   Shy Sarah saw six Swiss wristwatches.

   f.   One year we had a Christmas brunch with Merry Christmas mush to munch. But I don't think you'd care for such. We didn't like to munch mush much.

   g.   The view from the veranda gave forth a fine vista of waves and leafy foliage.

   h.   She sells seashells on the seashore.

   i.   While we waited for the whistle on the wharf, we whittled vigorously on the white weather-boards.

   j.   Grass grew green on the graves in Grace Gray's grandfather's graveyard.

   k.   Pete Briggs pats pigs.

        Briggs pats pink pigs.

        Briggs pats big pigs.

        Pete Briggs is a pink pig, big pig patter.

   l.   Amidst the mists and coldest frosts,

        With stoutest wrists and loudest boasts,

        He thrusts his fists against the posts,

        And still insists he sees the ghosts.

   Discussion: Try this as an in-class activity. It's enjoyable and it helps make students aware of the need for precise articulation. Students who want additional work on articulation should be encouraged to practice with the list outside of class.

Out-of-Class Speech Observation Worksheet

Your name _____   **Speaker** _____

Where was the speech presented? _____

What was the occasion for the speech? _____

VOCAL COMMUNICATION: *Record your observations about each of the following aspects of the speaker's voice.*

Volume _____

Pitch _____

Rate _____

Pauses _____

Vocal variety _____

Pronunciation _____

Articulation _____

PHYSICAL ACTION: *Record your observations about each of the following aspects of the speaker's physical action.*

Personal appearance _____

Movement _____

Gestures _____

Eye contact _____

OVERALL EVALUATION OF DELIVERY: *Explain how the speaker's delivery added to or detracted from the message.*

_____

_____

WHAT IT MEANS FOR ME: *Explain at least two techniques of delivery used by the speaker that you might want to try in your next speech.*

_____

_____

Using Visual Aids

Chapter Objectives

After reading this chapter, students should be able to:

1. Explain the major advantages of using visual aids in a speech.

2. Identify the kinds of visual aids available for use in speeches.

3. Apply the guidelines given in the chapter for preparing and presenting visual aids.

Chapter Outline

I. Visual aids offer a speaker several advantages.
   A. Visual aids enhance a speaker's credibility.
   B. Visual aids can improve a speaker's persuasiveness.
   C. Visual aids can help a speaker combat stage fright.
   D. Visual aids can increase the interest of a speaker's information.

II. There are many kinds of visual aids.
   A. Objects and models can work extremely well as visual aids.
   B. Photographs and drawings can be of great advantage to a speaker.
   C. Graphs are a good way to clarify and simplify statistics.
      1. Line graphs are best for illustrating statistical trends.

2. Pie graphs are well suited for demonstrating distribution patterns.

3. Bar graphs are effective for showing comparisons between two or more items.

D. Charts are a good choice when a speaker needs to summarize large blocks of information.

E. Video can be extremely effective as a visual aid.

F. Sometimes the speaker can use her or his own body as a visual aid.

G. PowerPoint presentations allow a speaker to combine charts, graphs, photographs, and video in the same talk.

1. When used properly, PowerPoint can be highly effective.

2. Speakers need a clear idea of exactly why, how, and when they will use PowerPoint in their presentations.

III. There are seven basic guidelines to follow whether creating visual aids by hand or by computer.

A. Speakers should prepare visual aids well in advance.

B. Speakers should keep visual aids simple.

1. A visual aid should be clear, straightforward, and uncluttered.

2. It should include only what is needed to make the speaker's point.

C. Speakers should make sure visual aids are large enough.

D. Speakers should use a limited amount of text in their visual aids.

E. Speakers should use fonts effectively in their visual aids.

F. Speakers should use color effectively in their visual aids.

G. Speakers should use images strategically in their visual aids.

IV. In addition to preparing visual aids effectively, speakers should follow seven guidelines when presenting visual aids during a speech.

A. Speakers should display visual aids where listeners can see them.

B. Speakers should avoid passing visual aids among the audience.

C. Speakers should display visual aids only while discussing them.

D. Speakers should explain their visual aids clearly and concisely.

E. Speakers should talk to their audience, not to their visual aid.

F. Speakers should practice with their visual aids when rehearsing the speech.

G. Speakers should check the room and equipment prior to speaking to ensure that their visual aids will work properly.

Exercises for Critical Thinking *(from text page 275)*

1. Watch a how-to television program (a cooking show, for example) or the weather portion of a local newscast. Notice how the speaker uses visual aids to help communicate the message. What kinds of visual aids are used? How do they enhance the clarity, interest, and retainability of the speaker's message? What would the speaker have to do to communicate the message effectively without visual aids?

    Discussion: This exercise helps attune students to the advantages and logistics of using visual aids in a speech. It works best if you assign a single program for the entire class to watch, so there is a common basis for class discussion. As an alternative, you can record segments of several programs yourself and show them to the class.

2. Consider how you might use visual aids to explain each of the following:

    a. How to perform the Heimlich maneuver to help a choking victim.

    b. The proportion of the electorate that votes in major national elections in the United States, France, Germany, England, and Japan, respectively.

    c. Where to obtain information about student loans.

    d. The wing patterns of various species of butterflies.

    e. The increase in the amount of money spent by Americans on health care since 1985.

    f. How to change a bicycle tire.

    g. The basic equipment and techniques of rock climbing.

    Discussion: This exercise is designed to get students thinking about how they might use visual aids in their classroom speeches. Handle the class discussion as a kind of brainstorming session and encourage students to be creative in their suggestions for visual aids. As the discussion progresses, you can also draw attention to the guidelines for using visual aids effectively.

3. Plan to use visual aids in at least one of your classroom speeches. Be creative in devising your aids, and be sure to follow the guidelines discussed in the chapter for using them. After the speech, analyze how effectively you employed your visual aids, what you learned about the use of visual aids from your experience, and what changes you would make in using visual aids if you were to deliver the speech again.

    Discussion: Some teachers assign a round of speeches—usually informative—in which students must use visual aids. Such an assignment has several advantages.

First, it gives students practical experience in creating and using visual aids. Second, it often reduces nervousness—because the visual aid heightens audience interest, helps divert the gaze of listeners from the speaker, and makes the speaker feel less self-conscious. Third, it encourages students to get away from their notes and to speak extemporaneously while explaining the visual aid.

Using Public Speaking in Your Career   *(from text page 266)*

As a veterinarian and owner of a small-animal practice, you work closely with your local humane society to help control a growing population of unwanted dogs and cats. You and your staff devote many hours annually in free and reduced-cost medical services to animals adopted from the society. Now you have been asked to speak to the city council in support of legislation proposed by the society for stronger enforcement of animal licensing and leash laws.

In your speech, you plan to include statistics that (1) compare estimates of the city's dog population with the number of licenses issued during the past five years and (2) show the small number of citations given by local law enforcement for unleashed pets during the same period of time. Knowing from your college public speaking class how valuable visual aids can be in presenting statistics, you decide to illustrate one set of statistics with a chart and the other with a graph.

For which set of statistics will a chart be more appropriate? For which set will a graph be more appropriate? Of the three kinds of graphs discussed in this chapter (bar, line, pie), which will work best for your statistics and why?

> **Discussion:** As with other Using Public Speaking in Your Career scenarios throughout the book, this one is designed to give students a sense of the many kinds of public speaking situations they can encounter once they leave college. In this case, the scenario also aims to help students understand the differences between charts and graphs, as well as the differences among the three kinds of graphs discussed in the chapter.
>
> The first set of statistics in the scenario—comparing estimates of the city's dog population with the number of dog licenses issued during the past five years—would be best illustrated with a graph. Although either a bar graph or a line graph could work effectively, the better choice would be a line graph, which is especially useful for showing statistical changes over time. It is conceivable that the second set of statistics—showing the small number of citations given by local law enforcement for unleashed pets during the past five years—could be represented with a line graph that contained only one line. But this would not be as effective as a chart that simply listed the figures for each year. Graphs are especially valuable for showing statistical trends or comparisons. Since that is not the primary purpose of the second set of statistics, a chart would be the better choice for them.

Additional Exercises and Activities

1. Show students Part Two of Introductions, Conclusions, and Visual Aids, which accompanies *The Art of Public Speaking*.

    Discussion: When it comes to teaching students about visual aids, a picture is truly worth a thousand words. Introductions, Conclusions, and Visual Aids is a 30-minute DVD produced exclusively to accompany *The Art of Public Speaking*. Part Two deals with the principles of effective visual aids and is illustrated with selections from a wide range of speeches. Use the DVD as a springboard for class discussion about the criteria discussed in the book for creating and presenting visual aids.

2. Develop a file of old visual aids you can bring to class to demonstrate for students the characteristics of effective and ineffective visual aids. Have the students identify which aids work well, which do not, and why. Ask students for ways to improve the ineffective visual aids.

    Discussion: This exercise complements Additional Exercise/Activity 1 above. Bringing old visual aids to class allows students to see how large the print or drawing must be; how important it is to keep an aid clean and uncluttered; how using bright, contrasting colors brings aids to life; how visual aids don't explain themselves, etc. It also allows you to illustrate the proper techniques for setting up and displaying visual aids, for explaining the point made by an aid, for communicating directly with the audience while discussing an aid, and so forth.

    Developing a file of visual aids is not very difficult. Simply collect the aids from your students after their speeches. Keep the aids in your office, so they will be at hand when you need to use them. After a few classes, you'll find that you have more than enough aids to demonstrate just about any point you wish to make. Some course directors keep a central file of visual aids from which instructors can draw as the need arises.

3. Show the class one or more of the speeches that use visual aids from the DVD of student speeches that accompanies this edition of *The Art of Public Speaking*. Use the DVD to illustrate points about the effective use of visual aids.

    Discussion: It is one thing to show students excerpts from speeches that use visual aids; it is another thing to show them full speeches that revolve around the effective use of visual aids. Doing so helps students understand the role visual aids play in relation to content, style, and delivery.

    The DVD of student speeches that accompanies this edition of *The Art of Public Speaking* contains a number of speeches that illustrate the proficient use of visual aids. One such speech—"Yoga: Uniting Mind, Body, and Spirit"—is a speech of demonstration that uses the speaker's body as a visual aid. For the text and discussion of "Yoga," see pages 288–291 of this manual.

The DVD also contains three informative speeches that demonstrate the use of PowerPoint: "Medical Robots: From Science Fiction to Science Fact," "Securing Yourself Online," and "The Hidden World of Chili Peppers." For the text and discussion of "Medical Robots," see pages 294–296 of the textbook; for the text and discussion of "Securing Yourself Online," see pages 299–302 of this manual; for the text and discussion of "Chili Peppers," see pages 308–311 of this manual.

Although students are most likely to use visual aids in their informative speeches, they can use them in persuasive speeches as well—as is illustrated on the DVD by "Phony Pharmaceuticals" and "The Horrors of Puppy Mills." For the text and discussion of "Phony Pharmaceuticals," see pages 318–320 of the textbook and pages 201–203 of this manual. For the text and discussion of "Puppy Mills," see pages A7–A9 of the textbook and pages 222–224 of this manual.

Speaking to Inform

Chapter Objectives

After reading this chapter, students should be able to:

1. Explain the four kinds of informative speeches discussed in the chapter.

2. Apply the six guidelines for informative speaking offered in the chapter.

Chapter Outline

I. Speaking to inform is one of the most important skills a student can develop.
    A. Public speaking to inform occurs in a wide range of everyday situations.
        1. There are endless situations in which people need to inform others.
        2. The ability to convey knowledge and understanding will prove valuable to students throughout their lives.
    B. There are three criteria for effective informative speaking.
        1. The information should be communicated accurately.
        2. The information should be communicated clearly.
        3. The information should be made meaningful and interesting to the audience.

II. Informative speeches can be classified into four types.
    A. Some informative speeches are about objects.
        1. Speeches about objects describe something that is visible, tangible, and stable in form.

2. Speeches about objects need to be sharply focused.

3. Speeches about objects can use a variety of organizational patterns.

    a. A speech about the history or evolution of an object would be arranged in chronological order.

    b. A speech about the main features of an object might be arranged in spatial order.

    c. Most informative speeches about objects will fall into topical order.

B. Some informative speeches are about processes.

    1. Speeches about processes explain how something is made, describe how something is done, or convey how something works.

    2. There are two kinds of informative speeches about processes.

        a. One type explains a process so the audience will understand it better.

        b. The other type explains a process so the audience will be able to perform the process themselves.

    3. Speeches about processes often require visual aids.

    4. Speeches about processes require careful organization.

        a. Speeches that explain a process step by step are arranged in chronological order.

        b. Speeches that focus on the major principles or techniques involved in performing the process are usually arranged in topical order.

        c. Whichever method of organization is used, each step in the process must be clear and easy for listeners to follow.

C. Some informative speeches are about events.

    1. Speeches about events can deal with any kind of happening or occurrence.

    2. There are many ways to organize a speech about an event.

        a. Speeches that recount the history of an event are arranged in chronological order.

        b. Speeches that deal with particular elements of an event are usually arranged in topical order.

D. Some informative speeches are about concepts.

    1. Speeches about concepts convey information concerning beliefs, theories, principles, or other abstract subjects.

    2. Speeches about concepts are usually arranged in topical order.

    3. Speeches about concepts are often more complex than other kinds of informative speeches.

        a. When discussing concepts, a speaker should avoid technical language and define terms clearly.

        b. A speaker should also use examples and comparisons to make concepts understandable to listeners.

E. The lines dividing speeches about objects, processes, events, and concepts are not absolute.

III. There are six guidelines for effective informative speaking.
- A. Informative speakers should be wary of overestimating what the audience knows.
  1. In most cases, the audience will be only vaguely knowledgeable about the speaker's topic.
  2. To avoid misunderstanding, the speaker must explain ideas thoroughly and clearly.
- B. Informative speakers should find ways to relate the subject directly to the audience.
  1. Informative speakers must recognize that what is fascinating to them may not be fascinating to everybody.
  2. Effective informative speakers work to get the audience interested—and to keep them interested.
- C. Informative speakers should avoid being too technical.
  1. An informative speech may be overly technical because the subject matter is too specialized for the audience or because of the speaker's use of jargon.
  2. Effective informative speakers select topics that are not too technical for the audience and use appropriate language.
- D. Informative speakers should avoid abstractions.
  1. Replacing tedious abstractions with specific details makes an informative speech more compelling.
  2. One way to avoid abstractions is through description.
  3. A second way to avoid abstractions is with comparisons.
  4. A third way to avoid abstractions is with contrast.
- E. Informative speakers should personalize their ideas.
  1. Nothing enlivens an informative speech more than personal illustrations.
  2. Whenever possible, informative speakers should try to dramatize their ideas in human terms.
  3. The best way to accomplish this is with examples—real or hypothetical—that personalize the subject matter.
- F. Informative speakers should be creative in thinking about ways to achieve their objectives.
  1. In public speaking, creativity involves using language imaginatively and resourcefully.
  2. Creativity can also influence any aspect of a speech, including a speaker's visual aids.

Exercises for Critical Thinking   *(from text page 297)*

1. Below is a list of subjects for informative speeches. Your task is twofold: (a) Select four of the topics and prepare a specific purpose statement for an informative speech about each of the four. Make sure your four specific purpose statements include at least one that deals with its topic as an object, one that deals with its topic as a process, one that deals with its topic as an event, and

one that deals with its topic as a concept. (b) Explain what method of organization you would most likely use in structuring a speech about each of your specific purpose statements.

hobbies	cultural customs
animals	education
science	media
sports	technology
music	

Discussion: This exercise gets students to work on developing specific purpose statements for informative speeches. It also leads them to apply what is said in the text about methods of organizing informative speeches. If you include Chapter 5, "Selecting a Topic and Purpose," or Chapter 9, "Organizing the Body of the Speech," in the unit on informative speaking, you may wish to forego this exercise in favor of the exercises in Chapters 5 and 9.

2. Analyze "Ramadan" in the appendix of sample speeches that follows Chapter 19 of the textbook. Identify the specific purpose, central idea, main points, and method of organization. Evaluate the speech in light of the guidelines for informative speaking discussed in this chapter.

Discussion: Highly informative, clearly organized, and effectively delivered, "Ramadan" is a good example of how speakers can combine personal experience with more traditional research materials to create an effective speech. A video is available online and on the DVD of student speeches that accompanies this edition of *The Art of Public Speaking*. Below is a synopsis.

Specific Purpose: To inform my audience about the history and practices of Ramadan.

Central Idea: Ramadan's rich history and sacred practices make it meaningful for Muslims around the globe.

Method of Organization: Topical

Introduction: The introduction consists of paragraphs 1–4. In paragraph 1, the speaker gains attention by mentioning that one billion people around the world skipped lunch during the previous month. Because the audience is composed mostly of non-Muslim American college students, who would not immediately think of Ramadan from such a perspective, the speaker's opening generates curiosity about her topic. At the end of the opening paragraph, she reveals that "last month" was the Muslim holy month of Ramadan. Paragraph 2 provides additional background for an audience unfamiliar with Ramadan.

Paragraph 3 opens with the speaker's credibility statement. Explaining her background and religious affiliation helps establish her personal expertise on the topic, while noting that she now celebrates Ramadan with other Muslim students "here on campus" relates the topic to the audience. Paragraph 4 states the speaker's specific purpose and previews the main points she will discuss in the body.

Body: Arranged in topical order, the body of the speech consists of two main points. The first is developed in paragraphs 5–7 and explains the history of Ramadan. Even though the speaker could recite this history from memory, she cites Karen Armstrong's history of Islam, thereby enhancing her credibility and letting the audience know that the speech is based on more than the speaker's personal experience. At the end of paragraph 5, the speaker builds common ground with the audience by explaining the role of the archangel Gabriel in the history of Ramadan. Because Gabriel is a part of the Jewish, Christian, and Muslim traditions, most listeners can relate to the speaker's point. Paragraph 7 further details the history of Ramadan by translating the name of the holiday and explaining why the dates of Ramadan change from year to year in the Western calendar.

Paragraph 8 provides a transition to the second main point and includes an internal preview of what the speaker will discuss in that point. Paragraphs 9-10 deal with fasting. As in other places, the speaker supplements her personal experience with information from expert authors. She displays potentially confusing words (*Sawm* and *Iftar*) on PowerPoint slides to ensure that the audience can follow along.

In paragraphs 11–12, the speaker deals with two other aspects of Ramadan—prayer and charity. Once again, she uses PowerPoint to display a potentially confusing term (*Tarawih*). She further builds common ground with the audience by noting, in paragraph 12, that gift giving at the end of Ramadan is comparable to gift-giving at Christmas. Paragraph 13 continues in the same vein by relating Ramadan to religious celebrations with which most non-Muslims in the audience are familiar.

As is apparent from the video of this speech, the speaker's sincere, conversational, and enthusiastic delivery plays an important role. She maintains excellent eye contact, gestures naturally and appropriately, and engages the audience with her ideas.

Conclusion: Paragraphs 14–15 constitute the conclusion. In paragraph 14, the speaker signals that her speech is coming to an end and summarizes her main points. To add a final personal touch, she explains the traditional greeting Muslims share with one another during Ramadan. The speaker's penultimate sentence—about Ramadan being sacred for one billion people around the globe—echoes the language of the introduction and provides a sense of psychological unity. Saying "Thank you" at the end is not always the most effective way to end a speech, but it works well in this case by conveying the speaker's appreciation for the audience's attention and for the opportunity to discuss a topic that is so important to her.

Using Public Speaking in Your Career   *(from text page 289)*

As a financial planner at a local investment firm, you have been asked to speak to a group of recent college graduates about long-term financial planning. After considering what recent college graduates need to know about saving for their future, you decide to organize your presentation around four general stages of investing:

1.   The early years of investing, which include putting aside small amounts of money that will grow over time.

2.   The years of acquisition, which include balancing investments with large expenses such as raising children and paying a mortgage.

3.   The years of accumulation, which include putting away as much money as possible in anticipation of retirement.

4.   The retirement years, which include living off of savings and adjusting investments as needed.

As you look over these stages of investing, you think back to the public speaking course you took in college. You remember that informative speakers should relate their speech directly to the audience, should not be too technical, should not overestimate what the audience knows about the subject, and should be creative. How might each of these guidelines influence your presentation to recent college graduates? Be specific.

> **Discussion:**   Like the other Using Public Speaking in Your Career scenarios throughout the book, this one is designed to show students that the principles of effective public speaking are as applicable outside the classroom as in it. This scenario is particularly helpful because it asks students to consider how informative speakers must adapt their remarks to their audiences.
>
> While there is not one right answer to the scenario, students should discuss how the guidelines for informative speaking would influence specific aspects of a financial planner's presentation. To relate the speech directly to the audience, for example, the speaker would likely explain that long-term financial planning begins with one's first job. To avoid overestimating what the audience knows, the speaker would need to remind the audience that retirement savings compound over time, so one's investments add up dramatically in subsequent decades, especially in the years just before retirement.
>
> At every stage of the presentation, however, the speaker would have to avoid using jargon related to economics and investments. Overly technical language would practically ensure that the audience had a difficult time understanding the information being presented. If the financial planner found some technical language necessary, he or she would have to explain the terminology carefully and provide clear descriptions of complex ideas. Using specific examples throughout the speech would also help ensure that the information is not too technical and not too abstract.

Being creative with a presentation on financial planning could involve any number of things, but visual aids could undoubtedly help the speech come alive. A line graph depicting compound interest over time, for example, would be a great way to show the importance of planning for one's future as soon as possible.

Additional Exercises and Activities

1. Show students the needs improvement version of "Medical Robots: From Science Fiction to Science Fact," which appears on the DVD of student speeches that accompanies this edition of *The Art of Public Speaking.* Have students analyze the speech by focusing on how well the speaker develops the introduction, body, and conclusion. Students should also pay attention to the speaker's delivery and visual aids.

Medical Robots: From Science Fiction to Science Fact
Needs Improvement Version

1 So, I was really cramped—I had to study for a calculus exam last night—so this didn't necessarily get done well. But let's just see how it goes, okay?

2 Basically, as a kid I watched *Star Wars* a lot, and I definitely loved seeing all the different kinds of robots there. Now that I want to be a doctor, I thought about looking into robots in medicine, and you definitely see them in hospitals all the time. So I thought that would be a good topic.

3 I also heard about a woman in New Jersey who had a kidney transplant operation done by a robot. Except there was a live surgeon that powered the robot, so they did it together.

4 First, though, there are orderly robots that carry stuff around the hospital, basically. Here's a picture of one. It's kind of like a square R2-D2, as you can see. Mark Weigel says these robots are fast and efficient, and they save hospitals a ton of time. So obviously that's important.

5 They use invisible light beams to get around. These beams are called "light whiskers." But because they are invisible, I actually can't show you a picture of them, unfortunately. I'm sure they're really cool still. I can tell you, though, the robots communicate with each other, so they can actually figure out how to get around the hospital efficiently.

6 The next robot is the remote-presence robot, and they are different than orderly robots. They actually let doctors see patients, and that's when the doctor isn't there. Normally, they can, obviously. But when the doctor is not there, they can still communicate. The doctor uses a camera to see the patient, and then the patient can see the doctor on the screen. Actually, you can see from these photographs that this is a remote-presence robot—kind of like Skype on wheels, so they can communicate.

7 These robots are actually really popular right now as well. I found a magazine article called *Hospital Management*, and it said that remote-presence robots are used in hundreds of hospitals. So obviously there is a trend in using these machines, and it's quite useful.

8   My favorite robot, though, is the da Vinci. It's named after the famous Italian painter. It's used for surgeries. I actually had a picture specifically of the robot, but I couldn't find it this morning when I double-checked. Obviously I'm here now and didn't have time. But it's definitely cool—the robot—and it's got a lot of arms, and it kind of looks like an octopus. Like Doctor Octopus, almost. It basically is the surgery machine.

9   According to an article I read, the doctor moves the arms from the terminal using a kind of controller. And he actually uses 3D imaging as well, so it's sort of like playing Xbox or Halo on a 3D TV. So it's probably fun. But the doctor himself doesn't ever touch the patient. Only the robot touches the patient.

10   In conclusion, that's my speech. I hope you see why I find robots so interesting. They are definitely changing medicine, and I'm sure they will all the way into the future for years to come. Thanks for listening.

Discussion: One of the most difficult things for students to grasp early in the term is the difference between an ordinary speech and a superior one. You can help them by showing the needs improvement version of "Medical Robots: From Science Fiction to Science Fact" followed by the final version of the same speech. When showing the needs improvement version, have students focus on how well the speaker develops the introduction, body, and conclusion of the speech, as well as the speaker's delivery and visual aids. Then show the final version of the speech. Follow with a class discussion that compares and contrasts the two versions and explores why the final version is superior.

Video of both versions is available online and on the DVD of student speeches that accompanies this edition of *The Art of Public Speaking*. The text and commentary for the final version is printed on pages 294–296 of the textbook. Below is a synopsis of the needs improvement version.

Introduction: The introduction, which consists of paragraphs 1–3, demonstrates that the speaker has not put enough time into his speech. Indeed, he begins by stating that he spent the previous night studying for a calculus exam, rather than working on his speech.

In paragraph 2, the speaker fulfills one of the objectives of a speech introduction by revealing the topic of his speech. However, he fails to relate the topic to the audience, save for a passing reference to *Star Wars*, a familiar film. In paragraph 3, he mentions a woman who had an operation involving a surgeon-controlled robot. But he does not explain the operation fully, and he does not tell the story in a way that draws the audience into the speech. The introduction ends without providing either a clear sense of the speaker's central idea or a preview statement of the main points he will discuss in the body.

In contrast, the final version of the speech fulfills all four objectives of an introduction—gaining the audience's attention, revealing the topic, establishing credibility and goodwill, and previewing the body of the speech.

Body: The body of the speech consists of paragraphs 4–9 and contains three main points. At the beginning of each point, the speaker provides a connective to help the audience follow along. However, the points themselves are poorly developed and ineffectually supported.

The first main point (paragraphs 4–5) deals with orderly robots. Testimony from Mark Weigel on the effectiveness of orderly robots is a good way to begin, but the speaker does not state who Weigel is or why he is a qualified source. In paragraph 5, the speaker attempts to describe light whiskers, but aside from calling light whiskers "invisible beams," he does not explain what they are or how they work. Describing technical subjects clearly and effectively is one of the major challenges facing informative speakers. This speaker does a much better of dealing with this challenge in the final version of his speech than in the needs improvement version.

The second main point (paragraphs 6–7) deals with remote-presence robots. The speaker's analogy between these robots and "Skype on wheels" is clever, but a careful speaker would take time to explain how doctors and patients actually interact through the robots. The speaker's citation in paragraph 7 of *Hospital Management* indicates that he has done some research, but a fully developed oral citation would include more than the title of the journal from which the information came.

The third main point (paragraphs 8–9) is equally problematic. Unsure of how the point should develop, the speaker launches into a free-association discussion of surgical robots, comparing them to a villain from *Spider-Man* and to a popular videogame franchise. He does not leave the audience with a clear sense of what surgical robots are or of how they work.

When comparing the needs improvement and final versions of the speech, students should notice that the body of both versions follows much the same structure. In the needs improvement version, the speaker has thought about the kinds of robots he wants to discuss, and he understands how to move the audience from one point to another. But, unlike the final version, he does not provide enough supporting materials to develop his ideas fully. The result is a speech with more promise than fulfillment.

Conclusion: Paragraph 10 serves as the conclusion. By saying "In conclusion," the speaker signals that the speech is coming to an end. He then reinforces his central idea when he mentions that robots are "definitely changing medicine." However, he does not attempt to end memorably or to leave a positive impression on the audience. Statements such as "that's my speech" and "thanks for listening" suggest that he put little thought into crafting his conclusion.

Delivery: As can be seen from the speech video, the speaker's delivery is animated and conversational. It is also fairly rapid and underscores the impression that the speaker is not properly prepared. He starts by taking a swig from his coffee cup—hardly a positive way to get attention at the outset. As the speech continues, he periodically leans on the lectern, inserts vocalized pauses, and loses his place—all of which reflect his lack of sufficient rehearsal.

The speaker's delivery is much better in the final version. He has excellent eye contact, gestures, and vocal variety, and he comes across as professional and fully prepared. He also speaks slowly enough that the audience can fully comprehend his technical information.

Visual Aids: Visual aids can greatly add to or detract from an informative speech. In the needs improvement version of "Medical Robots," the speaker's visual aids do little to enhance the information he is trying to convey. They fall far short of the guidelines discussed in Chapter 14 of the textbook.

The PowerPoint background that appears on screen at the beginning of the speech is cluttered and busy, drawing the audience's attention away from the speaker. The speaker's slide of an orderly robot (paragraph 4), is not as problematic as some of his other slides, but it lacks balance and effective composition when compared with the corresponding slide in the final version of the speech. More problems emerge in paragraph 5, where the speaker discusses light whiskers. Instead of thinking creatively about how to help the audience visualize light whiskers—as he does in the final version—he simply states that he can't show the light whiskers because they are not visible to the naked eye.

After discussing orderly robots, the speaker leaves his slide of an orderly robot on screen until he is partway through his next main point, on remote-presence robots (paragraphs 6–7). When he finally moves to a slide of remote-presence robots, it is cluttered and confusing. Chances are that the audience will spend more time puzzling over the visual aid than listening to the speaker.

When discussing surgical robots (paragraphs 8–9), the speaker displays a portrait of Leonardo da Vinci. While the portrait is interesting, it does not add to the speaker's explanation of the da Vinci surgical robot. The speaker again demonstrates his lack of preparation when he states that he had "a picture specifically of the robot," but he "couldn't find it this morning" when he looked for it.

Compared to the PowerPoint slides in the needs improvement version, those in the final version are carefully composed, visually appealing, and smoothly integrated into the speech. They are also creative, especially the slide used to illustrate the orderly robot's light whiskers. In addition to enhancing an audience's understanding of ideas, such creativity contributes to a memorable presentation that remains with listeners well after the speech has ended.

2. Show the needs improvement and final versions of "Securing Yourself Online" or "The Hidden World of Chili Peppers" from the DVD of student speeches that accompanies this edition of *The Art of Public Speaking*. Compare and contrast the two versions to illustrate the principles of effective informative speaking.

Discussion: Both the needs improvement and final versions of "Securing Yourself Online" and "The Hidden World of Chili Peppers" can help students avoid some of the most common problems facing informative speakers. When leading a class discussion on either speech, begin by showing the needs improvement version. Have students focus on the development of ideas as well as the speaker's delivery and visual aids. Then show the final version, having students focus on the same elements as they did in the needs improvement version. Conclude with a class discussion that compares and contrasts the two versions and explores why the final version is superior.

For the needs improvement and final versions of "Securing Yourself Online," see pages 296–302 of this manual. For the needs improvement and final versions of "The Hidden World of Chili Peppers," see pages 303–311 of this manual.

3. Popular nonfiction writing often provides helpful models of informative discourse on technical topics. Have each student select an article of interest from the medicine, science, or business section of *Time* or *Newsweek*. The student should prepare a brief report on the article answering each of the following:

a. How effectively does the author use definition, explanation, description, comparison, contrast, and examples to make the subject clear and interesting to ordinary readers? Identify two particular techniques used in the article that you might want to try in your next informative speech.

b. Are there some points in the story that you don't fully understand? If so, what information might the author have supplied to make the points clear to you?

c. Assume you will be giving a speech on the same topic as the article. What specific steps would you take to relate the topic directly to your classmates? To make it fully understandable to them? Consider not only what you might say in your speech, but also how you might use visual aids to enhance what you say.

Discussion: This can be a very helpful exercise if you have students give more than one informative speech or if you are teaching an advanced public speaking class. Because of its complexity, it does not always work well when beginning speakers are preparing their first informative speech.

4. Divide the class into groups of three to four students each. Have each group select one of the topics listed below (or other topics of your choosing). Each group has 15 minutes to work out a two-minute explanation designed for an audience that knows absolutely nothing about the topic. Each group should select one of its members to present the explanation orally to the class.

How to tie a shoe lace	How to build a campfire
How to change a car tire	How to lose weight
The basic rules of baseball	The basic rules of checkers

Discussion: This exercise drives home the complexity of giving information to listeners who are not already familiar with the topic. Like the preceding activity, it is usually too demanding for novice speakers who are working on their first informative speech. It can work very well in an advanced public speaking class or in the later stages of an introductory class with very good students.

5. Have students complete the Informative Speech Preparation Worksheet, which appears on pages 191–192 of this manual, or you can assign it from the assignments available in *Connect*.

Discussion: The Informative Speech Preparation Worksheet helps students develop their speeches systematically. It is best assigned early in the informative unit, so students can work on it throughout the speech preparation process. You can have students turn in the worksheet at the time of their initial preparation outline, or you can require that it be turned in on speech day. To help ensure that students take the worksheet seriously, many instructors make it a graded assignment.

6. Have students complete the Informative Speech Self-Assessment, which appears on page 193 of this manual.

Discussion: There is a great deal of research confirming the pedagogical value of self-assessments. The Informative Speech Self-Assessment asks students to write a full, objective evaluation of their informative speech. Assessment items include topic and purpose, organization, supporting materials, audience adaptation, delivery, language, visual aids, and overall performance.

Ideally, students will have a video of their speech in front of them when completing this assignment, especially when assessing their delivery. It is also best if students complete this assignment while their speeches are fresh in their minds. Most instructors require that the self-assessment be turned in no more than a week after the delivery of the informative speech.

Informative Speech Preparation Worksheet

Name _____   **Section** _____

1. What is the topic of your speech? Why is it appropriate for you?

   _____

   _____

   _____

2. Why is the topic appropriate for your audience?   _____

   _____

   _____

   _____

3. How is your topic narrowed to conform to the time limits for the speech assignment?

   _____

   _____

   _____

4. What is your specific purpose statement?   _____

   _____

   _____

5. Can you answer yes to all the questions on the Specific Purpose Checklist on page 87 of your textbook? _____

6. What is your central idea?   _____

   _____

   _____

7. Can you answer yes to all the questions on the Central Idea Checklist on page 92 of your textbook? _____

8. What method(s) of gaining attention do you use in the introduction?

   _____

   _____

9. How do you establish your credibility in the introduction?

   _____

   _____

   _____

— over —

10. Write the preview statement you will use in your introduction.

_____

_____

11. Can you answer yes to all the questions on the Speech Introduction Checklist on page 190 of your textbook? _____

12. What method of organization do you use in the speech?

_____

13. State in full sentences the main points to be developed in the body of your speech.

_____

_____

_____

_____

_____

_____

14. Can you answer yes to all the questions on the Main Points Checklist on page 176 of your textbook? _____

15. What steps have you taken to adapt the content of your speech so it will be clear and interesting to your audience? Be specific.

_____

_____

_____

_____

_____

_____

16. What method(s) of reinforcing your central idea do you use in the conclusion?

_____

_____

_____

_____

_____

17. Can you answer yes to all the questions on the Speech Conclusion Checklist on page 200 of your textbook? _____

Informative Speech Self-Assessment

Your task is to review your informative speech and to reach a full, objective assessment of its major strengths and weaknesses. Write a thoughtful evaluation of the speech in full-sentence and paragraph form with an introduction and a conclusion.

Be specific and concrete in your comments. Note in particular the areas in which you believe you did especially well and those areas in which you want to make special improvement in the next speech. Explain why you had difficulty with certain aspects of this speech and indicate the specific steps you will take to improve your next presentation.

Use the following questions to guide your self-assessment, though you do not need to answer each question individually in your paper. Be specific and concrete in your comments.

Topic and Purpose

Was the topic appropriate for the audience and the occasion?

Did you have a clear specific purpose that you could accomplish in the allotted time?

Organization

Was the speech well organized?

Did you fulfill all the major functions of a speech introduction?

Did you fulfill all the major objectives of a speech conclusion?

Were the main points of the body clear and easy to follow?

Did you use connectives effectively?

Supporting Materials, Audience Adaptation, and Language

Did you conduct adequate research when preparing the speech?

Did you adapt your speech so it would be relevant and interesting to your audience?

Did you follow the criteria in your textbook for the effective use of supporting materials?

Did you make a conscious effort to use clear, nontechnical language?

Delivery and Visual Aids

Did you begin and end your speech without rushing?

Did you use pauses, rate, pitch, and vocal variety effectively in delivering the speech?

Did your physical action add to or detract from the speech?

Did you maintain strong eye contact throughout the speech?

If you used visual aids, were they carefully prepared and smoothly integrated into the speech?

Did you follow the guidelines in your textbook for presenting visual aids?

Overall Assessment

What were you most pleased with in the speech? What were you least pleased with?

If you had an opportunity to deliver this speech again next week, what changes would you make? Be specific.

Speaking to Persuade

Chapter Objectives

After reading this chapter, students should be able to:

1. Define persuasion and explain why it is an important subject.

2. Explain why meeting ethical obligations can be especially challenging in persuasive speaking and identify the ethical responsibilities of persuasive speakers.

3. Clarify the differences between an informative speech and a persuasive speech and explain why speaking to persuade is especially challenging.

4. Explain what it means to say that audiences engage in a mental dialogue with the speaker as they listen to a persuasive speech.

5. Discuss the concept of target audience and its role in persuasive speaking.

6. Define a question of fact and give an example of a specific purpose statement for a persuasive speech on a question of fact.

7. Define a question of value and give an example of a specific purpose statement for a persuasive speech on a question of value.

8. Define a question of policy and give an example of a specific purpose statement for a persuasive speech on a question of policy.

9. Explain the difference between passive agreement and immediate action as goals for persuasive speeches on questions of policy.

10. Explain the three basic issues of need, plan, and practicality and their importance in persuasive speeches on questions of policy.

11. Discuss the four methods of organization used most often in persuasive speeches on questions of policy.

12. Identify the five steps in Monroe's motivated sequence.

Chapter Outline

I.   Persuasion is the process of creating, reinforcing, or changing people's beliefs or actions.

    A.   The ability to speak persuasively is beneficial in everything from personal relationships to career aspirations to civic deliberation.

    B.   The job of the persuasive speaker is that of an advocate, trying to affect the attitudes, beliefs, or actions of listeners.

II. Meeting ethical obligations can be especially challenging when one is speaking to persuade.

    A.   Persuasive speakers should keep in mind the guidelines for ethical speaking.

       1.   They should make sure their goals are ethically sound.

       2.   They should study the topic thoroughly so they won't mislead the audience.

       3.   They should learn about all sides of an issue and make sure they get the facts right.

       4.   They should be honest in what they say.

       5.   They should guard against subtle forms of dishonesty such as quoting out of context, portraying a few details as the whole story, and misrepresenting sources.

       6.   They should present evidence fairly and accurately.

    B.   Persuasive speakers should keep in mind the power of language and employ it responsibly.

III. Persuasion is a psychological process.

    A.   Of all the types of public speaking, persuasion is the most complex and the most challenging.

       1.   Persuasive speeches often deal with controversial topics that involve people's most basic attitudes, values, and beliefs.

       2.   No matter how skilled a speaker may be, some listeners are so committed to their own ideas that they cannot be persuaded to the speaker's point of view.

       3.   For this reason, persuasive speakers must enter a speech situation with realistic goals.

B.   When processing persuasive messages listeners engage in a mental give-and-take with the speaker.

   1.   Listeners do not sit passively and soak in everything a speaker says.

      a.   As they listen, they assess the speaker's credibility, delivery, supporting materials, language, and the like.

      b.   They may argue, inside their own minds, with the speaker.

   2.   Effective persuasive speakers regard their speeches as a kind of mental dialogue with the audience.

      a.   When preparing the speech, they try to put themselves in the place of the audience and imagine how they will respond.

      b.   Above all, they try to anticipate audience objections and to answer them in the speech.

C.   It is often helpful for persuasive speakers to think in terms of reaching their target audience.

   1.   The target audience is the part of the whole audience a speaker most wants to reach with his or her message.

   2.   In most situations, the target audience consists of uncommitted listeners, listeners who are inclining toward agreement with the speaker, and listeners who disagree with the speaker but who are open to persuasion.

   3.   Once a speaker knows where the target audience stands, she or he can adapt the speech to fit the values and concerns of the target audience.

IV.   Some persuasive speeches deal with questions of fact.

A.   Persuasive speeches on questions of fact seek to persuade an audience to accept the speaker's view of the facts on a particular issue.

B.   A persuasive speech on a question of fact is different from an informative speech.

   1.   The aim of an informative speech is to give information as impartially as possible, not to argue for a particular point of view.

   2.   Unlike speeches to inform, persuasive speeches on questions of fact take a partisan view of the information and try to persuade the audience to accept the speaker's view about that information.

C.   Most persuasive speeches on questions of fact are organized topically.

   1.   In such speeches, each main point will present a reason why the audience should agree with the speaker.

   2.   As in other speeches using topical order, persuasive speeches on questions of fact should subdivide the topic logically and consistently.

V.   Some persuasive speeches deal with questions of value.

A.   Questions of value require judgments based on a person's beliefs about what is right or wrong, good or bad, moral or immoral, etc.

B. When dealing with a question of value, a speaker needs to justify her or his value judgment in light of a clearly defined set of standards.

C. Speeches on questions of value are usually organized topically.

    1. The first main point establishes the standards for the speaker's value judgment.

    2. The second main point applies those standards to the speech topic.

VI. Most persuasive speeches deal with questions of policy.

A. Questions of policy deal with specific courses of action, deciding whether something should or should not be done.

B. There are two types of persuasive speeches on questions of policy.

    1. One type seeks to gain passive agreement that a policy is desirable, necessary, and practical.

    2. The second type seeks to motivate the audience to take immediate action.

C. Persuasive speeches on questions of policy must address three basic issues—need, plan, and practicality.

    1. First, speakers who advocate a change in policy must prove there is a need for the change.

    2. Second, after showing the need for change, a persuasive speaker must offer a specific plan—policy—that will solve the need.

    3. Third, speakers who advocate a new policy must show their plan is workable and will solve the need without creating new problems.

    4. The amount of time devoted to need, plan, and practicality in any given speech will depend on the topic and the audience.

VII. Four patterns of organization are especially effective for persuasive speeches on questions of policy.

A. The first pattern is problem-solution order.

    1. The first main point shows the need for a new policy by proving the existence of a serious problem.

    2. The second main point presents a plan for solving the problem and demonstrates its practicality.

B. The second pattern is problem-cause-solution order.

    1. The first main point shows the existence of a problem.

    2. The second main point analyzes the causes of the problem.

    3. The third main point presents a solution to the problem.

C. The third pattern is comparative advantages order.

    1. This pattern of organization is most effective when the audience already agrees there is a need for a new policy.

    2. Rather than dwelling on the need, the speaker devotes each main point to explaining why his or her plan is preferable to other solutions.

    D. The fourth pattern is Monroe's motivated sequence, which consists of five steps that follow the psychology of persuasion.

        1. The first step is to gain the attention of the audience.

        2. The second step is to show the need for a change.

        3. The third step is to satisfy the sense of need by presenting a plan that will remedy the need.

        4. The fourth step is to visualize the benefits and practicality of the plan.

        5. The fifth step is to urge the audience to take action in support of the plan.

Exercises for Critical Thinking *(from text pages 322–323)*

1. Look back at the story of Ramon Trujillo at the beginning of this chapter (pages 299–300 of the textbook). Like Ramon, most people do a certain amount of persuading every day in normal conversation. Keep a journal of your communication activities for an entire day, making special note of all instances in which you tried to persuade someone else to your point of view. Choose one of those instances and prepare a brief analysis of it.

    In your analysis, answer the following questions: (1) Who was the audience for your persuasive effort? (2) What were the "specific purpose" and the "central idea" of your persuasive message? (3) Did you rehearse your persuasive message ahead of time, or did it arise spontaneously from the situation? (4) Were you successful in achieving your specific purpose? (5) If you faced the same situation again, what strategic changes would you make in your persuasive effort?

    Discussion: This exercise emphasizes the extent to which most people engage in persuasion as part of normal conversation. It also provides a good springboard for discussion about the similarities between the kind of informal persuasive "speeches" we all give every day and the formal persuasive speeches students will present in class. Students should find that the strategic thinking they put into planning a formal persuasive speech is similar in many ways to the strategic thinking they use when trying to persuade someone in ordinary conversation.

2. Below are four specific purposes for persuasive speeches. In each case explain whether the speech associated with it concerns a question of fact, a question of value, or a question of policy. Then rewrite the specific purpose statement to make it appropriate for a speech about one of the other two kinds of questions. For instance, if the original purpose statement is about a question of policy, write a new specific purpose statement that deals with the same topic as either a question of fact or a question of value.

    a. To persuade my audience that a national sales tax should be adopted to help reduce the national debt.

b. To persuade my audience that it is unethical for doctors to receive money from pharmaceutical companies to promote their products.

c. To persuade my audience that violence in video games is a major cause of violent behavior among teenagers.

d. To persuade my audience to join Teach for America.

Discussion: This exercise works extremely well to help students understand the differences among questions of fact, value, and policy. Two possible variations follow each of the statements in the exercise.

a. To persuade my audience that a national sales tax should be adopted to help reduce the national debt.   (question of policy)

   Question of fact: To persuade my audience that a major source of new revenue is needed to help reduce the national debt.

   Question of value: To persuade my audience that a national sales tax is an equitable way to help reduce the national debt.

b. To persuade my audience that it is unethical for doctors to receive money from pharmaceutical companies to promote their products.   (question of value)

   Question of fact: To persuade my audience that doctors sometimes receive money from pharmaceutical companies to promote their products.

   Question of policy: To persuade my audience that doctors should be prohibited from receiving money from pharmaceutical companies to promote their products.

c. To persuade my audience that violence in video games is a major cause of violent behavior among teenagers.   (question of fact)

   Question of value: To persuade my audience that the federal government has a moral duty to monitor the amount of violence in video games.

   Question of policy: To persuade my audience that further reforms should be enacted to reduce the amount of violence in video games.

d. To persuade my audience to join Teach for America.   (question of policy)

   Question of fact: To persuade my audience that there is a serious shortage of participants in the Teach for America program.

   Question of policy: To persuade my audience that they have a civic obligation to join Teach for America after graduating from college.

3. Choose a topic for a persuasive speech on a question of policy. Create two specific purpose statements about that topic—one for a speech to gain passive agreement, another for a speech to motivate immediate action. Once you have the specific purpose statements, explain how the speech seeking immediate action would differ in structure and persuasive appeals from the speech seeking passive agreement. Be specific.

> **Discussion:** Understanding the distinction between seeking passive agreement and immediate action is crucial for effective persuasive speeches on questions of policy. This exercise helps students understand that distinction and the impact it has on the organization and strategy of a speech to persuade. The exercise works best when it is given as a homework assignment so students have plenty of time to work out their answers.
>
> As an alternative, the exercise can also be used as the basis for a small-group activity in class. Divide the class into groups and have each come up with its own answers. Designate one person to present the result of each group's work to the class.
>
> Here, as a general guide, is what the results might look like for a speech on the topic of cardiopulmonary resuscitation (CPR).
>
> a.   *Specific purpose statement for a speech seeking passive agreement*: To persuade my audience that everyone should learn CPR.
>
> b.   *Specific purpose statement for a speech seeking immediate action*: To persuade my audience to enroll in a CPR class at the Red Cross.
>
> c.   *Structure of the speech seeking passive agreement*: This speech would most likely be organized either in topical order (in which case each main point would explain a reason why everyone should learn CPR) or in problem-solution order (in which case the first main point would show why the lack of general CPR training is a problem and the second main point would present the speaker's plan to solve the problem).
>
> d.   *Structure of the speech seeking immediate action*: This speech could be organized in problem-solution order, but if it were, the speaker would have to be sure to include a call to action as part of the solution. A more effective organizational pattern would be Monroe's motivated sequence, which is specifically designed for speeches that aim to motivate listeners to take immediate action.
>
> e.   *Persuasive appeals of the speech seeking passive agreement*: This speech would focus on convincing the audience that it would be desirable for everyone to have training in CPR, but it would not try to persuade the audience to go out and learn CPR. As a result, the speaker could deal with the topic at a general level without having to confront the audience's objections to taking a CPR class themselves.
>
> f.   *Persuasive appeals of the speech seeking immediate action*: A speaker cannot motivate an audience to immediate action without relating the topic directly to

the audience and providing motivational appeals showing why they must change their behavior. It is also crucial that the speaker deal with the audience's potential reasons for not taking action—cost, lack of time, inconvenience, etc.

In the case of a speech on CPR, the speaker would need to show not just that there is a significant problem that can be solved by learning CPR, but also that it is necessary and practical for the listeners themselves to learn CPR. The speaker would have to anticipate the objections listeners might have to enrolling in a CPR class (too little time, not enough money, etc.) and answer those objections in the speech. The speaker might also rely more on emotional appeal in the speech seeking immediate action than in the speech seeking passive agreement. (See Chapter 17, pages 342–346, of the textbook for a discussion of emotional appeal in persuasive speaking.)

4. Analyze the sample speech with commentary at the end of Chapter 16 of the textbook ("Phony Pharmaceuticals," pages 318–320). Because this is a speech on a question of policy, pay special attention to how the speaker deals with the basic issues of need, plan, and practicality. Does the speaker present a convincing case that a serious problem exists? Does she offer a clear plan to solve the problem? Does she demonstrate that the plan is practical?

Discussion: "Phony Pharmaceuticals" is an instructive example of a persuasive speech on a question of policy. The commentary that accompanies the speech on pages 318–320 of the textbook points out a number of its major features. What follows is a more detailed analysis. Video of the speech is available online and on the DVD of student speeches that accompanies this edition of *The Art of Public Speaking*.

Specific Purpose: To persuade my audience that the federal government should pass legislation curbing the spread of phony pharmaceuticals.

Central Idea: Phony pharmaceuticals pose a serious problem that requires swift legislative action.

Method of Organization: Problem-solution

Introduction: The introduction consists of paragraphs 1–4. In paragraph 1, the speaker captures the audience's attention by displaying three PowerPoint slides, each of which shows a real prescription drug next to a phony one. The speaker's rhetorical questions about the pills gain attention and arouse the audience's curiosity. In paragraph 2, the speaker reveals the topic and notes how dangerous phony pharmaceuticals can be. In paragraph 3, she presents expert testimony to expand on the dangers of phony pharmaceuticals. In paragraph 4, she establishes her credibility by explaining her personal connection to the topic and noting that she has conducted a great deal of research for the speech. She then states her central idea and previews the main points she will discuss in the body.

Body: The body contains two main points—the first dealing with the need to curb the spread of phony pharmaceuticals, the second presenting a solution to the problem.

The first main point begins in paragraph 5, in which the speaker notes the dangers of fake drugs and quotes Graham Jackson, an expert on the problem. The examples of harmful ingredients found in phony pharmaceuticals help make the problem clear and vivid. In paragraph 6, the speaker illustrates the seriousness of the problem with an extended example about people killed by counterfeit heparin.

In paragraph 7, the speaker cites statistics and testimony to show that the heparin incident is not an isolated case. She relates the statistics to the audience by noting that the number of people killed each year by phony pharmaceuticals is "three times the number of people who live here in Madison." The first main point ends by showing that phony pharmaceuticals have become big business. Statistics from the FDA and a quotation from Tom Kubic, head of the Pharmaceutical Security Institute, document the extent of the problem. Comparing the profitability of phony pharmaceuticals to the heroin trade places the problem in vivid perspective.

Paragraph 9 begins with a transition to the solution section of the speech. The speaker then states that her solution is similar to legislation currently before the U.S. Congress. By stating that there are four steps to the solution, she prepares the audience to listen for each step.

The speaker discusses the steps of her plan in paragraphs 10–13. She begins each step with a signpost. As can be seen on the video, the speaker also highlights each step with a PowerPoint slide. This is an excellent strategy when communicating a multistep solution.

While the speaker does not have time to discuss all the intricacies of her plan, she stipulates its major elements clearly and concisely. In paragraph 10, for example, she notes that there should be no limit on jail time for a drug peddler whose phony pharmaceuticals result in death. The punishment, she states, "should fit the crime." In paragraph 11, she explains the current limits on the FDA's recall authority and notes that her plan will expand that authority.

In paragraph 12, the speaker moves to the third step of her plan. This paragraph is a good example of how a speaker can briefly but effectively note the practicality of a plan. In this instance, the speaker's analogy about inspectors for food and inspectors for drugs suggests that this part of the legislation is familiar and workable. By presenting the analogy in the form of a rhetorical question, the speaker invites the audience to draw the conclusion on their own.

In paragraph 13, the speaker deals with the fourth step of her plan. Because this step is more involved than the others, she cites an article from the *New York Times* to enhance the credibility of her information. She summarizes track-and-trace technology in sufficient detail to make her point understandable without getting bogged down in technical details.

Paragraph 14 presents further evidence that the speaker's plan is practical. Testimony from Representative Steve Israel of New York, a sponsor of the legislation before Congress, states that such a plan will "ensure that the domestic drug supply chain is secure for every American." The speaker ends the body by declaring that Congress must act swiftly to curb the spread of phony pharmaceuticals.

Conclusion: The conclusion begins in paragraph 15. The words "In conclusion" signal the end of the speech. The speaker then reinforces her central idea by reminding the audience of the problem and solution discussed in the body.

The most notable aspect of the conclusion comes in paragraph 16 when the speaker returns to the PowerPoint slides with which she opened the speech. In conjunction with language from the introduction, the slides tie the speech together and foster a strong sense of psychological unity. The parallel structure of the speaker's concluding sentences combine with the visual aids to create a memorable ending.

5. Select a television commercial that is organized according to Monroe's motivated sequence. Prepare a brief analysis in which you (a) identify the target audience for the commercial and (b) describe each step in the motivated sequence as it appears in the commercial.

> **Discussion:** Although this exercise does not deal directly with public speaking, it is a splendid way to get students to think about Monroe's motivated sequence and the structure of persuasive messages in general, and it almost always produces a lively class discussion. It works best when given as a homework assignment, so students have plenty of time to think about and to analyze the commercials they select. When discussing the commercials in class, be sure to make connections between the organization of the commercials and the organization of a speech.

Using Public Speaking in Your Career   *(from text page 317)*

After earning your teaching certificate, you landed a job in one of the best public school districts in the state. You've excelled in the classroom, and evaluations of your teaching are consistently outstanding.

But the newly announced state budget means drastic cuts for the district. Either 100 teachers will be laid off, or every teacher will have to accept a 10 percent pay cut. Because the newest teachers are the first to be fired, and you have been on the job for only three years, you know that the only way to keep your position is if all teachers agree to the pay cut. What's more, laying off 100 teachers will mean more students in each classroom, and that will harm the quality of education.

In one week, the school superintendent will hold an open meeting for teachers to voice their opinions. You plan on arguing for the pay cut, but you're unsure of how to organize your speech. Which of the following methods of organization will be most effective, and why: problem-solution, comparative advantages, Monroe's motivated sequence?

Discussion: Any of the methods of organization mentioned in the question could work for the teacher's speech. However, because most members of the audience already agree that a problem exists, comparative advantages would probably be the most effective. With comparative advantages, the speaker could systematically compare the two options—laying off 100 teachers or having every teacher accept a 10 percent pay cut—and show why the pay cut is preferable. This would also allow the speaker to highlight the disadvantages of not accepting the pay cut.

This exercise works well as a vehicle for class discussion on topics, occasions, audiences, and methods of organization in persuasive speaking. Divide the class into groups and give each a few minutes to come up with an answer to the question posed at the end of the scenario. Designate one person to present each group's answer to the class. Follow with a general class discussion.

Additional Exercises and Activities

1. Show one or more persuasive speeches from the DVD of student speeches that accompanies this edition of *The Art of Public Speaking*. Use the speeches to illustrate points about the principles of effective informative speaking.

    Discussion: The DVD that accompanies this edition of *The Art of Public Speaking* contains five complete persuasive speeches on questions of policy. For the text and discussion of "Phony Pharmaceuticals," see pages 318–320 of the textbook and pages 201–203 of this manual. For the text and discussion of "The Dangers of Cell Phones," see pages 346–349 of the textbook and pages 226–227 of this manual. For "The Horrors of Puppy Mills," see pages A7–A9 of the textbook and pages 222–224 of this manual. For "Bursting the Antibacterial Bubble," see pages A9–A11 of the textbook and pages 110–113 of this manual. For "Making a Difference Through the Special Olympics," see pages 345–349 of this manual.

2. Show students the needs improvement version of "Phony Pharmaceuticals" from the DVD of student speeches that accompanies this edition of *The Art of Public Speaking*. Have students analyze the speech by focusing on how the speaker develops the introduction, body, and conclusion. Students should also focus on the speaker's delivery and visual aids.

Phony Pharmaceuticals
Needs Improvement Version

1   So this one time, my sister took some medication for asthma, and it made her sick. I mean, it was totally fake, and it was really scary for my whole family.

2   I never heard of anything like this before, but guess what: She's not the only one who's been given fake medication. Lots of people end up with phony pharmaceuticals, and some of them even die.

3   Here's a picture of a phony pharmaceutical. See, it looks just like the real one. And that's the topic of my speech today.

4   Graham Jackson says fake drugs include things like boric acid, talcum powder, chalk, and even arsenic. In 2008, 81 people in the U.S. died from a phony pill. All over the world, 700,000 people will die this year. Think about how many people that is. That's a scary number. You don't want to be one of those people.

5   One reason there are so many phony drugs out there is that there are people who make a lot of money from them—more money, in fact, than from dealing heroin. So as you can see, the problem is only going to get worse. One website said that criminals make $75 billion a year.

6   We need to stop these phony pharmaceuticals from hurting any more people. My plan is to pass a bill and get it through Congress.

7   Firstly, criminal penalties should be increased. I mean, you can kill someone with fake drugs. Secondly, the government should have the power to get phony pharmaceuticals off the street. Thirdly, the FDA should check all the drugs everywhere to see if they're real or fake. We have health inspectors for food, why not for drugs? Finally, as all the experts agree, we need to have track-and-trace technology.

8   I know this plan sounds pretty complicated, but trust me, it will work. That's what all my sources say.

9   So we really need to pass this bill. We need to tell our congressmen and congresswomen. Let's do that so we can get phony pharmaceuticals off the streets. It's important to solve this problem.

10   That's the conclusion of my speech. Thank you.

Discussion: Like the other needs improvement speeches accompanying this edition of *The Art of Public Speaking*, the needs improvement version of "Phony Pharmaceuticals" can help students see the difference between an ordinary speech and an excellent one. When showing the needs improvement version, have students focus on how well the speaker develops the introduction, body, and conclusion, as well as on the speaker's delivery and visual aids. Then show the final version, having students focus on the same elements. Follow with a class discussion that compares and contrasts the two versions of the speech and explores why the final version is superior.

Video of the needs improvement and final versions of "Phony Pharmaceuticals" is available on the DVD of student speeches that accompanies this edition of *The Art of Public Speaking*. The text of the final version is printed on pages 318–320 of the textbook, and a detailed discussion appears on pages 201–203 of this manual. Below is a synopsis of the needs improvement version.

Introduction: The speaker begins with a story about her sister and phony pharmaceuticals—not a bad idea for gaining attention. However, she tells the story with few details and no sense of drama. She seems to be speaking off the top of her head, which suggests a lack of preparation. In the second paragraph, she states that lots of people have been given phony pharmaceuticals, but she provides no evidence to back up her claim. A statistic or piece of expert testimony would go a long way at this point in the speech. The speaker reveals the topic of the speech in paragraph 3, but she fails to preview the body. All told, the audience leaves the introduction with little sense of the speaker's central idea and no indication that she is qualified to speak on the topic.

Body: The body consists of paragraphs 4–8. The speaker begins paragraph 4 by paraphrasing Graham Jackson on the ingredients used to make counterfeit drugs. She does much the same thing in the final version of the speech. But in the needs improvement version, she fails to explain Jackson's credentials, thereby giving the audience no reason to accept his testimony. In paragraph 5, the speaker mentions "one Web site" as the source of her information, but she needs to provide further details, such as the name of the site, the sponsoring organization, the author's qualifications, and the date of the article.

In paragraph 6, the speaker begins to discuss her solution. She says that her plan is "to pass a bill and get it through Congress." Yet significant questions remain: Where did the bill come from? Why is the speaker qualified to write and propose legislation? Do other groups or individuals advocate a similar solution? Addressing these questions—which the speaker does in the final version—would make her plan considerably more credible.

As the solution section proceeds, the speaker includes signposts to demarcate the parts of her plan—a good strategy when explaining multistep legislation. But she needs to go into more detail about the plan to convince the audience that it is feasible and practical. Compare this section of the speech with the same section in the final version.

Conclusion: The conclusion consists of paragraphs 9 and 10. Even though the speaker communicates her passion for the subject, the conclusion remains underdeveloped. The speaker says, for example, that the audience should "tell" their Congressmen and Congresswomen, but she doesn't specify what the audience should tell Congress. The final paragraph signals that the speech is coming to an end, but it does not fulfill the other functions of a conclusion.

Delivery: The speaker states most of her points emphatically and seems genuinely concerned about the problem of phony pharmaceuticals, but she undermines her effectiveness by leaning on the lectern and twirling her hair. Although she has good eye contact in parts of the speech, her tone is too informal for such a serious topic. Compared to the delivery in the final version, that in the needs improvement version seems more like a practice session than a polished classroom speech.

Visual Aids: Comparing the visual aids of the needs improvement version with the visual aids of the final version is instructive for understanding the guidelines discussed in Chapter 14 of the textbook. In the needs improvement version, the speaker has a good idea—showing a phony pharmaceutical next to a legitimate drug in the introduction to help gain the audience's attention—but she does not use this approach as effectively as she might. In the final version, she uses three consecutive slides that build one upon the other to pull the audience into the speech.

When discussing her plan, the speaker presents a PowerPoint slide to identify the elements of her proposed legislation. However, the slide is overloaded with text, and the speaker turns her back to the audience when discussing it. She also leaves the slide on screen after she finishes discussing it. In contrast, the final version illustrates both how to prepare effective slides and how to present them so as to achieve the speaker's purpose.

3. Below are six statements. Explain whether each statement deals *primarily* with a question of fact, a question of value, or a question of policy.

   a. President Franklin D. Roosevelt knew in advance about the Japanese plan to attack Pearl Harbor and allowed it to happen.

   b. If Franklin D. Roosevelt knew in advance about the Japanese plan to attack Pearl Harbor, he was wrong in allowing it to happen.

   c. Using genetic profiles as screening devices for jobs in private business violates an employee's right to privacy.

   d. The use of genetic profiles in screening employees for private business should be banned by law.

   e. A federal law should be passed requiring the driver's seatbelt to be fastened in order for a car to operate.

   f. If the driver's seatbelt had to be fastened for a car to operate, we could save several hundred lives every year.

Discussion: These statements are somewhat more complex than those in Exercise 2 on pages 322–323 of the textbook. Dealing with them provides valuable extra work for students in distinguishing among questions of fact, value, and policy. It also helps demonstrate how one kind of question can have strong implications for a speech on one of the other types of questions.

a.   President Franklin D. Roosevelt knew in advance about the Japanese plan to attack Pearl Harbor and allowed it to happen.

(question of fact)

b.   If Franklin D. Roosevelt knew in advance about the Japanese plan to attack Pearl Harbor, he was wrong in allowing it to happen.

(question of value)

c.   Using genetic profiles as screening devices for jobs in private business violates an employee's right to privacy.

(question of value)

d.   The use of genetic profiles in screening employees for private business should be banned by law.

(question of policy)

e.   A federal law should be passed requiring the driver's seatbelt to be fastened in order for a car to operate.

(question of policy)

f.   If the driver's seatbelt had to be fastened for a car to operate, we could save several hundred lives every year.

(question of fact)

4.   Distribute copies of the Fact, Value, Policy Worksheet, which appears on page 213 of this manual.

Discussion: The Fact, Value, Policy Worksheet supplements the second Exercise for Critical Thinking on pages 322–323 of the textbook, as well as the third Additional Exercise/Activity above. You can use the worksheet either as a homework assignment or as the basis for a classroom activity.

5.   Conduct a class discussion on the ethics of persuasive speaking. Among the issues to consider are: (1) Is it ethical for one person to try to persuade another? (2) What is the most ethical approach for a speaker to take when trying to persuade an audience? (3) To what extent should a persuasive speaker reveal her or his true motives to the audience? (4) Are there any

situations in which it would be ethical for a speaker to distort the truth in order to persuade an audience? (5) Is it ethical for a speaker to use emotional appeal to sway listeners?

Discussion: Questions of ethics can arise every time a speaker seeks to persuade an audience. By dealing with the issue at the start of the unit on persuasive speaking, instructors can emphasize to students the importance of keeping a firm ethical rudder in their speeches. It may be helpful to have students review Chapter 2 of the textbook ("Ethics and Public Speaking") in preparation for discussion.

Although this exercise can work very well early in the unit on persuasion, some instructors prefer to discuss ethics in conjunction with the next chapter of the textbook, which contains a section devoted to the ethics of emotional appeal (text pages 342–346). For a similar exercise in Chapter 17, see page 351 of the textbook.

6. Bring to class a bag containing a half-dozen or so ordinary household items—rubber band, stapler, hairbrush, can of soda, etc. Also bring a bag containing an equal number of slips of paper on which you have identified potential speech audiences—retirees, college students, middle-class baby boomers, elementary-school students, etc. Divide the class into groups and have each group select an item from one bag and an audience from the other.

Give each group 10 minutes to compose a 1 to 2 minute speech designed to sell its object to the chosen audience. There are two special requirements. First, the group must come up with a completely new use for its item. For example, if the item is a can opener, the group must devise some use for it other than opening cans or bottles. Second, the speech must be organized according to Monroe's motivated sequence. Have one member from each group present its speech to the class. After each speech, ask the rest of the class if they can identify the target audience for the speech.

Discussion: Not only do students enjoy this activity, but it provides an excellent vehicle for discussion of two central concepts discussed in this chapter—the target audience and Monroe's motivated sequence. Encourage students to be creative in their speeches and expect a lively session.

7. As an alternative to the preceding activity, divide the class into groups and have each group prepare a 1 to 2 minute speech with the specific purpose, "To persuade my audience that all students should take a course in public speaking." The speech must be organized according to Monroe's motivated sequence. Have one member from each group present the speech to the class.

Discussion: There are an almost endless number of potential variations on this activity depending on the specific purpose you assign and the aspects of persuasive speaking you want to illustrate. It can also be adapted to provide a brief individual speech assignment rather than a group activity.

8. Have students complete the Persuasive Speech Preparation Worksheet, which appears on pages 211–212 of this manual, or assign the worksheet from the assignments available in *Connect*.

    Discussion: The Persuasive Speech Preparation Worksheet helps students develop their speeches systematically. It is best assigned early in the persuasive unit, so students can work on it throughout the speech preparation process. You can have students turn in the worksheet at the time of their initial preparation outline, or you can require that it be turned in on speech day. To help ensure that students take the worksheet seriously, many instructors make it a graded assignment.

9. Have students complete the Persuasive Speech Self-Assessment, which appears on page 214 of this manual.

    Discussion: There is a great deal of research confirming the pedagogical value of self-assessments. The Persuasive Speech Self-Assessment asks students to write a full, objective evaluation of their persuasive speech. Assessment items include topic and purpose, organization, supporting materials, audience adaptation, delivery language, visual aids, and overall performance.

    Ideally, students will have a video of their speech in front of them when completing this assignment, especially when assessing their delivery. It is also best if students complete this assignment while their speeches are fresh in their minds. Most instructors require that the self-assessment be turned in no more than a week after the delivery of the persuasive speech.

Persuasive Speech Preparation Worksheet

Name _____   **Section** _____

1. What is the topic of your speech? _____

2. Are you speaking on a question of fact, value, or policy? _____

3. What is your specific purpose statement? _____

    _____

    _____

4. Can you answer yes to all the questions on the Specific Purpose Checklist on page 87 of your textbook? _____

5. Is your speech meant to achieve passive agreement or immediate action from your audience?

    _____

6. What is your central idea? _____

    _____

    _____

7. Can you answer yes to all the questions on the Central Idea Checklist on page 92 of your textbook? _____

8. What is the target audience for your speech? How will you adapt your speech to be persuasive to your target audience? Be specific.

    _____

    _____

    _____

    _____

9. What method(s) of gaining attention do you use in the introduction?

    _____

    _____

10. How do you establish your credibility in the introduction?

    _____

    _____

    _____

— over —

11. Write the preview statement you will use in your introduction. _____

_____

_____

_____

12. Can you answer yes to all the questions on the Speech Introduction Checklist on page 190 of your textbook? _____

13. What method of organization do you use in the speech? _____

14. State in full sentences the main points to be developed in the body of your speech.

_____

_____

_____

_____

_____

15. Can you answer yes to all the questions on the Main Points Checklist on page 176 of your textbook? _____

16. What supporting materials do you use in developing each main point? Be specific.

_____

_____

_____

_____

_____

17. Can you answer yes to all the questions on the Evidence Checklist on page 334 of your textbook? _____

18. What steps have you taken to answer potential objections that your audience may have to your position? Be specific.

_____

_____

_____

_____

19. What method(s) of reinforcing your central idea do you use in the conclusion?

_____

_____

Fact, Value, Policy Worksheet

Below are four specific purpose statements for persuasive speeches. In each case explain whether the speech associated with it concerns a question of fact, a question of value, or a question of policy. Then rewrite the specific purpose statement to make it appropriate for a speech about one of the other two kinds of questions. For instance, if the original purpose statement is about a question of policy, write a new specific purpose statement that deals with the same topic as either a question of fact or a question of value.

1. To persuade my audience to get training in CPR.

    Does this specific purpose deal with a question of fact, value, or policy? _____

    Rewritten specific purpose statement: _____

    _____

    _____

2. To persuade my audience that pornography is a major cause of violence against women.

    Does this specific purpose deal with a question of fact, value, or policy? _____

    Rewritten specific purpose statement: _____

    _____

    _____

3. To persuade my audience that a national ban on private ownership of all kinds of guns should be adopted to help decrease violence.

    Does this specific purpose deal with a question of fact, value, or policy? _____

    Rewritten specific purpose statement: _____

    _____

    _____

4. To persuade my audience that it is unethical for U.S. clothing companies to employ foreign workers at substandard wages.

    Does this specific purpose deal with a question of fact, value, or policy? _____

    Rewritten specific purpose statement: _____

    _____

    _____

Persuasive Speech Self-Assessment

Your task is to review your persuasive speech and to reach a full, objective assessment of its major strengths and weaknesses. Write a thoughtful evaluation of the speech in full-sentence and paragraph form with an introduction and a conclusion.

Be specific and concrete in your comments. Note in particular the areas in which you believe you did especially well and those areas in which you want to make special improvement in the next speech. Explain why you had difficulty with certain aspects of this speech and indicate the specific steps you will take to improve your next presentation.

Use the following questions to guide your self-assessment, though you do not need to answer each question individually in your paper. Be specific and concrete in your comments.

Topic and Purpose

Was the topic appropriate for the audience and occasion?

Did you have a clear specific purpose that you could accomplish in the allotted time?

Organization

Was the speech well organized?

Did you fulfill all the major functions of a speech introduction?

Did you fulfill all the major objectives of a speech conclusion?

Were the main points of the body clear and easy to follow?

Did you use connectives effectively?

Supporting Materials, Audience Adaptation, and Language

Did you conduct adequate research when preparing the speech?

Were your ideas well supported and explained?

If you spoke on a question of policy, did you demonstrate a need to change current policy?

Did you present a clear plan to solve the need? Did you prove the practicality of your plan?

Did you follow the criteria in your textbook for the effective use of supporting materials?

Did you identify the target audience for your speech?

Did you use evidence to answer the potential objections of your target audience?

Did you present your ideas in clear, vivid, accurate, and appropriate language?

Delivery and Visual Aids

Did you begin and end your speech without rushing?

Did you use pauses, rate, pitch, and vocal variety effectively in delivering the speech?

Did your physical action add to or detract from the speech?

Did you maintain strong eye contact throughout the speech?

If you used visual aids, were they carefully prepared and smoothly integrated into the speech?

Did you follow the guidelines in your textbook for presenting visual aids?

Overall Assessment

What were you most pleased with in the speech? What were you least pleased with?

If you had an opportunity to deliver this speech again next week, what changes would you make? Be specific.

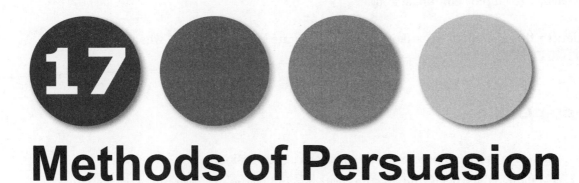

Methods of Persuasion

Chapter Objectives

After reading this chapter, students should be able to:

1. Explain the role of speaker credibility in persuasive speaking.

2. Define the differences among initial credibility, derived credibility, and terminal credibility.

3. Discuss three ways a speaker can enhance her or his credibility during a persuasive speech.

4. Explain why it is important for persuasive speakers to use evidence in their speeches.

5. Discuss the four tips presented in the chapter for using evidence in persuasive speeches.

6. Define reasoning from specific instances and explain the guidelines given in the chapter for using this method of reasoning.

7. Define reasoning from principle and explain the guidelines a speaker should follow when employing reasoning from principle.

8. Define causal reasoning and explain the two common errors speakers need to avoid when using causal reasoning.

9. Define analogical reasoning and explain how to judge the validity of an analogy.

10. Identify and explain the ten fallacies discussed in the chapter.

11. Explain the role of emotional appeal in persuasive speaking and discuss when it is ethical for a speaker to employ emotional appeal.

12. Identify three methods a speaker can use to generate emotional appeal when speaking to persuade.

Chapter Outline

I.   There is a perpetual interest in the methods of persuasion.
   A.   People have been studying the strategies and tactics of successful persuasion for thousands of years.
   B.   Scholars generally agree that listeners are persuaded by a speaker for one or more of four reasons.
      1.   Because they perceive the speaker as having high credibility.
      2.   Because they are won over by the speaker's evidence.
      3.   Because they are convinced by the speaker's reasoning.
      4.   Because their emotions are touched by the speaker's ideas or language.

II.   A speaker's credibility plays an important role in persuading the audience.
   A.   Credibility is the audience's attitude toward or perception of the speaker.
   B.   A speaker's credibility is affected by two primary factors—competence and character.
      1.   Competence refers to how an audience regards a speaker's intelligence, expertise, and knowledge of the subject.
      2.   Character refers to how an audience regards a speaker's sincerity, trustworthiness, and concern for the well-being of the audience.
   C.   There are three types of credibility.
      1.   Initial credibility is the audience's perception of the speaker before the speech begins.
      2.   Derived credibility is produced by everything a speaker says and does during the speech.
      3.   Terminal credibility is the audience's perception of the speaker at the end of the speech.
   D.   There are three strategies speakers can use to enhance their credibility.
      1.   Speakers can enhance their credibility by explaining their competence.
      2.   Speakers can enhance their credibility by establishing common ground with the audience.
      3.   Speakers can enhance their credibility by delivering their speeches fluently, expressively, and with conviction.

III. A speaker's use of evidence plays an important role in persuading the audience.

   A. Evidence consists of examples, statistics, and testimony used to prove or disprove something.

   B. To be persuasive, speakers must support their views with evidence.

      1. Careful listeners are skeptical of unsupported claims and generalizations.

      2. Strong evidence is particularly important when the speaker is not recognized as an expert on the speech topic.

      3. Strong evidence is also crucial when the target audience opposes the speaker's point of view.

   C. There are four tips persuasive speakers should follow to use evidence effectively.

      1. Persuasive speakers should use specific evidence.

      2. Persuasive speakers should use novel evidence.

      3. Persuasive speakers should use evidence from credible sources.

      4. Persuasive speakers should make clear the point of their evidence.

IV. A speaker's reasoning plays an important role in persuading the audience.

   A. Reasoning is the process of drawing a conclusion based on evidence.

   B. Public speakers have two major concerns with respect to reasoning.

      1. The first is to make sure the speaker's reasoning is sound.

      2. The second is to get listeners to agree with the speaker's reasoning.

   C. Persuasive speakers often use reasoning from specific instances.

      1. When speakers reason from specific instances, they progress from a number of particular facts to a general conclusion.

      2. Speakers should follow three guidelines when reasoning from specific instances.

         a. They need to beware of hasty generalizations based on insufficient evidence.

         b. They need to be careful with their wording so as not to overstate the facts.

         c. They need to reinforce their argument with statistics or testimony.

   D. Persuasive speakers often use reasoning from principle.

      1. When speakers reason from principle, they move from a general principle to a specific conclusion.

      2. Speakers should follow two basic guidelines when reasoning from principle.

         a. They need to make certain the audience will accept the general principle.

         b. They also need to make sure the audience will accept the minor premise.

   E. Persuasive speakers often use causal reasoning.

      1. Causal reasoning tries to establish the relationship between causes and effects.

      2. Speakers should follow two guidelines when using causal reasoning.

         a. They should avoid the fallacy of false cause.

b.   Speakers should also avoid the fallacy of assuming that events have only one cause.

F.   Persuasive speakers often use analogical reasoning.

1.   Analogical reasoning compares two similar cases to draw the conclusion that what is true in one case will also be true in the other.

2.   The most important guideline for speakers using analogical reasoning is to make sure the two cases being compared are essentially alike.

a.   If the cases being compared are essentially alike, the analogy is valid.

b.   If the cases being compared are not essentially alike, the analogy is invalid.

G.   Regardless of the method of reasoning they use, speakers must guard against logical fallacies in their presentations.

1.   A fallacy is an error in reasoning.

2.   There are ten fallacies that seem most common in student speeches.

a.   Hasty generalization occurs when a speaker jumps to a conclusion on the basis of too few cases, or on the basis of atypical cases.

b.   False cause occurs when a speaker assumes that because one event follows another, the first event is the cause of the second.

c.   An invalid analogy occurs when two cases being compared are not essentially alike.

d.   The bandwagon fallacy assumes that because something is popular, it is therefore good, correct, or desirable.

e.   The red herring fallacy introduces an irrelevant issue in order to divert attention from the subject under discussion.

f.   The *ad hominem* fallacy substitutes an attack on the person for discussion of the real issue in dispute.

g.   The either-or fallacy, sometimes referred to as a false dilemma, forces listeners to choose between two alternatives when more than two alternatives exist.

h.   The slippery slope fallacy assumes that taking a first step will lead inevitably to a second step and so on down the slope to disaster.

i.   The appeal to tradition fallacy occurs when a speaker assumes that something old is automatically better than something new.

j.   The appeal to novelty fallacy occurs when a speaker assumes that because something is new, it is therefore superior to something that is older.

V.   A speaker's emotional appeals play an important role in persuading the audience.

A.   Emotional appeals—often called motivational appeals—are intended to make listeners feel sad, angry, guilty, fearful, reverent, or the like.

B.   Speakers can generate emotional appeal in three ways.

   1.   One way to generate emotional appeal is with emotionally charged language.

   2.   A second way to generate emotional appeal is with vivid examples.

   3.   A third way to generate emotional appeal is to speak with sincerity and conviction.

C. Because emotional appeals have so much potential power, they need to be used with a strong sense of ethical responsibility.

   1.   Emotional appeals can be abused by unscrupulous speakers for detestable causes.

   2.   Emotional appeals can also be used by principled speakers for noble causes.

   3.   Ethical speakers make sure their emotional appeals are appropriate to the speech topic.

   4.   Even when trying to move listeners to action, a speaker should never substitute emotional appeals for evidence and reasoning.

   5.   When using emotional appeals, persuasive speakers should also keep in mind the guidelines for ethical speechmaking discussed in Chapter 2.

Exercises for Critical Thinking *(from text page 351)*

1. Research has shown that a speaker's initial credibility can have great impact on how the speaker's ideas are received by listeners. Research has also shown that a speaker's credibility will vary from topic to topic and audience to audience. In the left-hand column below is a list of well-known public figures. In the right-hand column is a list of potential speech topics. Assume that each speaker will be addressing your speech class.

    For each speaker, identify the topic in the right-hand column on which she or he would have the highest initial credibility for your class. Then explain how the speaker's initial credibility might be affected if the speaker were discussing the topic in the right-hand column directly across from her or his name.

Speaker	Topic
Hillary Clinton	Life in the NFL
Jon Stewart	The Future of Social Networking
Mark Zuckerberg	Pop Music and the Cult of Celebrity
Lady Gaga	Diplomacy in the 21st Century
Peyton Manning	The Comedy of Politics

Discussion: This exercise is almost certain to provoke a lively discussion and is a fine way to launch a class discussion on the importance of credibility in persuasive speaking. Here are some plausible responses to the questions about each of the speakers listed in the exercise:

Hillary Clinton: Although Clinton has likely seen several professional football games, she would have the highest credibility on "Diplomacy in the 21st Century." Indeed, as Secretary of State under President Obama, not to mention being a former first lady and senator, this is a subject she has addressed on many occasions.

Jon Stewart: Host of *The Daily Show*, a highly acclaimed television program that specializes in political satire, Stewart would command a rapt audience on "The Comedy of Politics." Although he maintains a presence on various social networks, he would have much less credibility on the future of social networking than Mark Zuckerberg.

Mark Zuckerberg: As the subject of a dramatized feature-length film, Zuckerberg might have a few words to say about the cult of celebrity. But as the founder of Facebook, the world's largest and most successful social network, he is perhaps the most qualified person on the planet to discuss "The Future of Social Networking."

Lady Gaga: Although Lady Gaga has spoken out on a range of social and political subjects, she is far from a recognized authority on "Diplomacy in the 21st century." However, as one of the most successful musicians in recent memory, she is perfectly able to discourse at length on "Pop Music and the Cult of Celebrity."

Peyton Manning: Quarterback for the Indianapolis Colts and member of a storied football family, Manning could speak with authority on "Life in the NFL." While he may have a sense of humor, few would trust what he had to say on "The Comedy of Politics."

2. Identify the kind of reasoning used in each of the following statements. What weaknesses, if any, can you find in the reasoning of each?

a. According to a study by the American Medical Association, men with bald spots have three times the risk of heart attack as men with a full head of hair. Strange as it may seem, it looks as if baldness is a cause of heart attacks.

Discussion: This statement is an example of causal reasoning. It is flawed by the fallacy of false cause. The fact that men with bald spots have three times the risk of heart attack does not mean their baldness is a cause of their heart attacks. If there is any connection between baldness and heart attacks, it is that both are brought on by similar factors—stress, heredity, diet, etc.—but medical researchers do not yet have an answer to this question.

b. We can see from its work all around the world that Women for Women International is a worthy charitable organization. It has helped women in Rwanda operate sewing machines and make clothing. It has given women in Kosovo the skills to operate businesses in their communities. It has shown women in the Democratic Republic of Congo how to create and market ceramics.

Discussion: This statement is an example of reasoning from specific instances. Whether it is flawed depends on whether the three specific instances mentioned in the statement are representative of the efforts of Women for Women International. And that cannot be determined in the absence of further evidence. One way to provide that evidence would be to follow the three instances with expert testimony and statistics about the charity's work. Even then, however, a skeptical listener could argue that the testimony is not conclusive or that the statistics are not sufficient to prove the speaker's point beyond doubt.

c.   The United States Constitution guarantees all citizens the right to bear arms. Gun control legislation infringes on the right of citizens to bear arms. Therefore, gun control legislation is contrary to the Constitution.

Discussion: This statement is an example of reasoning from principle. The reasoning is valid in that the movement from the general principle (The U.S. Constitution guarantees all citizens the right to bear arms) to the minor premise (Gun control legislation infringes on the right of citizens to bear arms) to the conclusion (Therefore, gun control legislation is contrary to the Constitution) is logically valid.

Logical validity, however, is judged by the form of an argument, not by its content. If the conclusion has been correctly inferred from the premises, the argument is valid regardless of whether or not the premises are true. It is possible to have a valid argument from principle that is patently unsound. For example:

1. All movie stars live in Hollywood.

2. Gwyneth Paltrow is a movie star.

3. Therefore, Gwyneth Paltrow lives in Hollywood.

This is a valid argument. If it is true that all movie stars live in Hollywood, and if it is also true that Gwyneth Paltrow is a movie star, then it must be true that Gwyneth Paltrow lives in Hollywood. In fact, however, it is not true that all movie stars live in Hollywood. Many live outside Hollywood; Gwyneth Paltrow lives in London. Even though the argument is valid, it is not sound.

A sound argument from principle is one in which the reasoning is valid and all the premises are true. For example:

1. To be elected a United States Senator, a person must be at least 30 years of age.

2. Al Franken was elected a United States Senator.

3. Therefore, Al Franken is at least 30 years of age.

In this case, the reasoning is valid and the premises are true. The argument is sound.

What about the argument regarding gun control? Is it sound as well as valid? That depends upon how one interprets the meaning of the clause of the U.S. Constitution ensuring citizens the right to bear arms. If one interprets that clause as meaning that all citizens have the right to own any kind of gun they please, then gun control legislation would certainly be contrary to the Constitution. If one interprets the right to bear arms in an 18th-century context as meaning that all citizens have the right to maintain their own weapons so as to be able to serve in the militia—a situation that is not relevant to U.S. life in the 21st century—then gun control legislation might not be contrary to the Constitution.

The persuasiveness of the argument in any given situation will depend on the ability of the speaker to convince the audience that he or she has the correct interpretation of the clause of the Constitution that guarantees citizens the right to bear arms. As with the example of reasoning from specific instances presented earlier, this case demonstrates that reasoning is not always a cut-and-dried matter.

    d. Almost every industrialized nation in the world except for the United States has a national curriculum and national tests to help ensure that schools throughout the country are meeting high standards of education. If such a system can work elsewhere, it can work in the United States.

Discussion: This statement is an example of analogical reasoning. Its validity depends upon whether the factors that allow a national curriculum and national testing to work successfully in most industrialized nations are also present in the United States. Advocates of nationalizing the educational system argue that the U.S. is similar enough to most other industrialized countries to conclude, on the basis of their experience, that a national curriculum and national tests would work successfully in the U.S. Opponents of nationalizing the educational system argue that U.S. society and its educational objectives are so unique that it is not possible to conclude, on the basis of other countries' experience, that a national curriculum and national testing can be successfully implemented in the U.S. In my opinion, the evidence is not yet conclusive enough to determine which side is correct. The important point is that students understand how one would judge the validity of the analogy.

3. Over the years there has been much debate about the role of emotional appeal in public speaking. Do you believe it is ethical for public speakers to use emotional appeals when seeking to persuade an audience? Do you feel there are certain kinds of emotions to which an ethical speaker should not appeal? Why or why not? Be prepared to explain your ideas in class.

Discussion: Because so much has been written over the years about the ethics of emotional appeal in persuasion, it is often valuable to take some time in class to discuss the issue. The purpose of the discussion is not so much for students to come away with the "correct" answer as it is for them to develop their own thinking about the ethics of emotional appeal.

4. Have students analyze "The Horrors of Puppy Mills" in the appendix of sample speeches that follows Chapter 19 of the textbook (pages A7–A9). Students should pay special attention to

the speaker's credibility, evidence, reasoning, and emotional appeal. Show the video from the DVD of student speeches that accompanies this edition of *The Art of Public Speaking* or have students view it in the online Media Library for this chapter at *Connect* so they can also assess the speaker's delivery and use of visual aids.

Discussion: "The Horrors of Puppy Mills" seeks both passive agreement and immediate action from the audience—passive agreement on legislation needed to solve the problem of puppy mills, immediate action on steps the audience can take to avoid purchasing a dog from a puppy mill. Here is a synopsis of the speech that focuses on how the speaker employs the methods of persuasion discussed in Chapter 17.

Specific Purpose: To persuade my audience that action needs to be taken to combat the problem of puppy mills.

Central Idea: Puppy mills are a serious national problem that can be combated by a combination of legislation and individual initiative.

Method of Organization: Problem-solution

Credibility: The speaker's credibility statement appears In paragraph 3, where he states that he is a dog lover whose research has led him to become aware of and concerned about the problem of puppy mills. He builds his credibility through the remainder of the speech by demonstrating that he has done sufficient research to speak intelligently about the issue. He relies on credible sources of evidence, such as the United States Humane Society, which in turn reinforces his own credibility. He also enhances his credibility by speaking with poise, confidence, and a strong sense of conviction.

Evidence: The speaker opens paragraph 1 with a dramatic scenario that gains the audience's attention and introduces the problem of puppy mills. In paragraph 2, he presents evidence from the Humane Society to define a puppy mill. In paragraph 4, he cites Stephanie Shain, the Society's Director of Outreach for Companionable Animals, to quantify the scope and seriousness of puppy mills. Had time allowed, the speaker could have presented evidence from additional sources, but given his time constraints, his decision to rely on statistics and testimony from the Humane Society was strategically sound.

In paragraphs 7–10, the speaker moves from print evidence to visual evidence, which he presents with PowerPoint. He uses two photographs to document the deplorable conditions found in puppy mills (paragraphs 7–8), and two photographs of rescued dogs to show what individual animals are forced to endure (paragraphs 9–10). When assessing the speaker's use of evidence, it is important to note how the photographs in paragraphs 7–10 reinforce the examples, statistics, and testimony presented earlier. Neither the visual evidence nor the print evidence would be as persuasive in isolation as they are in combination.

The speaker also uses evidence when presenting his solution to the problem of puppy mills. His proposal for legislative action (paragraphs 12–14) represents a synthesis of plans that have been presented in various states. Although he does not have time to mention the specific states, it is clear that he has done his research and has a well-thought-out plan. When talking about actions the audience can take as individuals (paragraphs 15–19), he draws upon recommendations of the U.S. Humane Society. He uses Power-Point to highlight each recommendation and to make it easier for the audience to remember.

Reasoning: When discussing the problem of puppy mills in the first main point of the body (paragraphs 4–10), the speaker relies primarily on reasoning from specific instances. As recommended in the textbook, he supplements the specific instances with testimony and statistics that show the instances are representative.

As is the case in many problem-solution speeches, "The Horrors of Puppy Mills" also uses causal reasoning. Puppy mills, the speaker says, are causing the mistreatment of dogs across the nation. His proposals should be adopted because they will bring puppy mills under control, thereby eliminating the cause of the problem.

Emotional appeal: "The Horrors of Puppy Mills" is an excellent example of how to use emotional appeal effectively and responsibly. The speech is replete with emotional appeal—from the opening scenario in paragraph 1 to the final lines of the conclusion. There is no doubt that the speaker is deeply concerned about the problem of puppy mills and wants the audience to share that concern. Yet he consistently lets his emotional appeal grow out of his evidence, rather than trying to impose it through his delivery. By emphasizing facts and documentation, his reportorial delivery style strengthens his case against puppy mills and prevents skeptical listeners from dismissing it as no more than an emotional exhortation. At the same time, the emotional content of the speech reinforces its persuasiveness for listeners who are inclined to support the speaker's position from the outset.

Using Public Speaking in Your Career   *(from text page 342)*

As the service manager for a local home improvement company, you have been pleased to see your company expand its size and scope, but you don't want that growth to come at the expense of customer service. In particular, you're worried about losing touch with one of the company's key demographics—women, who make up 55 percent of your customer base. To prevent this from happening, you have developed a plan for a range of personalized services targeted at women, including one-on-one teaching of do-it-yourself skills and free in-home consultations.

When you present your plan at a meeting of the company's management team, you listen as one executive argues in opposition. Among his points are the following: (1) If your plan is adopted, customers will expect more and more special services and eventually will demand free installation of flooring and carpeting; (2) Because a majority of the management team opposes your plan, it must not be a good idea; (3) One of your competitors tried a customer service plan specifically for women, but it did not succeed; therefore, your plan is doomed to failure.

In your response to the executive, you will point out the fallacy in each of his points. What are those fallacies?

> **Discussion:** Like the other Using Public Speaking in Your Career scenarios throughout the book, this one is intended to show how public speaking is used in everyday life and to challenge students to apply their critical-thinking skills to a wide range of practical situations. If you assign the scenario as a homework exercise, you can go over the answers with students in a class discussion. The fallacies in the scenario are as follows:
>
> (1) The claim that if the plan is adopted customers will expect more and more special services and eventually will demand free installation of flooring and carpeting is an instance of the slippery slope fallacy, which assumes that taking a first step will lead inevitably to a series of subsequent steps. If a speaker claims that taking a first step will lead inexorably to disastrous later steps, he or she needs to provide evidence or reasoning to support the claim. To assume that all the later steps will occur without proving that they will is to commit the slippery slope fallacy.
>
> (2) The claim that the plan is a bad idea because it is opposed by a majority of the management team is an instance of the bandwagon fallacy because it assumes that something is wrong simply because it is unpopular. It may be that the management team's majority is correct in its opinion, but that should be decided on the basis of analyzing all the factors involved in the plan and not simply on the fact that most of the management team has doubts about it.
>
> (3) To claim that the plan is doomed to failure because a competitor's plan aimed at female customers did not succeed is potentially a case of invalid analogy because it assumes that the proposed plan and the competitor's plan are essentially identical. It may be that the proposed plan is sufficiently different from the competitor's plan and that it will not fall prey to the same problems. On the other hand, it may be the case that the proposed plan is so similar to the competitor's plan that one can conclude that it will fail for the same reasons that the competitor's plan failed. But to be accepted as valid, such a conclusion must demonstrate that the two plans are essentially alike. Otherwise, the reasoning constitutes an invalid analogy.
>
> To give your students more work on fallacies, distribute the Fallacies Worksheet on page 231 of this manual.

Additional Exercises and Activities

1. Have students analyze the sample speech with commentary at the end of Chapter 17 of the textbook ("The Dangers of Cell Phones," pages 346–349). Students should pay special attention to the speaker's credibility, evidence, reasoning, and emotional appeal.

> **Discussion:** A speech seeking immediate action, "The Dangers of Cell Phones" is available online and as part of the DVD of student speeches that accompanies this edition of *The Art of Public Speaking*. The commentary that accompanies the speech on pages 346–349 of the textbook points out a number of its major features. Here is a synopsis that focuses on how the speaker employs the methods of persuasion discussed in the chapter.

> Specific Purpose: To persuade my audience to change the way they use their cell phones.

> Central Idea: Because of the health risks associated with cell phone radiation, you should avoid pressing your cell phone against your head while using it.

> Method of Organization: Monroe's motivated sequence

> Credibility: Given the controversial nature of the topic and the fact that the speaker is not an expert on it, establishing credibility is central to the success of the speech. To build her credibility in the introduction, the speaker mentions a CBS News report on the dangers of cell phones, plus the additional research she conducted for the speech. She also quotes epidemiologist Devra Davis.

> In paragraph 4, the speaker continues to build her credibility by creating common ground with and goodwill toward the audience. She assures her classmates that she is not seeking to persuade them to give up their cell phones, only to make a simple change in how they use their phones. Establishing goodwill in this manner encourages the audience to listen with an open mind. The speaker returns to the same point in paragraph 11 when discussing how her listeners can protect themselves against the potential dangers of cell phones.

> The speaker's credibility and goodwill are also strengthened by her delivery. Her sincere tone, warm smile, and caring demeanor communicate her interest in helping the audience avoid the dangers of cell phone radiation. Her delivery also reflects the fact that she is fully prepared and has done all she can to present a successful speech.

> Evidence: The body of the speech presents a substantial amount of testimony and statistical evidence documenting the dangers of cell phones. In paragraph 5,

she cites University of Pittsburgh cancer researcher Ronald Herberman. In paragraphs 6–7, she mentions studies from the World Health Organization and the *Journal of Occupational and Environmental Medicine*. In paragraph 9, she refers to Anne Gittleman's book *Zapped*. In paragraph 10, she turns to the owner's manuals issued by cell phone manufacturers themselves.

In paragraph 8, the speaker uses the extended example of Alan Marks to put the dangers of cell phones in human terms. The example is sharp, vivid, and memorable. The quotation from Marks at the end of paragraph 8 states his belief that he developed brain cancer from long-term use of his cell phone. In paragraph 13, the speaker uses another quotation from Marks, this time to reinforce her claim that holding one's phone away from one's head is an effective way to protect against the long-term dangers of cell phones.

Reasoning: This speech relies primarily upon causal reasoning. In the problem section, the speaker concludes that long-term use of cell phones can cause brain cancer and other problems. In the solution section, she reasons that holding the phone away from one's head will reduce the likelihood of those problems occurring. In the absence of substantial evidence, however, few listeners would be inclined to accept her conclusion. In this regard, her speech provides an instructive example of the interaction between reasoning and evidence.

The speaker is also served well by the care with which she states her claims. She does not argue that extended cell phone use always causes cancer or other problems. Nor does she argue that listeners should stop using their cell phones altogether. Her solution—to avoid holding one's cell phone next to one's ear for extended periods of time—seems reasonable given the evidence she provides.

Emotional appeal: The speaker does not use a great deal of explicitly emotional language. Instead, she lets her emotional appeals grow naturally out of the speech content. The primary emotion to which she appeals is fear—in this case, the fear that prolonged, long-term use of cell phones can cause brain cancer. The persuasiveness of her argument depends above all her use of evidence. It is reinforced by her delivery, which creates an emotional current of concern for the audience throughout the speech.

It is also worth noting that there is a great deal of research to indicate that the effectiveness of fear appeals depends partly on a speaker's ability to provide reasonable explanations of how to eliminate or cope with the sources of fear. In this speech, the speaker does an excellent job of explaining both why listeners should be concerned about the dangers of cell phones and of providing a practical course of action to guard against those dangers.

2. Have students complete the Fallacies Worksheet, which appears on page 231 of this manual.

    Discussion: The Fallacies Worksheet gives students practice in identifying the eight fallacies discussed in the chapter and supplements the second Exercise for Critical Thinking on page 351 of the textbook. Below are explanations of why each statement on the worksheet is fallacious.

a. I don't see any reason to wear a helmet when I ride a bike. Everyone bikes without a helmet.

    Discussion: This statement commits the bandwagon fallacy. Even if it were true that "Everyone bikes without a helmet," that does not mean it is a good idea to do so. It is fallacious to assume that an idea or course of action is correct just because it is popular.

b. It's ridiculous to worry about protecting America's national parks against pollution and overuse when innocent people are being endangered by terrorists.

    Discussion: This statement commits the red herring fallacy. By introducing the issue of terrorism, which is irrelevant to the question of protecting America's national parks against pollution and overuse, the speaker hopes to divert attention from the issue at hand.

c. There can be no doubt that the Great Depression was caused by Herbert Hoover. He became President in March 1929, and the stock market crashed just seven months later.

    Discussion: This statement commits the fallacy of false cause: *post hoc, ergo propter hoc*. That the stock market crashed just seven months after Herbert Hoover became President does not mean that Hoover caused the Great Depression. The Depression was caused by a number of complex forces, most of which had been in motion well before Hoover became President.

d. If we allow the school board to spend money remodeling the gymnasium, next they will want to build a new school and give all the teachers a huge raise. Taxes will soar so high that businesses will leave and then there will be no jobs for anyone in this town.

    Discussion: This statement commits the slippery slope fallacy. It assumes that taking a first step (remodeling the gymnasium) will lead inevitably to subsequent steps (building a new school and giving the teachers huge raises), and eventually to a disaster (people losing their jobs because of businesses leaving town to avoid high taxes). The fallacy does not result from claiming that the train of events will take place, but in assuming that it will without providing evidence or reasoning in support of the speaker's claim.

e.   Raising a child is just like having a pet—you need to feed it, play with it, and everything will be fine.

Discussion: This statement commits the fallacy of invalid analogy. One does need to feed and play with a child—just as one needs to feed and play with a pet—but that does not mean that raising a child is just like having a pet. There is much more involved in raising a child than in owning a pet. The differences between the two situations far outweigh their similarities.

f.   I can't support Representative Frey's proposal for campaign finance reform. After all, he was kicked out of law school for cheating on an exam.

Discussion: This statement commits the *ad hominem* fallacy. Instead of dealing with the substance of Representative Frey's proposal for campaign finance reform, the speaker rejects that proposal because Frey was kicked out of law school for cheating on an exam. Even if it is true that Frey was expelled from law school for cheating, that fact has no bearing on the merits of his proposal for campaign finance reform.

g.   One nonsmoker, interviewed at a restaurant, said, "I can eat dinner just fine even though people around me are smoking." Another, responding to a *Los Angeles Times* survey, said, "I don't see what all the fuss is about. My wife has smoked for years and it has never bothered me." We can see, then, that secondhand smoke does not cause a problem for most nonsmokers.

Discussion: This statement commits the fallacy of hasty generalization. Two examples are hardly enough to establish the claim that secondhand smoke does not cause a problem for most nonsmokers. Certainly it would be no problem for an opposing speaker to marshal the examples of two or more nonsmokers who are bothered by secondhand smoke.

h.   Our school must either increase tuition or cut back on library services for students.

Discussion: This statement commits the either-or fallacy. The speaker oversimplifies a complex issue by reducing it to a simple either-or choice. A critical listener might ask, "Is cutting library services for students the only alternative to increasing tuition? Why not reduce the amount of money spent on athletics? Why not cut back on spending by college administrators?"

3.   Distribute Mary Fisher's "A Whisper of AIDS" from pages 412–414 of this manual. Have students analyze the speech in light of how Fisher builds her credibility, employs evidence and reasoning, and generates emotional appeal. You may also want to have them examine how Fisher uses the resources of language discussed in Chapter 12 to bring her message home to listeners.

Discussion: One of the most acclaimed public discourses of recent decades, Mary Fisher's 1992 address to the Republican National Convention provides a masterful illustration of the art of public speaking. Not only does it utilize many of the methods of persuasion treated in this chapter, but it is strikingly eloquent in its use of the resources of language explored in Chapter 12. This exercise usually works best if you have students prepare their analyses of the speech as a homework assignment, so they will be fully prepared to deal with the speech in class. See pages 415–418 for a full analysis of the speech that you can use to help guide class discussion.

4. Have students complete the Persuasive Speech Preparation Worksheet, which appears on pages 211–212 of this manual, or assign the worksheet from the assignments available in *Connect*.

Discussion: The Persuasive Speech Preparation Worksheet helps students develop their speeches systematically. It is best assigned early in the persuasive unit, so students can work on it throughout the speech preparation process. You can have students turn in the worksheet at the time of their initial preparation outline, or you can require that it be turned in on speech day. To help ensure that students take the worksheet seriously, many instructors make it a graded assignment.

5. Have students complete the Persuasive Speech Self-Assessment, which appears on page 214 of this manual.

Discussion: There is a great deal of research confirming the pedagogical value of self-assessments. The Persuasive Speech Self-Assessment asks students to write a full, objective evaluation of their persuasive speech. Assessment items include topic and purpose, organization, supporting materials, audience adaptation, delivery language, visual aids, and overall performance.

Ideally, students will have a video of their speech in front of them when completing this assignment, especially when assessing their delivery. It is also best if students complete this assignment while their speeches are fresh in their minds. Most instructors require that the self-assessment be turned in no more than a week after the delivery of the persuasive speech.

Fallacies Worksheet

Identify the fallacy in each of the following statements and, in each case, explain why the statement is fallacious.

1. I don't see any reason to wear a helmet when I ride a bike. Everyone bikes without a helmet.

   _____

   _____

2. It's ridiculous to worry about protecting America's national parks against pollution and overuse when innocent people are being killed by terrorists.

   _____

   _____

3. There can be no doubt that the Great Depression was caused by Herbert Hoover. He became President in March 1929, and the stock market crashed just seven months later.

   _____

   _____

4. If we allow the school board to spend money remodeling the gymnasium, next they will want to build a new school and give all the teachers a huge raise. Taxes will soar so high that businesses will leave and then there will be no jobs for anyone in this town.

   _____

   _____

5. Raising a child is just like having a pet—you need to feed it, play with it, and everything will be fine.

   _____

   _____

6. I can't support Representative Frey's proposal for campaign finance reform. After all, he was kicked out of law school for cheating on an exam.

   _____

   _____

7. One nonsmoker, interviewed at a restaurant, said, "I can eat dinner just fine even though people around me are smoking." Another, responding to a *Los Angeles Times* survey, said, "I don't see what all the fuss is about. My wife has smoked for years and it has never bothered me." We can see, then, that secondhand smoke does not cause a problem for most nonsmokers.

   _____

   _____

8. Our school must either increase tuition or cut back on library services for students.

   _____

   _____

Speaking on Special Occasions

Chapter Objectives

After reading this chapter, students should be able to:

1. Explain the guidelines for an effective speech of introduction.

2. Discuss the purpose and major themes of a speech of presentation.

3. Discuss the purpose and major themes of a speech of acceptance.

4. Indicate the fundamental purpose of a commemorative speech and explain why a successful commemorative speech depends so much on the creative use of language.

Chapter Outline

I. Many special occasions provide opportunities for speechmaking.
    A. Ceremonies such as weddings, funerals, and dedications often include speeches.
    B. Speeches are part of what makes these occasions special and memorable.
    C. The primary aim of speeches on special occasions is neither to inform nor to persuade but to fulfill the special needs of the occasion.

II. Speeches of introduction present a speaker to an audience.
    A. A good speech of introduction achieves three goals.

        1.   It builds enthusiasm for the upcoming speaker.

        2.   It generates interest in the speaker's topic.

        3.   It establishes a welcoming climate that will boost the speaker's credibility.

    B.   There are several guidelines for speeches of introduction.

        1.   Speeches of introduction should be brief.

        2.   Speeches of introduction should be completely accurate.

        3.   Speeches of introduction should be adapted to the occasion.

        4.   Speeches of introduction should be adapted to the main speaker.

        5.   Speeches of introduction should be adapted to the audience.

        6.   Speeches of introduction should try to create a sense of anticipation and drama.

III.   Speeches of presentation are given when someone receives a gift or an award.

    A.   Speeches of presentation should usually be fairly brief.

    B.   The main purpose of a speech of presentation is to explain why the recipient is receiving the award.

        1.   The speech should point out the achievements for which the recipient is receiving the award.

        2.   The speech should discuss the recipient's achievements in a way that will make them meaningful to the audience.

    C.   If the recipient won the award in a competition, the speech of presentation should consider praising the other competitors as well.

IV.   Speeches of acceptance give thanks for a gift or an award.

    A.   A speech of acceptance should thank the people who are bestowing the gift or award.

    B.   A speech of acceptance should also acknowledge the people who helped the recipient win the award.

 V.   Commemorative speeches are addresses of praise or celebration.

    A.   Commemorative speeches pay tribute to a person, a group of people, an institution, or an idea.

    B.   The fundamental purpose of a commemorative speech is to inspire the audience—to heighten their admiration for the person, institution, or idea being praised.

    C.   Although it usually presents information about its subject, a commemorative speech is different from an informative speech.

        1.   The aim of an informative speech is to communicate information clearly and accurately.

        2.   The aim of a commemorative speech is to express feelings and arouse sentiments.

    D.   Commemorative speeches depend above all on the creative and subtle use of language.

        1.   Some of the most memorable speeches in history are commemorative addresses that we continue to find meaningful because of their eloquent expression.

2. Two aspects of language use are especially important for commemorative speeches.

   a. The first is avoiding clichés and trite sentiments.

   b. The second is utilizing stylistic devices such as those discussed in Chapter 12 to enhance the imagery, rhythm, and creativity of the speech.

Exercises for Critical Thinking   *(from text page 363)*

1. Attend a speech on campus. Pay special attention to the speech introducing the main speaker. How well does it fit the guidelines discussed in this chapter?

   Discussion: If you use this exercise, you may want to have students complete the worksheet on page 239 of this manual. Alternatively, you can assign the worksheet to students from the assignments available in *Connect*.

2. Observe several speeches of presentation and acceptance—at a campus awards ceremony or on a television program such as the Academy Awards, Grammy Awards, Emmy Awards, or Tony Awards. Which speeches do you find most effective? Least effective? Why?

   Discussion: This exercise works especially well if your class meets the day after a program such as the Academy Awards. While watching the program, each student should select his or her candidate for the best acceptance speech. After discussing all of the speeches in class, have students vote for the best acceptance speech. This often produces a spirited discussion while students defend their candidates for the best speech.

3. Analyze "Elie Wiesel," textbook page 361, in light of the criteria for commemorative speaking presented in this chapter.

   Discussion: Gracefully composed and confidently delivered, "Elie Wiesel" pays tribute to the internationally known writer, teacher, and human rights activist. It is also available online and on the DVD of student speeches that accompanies this edition of *The Art of Public Speaking*. Below is a synopsis.

   Introduction: The repetition of "A-7713" in paragraph 1 gains the audience's attention and arouses curiosity about the topic of the speech. In paragraph 2, the speaker reveals that A-7713 is Elie Wiesel. The recitation of Wiesel's major awards establishes his importance as a significant international figure, while a preview statement prepares the audience for the main points to follow in the body.

Body: Paragraphs 3–5 constitute the body of the speech. Paragraph 3 deals with Wiesel's accomplishments as an eloquent leader. The focal point of the paragraph is a moving quotation from Wiesel's acclaimed book Night that illustrates his "compelling prose and brutal honesty." The quotation also sheds light on the horrors of Auschwitz, where Wiesel was imprisoned during World War II.

Paragraph 4 begins with a transition noting that Wiesel is a fearless leader as well as an eloquent one. The speaker illustrates the point with a series of brief examples. By presenting each example in parallel structure, he enhances the rhythm of his prose and elevates the style of the speech.

In paragraph 5, the speaker turns to Wiesel's achievements as a selfless leader. Once again, he quotes Wiesel, this time using his Nobel Prize acceptance speech to illustrate his leadership qualities.

In all three main points the speaker does an excellent job of focusing on particular aspects of Wiesel's career. He provides enough details for the audience to understand and appreciate Wiesel's accomplishments without getting bogged down in biographical detail.

Conclusion: The conclusion consists of paragraphs 6–7. In paragraph 6, the speaker mentions Wiesel's ongoing "fight against the night," a reference to the novel mentioned in paragraph 3. Also in paragraph 6 the speaker returns to A-7713, originally mentioned in the introduction, thereby giving the speech a sense of psychological unity. Paragraph 7 closes with a final quotation from Wiesel. Combined with the speaker's elevated language and poised delivery, the use of Wiesel's own words—here and throughout the speech— gives voice to the moral principles that make him such an admirable figure.

Additional Exercises and Activities

1. Have students analyze "My Crazy Aunt Sue," which appears in the appendix of sample speeches that follows Chapter 19 of the textbook. Students should focus on how the speech exemplifies the principles of commemorative speaking discussed in this chapter.

    Discussion: "My Crazy Aunt Sue" is a heartfelt commemorative speech that focuses on how the speaker's aunt has turned what some would call a weakness into a strong mark of character. The speech shows how commemorative speeches can employ simple language and vivid imagery to affect the audience's emotions. A video of the speech is available online and on the DVD of student speeches that accompanies this edition of The Art of Public Speaking. Below is a brief synopsis.

Introduction: The introduction consists of paragraphs 1–2. Paragraph 1 uses vivid imagery and repetition to capture the audience's attention by arousing curiosity about the identity of the "strongest person" the speaker knows. Paragraph 2 reveals that the speaker is talking about her aunt Sue, who is afflicted with rheumatoid arthritis. After describing the daily torments of this disease, the speaker states her central idea—that her aunt Sue deserves commemoration because of her strength in dealing with such a debilitating condition.

Body: The body of the speech runs from paragraph 3 through paragraph 9. It revolves around three main points—Aunt Sue's courage and refusal to complain about her fate (paragraphs 3–4), her sense of humor (paragraphs 5–7), and the lessons she has taught the speaker about being happy for the things one has rather than worrying about what one does not have (paragraphs 8–9). In each main point, the speaker uses imagistic language and well-chosen examples to illustrate why her aunt Sue is so commendable. These examples provide information about Aunt Sue, but they are employed here for the purpose of praising her and inspiring the audience rather than for the purpose of presenting a biography of her life. This is a key difference between an informative speech and a commemorative speech.

The speaker also makes excellent use of the resources of language discussed in Chapter 11. Paragraph 1, with its series of sentences beginning "The strongest person I know," employs the time-honored rhetorical device of repetition. The first three sentences of paragraph 9 use both repetition and parallel structure, as the speaker begins each sentence with the phrase "I complain about" and ends each by noting that, despite her complaining, she is able to do things "pain free."

If you watch this speech on the video supplement that accompanies this edition of *The Art of Public Speaking*, you will see how the speaker uses her delivery to enhance the impact of her ideas. She has excellent eye contact, establishes a strong bond with the audience, and, most important for a speech of this nature, communicates her ideas with a powerful sense of commitment and sincerity.

Conclusion: The conclusion consists of the final paragraph—a single, memorable sentence that encapsulates the central idea and stresses the point that having a physical disability in no way diminishes a person's spirit or inner beauty. As in the rest of the speech, the language is strong, concise, and poignant.

2. Assign a speech in which each student introduces a famous person to the class. Tell students they should imagine themselves being able to invite any well-known figure, living or dead, to speak to the class on any topic of the student's choice. The task of each student is to prepare a two-minute speech introducing his or her chosen person to the class. In their speeches,

students should (a) provide some biographical information about the person and her or his contributions, (b) identify the topic of the person's speech, and (c) explain why the person's speech topic is important for this audience. Speeches should follow the guidelines for speeches of introduction discussed in the chapter.

Discussion: Like the previous activity, this assignment gives students practice in creating and presenting a speech of introduction. Unlike a speech introducing one of their classmates, however, this speech requires research so students can learn more about the person they are introducing. Indeed, one benefit of this assignment is that students can gain experience using the biographical aids available in the reference section of the library.

When making this assignment, it is extremely important to encourage students to be creative in their speeches. Otherwise, you are likely to get a series of dull recitations summarizing information from *Who's Who*, *Current Biography*, *Notable American Women*, and the like. For the most part, though, students are enthusiastic about this assignment, which provides a nice alternative to the usual informative and persuasive speeches. Because this presentation is only two minutes long, all students should be able to deliver their speeches in a single class session.

3. Have students analyze the speech by Sajjid Zahir Chinoy in the appendix of sample speeches that follows Chapter 19 of the textbook ("Questions of Culture") in light of the criteria for commemorative speaking discussed in the chapter.

Discussion: A superb commemorative address, "Questions of Culture" was presented extemporaneously, without notes, to an audience of 3,000 people at the 1996 University of Richmond commencement ceremonies and was widely reported in the press. In addition to being an outstanding student speech from a non-classroom situation, it deals with questions of cultural difference and similarity in a way that almost always provokes spirited discussion. For full analysis of the speech, see pages 164– 166 of this manual. The speech is also available online and on the DVD of student speeches that accompanies this edition of *The Art of Public Speaking*.

4. Distribute copies of "The Massachusetts 54th," the text of which appears on pages 424–425 of this manual. A video of the speech is available online and on the DVD of student speeches that accompanies this edition of *The Art of Public Speaking*. Have students analyze the speeches in light of the criteria for commemorative speaking discussed in the textbook.

Discussion: Part Five of this manual contains a number of commemorative speeches for analysis and discussion, one of which is "The Massachusetts 54th." The speech pays tribute to the first African-American regiment in the U.S. Civil War. It is particularly effective in showing students how to use various stylistic devices in their speeches. For analysis of the speech, see pages 426–427 of this manual.

In addition to "The Massachusetts 54th" are four other commemorative speeches: "Choices and Change," "James 'Cool Papa' Bell," "The Survivors," and "My Grandfather." All four illustrate how students can use language to create effective—even eloquent—commemorative addresses. For texts and analyses of these speeches, see pages 419–438 of this manual

5. Have students complete the Special Occasion Speech Self-Assessment, which appears on page 240 of this manual.

Discussion: There is a great deal of research confirming the pedagogical value of self-assessments. The Special Occasion Speech Self-Assessment asks students to write a full, objective evaluation of their special occasion speech. Assessment items include topic and purpose, organization, audience adaptation, language, supporting materials, delivery, and overall performance.

Ideally, students will have a video of their speech in front of them when completing this assignment, especially when assessing their delivery. It is also best if students complete this assignment while their speeches are fresh in their minds. Most instructors require that the self-assessment be turned in no more than a week after the delivery of the special occasion speech.

Speech of Introduction Observation Worksheet

Your name _____

Name of speaker you observed _____

Where was the speech presented? _____

Who was the speaker introducing? _____

Evaluate the speech of introduction as follows:

1. How long was the speech? Was it too long? Too short? About right? Explain.

2. As far as you can tell, was the speech accurate in its remarks about the main speaker? Explain.

3. Was the speech well adapted to the occasion? Explain.

4. Was the speech well adapted to the main speaker? Explain.

5. Was the speech well adapted to the audience? Explain.

6. Did the speech create a sense of anticipation and drama about the main speaker? Explain.

Special Occasion Speech Self-Assessment

Your task is to review your special-occasion speech and to reach a full, objective assessment of its major strengths and weaknesses. Write a thoughtful, objective evaluation of the speech in full-sentence and paragraph form with an introduction and a conclusion.

Be specific and concrete in your comments. Note in particular the areas in which you believe you did especially well and those areas in which you want to make special improvement in the next speech. Explain why you had difficulty with certain aspects of this speech, and indicate the specific steps you plan to take to improve your next presentation.

Use the following questions to guide your self-assessment, though you do not need to answer each question individually in your paper. Be specific and concrete in your comments.

Topic

Was the topic appropriate for the occasion?

Was the topic appropriate for the audience?

Did you deal with the topic creatively?

Organization

Did your introduction gain the attention and interest of the audience?

Were the main ideas of the speech easy to follow?

Did you use connectives effectively?

Did you conclude the speech in a memorable fashion?

Language

Was your language clear and concrete?

Was your language vivid and colorful?

Was your language appropriate to the topic, audience, and occasion?

Delivery

Did you begin and end your speech without rushing?

Did you use pauses, rate, pitch, and vocal variety effectively in delivering the speech?

Did your physical action add to or detract from the speech?

Did you maintain strong eye contact throughout the speech?

Overall Assessment

What were you most pleased with in the speech? What were you least pleased with?

If you had an opportunity to deliver this speech again next week, what changes would you make? Be specific.

Speaking in Small Groups

Chapter Objectives

After reading this chapter, students should be able to:

1. Provide definitions of a small group and a problem-solving small group.

2. Identify the four kinds of leadership that may occur in a small group.

3. Distinguish among the procedural needs, task needs, and maintenance needs of a small group.

4. Explain the five major responsibilities of every participant in a small group.

5. Identify the five stages of the reflective-thinking process and discuss the major tasks of a group at each stage.

6. Explain the methods for presenting orally the findings of a small group.

Chapter Outline

I. Speaking in small groups is an important form of communication.

    A. Small groups exist in virtually every area of life, including business, education, government, religion, community organizations, and volunteer associations.

B. As its name implies, a small group has a limited number of members.

    1. The minimum number is three.

    2. Most experts set the maximum number at eight, but some go as high as twelve.

C. Members of a small group assemble for a specific purpose.

D. This chapter deals with a particular kind of small group—the problem-solving small group.

    1. A problem-solving small group is formed to solve a particular problem.

    2. Speaking in a problem-solving small group involves many skills similar to those used in public speaking.

II. To be productive, a small group needs effective leadership.

A. There are several kinds of leadership in a small group.

    1. In some groups, there is no specific leader.

    2. In some groups, there is an implied leader—someone who may have the highest rank or the most expertise on the topic.

    3. In some groups, there is an emergent leader—someone who, by ability or personality, takes on a leadership role.

    4. Some groups have a designated leader—someone who is assigned or elected as leader when the group is formed.

B. Small groups have three kinds of leadership needs.

    1. Procedural needs are the "housekeeping" requirements of the group.

    2. Task needs are substantive actions that help the group complete its project.

    3. Maintenance needs involve interpersonal relations within the group.

III. Regardless of a small group's leadership, every member of a group has five responsibilities.

A. Members should commit themselves to the goals of the group.

    1. For a group to succeed, members must align their personal goals with the group's goals.

    2. Hidden agendas—in which individuals put personal goals over those of the group-are especially damaging.

B. Members should fulfill their individual assignments.

    1. A group can only be effective if each member fulfills his or her specific duties.

    2. No matter what other assignments they may have, all members of a small group have one vital assignment—listening.

C. Members should avoid interpersonal conflicts.

D. Members should encourage full participation in the group.

    1. One way to encourage participation is by listening attentively to other members.

    2. A second way to encourage participation is by inviting quiet members to speak.

      3. A third way to encourage participation is by offering supportive comments to other members.

   E. Members should work to keep the group's discussion on track.

IV. The reflective-thinking method is an effective procedure for organizing discussion in a problem-solving small group.

   A. The first step in the reflective-thinking method is defining the problem.

      1. The best way to define the problem is to phrase it as a question of policy.

      2. A group should follow four guidelines when phrasing the question for discussion.

         a. It should make the question as clear and specific as possible.

         b. It should phrase the question so as to allow for a wide variety of answers.

         c. It should avoid biased or slanted questions.

         d. It should pose only a single question.

   B. The second step in the reflective-thinking process is analyzing the problem.

      1. If a group analyzes the problem thoroughly, it will be in a much better position to devise a workable solution.

      2. When analyzing the problem, a group should pay special attention to two questions.

         a. How severe is the problem?

         b. What are the causes of the problem?

   C. The third step in the reflective-thinking method is establishing criteria for the solution.

      1. It is vital that a group set up criteria before discussing solutions.

      2. Setting up criteria gives the group a way to judge the appropriateness and practicality of potential solutions.

   D. The fourth step in the reflective-thinking method is generating potential solutions.

      1. At this stage, the group's goal is to come up with the widest possible range of solutions.

      2. Brainstorming is an effective way to generate potential solutions.

   E. The fifth step in the reflective-thinking method is selecting the best solution.

      1. The group should assess each potential solution in light of the criteria established for an ideal solution.

      2. In doing so, the group should try to reach consensus.

V. Once a group has reached a decision, it needs to present its recommendations clearly and convincingly.

   A. Although a group's recommendations are usually presented formally in writing, the written report is often supplemented with—or sometimes replaced by—an oral presentation.

   B. One kind of oral presentation is an oral report.

   C. A symposium is a second kind of oral presentation.

   D. A panel discussion is a third kind of oral presentation.

Exercises for Critical Thinking *(from text pages 381–382)*

1. Identify the flaw (or flaws) in each of the following questions for a problem-solving group discussion. Rewrite each question so it conforms with the criteria discussed in the chapter for effective discussion questions.

    a. What should be done to prevent the utterly ridiculous shortage of new computers for students at this school?

        Discussion: This question is biased or slanted. It should be rewritten more objectively. For example: "What steps should be taken to ensure that there are adequate computer facilities for students at this school?"

    b. What should be done about child abuse?

        Discussion: This question is too broad and ambiguous. It should be rewritten so as to be clear and specific. For example: "What steps should our local and state governments take to prevent child abuse?"

    c. What should state government do to reduce homelessness and to combat drunk driving?

        Discussion: This question poses two questions. It should be rewritten to ask a single question. For example: "What should state government do to reduce homelessness?" Or: "What should state government do to combat drunk driving?"

    d. Should the federal government institute a national sales tax to help reduce the national debt?

        Discussion: This question can be answered with a simple yes or no. It should be rewritten to allow for a wide variety of answers. For example: "What should the federal government do to reduce the national debt?

2. If possible, arrange to observe a problem-solving small group in action. You might attend a meeting of your city council, the school board, the zoning commission, a local business, a church committee. To what extent does the discussion measure up to the criteria for effective discussion presented in this chapter? What kind of leadership does the group have, and how well does the leader (or leaders) fulfill the group's procedural needs, task needs, and maintenance needs? How do the other members meet their responsibilities? What aspects of the meeting are handled most effectively? Which are handled least effectively?

    Discussion: This exercise gives students the opportunity to observe a small group in action. You may want to have students write a brief paper reporting their observations. Or you may want to arrange for the entire class to observe the same group meeting, so as to provide a common basis for class discussion.

3. Identify a relatively important decision you have made in the last year or two. Try to reconstruct how you reached that decision. Now suppose you could remake the decision following the reflective-thinking method. Map out what you would do at each stage of the method. Do you still reach the same decision? If not, do you believe the reflective-thinking method would have led you to a better decision in the first place?

    Discussion: This exercise requires students to sort out the steps of the reflective-thinking method and to apply them to the students' own decision making. Not only does this help familiarize students with the steps of the method, but it makes the point that the reflective-thinking method is not restricted to group discussion.

4. Attend a symposium or panel discussion on campus. Prepare a brief analysis of the proceedings. First, study the role of the moderator. How does she or he introduce the topic and participants? What role does the moderator play thereafter? Does she or he help guide and focus the panel discussion? Does she or he summarize and conclude the proceedings at the end?

    Second, observe the participants. Are the speeches in the symposium well prepared and presented? Which speaker (or speakers) do you find most effective? Least effective? Why? Do participants in the panel discussion share talking time? Does their discussion appear well planned to cover major aspects of the topic? Which panelist (or panelists) do you find most effective? Least effective? Why?

    Discussion: This can be handled much like Exercise 2. The questions in the exercise can also be used as the basis for evaluating symposia or panel discussions presented in class.

Additional Exercises and Activities

1. Have students perform the exercise "Lost on the Moon," as follows:*

    First, divide the class into groups of 4 to 6 members, and have each member complete the "Lost on the Moon" Individual Worksheet on page 250. Allow 10 minutes for this part of the exercise.

    Second, have each group discuss their individual answers and try to reach a consensus ranking of the 12 items. Each group should complete the "Lost on the Moon" Group Worksheet on page 251. Allow 25 minutes for this portion of the exercise.

---

*Adapted from Jay Hall, "Decisions, Decisions, Decisions," *Psychology Today*, 5 (November 1971), 51–54, 86–88.

For the third step of the exercise, have students compute their individual and group scores, as follows:

a. Provide students the correct ranking for each item, as given by NASA. Students should write this ranking in the column headed "NASA rank" on each of the two worksheets.

Item	NASA rank	NASA's rationale
box of matches	12	No oxygen on moon to sustain flame
food concentrate	4	Efficient means of supplying energy requirements
50 feet of nylon rope	6	Useful in scaling cliffs, tying injured together
parachute silk	7	Protection from sun's rays
two .45 caliber pistols	9	Possible means of self-propulsion
solar-powered portable heating unit	10	Not needed—temperature on the lighted side of the moon can exceed 100° C
two 100-pound tanks of oxygen	1	Most pressing survival need because of lack of oxygen on the moon
map of the moon's constellation	3	Primary means of navigation
self-inflating life raft	8	Some value for shelter or carrying. Also, CO_2 bottle in military raft may be used for propulsion.
magnetic compass	11	Worthless for navigation because magnetic field on the moon is not polarized
five gallons of water	2	Replacement for tremendous loss of liquid on lighted side of moon
solar-powered FM receiver-transmitter	5	For communication with command ship, but FM requires line-of-sight transmission and short ranges

b. For each item on both worksheets, students should enter the difference between their individual ranking or group ranking and the NASA ranking. It makes no difference which ranking is higher. For example, if the individual or group ranking is 12 and the NASA ranking is 8, the difference is 4. Likewise, if the individual ranking is 8 and the NASA ranking is 12, the difference is 4.

c. The total score for each worksheet is figured by adding all the numbers in the "Difference" column on each sheet.

Fourth, have students compare their individual scores with the group score. Also have students compare the average individual score of all members of each group with the group score. In almost every case the group's score will be better—closer to NASA's rankings—than either the individual scores or the average individual score of the group's members.

Fifth, conduct a general class discussion of the results and of the decision-making procedures used in the groups.

Discussion: This is an excellent exercise to acquaint students with the processes and benefits of small-group discussion. Students see how a small group can provide resources that allow it to improve upon the individual decisions of its members. Students also get firsthand experience in the difficult task of trying to reach consensus in a small group. In fact, because this exercise provokes so many questions and comments from students, you can use the general class discussion afterward to highlight any number of specific points about decision-making in small groups.

2.   Have students perform the "Hostages" exercise, as follows:*

First, divide the class into groups of 4 to 6 members, and have each member complete the "Hostages" Individual Worksheet on pages 252–253. Allow 10 minutes for this part of the exercise.

Second, have each group discuss their individual answers and try to reach a consensus ranking of the eight hostages. Each group should complete the "Hostages" Group Worksheet on page 254. Allow 20 minutes for this part of the exercise.

Third, have each group report its rankings to the rest of the class. Afterward, conduct a general class discussion of the results and of the decision-making procedures used in the groups.

Discussion: Like "Lost on the Moon," this is an excellent exercise to acquaint students with the processes of small-group discussion. But whereas "Lost on the Moon" deals with scientific and technical matters on which there are right and wrong answers, "Hostages" revolves around subjective personal values that cannot be incontestably established as right or wrong. As a result, you should be prepared for some fairly intense discussions in the individual groups. You should also be prepared for that intensity to spill over into the general class discussion afterward. You may need to work to keep that discussion focused on the process of small-group communication rather than allowing it to turn into an extended debate on the specific decisions of each group regarding which hostages to save.

---

*Adapted from Anne L. Haehl, "Adapting to Non-Traditional Students," *Speech Communication Teacher* (Winter 1988), 12–13.

3.   Assign students the Twelve Angry Men group consultation project, as follows:*

First, divide the class into groups of 5 to 6 members. The task of each group is to view the classic film *Twelve Angry Men,* which revolves around the efforts of eleven members of a jury in a murder trial to convince one member to change his "not guilty" vote to "guilty." The film dramatizes many of the aspects of small-group discussion covered in the textbook, including the kinds and functions of leadership, interpersonal conflict, hidden agendas, and the creation of consensus. Because the film is 96 minutes long, each group will have to arrange a time to view it out of class.

Second, give each group the following instructions: For this assignment, your group is to act as a consultant to the jury in the movie *Twelve Angry Men.* The purpose of this assignment is for you to demonstrate your knowledge of group processes by evaluating a group's decision making. There is no single correct answer to this assignment. Your task as a group is to demonstrate that you understand and can apply the concepts of small-group discussion presented in the textbook and in class.

Third, have each group consider the following questions in its analysis:

a.   What are the strengths of the group portrayed in Twelve Angry Men?

b.   What are the weaknesses of the group?

c.   What kinds of leadership does the group demonstrate?

d.   What role do hidden agendas play in the deliberations of the group?

e.   If you were the leader of the group, what would you do to eliminate some of its interpersonal conflict?

f.   Who are the most effective communicators in the group? The least effective? Why?

g.   How could the group improve its decision making and problem solving?

Fourth, conduct a general class discussion in which each group reports a summary of its deliberations and recommendations. Use the discussion to illustrate points about speaking in problem-solving small groups.

Discussion: This assignment is particularly valuable in helping students understand the dynamics of the group process. It can also be used as an alternative to the major problem-solving group discussion explained on page 31 of this manual. If so, however, it should probably be supplemented with a requirement that each student prepare either a written report or a journal of her or his group's activities—as explained in Additional Exercises/Activities 5 and 6 below.

4.   Divide the class into groups of 5 to 6 students each and distribute the Classroom Speech Deliberation Worksheet from page 255 of this manual. The task of each group is to review the

---

*Adapted from Bruce C. McKinney, "The Group Process and 'Twelve Angry Men,'" *Speech Communication Teacher* (Winter 1990).

previous round of classroom speeches according to the questions on the worksheet and to provide constructive suggestions to help improve the next round. Have each group present its thinking in a panel discussion.

Discussion: This assignment can be a helpful way to integrate group discussion into a public speaking class. Groups should be assigned before the start of the round of speeches they are to analyze. Be sure to tell the groups that this assignment will require them to meet outside of class and to reach consensus on their judgments about their classmates' speeches.

This assignment can also be used as an alternative to the major problem-solving group discussion described on page 31 of this manual. If so, however, it should probably be supplemented with a requirement that each student prepare either a written report or a journal of their group's activities—as explained in Additional Exercises/Activities 5 and 6 below.

5. If you assign students a major group project that requires work outside of class, have them prepare a 2- to 3-page written report on the deliberations of their group. To guide their writing of the report, students should follow the Group Discussion Self-Assessment, which appears on page 256 of this manual.

Discussion: This assignment helps students think critically about their small-group experience in light of the principles discussed in Chapter 19. The Group Discussion Self-Assessment guides students through their reports by focusing on leadership, the responsibilities of group members, use of the reflective-thinking method, and overall performance of the group.

To help with this assignment, each student should be encouraged to keep a journal of his or her group's deliberations. The journal should note what happens at each meeting of the group and what developments take place over time as the group works on its project. Because this assignment requires a substantial investment of time, some teachers count it as a major part—25 percent or more—of the student's grade for the unit on group discussion. For an alternative to this assignment, see the next Additional Exercise/ Activity.

6. As in the preceding assignment, encourage students to keep a journal of their group's deliberations. The journal should note what happens at each meeting and what developments take place over time as the group works on its project. When the project is completed, have each student turn in a Group Discussion Participant Evaluation Worksheet (page 257) assessing the work of each participant in the group other than himself or herself.

Discussion: This is an alternative to the detailed evaluation called for in the preceding Additional Exercise/Activity. Because this evaluation focuses on individual group members, it usually gives a pretty clear picture of who met their responsibilities and who did not. As a result, it can be an excellent aid in assigning students individual grades for their group projects.

"Lost on the Moon" Individual Worksheet

Instructions:

Your spaceship has just crash-landed on the lighted surface of the moon. You were scheduled to rendezvous with a command ship 200 miles away, also on the lighted side of the moon, but the rough landing has ruined your ship and destroyed all the equipment on board, except for the 12 items listed below.

Your crew's survival depends on reaching the command ship, so you must choose the most critical items available for the 200-mile trip. Your task is to rank the 12 items according to their importance in allowing your crew to survive the 200-mile journey to the command ship. In the column titled "Your rank," place the number 1 by the most important item, the number 2 by the second most important item, and so on through number 12, the least important.

You have 10 minutes to complete this worksheet.

Item	Your rank	NASA rank	Difference
box of matches	_____	_____	_____
food concentrate	_____	_____	_____
50 feet of nylon rope	_____	_____	_____
parachute silk	_____	_____	_____
two .45 caliber pistols	_____	_____	_____
solar-powered portable heating unit	_____	_____	_____
two 100-pound tanks of oxygen	_____	_____	_____
map of the moon's constellation	_____	_____	_____
self-inflating life raft	_____	_____	_____
magnetic compass	_____	_____	_____
five gallons of water	_____	_____	_____
solar-powered FM receiver-transmitter	_____	_____	_____

"Lost on the Moon" Group Worksheet

Instructions:

Your task is to reach a consensus ranking of the 12 items needed to survive the journey to the command ship 200 miles away. This means that the ranking for each of the 12 items should be agreed upon by each member of the group before it becomes a part of the group's decision. Here are some guides to use in reaching consensus:

1. Don't argue stubbornly for your own point of view just because it is yours. Listen to other members of the group and be willing to change your views on the basis of reason and logic.

2. On the other hand, don't change your mind simply to avoid disagreement. Seek out differences of opinion and try to get every member involved in the decision-making process. The more information you have, the better chance you will have of making a sound decision.

3. Avoid such techniques as majority vote, averaging, flipping coins, and bargaining.

After your group has reached consensus on how to rank the 12 items, fill in the "Group rank" column below. You have 25 minutes to complete this phase of the exercise.

Item	Your rank	NASA rank	Difference
box of matches	_____	_____	_____
food concentrate	_____	_____	_____
50 feet of nylon rope	_____	_____	_____
parachute silk	_____	_____	_____
two .45 caliber pistols	_____	_____	_____
solar-powered portable heating unit	_____	_____	_____
two 100-pound tanks of oxygen	_____	_____	_____
map of the moon's constellation	_____	_____	_____
self-inflating life raft	_____	_____	_____
magnetic compass	_____	_____	_____
five gallons of water	_____	_____	_____
solar-powered FM receiver-transmitter	_____	_____	_____

"Hostages" Individual Worksheet

Instructions:

A plane has been hijacked! The hijackers offer to release four passengers to the U.S. embassy. In return for this gesture, the government of a neutral country will agree to allow the plane to land at its airport and refuel.

The captors insist, however, that U.S. authorities select the four to be released from the following list. The President has given your group the job of making the selection. If you do not select the people, the hijackers are perfectly willing to allow the plane to run out of gas and crash, killing all passengers. You must reach a decision by consensus, and you must do so within the next half hour.

You may assume the terrorists are honest about releasing those who are chosen to be released. You do not know what will happen to those who remain on the plane, but given what is known about this particular terrorist group, you expect most or all of the remaining hostages probably will die.

Quickly rank the following passengers in the order in which you would choose them to be released. In the column titled "Your rank," place the number 1 by the hostage you would save first, the number 2 by the one you would save second, and so on through number 8, the hostage you would save last.

You have 10 minutes to complete this part of the exercise, after which you will discuss the matter with your group and reach an agreement.

Hostages   **Your rank**

1. Brenda Jones, age 27, has three children by three different fathers, none of whom she has married. She loves her children, however, and has resolved to get her life together for the children's sake. Her mother is caring for them so Brenda can attend a six-week training program for women who lack job skills.   _____

2. Fr. John O'Brien, 65 years old, is in excellent health. A Roman Catholic priest, he has dedicated his life to working with the poor in an inner-city ghetto. He is taking this flight to arrange for funding and personnel that will enable him to set up a program to carry on his life's work after he becomes unable to work. Should he die at this time, the work probably will end.   _____

3. Juan Garcia is 45. He has a history of heart trouble and might not survive the stress of a prolonged hostage situation. He is a wealthy businessman whose estate would easily provide for his wife and three young children, even if he should die in the hijacking. His business, however, which has employed and given dignity to many Hispanic people, probably would fold without his vision and drive, putting many people out of work who will not be able to find jobs.   _____

4. Elijah Brown is 52. He did time in jail for armed robbery. Since his release two years ago, he has worked hard, gone to school part time, and supported his invalid wife and youngest child (the only one remaining at home). There would be no money to provide for his family in the event of his death. _____

5. Betsy Bates, 29, is a well-known and successful model. Married a little over a year to rock star Duke, she has just found out that she is pregnant, a discovery she views with mixed feelings. _____

6. Congresswoman Jan Perkins is 47. Widowed young, when her husband died in the crash of an Air Force plane while on a diplomatic mission for the State Department, she has devoted her life to politics. She has been an effective and eloquent worker for peace and for the rights of women and minorities. Her death would be a crushing emotional blow to her elderly parents, though she has provided for them financially in her will. Perkins is widely seen as the most likely candidate for the first woman President of the United States. _____

7. D. B. Calhoun is 43. Little is known about him, except that he is a very bigoted person with an unstable employment history. He reads *Soldier of Fortune* and similar magazines, and dreams about being a mercenary. It is quite possible that he will try some hostile action against the hijackers and ruin any chance of getting the remaining hostages out alive. _____

8. Andrea Ohms, at 19, is already a distinguished pianist, having started performing professionally at age 8. Her performances give immense pleasure to thousands of people around the world. She is engaged to be married. _____

"Hostages" Group Worksheet

Instructions:

Your task is to reach a consensus ranking of the four hostages to be released by the terrorists. This means that the ranking for each of the four should be agreed upon by each member of the group before it becomes part of the group decision. Here are some guidelines to use in reaching consensus.

1. Don't argue stubbornly for your own point of view just because it is yours. Listen to other members of the group and be willing to change your views on the basis of reason and logic.

2. On the other hand, don't change your mind simply to avoid disagreement. Seek differences of opinion and try to get every member involved in the decision-making process. The more information you have, the better chance you will have of making a sound decision.

3. Avoid such techniques as majority vote, averaging, flipping coins, and bargaining.

After your group has reached consensus on how to rank the hostages, fill in the "group rank" column below. You have 20 minutes to complete this phase of the exercise.

Hostage	Group Rank
1. Brenda Jones	_____
2. Fr. John O'Brien	_____
3. Juan Garcia	_____
4. Elijah Brown	_____
5. Betsy Bates	_____
6. Jan Perkins	_____
7. D. B. Calhoun	_____
8. Andrea Ohms	_____

Classroom Speech Deliberation Worksheet

Your group's task is to review the previous round of classroom speeches by answering the questions below. Try to reach consensus in your answers, and make sure you provide constructive suggestions to help improve the next round of speeches. Present your group's recommendations in a panel-discussion, which is described on pages 379–380 of your textbook.

a. How well did the class as a whole perform in narrowing their topics and adapting their speeches to this audience?

- Were specific purposes sharply defined? Were they too broad? Too narrow? Too technical? Too trivial?
- Which speeches were especially well adapted to the background, knowledge, and interests of the audience? What methods of audience adaptation were used in these speeches?
- What advice would you give to the class about audience analysis and adaptation for the next round of speeches?

b. How well did the class as a whole perform in the area of speech organization?

- Which introductions worked especially well? Why?
- Which conclusions were particularly effective? Why?
- Did speeches follow a clear method of organization? Which speeches were especially strong in this respect?
- Did speakers make effective use of connectives to help listeners follow their ideas? Which speeches stood out in this regard?
- What advice would you give to the class about organization for the next round of speeches?

c. How well did the class as a whole use supporting materials in this round of speeches?

- Which speakers made especially good use of examples? What made their use of examples so effective?
- Which speakers made especially good use of statistics? What made their use of statistics so effective?
- Which speakers made especially good use of testimony? What made their use of testimony so effective?
- What advice would you give to the class about the use of supporting materials in the next round of speeches?

d. How well did the class as a whole deliver this round of speeches?

- Did speakers sound fluid, confident, and conversational?
- Did speakers manage their notes effectively and establish strong eye contact with listeners?
- Did speakers avoid distracting mannerisms? Did they use gestures to help communicate their ideas?
- Did speakers use visual aids effectively? Which speeches were especially noteworthy in this respect?
- What advice would you give to the class about delivery in the next round of speeches?

Group Discussion Self-Assessment

Your task is to reach a full, objective assessment of the major strengths and weaknesses of your small group and of your performance in the group. Write a thoughtful, objective evaluation in full-sentence and paragraph form with an introduction and a conclusion.

Use the following questions to guide your self-assessment, though you do not need to answer each question individually in your paper. Be specific and concrete in your comments.

Leadership

Did your group have a designated leader?

If you did not have a designated leader, what kind of leadership developed in the group?

Which members were most effective in meeting the group's procedural needs?

Which members were most effective in meeting the group's task needs?

Which members were most effective in meeting the group's maintenance needs?

Responsibilities of Group Members

How fully did members commit themselves to the goals of the group?

How well did members carry out their individual assignments?

Did the group avoid interpersonal conflict by keeping disagreement at the task level?

Did vocal members encourage full participation by other members of the group?

Did group members work to keep discussion on track?

Use of the Reflective-Thinking Method

Did the group define the question for discussion clearly?

Did the group analyze the problem thoroughly before attempting to map out solutions?

Did the group establish criteria for an ideal solution?

Did the group brainstorm to generate a wide range of potential solutions?

Did the group evaluate each potential solution in light of the criteria for an ideal solution?

Did the group make a determined effort to reach consensus about the best solution?

Did the group achieve consensus? Why or why not?

Overall Evaluation

Are you satisfied with the work of the group and with your role in the group?

If the group were to start its project over again, what changes would you recommend to help the group work more effectively? Be specific.

Group Discussion Participant Evaluation Worksheet

Person being evaluated _____

Your name _____   Group _____

For each item, circle the number that best reflects your evaluation of the participant's contribution to the group.

poor	fair	average	good	excellent	
P	F	A	G	E	Appeared committed to the goals of the group
P	F	A	G	E	Participated frequently in group deliberations
P	F	A	G	E	Comments were clear, relevant, and helpful
P	F	A	G	E	Carried out individual assignments promptly
P	F	A	G	E	Assisted with procedural leadership functions
P	F	A	G	E	Assisted with task leadership functions
P	F	A	G	E	Assisted with maintenance leadership functions
P	F	A	G	E	Avoided interpersonal conflict with group members
P	F	A	G	E	Encouraged participation by other group members
P	F	A	G	E	Helped keep discussion on track
P	F	A	G	E	Overall contribution in comparison to other group members

Comments: (this space must be filled in)

Part Five

Speeches for Analysis
and Discussion

New Game, New Life

1   It was seven minutes into the second half of my soccer game. A tall, red-headed striker from the other team collided with me. After flipping into the air, I was flat on the ground with a fractured back. I was out for the season, and I had to wear a back brace for months.

2   My injuries were physical, but they initiated a process of mental change. As I coped with them, I discovered a new sense of self and gained a different perspective on life and relationships.

3   Before the injury, when people would ask me about myself, the first thing I would say was, "I'm a soccer player." After I broke my back, my self-image began to change. I had a chance to branch out, and I realized there was more to me—and to life—than just athletics.

4   I joined the school play and realized I loved working backstage. The people I met were relaxed, and they liked trying on silly costumes and playing with props. I had always been close to the girls on my soccer team, but I enjoyed my new friends just as much.

5   Without soccer, I was able to spend more time with my family. Every Sunday, my parents, my sister, and I would eat breakfast together. We'd sit around the table and talk until lunchtime, without being interrupted by a game or practice. These talks drew me closer to my family and made me aware of just how important they are to me.

6   Eventually, I went back to play for my high school soccer team; I was just no longer the star player I used to be. I learned not to take myself too seriously, and now I see soccer as a hobby instead of my entire identity. At the time it happened, breaking my back seemed to make my whole world come to a stop. But in reality I was able to discover a new world and a fuller sense of who I am.

New Game, New Life

Commentary

Developed around the theme of personal growth, "New Game, New Life" follows a narrative structure. After explaining how she broke her back during a soccer game, the speaker focuses on how she grew personally and relationally while recovering from her injury. A video of the speech is available online and on the DVD of student speeches that accompanies this edition of *The Art of Public Speaking*. Below is a synopsis.

Specific Purpose: To introduce myself to the audience by explaining how my soccer injury opened new possibilities in my life.

Central Idea: Breaking my back on the soccer field changed my life in ways I never could have imagined.

Method of Organization: Topical

Introduction: The introduction consists of the first two paragraphs. In paragraph 1, the speaker gains the audience's attention by telling the story of her back injury. She includes specific details to make the story vivid and engaging. In paragraph 2, she reveals the topic of the speech and previews the main points she will discuss in the body. Even in speeches of self-introduction, a clear statement of the central idea is needed to orient the audience to what will happen in the rest of the speech.

Body: The body consists of paragraphs 3–5. The first main point (paragraph 3) deals with the speaker's self-image as a soccer player and how her injury changed that image. The second main point (paragraph 4) provides a specific example of how the speaker realized there was more to life "than just athletics." No longer a star athlete, she finds fulfillment as a stagehand for the school play. The third main point (paragraph 5) covers the speaker's new relationship with her family. She creates a vivid picture of talking with her family for hours around the breakfast table—an image to which many audience members can relate.

Conclusion: The conclusion consists of paragraph 6. By mentioning her return to the soccer field, the speaker provides closure to her back-injury story and creates a sense of psychological unity. She then reinforces her central idea by noting that her outlook on life has changed forever. The speaker's closing thought—that breaking her back was a blessing in disguise—provides the right tone for the end of the speech.

A Heart Worn on My Hand

1   The blistering sun beats on my forehead. I grip my fingers along the red stitching of the leather softball nestled in my hand. The batter steps up to the plate and I dig the toe of my cleats further into the pitching mound. As I prepare to pitch, my focus lies on nothing but the catcher's glove. I know my next pitch will be a strike. As I throw the ball with all my strength, the batter unleashes a hard line drive right back at me. But it's all right because I catch the ball in my glove and the batter is out.

2   Not only has my softball glove saved me from physical harm, but it contains hidden clues to my personality, my background, and the experiences that have helped shape who I am today.

3   On the outside of my glove, you notice my name scribbled in black permanent marker. My name is unique and I feel this has given me the courage to be different and stand out from my peers throughout my life. Surrounding my name you notice water stains on the leather of my glove. These stains come from practicing in the rainy spring weather in Milwaukee, Wisconsin, where I attended high school.

4   As you try on my glove, you notice how easily it conforms to the shape of your hand. As you open and close the glove, you notice that all the individual fingers move together with ease. This reflects how important teamwork is to me. I was captain of my softball team my senior year in high school, and I know that to accomplish any major task, everyone must move in the same direction, together.

5   If you look closely at the seams of my glove, you can imagine all the experiences they—and I—have been through. You can see me playing catch with my dad for the first time in my backyard. You can feel the dirt from my hand after I hit a home run and the joy I experienced after being named first team all-conference. You can see my mom, dad, younger sister, and older brother always there to support me by cheering at the games.

6   Over time, my softball glove has changed in appearance. Not only does it reveal aspects of my personality, my background, and my experiences, but the warm tone of the leather shows my own aging and transformations as I have grown up. As the famous basketball coach John Wooden once said, "Sports do not build character, they reveal it." Through my softball glove, my character is revealed.

A Heart Worn on My Hand

Commentary

Clearly organized and confidently delivered, "A Heart Worn on My Hand" is a speech of self-introduction based on a personal object—in this case, the speaker's softball glove. Notice, as the speech progresses, how the speaker does not focus on describing the glove, but on how the glove provides insight into the speaker herself. The speech is also available online and on the DVD of student speeches that accompanies this edition of *The Art of Public Speaking*. Below is a synopsis.

Specific Purpose: To introduce myself to the audience by explaining how my softball glove reveals important aspects of my life and personality.

Central Idea: A close look at my softball glove provides insight about my personality, my background, and the experiences that have shaped my life.

Method of Organization: Topical

Introduction: The speaker begins in paragraph 1 with a story that gains attention and arouses curiosity about where the speech will go next. Her vivid descriptions and specific details make the introduction much more effective than if she had simply said, "I used to pitch softball when I was in high school." She completes the introduction in paragraph 2 by stating the central idea, which lets the audience know what to listen for in the body.

Body: Paragraphs 3–5 make up the body of the speech. If you watch the video, you will notice that the speaker picks up her softball glove from the table and shows it to the audience as she discusses it, perfectly coordinating her words with her actions as she goes through each main point. Focusing on the outside of the glove in paragraph 3, she mentions the uniqueness of her name and refers to her upbringing in Milwaukee, Wisconsin. Focusing on the feel of the glove in paragraph 4, she explains the importance of teamwork by discussing her high-school softball team. Focusing on the seams of the glove in paragraph 5, she talks about her relationship with her family and some of the things she experienced while growing up. None of this information is overly dramatic, but it engages the audience because of the creative way it is worked into the speech.

Conclusion: The conclusion consists of paragraph 6. The speaker summarizes her main points by noting how she has grown through the experiences represented by her softball glove. The final sentence, preceded by the quotation from John Wooden, reinforces the central idea and ends the speech on a strong note.

Pot, Soil, Water
Needs Improvement Version

---

1   So the assignment is to choose an object and talk about it and how it's like us. So I chose a plant from my dorm room. Anyway, it's a lot like me because it has a pot and soil and water.

2   My family is really important to me and keeps me together. My mom and dad have a lot of houseplants. They're really great people. I can talk to them about anything—well, most things, anyway.

3   Plants need to be potted in soil. The dirt helps the roots. Similarly, I have a lot of great friends. I'm not trying to say that my friends are like dirt, but they always help me out and give me a lot of advice.

4   I have a lot of interests, too. Speaking of water, one of my interests is swimming. I was on the swim team in high school, and it was a great experience. Without water, I wouldn't survive. Plants need water, and I do too.

5   So, like the plant in my dorm room, I have a lot of things that make me who I am.

Pot, Soil, Water
Needs Improvement Version

Commentary

Showing sample speeches can be of great help to students as they work on their initial presentations. This edition of *The Art of Public Speaking* offers both a needs improvement and a final version of "Pot, Soil, Water," a student speech of self-introduction based on a personal object. When showing the needs improvement version, have students focus on the speaker's organization, delivery, and development of ideas. Follow with a brief class discussion about each of these aspects of the speech. Then show the final version of the speech, which appears on page 00 of this manual. Again have students focus on the speaker's organization, delivery, and development of ideas. Follow with a class discussion that compares and contrasts the two versions and explores why the final version is superior.

Both versions of the speech are available on the DVD of student speeches that accompanies this edition of *The Art of Public Speaking*. Here is a synopsis of the needs improvement version.

Introduction: The introduction consists of paragraph 1. The opening line simply restates the assignment and suggests that the speaker has not given a great deal of thought to how she will begin. That perception is reinforced by the sickly looking plant from her dorm room, which gives the impression that she grabbed whatever was lying around for use in the speech. Her central idea—that the plant is like her because it has a pot, soil, and water—is clearly stated and, as can be seen from the final version, has promise. It would have been more effective here, however, if the speaker had been more specific about the comparison before moving into the body of her speech.

Body: Paragraphs 2–4 make up the body of the speech and revolve around the similarities between the speaker's life and the plant's pot, soil, and water. Paragraph 2 says that the speaker's parents have helped keep her life together, but it does not state explicitly the comparison between her parents and the houseplant. Paragraph 3 starts off better as it compares the plant's soil with the speaker's friends, but it breaks down when the speaker suddenly realizes the negative connotations of the comparison and states that she does not mean "my friends are like dirt." Paragraph 4 is somewhat better in that it tells the audience a little about the speaker's interests—in this case, swimming—but it, too, is less effective than the final version.

Apart from its weaknesses in content, the message sent by the body of this speech is that the speaker is not well prepared. She makes a genuine effort to speak extemporaneously, and she has fairly good eye contact, but she is not poised in her mannerisms and she does not have strong command of what she wants to say. Despite the fact that the main points are well organized and easy to follow, there is a stream-of-consciousness quality to the speaker's ideas that suggests she is making things up as she goes. Part of that might be due to her nervousness, but one way to control nervousness is to be fully prepared. Had the speaker put more time into her preparation and rehearsal, she would have been more confident.

Conclusion: The conclusion consists of the single sentence in paragraph 5. It lets the audience know the speech is coming to an end, and it alludes to the central idea, but it does nothing to counter the impression that the speaker needed to take the assignment more seriously and prepare more thoroughly.

All told, the needs improvement version of "Pot, Soil, Water" illustrates the difference between having a good idea for a speech and turning that idea into a good speech. The speaker came up with a creative comparison, but she was not creative in developing the comparison. The final version provides an instructive contrast in content and delivery.

Pot, Soil, Water
Final Version

---

1   Those of you with a green thumb know that a healthy houseplant like this one needs a number of things to grow, including a good pot, rich soil, and adequate water. The pot is the plant's home, the comforting place where it grows up. The soil gives the plant nutrients and helps its roots expand. Water is the basis of all life and allows the plant to thrive. Like this plant and the pot, soil, and water it requires to grow, you can get a sense of my growth by looking at my family, my friends, and my interests.

2   The pot represents my family. A pot holds the plant together just like my family holds me together. My mom and dad not only gave me life but a loving home to grow up in. If I ever had a bad day, they kept me from falling apart. As the plant protects the roots and the soil, my family protected me as I grew through my childhood.

3   The soil represents my friends, who have supported me as I branched out into new experiences. Here on campus, my three best friends have helped me adjust to college by showing me around, by introducing me to new people, and by helping me with my assignments. They encourage me to follow my dreams and are always willing to offer advice. As the nutrients from the soil feed the plant, my friends have helped me grow and develop.

4   The water represents my interests. Without water, this plant would turn brown and dull, but with water, the plant is bright and full of life. Like water for this plant, my interests help me flourish rather than wilt. I have a broad range of interests, including music, art, swimming, and watching movies. My interests make my personal colors more vibrant and allow me to bloom.

5   I wouldn't be who I am today without my family, my friends, and my interests. But like this plant, I still have some growing to do—more things to learn and more things to experience. Luckily, because of my own pot, soil, and water, I'm confident I will bloom into the person I want to be.

Pot, Soil, Water
Final Version

Commentary

The final version of "Pot, Soil, Water" provides an excellent vehicle for helping students understand the elements of a speech of self-introduction. Unlike the needs improvement version, the final version is clearly organized and creatively developed. A video of the speech is available online and on the DVD of student speeches that accompanies this edition of *The Art of Public Speaking*. Below is a synopsis.

Specific Purpose: To introduce myself to the audience by explaining how a common houseplant represents important aspects of my life.

Central Idea: The pot, soil, and water of a common houseplant illustrate the importance of my family, friends, and interests.

Method of Organization: Topical

Introduction: The introduction, which consists of paragraph 1, captures the audience's attention, reveals the topic of the speech, and previews the points that will be discussed in the body. By referring to a houseplant and what it needs to grow, the speaker provides a creative touch that runs through the entire speech. By bringing a houseplant to class with her, she helps the audience visualize her main points. At the end of the introduction, she links the plant's pot, soil, and water to her family, friends, and interests. Doing so gives the audience a clear sense of what to expect as the speech unfolds.

Body: The body consists of paragraphs 2–4. Each paragraph utilizes a different part of the houseplant to reveal a different aspect of the speaker's life. In paragraph 2, the speaker uses the pot to discuss the importance of her family. In paragraph 3, she uses the soil to discuss how her friends have helped her grow as a human being. In paragraph 4, she uses the water needed for a healthy houseplant to discuss how her interests nurture and sustain her life. It is important to notice that the speaker does not focus on describing the plant itself, but on how it provides insight into the speaker herself. Each paragraph in the body is carefully woven into the overall theme of the speech and is developed with examples and illustrations from the speaker's life.

Conclusion: The conclusion, which consists of paragraph 5, begins with a brief reminder of the speech's main points. The speaker completes the comparison with the houseplant by stating that she is not finished growing. She then ties everything together and ends on a positive note.

My Life from Toe to Head

---

1   Good afternoon, everyone. My name is Allie, and today I'm here to introduce you to me and my life, from toe to head—starting with the toes.

2   I have ten of them. In July 1985, my parents gave birth to a happy, healthy, blue-eyed girl with ten toes and ten fingers. Unfortunately, I was born with two left feet. Although all my toes were in their correct places, my right foot curved the wrong way. So I had two left feet, and the doctors were stumped, and so they put a tiny plaster cast on my right foot in order to reshape it.

3   I spent the first two months of my life with a cast on my foot, while my mother spent time explaining why her precious baby was already in a cast. Well, today I realize how lucky I am to have normal feet. I played eight years of hockey, three years of tennis, and two years of volleyball. I love to dance and jog and buy shoes. Try doing those things with two left feet!

4   Next are my legs. As you can see, I'm very tall. When a six-foot-seven-inch man marries a five-foot-ten woman, they tend to create big children. And it isn't easy growing up taller than all of your friends, and taller than most boys too.

5   My height has taught me a lot. For a while, I was self-conscious and I thought I stuck out and was different from everyone else. But then I learned to love my height, the attention that I got, and the fact that I was unique. And my height has taught me to be comfortable with myself and my appearance.

6   Finally, moving up to the head—the most important part. I have a good head on my shoulders. You may notice the hair, which has been highlighted. Last summer I worked as a receptionist at a local hair salon, but I like to think of it more as an experience than as a job. I learned a lot about life and responsibility, as well as what can happen when ten people—mostly middle-aged women—work in close quarters with each other.

7   So now you've all met me, Allie, from toe to head. I'm an active, fun-loving, proud, and motivated person who is ready to take on the world. Being a freshman in college is a new experience, but I know that all six feet of me will be successful.

My Life from Toe to Head

Commentary

Creative, carefully developed, and clearly organized, "My Life From Toe to Head" exemplifies the most important aspects of a speech of self-introduction. Its central theme is how the speaker's height has influenced her character and outlook. Here is a synopsis.

Specific Purpose: To introduce myself to the audience by explaining how my height has influenced my perspective on life.

Central Idea: The fact that I am so tall has taught me a lot about my character and my view on the world.

Method of Organization: Spatial

Introduction: The introduction consists of paragraph 1, which greets the audience, reveals the purpose of the speech, and announces its pattern of organization. Although only two sentences in length, the introduction accomplishes everything it needs to in that brief compass.

Body: The body of the speech runs from paragraph 2 through paragraph 6. Paragraphs 2–3 deal with the speaker's feet. She explains how being born with two left feet shaped the first years of her life and how that condition was corrected so as to allow her eventually to participate in a variety of sports and other activities. In paragraphs 4–5, the speaker shifts the focus to her legs and her above average height. Paragraph 4 reveals the interesting fact that both her parents are extremely tall, while paragraph 5 explains how the speaker's height has taught her to be self-confident and to appreciate her appearance. Paragraph 6 brings the speaker to her head—"the most important part." She discusses her experience working at a beauty salon and what it taught her about interpersonal relationships. Although the use of spatial organization is unusual for an introductory speech, it works perfectly in this case and makes the presentation much more interesting than if the speaker had simply recounted the facts of her life in chronological order.

Conclusion: As in most introductory speeches, the conclusion is brief and succinct. Consisting of paragraph 6, it summarizes the central idea and ends with the speaker's enthusiasm about being a college freshman. The final words tie the entire speech together by restating the theme of the speaker's height.

My Eye on the World

1   Gordon Parks once said, "I choose my camera as a weapon against all the things I dislike about America—poverty, racism, discrimination." Parks, an extraordinary photographer, gives insight into my character, passions, and concerns in this one profound quotation.

2   I began photography during the fall of my freshman year in high school. After learning simple techniques of printing in the darkroom and studying the works of influential photographers, I developed an interest in this art that I have continued to pursue ever since. In addition to taking three other photo courses, I worked as a photographer and even received awards for some of my photographs.

3   My camera is therefore an effective tool that expresses my values, ambitions, and views in a literal sense. Being able to capture an idea or moment in a tangible art has always amazed me. The product that I create by the snap of a shutter greatly describes the way I see the world around me. The different angles, the way I choose to frame a photo, and my subject matter—all shed light on describing who I am as a person.

4   By photographing the world around me, I can also express my sense of beauty. This may include an abstract silhouette of the contours of a woman's body, the way the sun accents a stairwell at a certain time of day, the motion of water flowing down a channel of rocks, or the smile on a child's face.

5   My camera sheds light on my emotions and concerns as well. It can describe a feeling or an issue in a single moment—the loneliness of a stark, dreary winter day or the hunger in a homeless child's eyes.

6   So you can see photography is an outlet for my energy, my ideas, my creativity, and even my frustrations. Through the lens of a camera I can articulate my feelings and express myself to the world.

My Eye on the World

Commentary

"My Eye on the World" is a 2-minute speech of self-introduction. It uses the speaker's interest in photography to reveal significant aspects of her life. Here is a synopsis of the speech.

Specific Purpose: To introduce myself to the audience by explaining how my hobby of photography provides insight into my character, passions, and concerns.

Central Idea: Through photography, a hobby I have pursued since high school, I am able to express my character, passions, and concerns.

Method of Organization: Topical

Introduction: The introduction consists of paragraph 1, which opens with an attention-getting quotation from famous photographer Gordon Parks. The speaker then moves from this quotation to indicate how her hobby of photography reveals a great deal about her character, passions, and concerns. Although only two sentences in length, the introduction accomplishes everything it needs to in that brief compass.

Body: The body of the speech runs from paragraph 2 through paragraph 5. In paragraph 2, the speaker notes how she first became interested in photography and explains the role it has continued to play in her life. Paragraphs 3–5 focus on specific aspects of photography and what they reveal about the speaker. Rather than speaking in general terms, the speaker uses sharp imagery and concrete, descriptive language to convey her ideas. Consistent with the visual images created by a photograph, the speaker provides linguistic images for her listeners.

Conclusion: As in most introductory speeches, the conclusion is brief and succinct. Consisting of paragraph 6, it summarizes the central idea of the speech and ends with a strong final sentence.

The Rare Phobia

---

1   Everyone in the world today suffers from some kind of fear. However, about 4 to 5 percent experience a more severe form of fear known as phobias. Some of the most common phobias are claustrophobia; agoraphobia, which is the fear of public spaces; and arachnophobia, the fear of spiders. Then there are the more uncommon phobias—such as peladophobia, the fear of bald people, or geniophobia, the fear of chins. There is even a name for the fear of Friday the 13th—paraskevidekatriaphobia.

2   According to the latest count, there was a total of 530 named phobias. However, my particular phobia is so rare that it doesn't even have a name. It is simply called the fear of baseballs. That's right, you heard me, the fear of baseballs. I know it sounds stupid, but it's true. I am terrified of baseballs. Even holding one in my hand sends shivers down my spine.

3   People don't understand this. They do not understand that this is a real fear. I know it's been said that the only thing to fear is fear itself. But that's not true. I'm not scared of being scared of baseballs. I'm scared of the ball itself—the hard, round object that is usually flying fast through the air.

4   But some people will fight to the death with me about this. For example, just this weekend I was at my friends' apartment and they found out that I have an extreme fear of baseballs. So what do they do? They decide they're going to help cure me of this fear by playing catch with the ball over my head. I get so scared that I have to leave the room and sit on the stairway. And believe me, this is not the first time something like this has happened.

5   You may be wondering how I acquired this phobia. I was about four years old and on a tee-ball team. I was just learning, so my catching skills weren't quite as good as they needed to be. Then, one day at practice, some guy threw a ball at me as hard as he could. He hit me directly in the head and knocked me out cold. Needless to say, I didn't stick with the sport, and ever since I've been scared to death of baseballs.

6   Now it's not like I hate the sport of baseball. I'm a huge Chicago Cubs fan—I can just never attend the games in person.

7   In conclusion, my unusual fear of baseballs is something real that I have to live with. And while it is inconvenient at times—like when I can't attend the Cubs' games or occasionally have to leave social situations—I take comfort in the fact that at least I'm not afraid of bald people, or public places, or spiders, or even Friday the 13th. So I suppose it could be worse.

The Rare Phobia

Commentary

Delivered with strong eye contact and vocal variety, "The Rare Phobia" is a creative, entertaining speech of self-introduction. Below is a synopsis.

Specific Purpose: To introduce myself to the audience by explaining my fear of baseballs.

Central Idea: While most people are scared of something, my particular phobia—the fear of baseballs—is so rare that there is no technical name for it.

Method of Organization: Topical

Introduction: Consisting of paragraphs 1 and 2, the introduction is at once playful, informative, and attention-grabbing. The first paragraph arouses the audience's curiosity and pulls them progressively into the speech, while the second paragraph reveals the specific phobia from which the speaker suffers. This would be an outstanding introduction even for a speech presented much later in the term.

Body: Paragraphs 3–6 cover the body of the speech. In paragraph 3, the speaker clarifies the nature of her phobia, juxtaposing her fear with the famous words of Franklin D. Roosevelt's first inaugural address that "the only thing we have to fear is fear itself." Paragraph 4 presents a brief example of how the speaker's fear of baseballs has affected her life. The story of her friends playing catch above her head is an amusing way to illustrate just how fearful she is of baseballs. In paragraph 5, the speaker explains how she developed her fear of baseballs, while in paragraph 6, she emphasizes that it is the baseball itself she fears, not the game of baseball. The fact that she loves the Chicago Cubs but cannot attend their games in person highlights once more the rare nature of her phobia.

Conclusion: The conclusion is paragraph 7. The speaker reiterates that her phobia is real and indeed inconvenient, but she makes it clear to the audience that she's not asking for their sympathy. By reminding her listeners of the other phobias out there, she echoes the introduction and concludes that hers could be a lot worse.

A Mile in My Shoes

1   Someone once said, you don't really know a person until you walk a mile in their shoes. Whoever said this must have met many a person like me. Where one's shoes have been and what they have done can give you a great deal of insight into a person. I think my shoes reveal a lot about me—not only my everyday activities and hobbies, but the events that have shaped my inner self.

2   If you closely examine my shoes, you'll notice many things that connect me to what I do. I am an artist. You may see a speck of paint that fell from the brush as I worked on my latest still-life oil painting. Or you may notice a fair amount of clay, a result of my aggressive wrestling with the medium on a potter's wheel.

3   Also evident on my shoes is my major on campus. I'm a Meat and Animal Science major, and my shoes bear full documentation of my involvement in this program. The shoelaces are frayed from the sheep that chew on them while I work in the barns. The leather is marred from the hooves of animals stepping on my feet. If you're unfortunate enough, you may find something in the treads that I accidentally stepped in.

4   The exterior of my shoes can tell you a lot about what I do, but they also can provide clues to who I am and where I have been. I have always been an explorer and traveler. My father says that I was born under a wandering star. My shoes have been on my feet for many of my spiritual and physical wanderings. They've walked up into the Alps, across the cliffs of Ireland, and through 14 countries. They've been on numerous backpacking trips throughout the nation and on hikes in the northern Wisconsin woods. They've been witnesses to archeological digs and rowing regattas. They were on my feet the day I took my first hike with my fiancé and the day we took the walk that ended in his proposal.

5   So you can see my shoes have been through a lot, and they're beginning to show the wear and tear a bit. They've been witnesses to my everyday adventures and the epic journeys that have shaped my life. You could learn a lot about me by looking at my shoes, but you could learn a great deal more by walking a few miles in them.

A Mile in My Shoes

Commentary

"A Mile in My Shoes" is a speech of self-introduction based on a personal object. Clearly organized and effectively delivered, it provides a fine example of how students can approach the introductory speech creatively. The ideas of the speech are fairly ordinary, but the manner in which the speaker expresses and communicates those ideas lifts the speech well above the ordinary. Here is a synopsis.

Specific Purpose: To introduce myself to my audience by explaining how my shoes reveal my everyday activities, my hobbies, and the events that have shaped my inner self.

Central Idea: My shoes reveal that I am an artist, a Meat and Animal Science major, and a wanderer and traveler.

Method of Organization: Topical

Introduction: The introduction consists of the first paragraph. The speaker gains attention by opening with the old adage about walking a mile in a person's shoes. She moves from the adage to note that one's shoes can reveal a great deal about a person. In her case, she says, one can learn about her hobbies, her everyday activities, and the events that have shaped her inner self. Crisp and concise, the introduction leaves no doubt about the topic of the speech or the major points to be covered in the body.

Body: There are three main points in the body of this speech, each of which reveals something different about the speaker. The first tells us that the speaker is an artist (paragraph 2). The second tells us that she is a Meat and Animal Science major (paragraph 3). The third tells us that she has traveled a great deal, has participated in activities from rowing regattas to archaeological digs, and is engaged to be married (paragraph 4).

Because the speech assignment required students to use a physical object to help introduce themselves to the class, the speaker uses her shoes as a visual aid in paragraphs 2–3. But even if this had not been the assignment, using the shoes would have been an excellent idea. Not only do they make the speech more interesting, but they give the speaker something to do other than worry about her nervousness. She does an excellent job of using the shoes to reinforce her ideas; her words are perfectly coordinated with her actions; and she maintains strong eye contact with the audience every step of the way.

Conclusion: The speaker concludes in paragraph 5, in which she summarizes the major themes of the speech and provides a sense of psychological unity by referring back to her opening line. Here, as elsewhere, she chooses her words carefully and communicates them extemporaneously.

Kiyomi and Me

1 Her name was Kiyomi. She was a mysterious Japanese dancer. Last autumn I got to meet her. How, you ask. Well, actually, she was a character in a play. I met her the day I became her. That day was one of the happiest days of my life. I wanted that part so desperately it was all I could think about. Being Kiyomi was one of the most memorable experiences of my life.

2 When I first read the script for the play *A Wind of a Thousand Tales*, I couldn't believe it. The description of the character Kiyomi was perfect. She was everything I ever wanted to be in life. She was beautiful, humble, shy, loving, loved, and, most of all, she was graceful. To me, she was the ideal woman. So, obviously, I tried out for the part.

3 I had to wait an entire weekend to find out if I got the part or not. Now I know that doesn't seem like a long time, but to me it felt like an eternity. So when I found out I got the part that Monday, I was so excited that I memorized all my lines that night.

4 Yet it wasn't getting the part that made so much of a difference in my life. The most important experience came after all the rehearsals, when it was finally time to perform the play. I was performing on stage, when gradually I forgot who I was. I said all the lines and performed all the actions—but not as Priya acting as Kiyomi, but as Kiyomi herself. It was the strangest experience of my life. I had become a completely different person. Even after the play was over, it took me a good five minutes to snap out of it.

5 After finding myself again, I realized why I had this strange experience. I needed this experience to appreciate who I was. I realized that I should be myself and not long to be someone else. So what if I'm not the most graceful or feminine person? So what if I don't possess all the wonderful characteristics of Kiyomi? I am still me—not a character in a play. Yet by playing that character, I learned one of the most important lessons of my life. I learned that by becoming a woman who never was, I became proud of who I am.

Kiyomi and Me

Commentary

A narrative speech of self-introduction, "Kiyomi and Me" is clearly organized and creatively developed. Here is a synopsis.

Specific Purpose: To introduce myself to the audience.

Central Idea: Playing the role of Kiyomi in *A Wind of a Thousand Tales* was one of the most memorable experiences of my life.

Method of Organization: Chronological

Introduction: The introduction consists of paragraph 1 and provides an excellent example of how students can gain the audience's attention by arousing curiosity about the speech topic. After beginning with the opening words, "Her name was Kiyomi," the speaker gradually reveals the identity of Kiyomi as a character in a play. She ends the introduction by making clear that the rest of the speech will explain why playing the role of Kiyomi was one of the most memorable experiences of the speaker's life.

Body: Running from paragraph 2 through paragraph 4, the body of this speech is organized chronologically and presents a narrative about the speaker's experience playing Kiyomi. In paragraph 2, the speaker begins her narrative by recalling the day she read the script of A Wind of a Thousand Tales and how captivated she was by the character of Kiyomi. In paragraph 3, the speaker describes waiting for the results of her audition and her excitement when she learned that she was chosen to play Kiyomi. In paragraph 4, she explains how she found herself so absorbed by the role of Kiyomi during the play that she became "a completely different person." It was, she says, "the strangest experience of my life." As with most good narratives, this one is clearly structured and communicated. The speaker uses vivid, descriptive language and provides enough details for the audience to understand what occurred, but not so many as to make the speech run over the time limit.

Conclusion: Consisting of paragraph 5, the conclusion is especially effective. Having presented her narrative in the body of the speech, the speaker now explains why her experience playing Kiyomi was so significant. In doing so, she makes a larger point about the importance of being true to one's self. The final two sentences end the speech on a dramatic and thought-provoking note.

Brooklyn Roads

---

1   As the poet E. E. Cummings once said, "To be nobody but yourself in a world which is doing its best, day and night, to make you everybody else means to fight the hardest battle which any human being can fight." As a young boy, your classmate Danny made a promise to himself to fight for his individuality, and to this day he has not given up on that promise.

2   Growing up in a poverty-stricken Brooklyn neighborhood, Danny had hopes of making his individual mark in the world. He saw the struggles his parents endured because they didn't have the same opportunities as kids today. With his parents' support, he ventured outside Brooklyn to Manhattan, where he attended grammar school and high school. While in high school, Danny decided that he wanted to attend college, something that neither of his parents had the chance to do.

3   When choosing a school, Danny again showed his individuality. While most of his friends and classmates stayed in their comfort zone by attending college close to home, Danny has traveled 812 miles to attend the University of Wisconsin, where he hopes to study engineering.

4   Danny shows his individuality in other ways as well. He started playing billiards in high school, and it's been a hobby of his ever since. Unlike pool, which is based on shooting balls into pockets, billiards has no pockets and is much more challenging than pool. Danny also plays handball, another game with a loyal following but definitely outside the football-basketball-baseball mainstream. Then there was Danny's decision to ignore the instant popularity of iPods. Instead, he checked out all the options and bought a ZEN mp3 player. If you have the time, Danny will gladly tell you all of the virtues of ZEN.

5   For Danny, being an individual in a world of trends hasn't been the easiest of battles. But, he says, it's worth the effort. After all, would you want to lose what makes you who you are?

Brooklyn Roads

Commentary

Organized around the theme of individuality, "Brooklyn Roads" is a 2-minute speech introducing a classmate. Video of the speech is available online and on the DVD of student speeches that accompanies this edition of *The Art of Public Speaking*. Here is a brief synopsis.

Specific Purpose: To introduce my classmate Danny to the audience.

Central Idea: Throughout his life Danny has demonstrated his individuality.

Method of Organization: Topical

Introduction: Paragraph 1 serves as the speaker's introduction. The opening quotation gains the audience's attention, while the second sentence identifies the speech's theme—namely, Danny's individuality. Because every paragraph deals with Danny's individuality, identifying the theme also previews the body of the speech.

Body: The body contains three main points, each of which deals with an aspect of Danny's individuality. In paragraph 2, the speaker focuses on Danny's background and early education. The point culminates with Danny's desire to be the first in his family to attend college. In paragraph 3, the speaker focuses on Danny's decision to attend the University of Wisconsin, a school that is "812 miles" away from Danny's Brooklyn home. The figure adds specificity to the point and is more memorable than if the speaker had simply said, "Danny has traveled several hundred miles." Paragraph 4 constitutes the third main point, which deals with other ways Danny has shown his individuality. The ideas are presented clearly and concisely, and they are developed through specific examples from Danny's life.

Conclusion: The conclusion consists of paragraph 5. The speaker begins it by restating the speech's theme. He then poses a serious question that reinforces the importance of maintaining one's individuality.

Rhymes with Orange

1   Paul Madsen's first memory in life was sitting on his grandmother's lap and being fed his favorite food—an orange. Surprisingly, there are actually many similarities between Paul and his favorite food.

2   Much like an orange has tough skin, so does Paul, which is evident by his choice of a major hobby—playing rugby. Paul started playing rugby while he was growing up near London, England. Rugby is described by many as the roughest sport in the world, a fact Paul can attest to since he has broken two ribs, two bones in his foot, and fractured his jaw while playing the sport. But rugby's brutal nature hasn't stopped Paul from pursuing the sport to its highest level, including leading his local team to the European championship game for its age group.

3   But like an orange, Paul's tough skin can be misleading. Just as an orange has a softer inside, so does Paul. He is both a caring person and a humanitarian. He has done lots of charity work throughout his life, and this past summer he went to Namibia in Southern Africa and helped build schools so the local children could have a chance to be educated. Paul also helped teach some of the children English and distributed basic health products that the children had been lacking. Paul views it as an obligation to give back to those less fortunate than him because he has been so blessed in life—especially by his loving family, which includes his mother, father, and three younger brothers.

4   Like an orange about to be picked from the tree, Paul has absolutely no idea where he will end up. After growing up in England, he's spending his first full year away from his homeland and is just starting to adjust to American culture. So far he's enjoying his new home immensely and is very much looking forward to furthering his education here at the university. As for a profession, Paul is not sure yet what he wants to do. He thinks he would like to have a job doing some sort of charity-related work, or he might want to coach rugby back in England.

5   But no matter where life takes him, one thing is for sure—Paul will eat lots of oranges along the way.

Rhymes with Orange

Commentary

"Rhymes with Orange" is a brief speech introducing a classmate. Developed through the theme of an orange, it provides an excellent example of creativity in the first classroom presentation. A video is available online and on the DVD of student speeches that accompanies this edition of *The Art of Public Speaking*. Here is a brief synopsis.

Specific Purpose: To introduce my classmate Paul to the audience.

Central Idea: There are many similarities between Paul's life and oranges, his favorite food.

Method of Organization: Topical

Introduction: The introduction consists of paragraph 1. The opening sentence gains attention and the second identifies the central idea that will be developed in the body. Though brief, the introduction accomplishes exactly what is needed for an introductory speech.

Body: The body contains three main points. In the first (paragraph 2), the speaker uses a comparison with the tough skin of an orange to discuss Paul's major hobby—playing rugby. This continues the theme advanced in the introduction and provides a creative element that will run throughout the speech. In the second main point (paragraph 3), the speaker moves from the tough skin of an orange to its softer inside as a way to discuss Paul's humanitarian activities. In the third main point (paragraph 4), the speaker continues the theme by comparing Paul to an orange about to be picked from the tree. He presents each point extemporaneously, with excellent vocal variety and eye contact.

Conclusion: The speaker concludes in paragraph 5 by returning to the central theme of his speech. The final words bring everything together and add a light touch of humor.

Steady and True

---

1   As you hit the road with your best friend on a trip cross country in an old convertible, you see so many different sights that it's easy to overlook the one constant that is always in the same place and is always there. The lane divider is always present—dead center in the middle of the road. Our classmate Beth Michalski fits right in the middle—just like the lane divider.

2   Beth was born right between her older sister Katie and her younger brother Max, by her parents Carol and Phil. Perhaps it is not surprising, then, that when it comes to having fun, Beth usually sticks to the middle of the road. Even though she is a shy person, she loves to goof around and have a good time. She loves any water sport, whether it's water skiing, swimming, or riding a wave runner, but she won't take it to the extreme by bungee jumping or skydiving. On the other hand, you won't catch Beth sitting around all day turning into a couch potato.

3   In fact, one of Beth's favorite activities is playing competitive volleyball. Her love for this game gives her a thirst comparable to the one you would get if you were on the open road on a hot day. And when you speed up while driving on the road, the lines speed faster too. This same thing happened to Beth while she played varsity volleyball in high school for three years—the competition increased, and so did her level of play.

4   She loves the game and plays with a fierce passion, but she knows it's not everything in life. She thought long and hard about whether she was going to play here at the university, but her thirst for the game was conquered by her hunger to achieve academic success, and so she decided to focus solely on her schoolwork.

5   Beth followed a road to college that was already paved and, to her, very familiar. She was born and raised here in Madison, Wisconsin, and she attended Edgewood High School, where she was a superb student. When it came time for college, she chose to stay close to home and attend the University of Wisconsin.

6   But just because Beth's going to college close to home doesn't mean she will never move in another direction. She aspires to become an interior decorator and designer in a large city such as New York. While there is no way to know whether she will in fact achieve this dream one day, we can all be sure that as Beth travels down the road of her life, she will be steady and constant as that middle lane divider.

Steady and True

Commentary

A brief speech introducing a classmate, "Steady and True" shows how one can use creativity to craft an interesting first speech. The theme of the lane divider allows the speaker to convey information about his classmate through a clear, easily understandable visual metaphor. Below is a brief synopsis.

Specific Purpose: To introduce my classmate to the audience.

Central Idea: Beth's steady and true course in life has carried her into college and will carry her beyond.

Method of Organization: Topical

Introduction: The introduction consists of paragraph 1. The speaker opens with a hypothetical scenario that relates to the audience and establishes an image that will run throughout his speech—driving down the road and seeing the center lane divider. The last sentence of paragraph 1 connects the image of the lane divider to Beth, the classmate who is being introduced.

Body: Paragraphs 2–5 constitute the body of the speech. In paragraph 2, the speaker presents information about Beth's parents and siblings. Just as she was born in the middle, the speaker says, she usually sticks to the middle of the road when having fun. He continues with the same theme as he discusses Beth's other interests. In paragraph 3, he compares Beth's experience playing competitive volleyball in high school to the way the lines move faster as one speeds up while driving down the road. Paragraph 4 carries Beth's past love of volleyball into the present, explaining how she has balanced her thirst for the game with her hunger for academic success. In paragraph, 5 the speaker continues to employ the same imagery he has used throughout the speech as he recounts the "road" Beth followed in deciding to attend the University of Wisconsin.

Conclusion: In paragraph 6, the speaker projects Beth's steady and true course into life after college by mentioning her dream of becoming an interior designer in a city such as New York. He ends by returning to the imagery of the middle lane divider, giving the speech a unified structure and thematic consistency.

A Family Tradition

1   Drawers pulled open. Clothes scattered all over the floor. A little girl with white blonde curls is digging through her father's chest of drawers. "At last," she exclaims, "I found you." She pulls the expensive European cigars out from the drawer and holds them triumphantly to the sun. Little Reva was not going to let her father ruin his health. Without hesitation, she hoists the cigars out the open window and skips out of the room.

2   Reva's parents were not sure what to make of their five-year-old daughter and her precocious antics. Thirteen years later, Reva, your classmate, continues to astound her parents. She likes to meet new people; she loves to party; and she left her home state of Indiana to come here to the University of Wisconsin. They attribute her daring to the American culture. But I contend that, more than anything, she embodies the values of her family.

3   Reva's parents were born in a small backwater town in the Netherlands, just 10 miles from the German border. Both parents were raised in traditional Dutch Catholic families where 10 to 12 children were the norm. However, Reva's parents turned out to be anything but traditional. They renounced both Catholicism and traditional Dutch life. Reva's mother had never seen an orange, a person of color, or even a Protestant, yet she decided she was going to America. Knowing little English, the young couple set off to build a new life in a new land.

4   Surrounded by a new people, a new language, and a new culture, the young couple struggled to make their growing family belong. Reva remembers her father's daring and sometimes dangerous stunts to give her an authentic American childhood. One Christmas Eve, Reva was snuggling under her covers, waiting for the night to pass, when, all of a sudden, a rapid stomping shook the ceiling above. The children screamed as the roof rumbled and roared. They went scurrying down the stairs only to watch as large, dusty bundles dropped down the chimney into the fireplace. Meanwhile, Reva's father was wrestling wind and ice atop the roof, losing several toys and nearly his life in his struggle to give his children a genuine "Santa and Reindeer" Christmas.

5   Today, Reva's family is fully comfortable in American life and society. Her father travels the country in his work as an engineering specialist. Her oldest sister, Amy, attends Washington University Medical School in St. Louis, while her other sister is a junior at MIT. Clearly, Reva's family has accomplished a great deal.

6   How many of us can imagine leaving our families and everything we own to travel thousands of miles across the ocean to a land where we have no guarantee of success? Furthermore, a land where we don't even speak the language. And yet, once here, Reva's family was able to carve out an extremely successful lifestyle.

7   This is why I think Reva's daring nature is not simply a result of an American life. Rather, I would contend that Reva's parents passed on to her their own adventurous spirit, which allowed them to break tradition; their own courage, which enabled them to leave their homeland; and their own creativity, which they used to weave their traditions into the fabric of American society. If, as it's been said, one is inevitably the product of one's own family, then Reva is truly blessed indeed.

A Family Tradition

Commentary

Marked by expressive language and dynamic delivery, "A Family Tradition" is a fine example of an ice breaker speech introducing a classmate. Here is a synopsis of the speech.

Specific Purpose: To introduce my classmate Reva to the audience.

Central Idea: Reva's daring nature is attributable primarily to the values of her family.

Method of Organization: Chronological

Introduction: The introduction consists of paragraphs 1–2. It opens in paragraph 1 with a story about the speaker's classmate Reva as a little girl. Featuring colorful, descriptive language and sharply etched details, the story does an excellent job of gaining the audience's attention. Paragraph 2 moves from Reva's childhood into her current interests as a student at the University of Wisconsin. It also introduces the main theme of the speech—that Reva's daring nature is attributable above all to the values of her family.

Body: Running from paragraph 3 through paragraph 6, the body focuses on several aspects of Reva's family that reveal her adventurous spirit and willingness to break with tradition. Paragraph 3 explains how Reva's parents boldly decided to leave the Netherlands and emigrate to the United States. Paragraph 4 situates Reva and her family in the U.S. and discusses her parents' efforts to provide their children a "genuine" American childhood. Paragraph 5 brings the sketch of Reva's family up to the moment, while paragraph 6 reinforces the family's achievements by asking the audience to imagine whether they could succeed under the same conditions.

Conclusion: The speech concludes in paragraph 7 by reemphasizing the extent to which Reva's parents passed on to her their courage, creativity, and adventurous spirit. The final sentence brings the entire speech together and adds a touch of eloquence.

Yoga: Uniting Mind, Body, and Spirit

---

1   What do you think of when I do this? If you said "Yoga," you are absolutely correct. For 5,000 years, people have been practicing yoga in order to enhance their mental, physical, and emotional health.

2   "Yoga" comes from the Sanskrit word meaning to "unite" or to "join." As Stella Weller says in her book *Yoga: Finding Balance and Serenity in Everyday Life*, yoga is the practice of uniting one's mind, body, and spirit.

3   I've been practicing yoga for over eight years, and I'm in the process of getting my certification to become a yoga instructor. Although there are many dimensions to yoga, today I'm going to focus on two—yoga breathing and yoga postures. Along the way, I'm going to share with you some of the health benefits that come along with these simple yoga practices. First, I'm going to go over yoga breathing.

4   Breathing has been an essential part of yoga for centuries. There are four major stages in the breathing process. The first is inhalation; the second, pause; the third, exhalation; and the fourth, a pause.

5   It goes something like this. When you inhale, you feel the breath coming from deep within your belly. And as you pause, you will feel the breath rising up. You focus to feel the breath around your heart. As you exhale, you feel the breath moving slowly from your throat and out of your mouth. As you pause the final time, it needs to be prolonged and deliberate, because this is what completes the cycle of yoga breathing until the new inhalation begins.

6   Now, you may be asking yourselves: Why does yoga concentrate on something so ordinary like breathing? Well, the reason is this: When you breathe properly, the amount of oxygen that enters your brain and your bloodstream allows your body to relax, and it allows you to concentrate better than you normally would. For example, as Vimla Lalvani, author of *The Power of Yoga*, writes: "Correct breathing rejuvenates the entire system by sending increased oxygen into the bloodstream to nourish and revitalize the internal organs. . . . The deeper you breathe, the calmer the mind becomes."

7   Now that we've learned about yoga breathing, I'm going to move on to yoga postures. I'm going to demonstrate three postures that I find extremely beneficial to me—the tree pose, the triangle bow pose, and the king of the dance pose.

8   First, let's start with the tree pose. So I'm going to start and shift all of my weight onto my left foot. I'm then going to take my right foot and insert it into my left thigh. I'm going to take my hands in front of me and press my palms together. And as I raise my arms over my head, I'm going to stare at a fixed point ahead of me. I usually hold this pose for about thirty seconds to a minute. This pose helps to strengthen your thighs, calves, ankles, and your back. It also helps to improve your balance.

9   The second pose that I'm going to do is the triangle bow pose. You start with your feet a little bit wider than your shoulders. You then take your arms straight out across your body with your palms facing down. You then touch your left hand to the floor while the opposite arm stretches towards the ceiling. You then take your head and gaze up towards the ceiling. This pose helps with your blood circulation and it stretches your torso and your neck.

10   The third and final pose I'm going to do today is the king of the dance pose. You take your right foot into your right hand and extend your let arm forward. And as you raise your left arm, you raise your right leg as high as possible. Your hold this pose also for thirty seconds to a minute. Not only does this pose help greatly with balance, but it also stretches out your hips, legs, and your torso.

11   So today we've learned about two important dimensions of yoga—yoga breathing and yoga postures. Developed across centuries and now practiced worldwide, yoga is helping millions of people to unite their mind, body, and spirit.

12   Donna Farhi, author of five books on yoga, emphasizes that yoga affects the whole body and the whole person. "Each movement," she says, "demands that we hone some aspect of our consciousness and use ourselves in a whole new way." As yoga practitioners have known for centuries, a few simple movements can do a whole lot of good.

13   Thank you.

Yoga: Uniting Mind, Body, and Spirit

Commentary

An exemplary speech of demonstration, "Yoga: Uniting Mind, Body, and Spirit" illustrates how the speaker's body can function as a visual aid. It also provides a fine model of extemporaneous delivery and is best discussed after watching the video online or on the DVD of student speeches that accompanies this edition of *The Art of Public Speaking*. Here is a synopsis of the speech.

Specific Purpose: To inform my audience about the practice and health benefits of yoga breathing and yoga postures.

Central Idea: Yoga breathing and yoga postures follow specific procedures and are highly beneficial for one's mind, body, and spirit.

Method of Organization: Topical

Introduction: The introduction consists of the first three paragraphs. The speaker opens with a question that draws the audience's attention, at which point she assumes a traditional yoga pose. While holding the pose for the remainder of the first paragraph, she reveals the topic of her speech and notes that yoga has been practiced around the world for 5,000 years.

In paragraph 2, the speaker explains the origins of the word "yoga" and explains that it is the practice of uniting one's mind, body, and spirit. As will occur throughout the speech, she uses expert testimony to establish the health benefits of yoga. Indeed, one of the strongest aspects of this speech is the way it combines traditional research with the speaker's personal experience.

Paragraph 3 establishes the speaker's credibility and previews the body of the speech. The speaker explains that she has been practicing yoga for more than eight years and is pursuing her certification as a yoga instructor. She then previews the body of the speech by stating that she will focus on two aspects of yoga—yoga breathing and yoga postures. All in all, this is an excellent introduction that fulfills all the objectives of an introduction discussed in Chapter 10 of the textbook.

Body: Divided into two main points, the body runs from paragraph 4 through paragraph 10. The first main point deals with yoga breathing and is presented in paragraphs 4–6. After identifying the four steps of yoga breathing in paragraph 4, the speaker demonstrates each step in paragraph 5. In paragraph 6, she explains the health benefits of yoga breathing. Once again she turns to a respected authority, quoting Vimla Lalvani, author of *The Power of Yoga*, on the manner in which yoga breathing rejuvenates the entire body by sending increased oxygen into the bloodstream.

Paragraph 7 begins with a transition from the first main point to the second. It then provides an internal preview specifying the three yoga poses to be demonstrated in main point two.

Paragraph 8 demonstrates the tree pose, paragraph 9 the triangle bow pose, and paragraph 10 the king of the dance pose. The speaker demonstrates each pose effortlessly while explaining it clearly. Her words and movements are perfectly coordinated, and she explains each pose extemporaneously while maintaining excellent eye contact with the audience. In addition to making for an entertaining demonstration, this reflects the speaker's careful preparation and enhances her credibility.

Conclusion: The speaker begins paragraph 11 with a signal that she is moving into the conclusion. She reinforces the central idea in the second sentence of paragraph 11 and in paragraph 12, where she quotes Donna Farhi, author of five books on yoga. She ends in paragraph 13 with a simple "Thank you." This is not always recommended as the best way to finish a speech, but it works in this case because of the speaker's delivery, which reflects her enthusiasm about the topic and the opportunity to share it with her audience.

Sign Language

1   [The speaker begins by using Signed English to express the words, "You are my friend."] Do you know what I just told you? The message I communicated probably escaped most of you. Communication through hand motions is something we do all the time without even thinking about it. For most of us, it's a supplement to spoken language. But for many deaf and hearing-impaired people, sign language isn't just a supplement, it's a primary mode of communication.

2   I'm not an expert in sign language, but I've been interested in it for several years. My father is the treasurer for a group of deaf and hearing-impaired people, and I've attended some functions with that group. At those times, I had a chance to learn bits and pieces of sign language. I also had the chance to learn more in researching for this speech.

3   In the speech, I'd like to first give you a bit of background about sign language. Then I'd like to teach you how to sign one important sentence, the one I started with: "You are my friend." By sharing this sentence with you, I hope to help you realize that sign language is just as expressive as spoken language. Let's start with a little background.

4   There are two broad categories of sign language used in America. One is Signed English, and the other is American Sign Language. Both use most of the same hand gestures. Signed English usually uses one hand gesture for each spoken word and presents the signs in the same order as the spoken words. On the other hand, American Sign Language—also called ASL—doesn't always have exactly one sign for each spoken word, and might present them in a different order. This distinction will become clear during the demonstration.

5   No one knows exactly how many people use sign language as their primary language today. The National Center for Health Statistics estimates that about 20 million Americans have some sort of hearing impairment. Depending on the exact definition of "deafness," about half a million to 2 million of these people are deaf. Most sources agree that American Sign Language is the fourth most used language in the United States today, after English, Spanish, and French.

6   Some people think that sign language is a primitive substitute for spoken language, but in fact sign language is just as rich and expressive as spoken language. For example, Karen Nakamura states in the online *Deaf Resources Library* that American Sign Language "should not be considered in any way to be a broken, mimed, or gestural form of English." According to Nakamura, ASL is a complex, full, and natural language in its own right, with "its own beautiful grammar."

7   Keeping these points in mind about sign language, let's return to the sentence I started with and see if we can learn the signs for "You are my friend." [At this point, the speaker begins her demonstration of how to sign, "You are my friend." Each of the signs she discusses in paragraphs 7–13 is accompanied by a demonstration that explains the steps in making the sign.]

8   First, make the sign for "you" with your right hand. Extend your index finger and point at a classmate.

9   The word "are" is interesting because it starts with the letter "R." To make the sign for the letter "R," extend your index finger and wrap your next finger around it. This is the sign for the letter "R." Now we're going to make the word "are." Just put your fingertips under your chin and arc outward.

10   "My" is easy. It's just an open right hand. Put your palm inward on your chest.

11   "Friend" is a little trickier. It takes both hands. Extend your index finger on each hand, with your fingers folded down. And now bend each index finger. Now you're going to hook them together, hanging the back and knuckles of your right hand outward from your left hand. And now reverse, with the back and knuckles of your left hand hanging outward from your right hand.

12   Now please tell a classmate these four signs slowly: "You are my friend." And now try to sign the whole sentence quickly: "You are my friend."

13   What you just learned was Signed English. In American Sign Language, the word "are" is generally implied, so you wouldn't need to use it. The sentence in ASL would usually just be "You're my friend."

14   In closing, I hope you learned that sign language is just as expressive as spoken language. Think back to the way we signed "friend." That sign isn't an arbitrary combination of empty symbols. It's a visual depiction of the way friends really are—interdependent, interlocked. In addition to learning how to sign the sentence "You are my friend," I hope you'll also take away from this speech a new appreciation for the complexities of sign language.

Sign Language

Commentary

A first-rate informative speech, "Sign Language" illustrates how a speaker can use a demonstration, as well as audience participation, to communicate ideas and to get listeners involved in the speech. Here is a synopsis.

Specific Purpose: To inform my audience about the richness of sign language and the steps involved in signing a simple sentence.

Central Idea: By learning how to sign a simple sentence, we can see that sign language is just as expressive as spoken language.

Method of Organization: Topical

Introduction: The introduction consists of the first three paragraphs. The speaker gains the audience's attention in paragraph 1 by making a series of gestures while she remains silent. Doing so arouses the curiosity of the audience, a move that the speaker reinforces by asking, "Do you know what I just told you?" After noting that, for most people, gestural communication is a supplement to spoken language, the speaker ends paragraph 1 by revealing that the topic of her speech is the use of sign language by deaf and hearing-impaired people.

Paragraph 2 provides an excellent example of how classroom speakers can establish their credibility. After acknowledging that she is not an expert on sign language, the speaker explains that she has long been interested in the topic as a result of her interaction with a group of deaf and hearing-impaired people, that she learned some sign language from this group, and that she has done further research on the topic. The fact that she cares about the subject and seems qualified to talk about it further boosts audience interest at this early stage of the speech.

Paragraph 3 begins with a concise preview statement of the two main points to be discussed in the body of the speech. The speaker then states her central idea: that sign language is just as expressive as spoken speech. She will reinforce this idea by restating it again in the body of the speech and in the conclusion. An excellent signpost—"Let's start with a little background"—completes the introduction and provides a bridge to the body of the speech.

Body: The first main point in the body provides background information about the two types of sign language used in the United States. In paragraph 4, the speaker identifies those types as Signed English and American Sign Language. In paragraph 5, she uses figures from the National Center for Health Statistics to show the number of Americans with hearing impairments and to document the fact that American Sign Language is the fourth most used language in the United States. In paragraph 6, she uses expert testimony to emphasize the richness and complexity of sign language. In keeping with the guidelines for using supporting materials, she identifies the source of her testimony (Karen Nakamura) and where the testimony was obtained (the online *Deaf Resources Library*).

In her second main point, the speaker demonstrates how to sign the sentence "You are my friend" (paragraphs 7–13). Because of the speaker's demonstration, this speech is highly instructive for illustrating the interaction of language and physical action. Based on words alone, the speaker's explanation in paragraphs 7–13 is as clear as it can be. But the effectiveness of the explanation increases dramatically once the speaker's physical demonstration is added to her words.

Conclusion: The speaker concludes in paragraph 14. She begins by re-emphasizing her central idea that sign language is just as expressive as spoken English. Once again, she supplements her verbal message with physical action—this time when showing the manner in which the sign for "friends" depicts visually the interlocked and interdependent nature of true friends. She ends by noting that she hopes her audience has gained a fuller appreciation of the complexities of sign language in addition to learning how to sign "You are my friend." Here, as elsewhere, the speaker does an excellent job of connecting her specific demonstration to a larger set of ideas about the nature and importance of sign language.

Securing Yourself Online
Needs Improvement Version

---

1   Okay, ready? How much do you know about computer security problems? They're really serious, especially for college students like us. You wouldn't believe how many computers are infected and compromised.

2   I've always been interested in computers, and I use mine all the time. So today I'm going to talk about computer safety and explain some things you can do to secure yourself when you're online.

3   First, you should use a strong password. What makes a strong password? Take a look at this example. Okay, that's it. Here's the right one. This is a long password, which is good. You need lots of characters. All my sources say this will help keep you safe.

4   Using a secure connection is important, too. That means your connection is encrypted. How do you know if your connection is secure? Here are two screen shots I copied from my computer. This one shows a secure connection. It says *https* at the top. You may not be able to see it, but it will keep you safe.

5   Here's an insecure connection. As you can see, it doesn't have an *s*—there, after the *http*.

6   It also helps to double check links before you click them. Sometimes you get e-mails like this one from your bank or someone pretending to be your bank. But the e-mail is not really from your bank; it's from a hacker who wants your financial information. If you check this out before clicking on the link, you can save yourself a lot of trouble and also maybe a lot of money.

7   So, I guess that's it. Protecting yourself online is extremely important in today's world. I hope you know more about this as a result of my speech.

Securing Yourself Online
Needs Improvement Version

Commentary

The needs improvement and final versions of "Securing Yourself Online" can help students understand the difference between a weak speech and a strong one. When analyzing the speech, have students focus on the speaker's organization, development of ideas, delivery, and use of visual aids. Follow with a brief class discussion about each of these aspects of the speech. Then show the final version of the speech. Again have students focus on the speaker's organization, development of ideas, delivery, and use of visual aids. Follow with a class discussion that compares and contrasts the two versions of the speech and explores why the final version is superior.

Both versions of the speech are available on the DVD of student speeches that accompanies this edition of *The Art of Public Speaking*. The text of the final version, followed by an analysis, is printed on pages 299–302 of this manual. Here is a synopsis of the needs improvement version.

Introduction: The introduction consists of paragraphs 1–2 and shows how not to begin a speech. Rather than approaching the lectern confidently and establishing eye contact with his audience before starting to talk, the speaker keeps his head down, pulls his speaking notes out of his back pocket, and starts talking before making sure the audience is paying attention. His opening words—"Okay, ready"—do not provide an attention-getter.

The speaker makes an effort to relate the topic to his audience by noting that computer security problems are "really serious, especially for college students." The statement is true, but it would be more effective—as in the final version—if it were buttressed by supporting materials showing how serious the problems are.

In paragraph 2, the speaker says he is interested in computers and uses his all the time. This is not enough, however, to establish his credibility on the topic of online security, which requires specialized knowledge beyond that of the typical computer user. The preview statement at the end of paragraph 2 is perhaps the most effective part of the introduction, but it would have been stronger had the speaker stated exactly what points he was going to discuss in the body.

Body: The body consists of paragraphs 3–6, in which the speaker develops three main points. The points are arranged in topical order, and it is easy to follow the speaker from point to point. His problems are less with organization than with the development and explanation of his ideas. The main points are underdeveloped, his visual aids are poorly designed, and his delivery is not strong enough to boost his credibility or to get the audience engaged in the speech.

The first main point, discussing the importance of having a strong password, is presented in paragraph three. Unfortunately, the speaker's PowerPoint slide is almost impossible to read. The composition of the slide, the color scheme, the choice of font, the unnecessary use of clip art, and the speaker's confusion about which slide he is display-ing make this a textbook example of how not to use PowerPoint. The problem is com-pounded by the speaker's failure to provide an adequate explanation of the slide. He states that a strong password should contain "lots of characters," but he does not indi-cate how many characters that might be. Nor does he cite any sources that support the importance of a strong password.

The second main point of the body consists of paragraphs 4–5 and focuses on the need for students to use a secure connection when they are online. Again, the speaker il-lustrates with PowerPoint. And again he does so badly. The slides are too small and too cluttered to communicate his point. Moreover, as in main point one, he again fails to pro-vide a satisfactory explanation of his slide.

In paragraph 6, the speaker presents his third main point, which stresses the im-portance of double checking links before clicking on them. This is important information, but the speaker does not explain it clearly, and his PowerPoint slide is too small to be seen clearly. In contrast, the final version of the speech uses two large, well-designed slides in this section, and the speaker goes through his points step by step to make sure the audience understands them.

Conclusion: The speech concludes in paragraph 7 and reinforces the perception that the speaker is not fully prepared. Not only is the content weak, but the delivery is halting and tenta-tive. Because the speaker forgot to exit from the PowerPoint slide he displayed in main point three, that slide is still on display during his conclusion. He discovers his error as he is leaving the lectern, and he dashes back to turn off the slide, but because he did not in-sert a blank slide at the end of his presentation, he cannot clear the screen before return-ing to his seat.

Securing Yourself Online
Final Version

---

1   You are at risk. All of us are at risk. I'm not talking about STDs, global warming, or terrorism. I'm talking about your life online. You're at risk of having your computer taken over so that perfect strangers can read your e-mail, access your bank accounts, pilfer your credit card numbers, and even steal your identity.

2   I've seen this over and over again at my summer job as a computer technician at a nationwide computer store. You wouldn't believe how many computers are compromised and infected.

3   As college students, we're particularly vulnerable because we spend so much time online. According to David Tatar, manager of Wisconsin's Consumer Office of Privacy Protection, 32 percent of all identity theft claims are filed by people between the ages of 18 and 29 years old. That's the largest percentage of any age group.

4   Today I'd like to explain three steps that experts recommend for online security—using strong passwords, using secure connections, and double checking links before clicking on them.

5   Step one: The first step is using strong passwords—for e-mail accounts, bank accounts, and everything else that you do online. What makes a strong password? Take a look at this example: *IwbiP;;4387-CSamFF*. Now this is a long password, but that's part of its strength. The first criterion of a strong password is having 10 characters; 15 or more is even better—like the one I showed you. It should also include uppercase and lowercase letters, numbers, and punctuation such as semicolons, hyphens, and underscores.

6   According to Microsoft's online guide to creating strong passwords, when your passwords contain long combinations of seemingly random letters, numbers, and punctuation, your security increases exponentially—meaning that a password like the one I showed you is literally billions of times more secure than something short and ordinary like *hot dog* or *college*.

7   In addition to having a strong password, you should use a secure connection whenever possible. How do you know if a connection is secure or insecure? Here's an insecure connection. If you look at the address bar, you'll see the first letters are *http*—highlighted here with the red arrow. Whenever you see *http* in a Web site address, your connection is not secure. It's fine to read Web sites with this kind of connection, but you should never transmit sensitive information over *http*. When the connection is secure, it will begin with *https*—as in this example. Think of the *s* as standing for safe or secure.

8   So far we've seen the importance of having a strong password and of using secure connections whenever transmitting sensitive data. The third step is double checking links before you click them. This is a little more involved than the previous steps, but it's just as important.

9   For example, here's an e-mail that was supposedly sent from my bank, Franklin Bank. It tells me that I need to click on the blue link in order to update my account information. But if we take a closer look, we can see that while the link says *BankFranklin.com*, the actual destination is another site entirely. If I hold my cursor over the link for a second or two without clicking on it, the yellow box that pops up will show the real Web site—not Franklin Bank, but something called *ssedu.org.cn/dede*.

10   This looks like it might be my bank's information, but it's not. It's a fraudulent Web site run by a hacker who's trying to gain access to my financial information. By double checking potentially questionable links before you click on them, you can avoid scams like this one.

11   What do you do if the e-mail link doesn't match the one your cursor reveals? The answer is: Don't click. It's as simple as that.

12   At the beginning of this speech I said that you're at risk. And that's true. But you're not helpless. I've shared three proven ways to protect yourself—strong passwords, secure connections, and double checking links. I hope you'll find this information helpful as you fight this endless battle for online security.

Securing Yourself Online
Final Version

Commentary

The final version of "Securing Yourself Online" provides a good example of an informative speech on a technical topic. Better prepared than the needs improvement version, it explains key concepts clearly and uses visual aids to maximum advantage. By showing it after the needs improvement version, you can help students grasp the principles of informative speaking discussed in Chapter 15.

Both versions are available on the DVD of student speeches that accompanies this edition of *The Art of Public Speaking*. For text and commentary on the needs improvement version, see pages 296–298 of this manual. Below is a synopsis of the final version.

Specific Purpose: To inform my audience about three steps for protecting themselves online.

Central Idea: Using strong passwords, using secure connections, and double checking links are three ways for college students to keep themselves safe online.

Method of Organization: Topical

Introduction: The introduction consists of paragraphs 1–4 and fulfills all the major objectives of an introduction discussed in Chapter 10.

In paragraph 1, the speaker gains his listeners' attention with the startling statement, "You are at risk." He then explains that he is referring to the dangers they face when using their computers. He relates the topic directly to the audience both by mentioning the specific dangers they face and by personalizing those dangers with the use of "you" and "your."

The speaker establishes his credibility in paragraph 2 by referring to his job as a computer technician at a nationwide computer store. In paragraph 3, he cites David Tatar, manager of Wisconsin's Consumer Office of Privacy Protection, to document how serious an issue computer security is for people of college age. In paragraph 4, he presents a concise preview of the main points he will cover in the body.

It is also worth contrasting the speaker's nonverbal behavior in this version with that in the needs improvement version. Rather than rushing to the lectern and starting his speech with "Okay, ready," he gives himself time to get set, establishes eye contact with the audience, and makes sure they are paying attention before he starts to talk. Despite being nervous, he does his best to appear calm and confident, which in turn boosts his confidence by getting his speech off to a good start.

Body: The body of the speech runs from paragraph 5 through paragraph 11 and presents three steps students can take to make themselves more secure online: using strong passwords, using secure connections, and double checking links before clicking on them.

The first point is developed in paragraphs 5–6. As in the needs improvement version, the speaker uses a PowerPoint slide to illustrate the traits of a strong password, but in this version the slide is readable and the speaker presents it without fumbling. Also unlike the needs improvement version, he cites testimony from Microsoft to document how important a strong password is to maintaining personal security online.

The speaker presents his second main point in paragraph 7. He illustrates the difference between secure and insecure connections with two excellent PowerPoint slides, both of which zoom in on essential information and fade unnecessary details into the background. A bright red arrow directs attention exactly where the speaker wants it.

The third main point—double checking links before clicking on them—is presented in paragraphs 8–11. The speaker does an excellent job of explaining this point in conjunction with his PowerPoint slides. The slides are clear and simple, but they reflect a great deal of time and thought on the speaker's part.

The clarity of the speech is enhanced by the speaker's use of connectives throughout the body to help listeners keep track of his ideas. Paragraph 5 begins with a signpost ("Step one") followed by a clear statement of main point one. Paragraph 7 opens with a transition from the first main point to the second. Paragraph 8 begins with an internal preview, followed by a transition to the speaker's third main point. The speaker also uses questions as signposts: "What makes a strong password?" (paragraph 5) and "How do you know if a connection is secure or insecure? (paragraph 7). As noted in Chapter 9, such questions invite subliminal answers and help get the audience more involved with the speech.

Conclusion: The conclusion (paragraph 12) signals the end of the speech and reinforces the central idea. By referring back to the introduction, the speaker provides a sense of psychological unity. By restating his main points, he reminds the audience of the key ideas he wants them to remember. The final sentence is not overly dramatic, but it ends the speech on a strong note by reiterating the importance of the struggle for online security.

Like the rest of the speech, the conclusion relates the speaker's ideas directly to the audience with the use of "you" and "your." As explained in Chapter 15, this is an excellent way to personalize ideas in any informative speech, but it can be especially valuable when dealing with a technical topic. In addition to its other virtues, "Securing Yourself Online" shows how speakers can explore technical subjects in clear, nontechnical language.

Delivery: The speaker's delivery is much better in the final version than in the needs improvement version. He is nervous, but he fights through his nerves and keeps his composure throughout. Because he is more fully prepared, he has stronger command of the material, is more poised and confident, and does a better job presenting his visual aids. At times, he is more tied to his note cards than would be ideal, but for the most part he talks in a conversational tone and maintains eye contact with the audience.

The Hidden World of Chili Peppers
Needs Improvement Version

---

1   Okay. Chili peppers can be incredibly hot, but they're still one of my favorite things to eat. Whether it's Mexican food, Thai food, or plain old Texas chili, the spicier the better in my view. So when thinking about a speech topic, I thought it'd be a really neat idea to do it on chili peppers.

2   Chili peppers have been around for thousands of years. Their scientific name is *capsicum*—I think that's how it's pronounced. They're different from black peppers, which come from Asia. Chili peppers come from South America. In fact, as you can see from this map, they began somewhere around Bolivia or Brazil. They spread everywhere else after Columbus came to the New World.

3   The pleasure and pain of eating chili peppers comes from a chemical called caps, caps, capsaicin—something like that. Here's a chili pepper that I cut in half. I know it's kind of small, you can't see it, but there are these veins and seeds in there. And that's where the capsaicin is held. That's where all the heat is.

4   As one of the books I read said, there are two ways to measure the heat of a chili pepper. The HPLC method is more scientific, so scientists prefer to use it.

5   This guy that I held up is an orange habanero pepper, and if you eat it, it'll burn your mouth up.

6   So if you do eat a hot pepper, don't try rinsing out your mouth with water. Instead drink some milk or eat some yogurt or some other stuff like that. Milk also helps if you burn your skin from contacting with a pepper.

7   If you're attacked by a mugger or a robber, you can protect yourself by using a pepper spray. The spray burns the eyes and skin and gives you enough time to escape.

8   According to Jack Challem, chili peppers also have lots of medical benefits. They're used to reduce arthritis pain, to help with indigestion, and cure baldness.

9   Um, well, I guess that's all I have to say about chili peppers. Can you imagine life without chili peppers? I know I can't. So, thank you.

The Hidden World of Chili Peppers
Needs Improvement Version

Commentary

When showing the needs improvement version of "The Hidden World of Chili Peppers," have students focus on the speaker's organization, development of ideas, delivery, and use of visual aids. Follow with a brief class discussion about each of these aspects of the speech. Then show the final version of the speech. Again, have students focus on the speaker's organization, development of ideas, delivery, and use of visual aids. Follow with a class discussion that compares and contrasts the two versions of the speech and explores why the final version is superior.

Video of both versions of the speech is available on the DVD of student speeches that accompanies this edition of *The Art of Public Speaking*. For the text and a detailed discussion of the final version, see pages 308–311 of this manual. Below is a synopsis of the needs improvement version.

Organization: The introduction consists of paragraph 1. The speaker does a good job revealing the topic, but he fails to relate it to his audience, noting only that chili peppers are one of his favorite foods and are therefore a topic of interest to him. Nor does he establish his credibility. Presumably his interest in the subject has led him to do research on it in preparation for the speech, but there is no mention of it in the introduction. The introduction also lacks a preview statement of the main points that will be covered in the body of the speech.

In discussing this introduction, it is also worth noting the speaker's opening word: "Okay." This may reflect a degree of stage fright, or perhaps simply be a symptom of the fact that he is not fully prepared. In either case, it provides an instructive example of how not to begin a speech. As discussed in Chapter 13, speakers should approach the lectern in a poised, confident manner despite the nervousness they may be feeling inside. They should have their notes arranged just as they want them, they should establish eye contact with the audience, and they should not begin with words such as "Okay," "I'm really nervous today," or "I'm afraid I don't have a lot to say on this topic." As students work on their speeches early in the term, remind them to spend a little time rehearsing how they will behave once they arrive at the lectern. It is one of the easiest things they can do to help get off to a strong start.

The body of the speech is organized in topical order. The first main point deals with the history of chili peppers (paragraph 2), the second with the reasons why some chili peppers are so hot (paragraphs 3–5), the third with how to counteract the effects of a too-hot pepper (paragraph 6), and the fourth with nonculinary uses of chili peppers (paragraphs 7–8). These are the same main points as in the final version of the speech, but they are much less effective in this version. One reason, as we shall see shortly, is that the ideas are woefully underdeveloped. Another reason is that the main points are not clearly stated in the speech and the speaker does not provide connectives to help the audience follow him from point to point. As a result, there is an almost random quality to the progression of ideas in the body, unlike the final version of the speech, in which the main points emerge crisply and clearly.

The speaker concludes in paragraph 9. He begins the conclusion by saying, "Um, well, I guess that's all I have to say about chili peppers." Two sentences later he ends the conclusion weakly by stating, almost as an afterthought, "So, thank you." As in other parts of the speech, there are some positive aspects to the conclusion, but the overall impression is of a speaker who has not prepared as fully as he should have.

Development of Ideas: The most important ingredient in a good speech is having something to say. It is clear from the final version of "The Hidden World of Chili Peppers" that there is a great deal to say about this subject. In contrast, the needs improvement version skips along the surface of ideas and does not provide sufficient supporting materials for any of its four main points.

In main point one, for example, the speaker touches lightly on the differences between black pepper and chili peppers, but he does not provide the technical name for black pepper and he botches the pronunciation of *capsicum*, the scientific name for chili peppers. He states that chili peppers spread to the rest of the globe after Columbus came to the New World, but he does not provide any of the details found in the final version of the speech. Equally important, the needs improvement version does not cite the sources of the speaker's information, leaving the audience with questions about its reliability.

As in the first main point, the second main point is developed much more fully in the final version than in the needs improvement version. Indeed, while the needs improvement version states that there are two methods of measuring the heat of a chili pepper, the speaker identifies only one of them—the HPLC method—and he does not explain how this method works. In contrast, the final version explains both methods fully and clearly. The same lack of development is evident in the needs improvement version's discussion of the orange habanero pepper.

Main point three deals with one of the questions people invariably have about chili peppers—what to do if one eats a too-hot pepper. This was an excellent item to include in the speech, and the information about it in the needs improvement version is fundamentally accurate. Again, however, it is cursory in comparison to the final version, which explains both what to do and why dairy products are more effective than water in counteracting the heat of a chili pepper. The final version is also more credible because the speaker identifies the sources of his information. There is no way of knowing from the needs improvement version whether the speaker's information is accurate.

The fourth main point continues the pattern we have seen in the first three main points. The needs improvement version is less developed and less credible than the final version. Unlike main point three, main point four does identify a source for the speaker's information—Jack Challem—but it does not explain who Challem is or why his ideas should be taken seriously. The needs improvement version also implies that it is a matter of scientific fact that chili peppers can be used to cure baldness, while the final version explains that this is only a hypothesis stemming from preliminary research.

Delivery: While the speaker in the needs improvement version has done some rehearsal for the speech, it is clear that he has not rehearsed enough. He speaks personably and extemporaneously, and he usually has good eye contact with the audience. These are all commendatory. At the same time, the speaker often seems unsure where he is in the speech and has to rearrange his note cards to get them in the proper order as he moves from point to point. In paragraph 2, he is unsure how to pronounce the word capsicum and in paragraph 3 he stumbles over "capsaicin," the chemical responsible for the heat in chili peppers. These are technical terms, and someone running across them for the first time might struggle to find the right pronunciation. However, audiences expect speakers to be fully enough prepared to handle whatever technical terms they include in the speech.

The speaker's body language in the needs improvement version is also much less effective than in the final version. He does not establish a strong physical presence in the needs improvement version, he does not handle his note cards as well as in the final version, and his gestures are less confident and purposeful. All in all, the delivery of the needs improvement version does not convey the sense of a fully prepared speaker in full command of his information.

Visual Aids: As with many informative speeches, "The Hidden World of Chili Peppers" needs visual aids to help communicate the speaker's ideas. To his credit, the speaker in the needs improvement version recognizes this and incorporates several visual aids into his presentation. Unfortunately, he does not use them nearly as well as he might have.

In paragraph 2, for example, he uses PowerPoint to show a map of South America, but he displays the map against a "fireworks" background, which distracts the viewer's eye from the map. Also, the map is too small, is confined to the lower left-hand corner of the screen, and the speaker does not specify which part of the map he is referring to. In paragraph 3, the speaker uses the same distracting background when he displays the word "capsaicin," and he has trouble operating the slides smoothly. In comparison, the speaker has complete control of his slides in the final version. They are large enough to be seen clearly throughout the room; the information is centered on the screen and is presented against a nondistracting background; and the speaker has rehearsed to make sure the PowerPoint slides are perfectly timed with his words.

Another difference between the two speeches revolves around the speaker's decision of what visual aids to use and when to incorporate them into the speech. In the needs improvement version, he does not use visual aids to help clarify his explanation in paragraph 4 of how to measure the heat of a chili. Contrast this with his adroit use of visual aids in the same section of the final version. The use of visual aids here is crucial to explaining technical information about Scoville Heat Units and the High Performance Liquid Chromatography Test for measuring the heat of a chili pepper.

On the other hand, there is no need for a visual aid when the speaker states that consuming a dairy product such as milk or yogurt is the best way to reduce the burning sensation caused by a hot pepper. The PowerPoint slide showing a glass of milk and a container of yogurt in the needs improvement version is superfluous. Moreover, the speaker forgets to take the slide off the screen when he is finished with it, thereby distracting the audience's attention from his next point.

The speaker also has trouble in paragraph 3 when he holds up an orange habanero pepper cut in half. Introducing a visual aid by saying "I know this is too small for you to see" is a sure sign that the speaker should look for a different kind of visual aid—which is what he does in the final version of this speech. Instead of cutting an orange habanero in half to show its veins and seeds, he uses PowerPoint to display a photograph in which the veins and seeds are clearly visible.

The speaker does display an orange habanero in the final version of this speech, but when he does so it is simply to show how small and unimposing the habanero is notwithstanding its status as the hottest pepper on record. He also holds it by the stem to emphasize the fact that people can have an allergic reaction simply from touching the outside of the pepper. In this case, a photograph would not work nearly as well; showing the actual pepper is appropriate for the speaker's point and adds visual interest to the speech.

The Hidden World of Chili Peppers
Final Version

---

1   Imagine your mouth burning like wildfire, your eyes squirting out uncontrollable tears, and your face red and sweating profusely. Are you sick? No, you just took a bite of a screaming hot chili pepper. Congratulations. You're partaking in a worldwide tradition that has been spicing up lives and diets for thousands of years.

2   My own desire for spicy meals led me to investigate why I get red in the face and salivate over the mere thought of eating a spicy chili. In the process, I've discovered there's a lot more to chili peppers than I'd ever imagined. Today I'd like to share with you what I've learned about the history of chili peppers, why they can be so spicy, what to do if you eat a too-hot pepper, and some of the ways peppers are used other than in foods.

3   The chili pepper has a long and fascinating history. Its scientific name is *Capsicum*. This is different from the common black pepper you have on your dining room table, whose scientific name is *Piper nigrum*. Black pepper was first cultivated in Asia and was prized in the West as early as the Roman Empire. In contrast, the chili pepper originated more than 5,000 years ago in South America, near what is today Bolivia and Brazil. Over time, it spread to Mexico, Central America, and the Caribbean.

4   But it wasn't until Columbus came in the 1490s that the chili pepper became known to the rest of the world. As stated in *The Cambridge World History of Food*, within fifty years after Columbus returned to Spain with sample plants, chili peppers could be found growing in coastal areas from Africa to Asia. From there, they spread inland, until they took hold of the taste buds of people around the globe. Today they're most widely used in Mexico, Central and South America, Africa, Asia, the Balkans, and the United States. Carolyn Dille and Susan Belsinger, authors of *The Chili Pepper Book*, estimate that 25 percent of the world's adult population uses chili peppers as a part of their daily diet.

5   Now that we know a little bit about the history of chili peppers, let's see why they can put such a fire in our belly. The pleasure and pain involved in eating chili peppers comes from a chemical called capsaicin. Capsaicin is concentrated in the pepper's veins and seeds. To enjoy the flavor of a chili pepper without burning your stomach or mouth, avoid the veins and seeds when cooking or eating them.

6   P. W. Bosland tells us in the book *Spices, Herbs, and Edible Fungi* that chili pepper intensity is measured in two ways. The first was developed by Wilbur L. Scoville in 1912. This method uses trained testers to measure chili peppers in Scoville Heat Units. These range from zero to 300,000. According to Bosland, this test is subjective because it relies on the individual tester's sensitivity to capsaicin.

7   The second, more widely used test is called the High Performance Liquid Chromatography test, more commonly known as HPLC. This is also measured in Scoville Heat Units, but it's more objective. The chili pods are dried and ground, and then the chemicals responsible for the heat are analyzed and rated according to pungency.

8   The hottest pepper on record is the deceptively small and unimposing orange habancro pepper. It's been rated as high as 300,000 Scoville Heat Units, and it's so powerful that some people have an allergic reaction just by touching it, which is why I'm holding it by the stem. The mildest pepper is the standard green bell, which you see at the grocery store everyday. It's been rated at zero Scoville Heat Units.

9   If you eat an orange habanero pepper, it's important to know how to deal with the burning sensation. Whatever you do, do not rinse your mouth with water. Dave DeWitt in *The Chili Pepper Encyclopedia* tells us capsaicin is not soluble in water. And even if you drink a gallon of ice water, it's not going to help. According to the Chili Pepper Institute at New Mexico State University, the best solution is to consume a dairy product such as milk or yogurt, which contain a substance that strips away capsaicin from the interior cells of your mouth. This is why some hot foods, like Indian foods, are served with yogurt sauce.

10   If you burn your skin, the Institute recommends cleaning the area with rubbing alcohol and then soaking it with milk. Above all, remember two things: First, always wear gloves when you cut a hot pepper such as a habanero. Second, never rub your eyes when working with hot chili peppers.

11   Although chili peppers are prized above all for the flavor they add to food, they have other benefits as well. Pepper sprays have become a standard weapon for the personal protection of individuals and law-enforcement agencies. The *New York Times* reports that sales of pepper sprays have risen steadily and show no sign of slowing.

12   Chili peppers are also valued for their medicinal properties. According to Jack Challem, author of *The Nutrition Reporter*, there have been more than 1,300 medical studies on capsaicin, the active ingredient in peppers. Moderate doses have been proved to aid digestion, reduce hypertension, improve circulation, and help dissolve blood clots. Preliminary research by Professor Kenji Okajima at Japan's Kumamato University School of Medicine suggests that a combination of chili peppers and soybeans can promote hair growth and might hold promise as a cure for baldness.

13   In closing, it's difficult to imagine our lives without the spice added by chili peppers. From their origins in South America to their current popularity around the world, peppers have been used not only to flavor our food but also to improve our health and personal safety. While it remains to be seen whether or not chili peppers can actually cure baldness, we can be sure this ancient plant will continue to find new uses in our modern age.

The Hidden World of Chili Peppers
Final Version

Commentary

Clear, well-supported, and sharply organized, the final version of "The Hidden World of Chili Peppers" is a good model of the guidelines for informative speaking presented in Chapter 15. Both it and the needs improvement version are available on the DVD of student speeches that accompanies this edition of *The Art of Public Speaking*. You'll find the text and discussion of the needs improvement version on pages 303–307 of this manual. Here is a brief synopsis of the final version.

Specific Purpose: To inform my audience about the history of chili peppers, why they can be so spicy, strategies for dealing with a too-hot pepper, and some of the nonculinary uses of peppers.

Central Idea: There is much more to chili peppers than most people imagine.

Method of Organization: Topical

Introduction: The introduction consists of paragraphs 1 and 2. The first paragraph uses several methods to gain attention and interest. The vivid description of sentence one is followed by a question that arouses curiosity about the subject of the speech. The third sentence reveals that the speaker is discussing chili peppers, while the final sentence suggests that the topic is important because of the long use of chili peppers by people around the globe. This paragraph also relates the topic directly to the audience by using the words "you" or "your" six times.

The second paragraph establishes the speaker's credibility and indicates that there is much more to the subject of chili peppers than most people might imagine. The paragraph ends with a succinct preview statement that provides a strong lead-in to the body of the speech.

Body: Arranged in topical order, the body of the speech consists of four main points. The first main point is developed in paragraphs 3–4 and explains the history of chili peppers. Noting the differences between black pepper, which originated in Asia, and chili peppers, which originated in South America, the speaker explains how chili peppers spread around the globe after Columbus came to the New World. Because the speaker is not an expert on chili peppers, he is careful to identify the sources of his information.

A transition at the beginning of paragraph 5 alerts the audience that the speaker is moving into his second main point, in which he explains why chili peppers affect people as they do (paragraphs 5–8). In paragraph 5, he points out that the pleasure and pain involved in eating chili peppers comes from a chemical called capsaicin, which is concentrated in a pepper's veins and seeds. Paragraphs 6 and 7 look at the two major methods of measuring the intensity of a chili pepper.

Although the information in paragraphs 5–7 is technical in nature, the speaker explains it clearly and with a minimum of technical language. When he cannot avoid technical language, he uses visual aids to make sure the audience understands terms such as "capsaicin," "Scoville Heat Units," and "High Performance Liquid Chromatography." As can be seen from the video of the speech, the visual aids are well-designed and are perfectly timed with the speaker's words. This is also true of the visual aids in other parts of the speech.

In paragraph 8, the speaker focuses primarily on the orange habanero. This pepper, he states, is so hot that some people have an allergic reaction just from touching it. As he discusses the orange habanero, the speaker holds one by the stem so the audience can see just how small and unimposing it is. He then contrasts it with the standard green bell pepper that we see in the grocery store every day. Although it might seem to be a minor matter, the speaker's use of the peppers as visual aids makes his discussion much more interesting than it would have been otherwise.

The speaker develops his third main point in paragraphs 9–10, which explain how to deal with the effects of eating or handling a too-hot pepper. As in the rest of his presentation, the speaker relies on expert sources and covers his points clearly and concisely. Not only does the speaker explain what to do in dealing with a hot pepper, he also explains why rinsing one's mouth with water is less effective than consuming a dairy product such as milk or yogurt. This kind of detail provides depth and texture that goes beyond the level of an ordinary informative speech and leaves the audience feeling that they have truly learned something new.

Paragraphs 11–12 constitute the fourth main point and discuss the nonculinary uses of chili peppers. Paragraph 11 deals with the use of pepper sprays for self-defense by individuals and law-enforcement agencies. Paragraph 12 focuses on the medicinal properties of chili peppers. By citing Jack Challem, author of *The Nutrition Reporter*, on the number of medical studies conducted on capsaicin, the speaker establishes the credibility of his information. In addition to noting that moderate doses of chili peppers can be used for such purposes as aiding digestion and improving circulation, he mentions the intriguing possibility that a combination of chili peppers and soybeans might hold promise as a cure for baldness

Conclusion: The conclusion consists of the final paragraph. After summarizing his main points, the speaker ends by stating that whether or not chili peppers actually prove to be a cure for baldness, they will doubtless continue to be used in new ways as time goes by. The tone of the final sentence is just right for a speech on this subject and brings it to a successful end.

All in all, "The Hidden World of Chili Peppers" illustrates how students can produce an interesting and highly informative speech on a seemingly ordinary topic. The speaker's enthusiasm, knowledge of the subject, fascinating supporting materials, extemporaneous delivery, and adroit use of visual aids combine to produce a top-notch presentation.

Acupuncture: New Uses for an Ancient Remedy

1   Six months ago, my 78-year-old grandmother was quickly losing her independence. Severe arthritis in both knees hampered her ability to take care of herself. Shopping, getting around the neighborhood, even walking down her front steps was becoming almost impossible. Pain medications helped somewhat, but the side effects created their own problems.

2   Then her doctor suggested acupuncture. My grandmother was skeptical at first, but she was willing to try just about anything. She did, and the results were miraculous. After six weeks, her pain and stiffness were significantly reduced, she was able to take care of her apartment again, she could get out on her own to go shopping, to visit friends and family, and to do the other things her arthritis had prevented in the past. Acupuncture restored her quality of life and her independence.

3   My grandmother's story is not unique. Performed for well over 2,000 years in China and other parts of Asia, acupuncture is becoming more and more popular in the U.S. and other Western countries for one simple reason—it works. Impressed by my grandmother's experience, I began acupuncture treatments for my migraine headaches, and now my headaches are completely gone.

4   Not surprisingly, I wanted to learn more about this treatment that produced such miraculous results for both my grandmother and myself. Today I will share part of what I have learned by explaining what happens when you receive an acupuncture treatment, how acupuncture works, the kinds of medical conditions that can be treated by acupuncture, and the growing use of acupuncture in combination with Western medical techniques. Let's start by looking at a typical acupuncture treatment.

5   Acupuncture is the insertion of needles into the skin to achieve a balanced flow of energy, which in turn restores and preserves health. To prevent any chance of contamination from one person to another, acupuncturists in the U.S. use sterilized needles that are individually packaged and are disposed of after a single use.

6   I realize that the notion of having needles stuck into you may seem frightening, but the needles are so thin that the process is painless. Acupuncture needles are much smaller than the needles used for drawing blood or getting shots. Here are some needles that I received from my acupuncturist. After my speech I'll pass them around so you can see how incredibly light and small they are. They are so thin—about the thickness of a human hair—that you can hardly tell when they're inserted. And there's usually no sensation other than pain relief once they have been inserted. After being left in for 20 or 30 minutes while you lie in a darkened room, the needles are removed and the treatment is over.

7   Now that you know what happens when you're treated by an acupuncturist, you're probably wondering how acupuncture works. The process is explained by Dr. Felix Mann, President of the Medical Acupuncture Society, in his book *Acupuncture: The Ancient Chinese Art of Healing and How It Works Scientifically.* According to traditional Chinese medicine, every life process is based on the flow of vital energy through the body. This energy is known in Chinese as *qi* and flows along channels or pathways called meridians.

8   The meridians are shown in this visual aid. As you can see, they cover the entire body, running from the top of the head to the bottom of the feet and down both arms. When the free flow of energy through these meridians is blocked, the result is pain, illness, disease, or other physical problems.

9   The aim of acupuncture is to restore the open flow of energy through these meridians. This is done by placing needles at specific points on the meridians. Altogether there are more than 1,000 acupuncture points on the meridians. These points have been mapped out over the centuries with scientific precision. In China there is a saying: "There is no pain if there is free flow; if there is pain, there is no free flow."

10   Although acupuncture is based on a different view of the body from that held by Western doctors, the evidence is clear that it works in treating a wide range of medical conditions. The World Health Organization lists more than 40 conditions that can be effectively treated with acupuncture, including ear, nose, and throat ailments; asthma and other respiratory problems; and nervous system and muscular disorders. A study in the *Annals of Internal Medicine* confirms that acupuncture can relieve low-back pain, while the American Cancer Society reports that acupuncture may even help smokers kick the habit.

11   People also use acupuncture to build their immune system, to control allergies, and to combat depression and anxiety. Of course, you can't use acupuncture to heal a broken arm. But people in Asia often use acupuncture during surgery instead of Western anesthesia, and it can speed recovery time after surgery.

12   In light of all this, it is not surprising that a number of clinics and hospitals are combining acupuncture with Western medicine in an effort to provide patients the benefits of both. For example, Massachusetts General Hospital in Boston, the third oldest hospital in the U.S., has added acupuncture to its wellness center. Positive results have also been seen at the Mattel Children's Hospital at UCLA. Dr. Lonnie Zeltzer, director of the hospital's pediatric pain program, confirms that acupuncture "really does help. Most children accept acupuncture, and in fact, really feel good about it."

13   Another example of the integration of acupuncture with Western medicine is the Wasser Pain Management Center at Mount Sinai Hospital in Toronto, Canada. Neurologist Allan Gordon, Director of the Center, says that introducing acupuncture into the hospital "expands the treatment available to chronic pain sufferers" and provides "multiple options for care to our patients." The National Institutes of Health report that more than 8 million Americans have tried acupuncture, and its use throughout the rest of the Western world is growing fast.

14   Today we have learned what happens during an acupuncture treatment, how acupuncture works, some of the illnesses that can be treated with acupuncture, and the growing integration of acupuncture with Western approaches to medicine. I hope you now know more about this ancient medical practice and the benefits it can provide.

15   After years of skepticism about acupuncture, the West is finally beginning to recognize that acupuncture is a highly effective way to improve health and reduce pain and suffering. Just ask my grandmother.

Acupuncture: New Uses for an Ancient Remedy

Commentary

"Acupuncture: New Uses for an Ancient Remedy" takes what could be a dry, technical topic and makes it interesting. The speech is crisply organized, contains well-chosen supporting materials, and uses concrete language and personal examples to clarify ideas. A video is available online and on the DVD of student speeches that accompanies this edition of *The Art of Public Speaking*. Here is a synopsis.

Specific Purpose: To inform my audience about the role of acupuncture in modern society.

Central Idea: Based on traditional Chinese medicine, acupuncture is a safe procedure used to treat a wide range of health conditions.

Method of Organization: Topical

Introduction: The introduction consists of paragraphs 1–4. The speaker starts with an extended example that captures attention and interest. In this case, the example works particularly well because it is personally related to the speaker. It is also richly detailed and vividly drawn. As the speaker continues her opening example in paragraph 2, she introduces the subject of her speech by talking about her grandmother's positive experience with acupuncture. Giving specific examples about the improvements in her grandmother's life is much more effective than if the speaker had simply stated that her grandmother got better. At the same time, the examples personalize the benefits of acupuncture.

In paragraph 3, the speaker mentions her personal experience with acupuncture, which helps build her credibility. In the following paragraph, she continues building her credibility by referencing the additional research she conducted for the speech. The speaker then previews the main points to be discussed in the body.

Body: Paragraph 5 begins the body of the speech. The information in this paragraph and the subsequent paragraph answers the audience's questions about what happens during an acupuncture treatment. Knowing that many people are squeamish about being poked with needles, the speaker explains that the needles used in acupuncture are small and essentially painless. As you can see from the video, the speaker does not pass the needles around during her speech. As mentioned in Chapter 14, putting visual aids in the hands of the audience during a speech is an almost certain recipe for disaster because listeners will end up paying more attention to the visual aids than to the speaker's words.

The second main point begins in paragraph 7. The speaker includes a transition to help the audience move from the discussion of what acupuncture is to a discussion of how acupuncture works. As in other parts of the speech, she cites the sources of her information and relates to the audience by speaking in terms of "you." In paragraph 8, she uses a visual aid to show the meridians of the human body—an effective way to clarify potentially confusing information. The entire main point, in fact, is a good example of how to communicate technical information in everyday language. The quotation at the end of paragraph 9 nicely sums up this section of the speech.

A signpost at the beginning of paragraph 10 signals that the speaker is moving to her third main point, in which she explains some of the medical conditions that can be treated with acupuncture. Again, she relies on credible sources and identifies them clearly. Because the speaker is not an expert on acupuncture, citing high-quality sources helps establish the reliability of her information.

The speaker's final main point, which consists of paragraphs 12–13, deals with the growing integration of acupuncture with Western medical techniques. The speaker uses a mix of examples, testimony, and statistics to illustrate her point. By citing Massachusetts General Hospital, the Mattel Children's Hospital, the Wasser Pain Management Center, and the National Institutes of Health, she gives the audience multiple examples of where acupuncture is meeting Western medicine. She also provides brief, well-chosen quotations. All in all, this speech provides an excellent case study in how to use supporting materials to buttress an informative presentation.

Conclusion: The phrase "Today we have learned" at the start of paragraph 14 signals that the speaker is moving into her conclusion. What follows is a concise summary of the main points developed in the body. In paragraph 15, the speaker reinforces her central idea about the benefits of acupuncture and then refers back to her grandmother, whom she had discussed in the introduction. This unifies the entire speech and ends it on a personal note.

Feng Shui

1   It's move-in day. While most everyone is rushing about carrying boxes, computers, TVs, and stereos to make their dorm rooms feel a little more like home, my mom is carrying—wind chimes. Don't wind chimes belong outside? In a garden? On a patio? Anywhere but a dorm room? My mom had strategically placed them so that each time I opened the door, it would swing into them. It was all because of feng shui.

2   According to Simon Brown, author of the book *Practical Feng Shui*, feng shui, which literally means wind and water, "is the art of designing your home to promote success in life, health, wealth and happiness." Feng shui originated in China over 4,000 years ago and is still practiced throughout the world today.

3   While it may seem like only ancient Chinese philosophers can master this art, even college students like us can learn simple techniques for improving the flow of energy in our dorm rooms, homes, or apartments. With my mom's enthusiasm behind me, I decided to research this topic some more on my own. First I'll explain a bit more about what feng shui is and then give you some tips on putting this ancient art into practice.

4   As I mentioned in my introduction, the ancient Chinese art of feng shui is a method of maximizing energy flow by manipulating your environment. Pam Kai Tollefson, director of Feng Shui Design, believes that feng shui changes and harmonizes the environment. There are many components of feng shui, the most important of which is chi. According to Sarah Rossbach, author of the book *Feng Shui: The Chinese Art of Placement*, chi is defined as the energy flow that connects all things, and it has a profound impact on our lives. Simon Brown describes chi as carrying thoughts, ideas, emotions, dreams, and energy from the environment. Practitioners of feng shui maintain that chi can move through air, people, buildings, windows, and doors. The flow of chi is the basis of feng shui.

5   The aim of feng shui is to improve your chi, which is accomplished by altering your surroundings. There is good and bad chi that flows throughout buildings such as this one. For example, the sharp corners on this lectern create negative chi because sharp corners cause chi to swirl, creating confusion or illness. Another problem in this room is that there are no windows. Sunlight is crucial because it's the main medium that keeps chi moving.

6   According to its followers, feng shui has many benefits once a home or office is arranged according to the principles of feng shui. Decreased stress and a better night's sleep are one advantage of feng shui. Improved health, motivation, relaxation, love, and romance can even occur. Feng shui helps create more harmonious family relationships. Overall, it can help you feel more in control and might even win you fame and respect.

7   Nancilee Wydra, author of the book *Feng Shui: 150 Simple Solutions for Health and Happiness in Your Home or Office*, believes that feng shui is beneficial in the workplace as well. Balanced chi creates a good start to a new career and a growing business, while evenly circulated chi throughout the body can help you become more assertive in the workplace.

8   Now that we've taken a look at what feng shui is, let's put this newfound knowledge into practice. To illustrate, we'll look at how feng shui works in a typical dorm room. Since we don't have control over the actual structure of our dorm rooms, we're forced to work with what we have.

9   Let's start with the ideal floor covering. Winifred Gallagher, in *The Power of Place*, says that soft materials slow chi energy and create a relaxing atmosphere. Few dorm rooms are carpeted, so make sure to cover your floor with a soft, fitted carpet.

10   Next, we'll look at the placement of your bed in your dorm room. In *Practical Feng Shui*, Simon Brown claims that "the direction you sleep in affects your whole life as well as how well you sleep." Feng shui recommends having the head of the bed face east because it's good for career building, ambition, getting things done, and ideal for growth. Or, if you're having trouble sleeping, try having the head of the bed face the north. This will enhance feelings of peace, tranquility, and spirituality. No matter what direction the head of your bed faces, make sure you can see the door and the window from your bed.

11   Once it's located in the ideal position, make sure to cover your bed with cotton, linen, or silk sheets to create a harmonious flow. Synthetic materials have a negative effect on chi. Finally, keep your curtains tightly closed at night to slow the flow of chi energy through your window.

12   Now that we've looked at the possibilities with what's already in your dorm room, let's see what we can add to enhance the already flowing chi.

13   For starters, try adding a wide mirror on one end of your dorm room to reflect the energy across the entire room. Most dorms provide harsh, electric lighting. To soften this light, bring in lamps with shades on them.

14   You can also add simple elements to enhance the flow of chi. Plants are always a good addition to a room because of their soothing effect. As my mom insisted, try placing wind chimes next to your door so they sound every time you open it. Lurrae Lupone, author of *Feng Shui: Therapy for the New Millennium*, says that wind chimes cleanse and purify the chi energy already in your room.

15   In addition to hanging wind chimes near your door, you can hang crystals such as this one in a window. The crystals bring energy from the outside environment into your dorm room. Adding water, such as a bowl of water or a fish tank, can also bring fresh chi energy into the room. If you place a bowl of water in your room, place it in the east or the southeast and refill it every day. According to advocates of feng shui, the water element can help you attain your goals and might even help you study for those midterms.

16   Finally, for those of you who tend to be a bit messy, beware. Untidiness slows the flow of chi energy. Make sure to store everything in cupboards or storage areas, and remember to stay organized.

17   In conclusion, we have taken a look at one of China's most time-honored traditions. We've seen what feng shui is and then put this ancient art into practice. Although we looked at how feng shui works in a typical dorm room, you can apply the principles of feng shui to your home, office, or apartment.

18   Now as I walk into my dorm room, I no longer cringe at those wind chimes' loud clanging or avoid touching them at all costs. Instead, I swing the door right into them and smile. It may be noisy, but it sure is good chi.

Feng Shui

Commentary

An outstanding informative speech, "Feng Shui" is well researched, clearly organized, and adroitly tailored to the audience. Here is a synopsis of the speech.

Specific Purpose: To inform my audience about the principles of Feng Shui.

Central Idea: The aim of Feng Shui is to improve the flow of positive energy by the harmonious arrangement of one's physical surroundings.

Method of Organization: Topical

Introduction: The introduction of "Feng Shui" consists of paragraphs 1–3. The speaker begins in paragraph 1 with a brief story about her mother helping her move into her dorm room. Although this would not have been a good attention-getter for an audience of older students, it was perfectly suited to the speaker's classmates, almost all of whom were 18- to 19-year-old first-semester students. In paragraph 2, the speaker defines feng shui and takes note of its 4,000-year-old tradition. Because few of her listeners were familiar with feng shui, the speaker used an overhead transparency to show how the term is spelled and to help her classmates remember it.

In paragraph 3, the speaker again relates the topic to her audience and then establishes her credibility by mentioning her research on the topic. (The extent of that research will become evident in the number and variety of sources she cites as the speech progresses.) The introduction ends with a concise preview of the main points to be discussed in the body.

Body: The body of this speech provides a superb example of how to organize ideas for effective communication. The first main point runs from paragraph 4 through paragraph 7 and explicates the philosophy of feng shui. It deals with the role of chi as the major component of feng shui (paragraph 4), the manner in which feng shui seeks to improve the flow of chi by altering one's surroundings (paragraph 5), and the benefits of feng shui in both the home and the workplace (paragraphs 6–7).

A transition at the start of paragraph 8 marks the speaker's move to her second main point, in which she illustrates the principles of feng shui by showing how they can be applied in a typical dorm room (paragraphs 8–16). Given the fact that almost all her classmates were living in the dorms, this was an excellent way for the speaker to make her ideas more applicable to her audience. As in her first main point, the subpoints are clearly organized and explained. First the speaker discusses floor coverings, bed placement, and bed coverings (paragraphs 9–11). After a transition in paragraph 12, she turns to items that can be added to a dorm room: mirrors, lamps, plants, wind chimes, crystals, and water (paragraphs 13–15). She ends the second main point by discussing the need for tidiness to maintain the flow of chi (paragraph 16).

The speech is also noteworthy for its use of testimony to support the speaker's ideas. Because the speaker is not an expert on feng shui, she repeatedly refers to the opinions of experts. All told, she cites six different books. These citations boost the speaker's credibility and make clear that she has done her research. Also noteworthy is the way the speaker relates her ideas to the audience. Not only does she illustrate the principles of feng shui by applying them to a college dorm room, but she repeatedly addresses the audience directly by using "you" and "your."

Conclusion: Consisting of paragraphs 17–18, the conclusion is concise and effective. Paragraph 17 reminds listeners of the significance of the topic and summarizes the main points. Paragraph 18 provides a sense of psychological unity by referring to the story told in the introduction. As with the rest of the speech, the conclusion is delivered conversationally and with superb eye contact.

Dying to Be Thin

---

1   I was Julie's best friend. I watched her grow from a little girl who was doted on by her parents into a tomboy who carried frogs in her pockets. I watched her become a young woman, fussing with her hair and trying on every outfit in her closet before her first date. I always wanted to be just like her.

2   But then something went terribly wrong. Julie's shiny hair became dull and brittle. Her eyes lost their sparkle, and she didn't smile that brilliant smile anymore. I watched now as she stepped on to the scale seven times a day, wore baggy clothes to cover her shriveled frame, and kept muttering about losing those last two stubborn pounds. Julie had become anorexic.

3   One in every 100 teenage females in America suffers from anorexia, and the New York Times says this number is rising by 5 percent every year. Although this disease does strike men, says the Times, 90 percent of its victims are women, and 44 percent of those victims are college-age females.

4   From my research and my personal experience with Julie, I have discovered that anorexia is an extremely serious disease that strikes a large number of Americans. Today I will tell you what anorexia is, what causes it, and what methods are used to treat it. Let's start by examining what anorexia is.

5   Anorexia nervosa, one of a number of eating disorders, is a disorder of self-starvation. Simply put, a person who is anorexic refuses to eat normal amounts of food. An article in Maclean's states that there are four characteristics of all anorexics: (1) refusal to maintain normal body weight, (2) loss of more than 15 percent of original body weight, (3) a distorted image of one's own body, and (4) an intense fear of becoming fat.

6   The refusal of anorexics to eat has many serious physical consequences. Hair and skin become dry and brittle, and a fine growth of hair may cover the entire body in an attempt to compensate for a lower body temperature. As the anorexia progresses, lack of calcium causes bones to become brittle and break easily. According to an article in Sports Illustrated, "The X-rays of a young person who has been anorexic for five to six years and those of a 70-year-old are almost identical." Lack of nutrition can also cause brain damage, blackouts, and a decreased pulse rate. In the most severe cases, anorexia can prove fatal.

7   In Julie's case, she suffered from many of the symptoms of anorexia. I saw her 5-foot-7-inch frame drop to 86 pounds. She became weak and pale. Even in the middle of the summer, she was cold all the time. I just wanted to say to her, "Julie, please, can't you see what you're doing to yourself!" But, like most anorexics, she just couldn't see.

8   What causes people like Julie to become anorexic? Scientists have identified three main causes of anorexia. An article in Newsweek attributes the rise in cases of anorexia to the pressure in our society to be thin. The media constantly bombards us with images of thin people as ideals. Fat-free products and diet aids have become multimillion-dollar industries. These images and these industries project the idea that being anything but slender is something to be feared and shunned.

9   The second major factor in causing anorexia is the personality of the victim and his or her reaction to the pressures of society. The book *Dying to Please* states that most anorexics fit a basic profile. Many are overachievers or perfectionists. They excel in school and are involved in a variety of extracurricular activities. They seek to please parents, teachers, and friends. Anorexics see being thin as a way to please others. In fact, most will limit their food intake to try to fulfill expectations of perfection from family and friends.

10   A third possible cause of anorexia has only been discovered within the past year. Doctors at the University of Pittsburgh School of Medicine found that when anorexics don't eat, they experience a rise in their level of opiates, natural brain chemicals that produce a sense of happiness. The researchers also found that when anorexics do eat, their bodies produce higher than normal levels of serotonin, a brain chemical that causes a sense of anxiety. According to the doctors, these chemical changes may make anorexia as physically addictive for the anorexic as alcohol or drugs are for the alcoholic or drug addict.

11   Julie always wanted to be perfect. She was prom queen, a straight-A student, and a member of every team, club, and organization imaginable. But then Julie decided she needed to go on a diet. She started constantly comparing herself to pictures of models in magazines. She was just sure that if she could look like the models, her life would truly be perfect. But losing weight never made Julie's life perfect.

12   What kinds of treatment could have helped Julie and others like her? Treatment of anorexia is a lifetime process. According to Dr. Katherine Halmi, director of the eating disorders clinic at New York Hospital, people think that eating disorders are "minor disorders than can be overcome with a little willpower and effort, but these are serious, incapacitating illnesses that require professional intervention."

13   Methods of treatment used to treat anorexia include group therapy, drug therapy, and individual counseling. In severe cases, hospitalization and forced feeding are used to provide nutrition for the anorexic until he or she will eat a sufficient amount. Most anorexics are never cured and must fight the disease daily. Another article in the *New York Times* states that more than 80 percent of anorexics will have several relapses before they are cured. As Angie Melnyk, a 14-year-old who has been anorexic for two years, stated, "If you could cure anorexia in 30 days, it would be a lot less trouble."

14   As I mentioned before, for some anorexics, no treatment is successful. For 18 percent of diagnosed anorexics, the disease proves fatal.

15   We have seen that anorexia is a serious disease with deep-seated causes and devastating, potentially fatal effects. Julie was one of those who couldn't beat anorexia. She died when she was only 17. We will never go to college together and share a dorm room. She will never fulfill her dream of becoming a nurse. And we will never grow old living beside each other and watching our kids grow up together. Anorexia killed my beautiful, vibrant friend.

Dying to Be Thin

Commentary

Clear, well-supported, and sharply organized, "Dying to Be Thin" shows how students can apply the guidelines for informative speaking presented in Chapter 15. Here is a brief synopsis of the speech.

Specific Purpose: To inform my audience about the symptoms, causes, and treatment of anorexia.

Central Idea: A serious, potentially fatal disorder, anorexia has several major causes and no easy cure.

Method of Organization: Topical

Introduction: The introduction consists of paragraphs 1–4. The first two paragraphs gain attention and gradually reveal the topic of the speech. Paragraph 3 quantifies the problem of anorexia and relates it to a college-age audience. Paragraph 4 reinforces the speaker's credibility and previews the main points to be discussed in the body of the speech. All in all, this is a very effective introduction.

Body: Arranged in topical order, the body of the speech consists of three main points, the first of which explains the nature and symptoms of anorexia (paragraphs 5–7). After defining anorexia as a disorder of self-starvation, the speaker identifies the four major traits of all anorexics (paragraph 5). She then explains the physical consequences of anorexia, which range from dry skin and brittle hair to a decreased pulse rate and even death (paragraph 6). In paragraph 7, the speaker returns to the story of her friend Julie that she began in the introduction. In addition to illustrating the speaker's ideas, this story provides a unifying element to which the speaker will return throughout the speech.

A signpost at the beginning of paragraph 8 alerts the audience to the fact that the speaker is moving into her second main point, in which she explains why people become anorexic (paragraphs 8–11). The speaker identifies three major causes of anorexia: societal pressure to be thin (paragraph 8), individual personality traits (paragraph 9), and chemical reactions in the body that may make anorexia physically addictive (paragraph 10). She ends the second main point in paragraph 11 by once again talking of Julie, who tried to make herself perfect by losing weight.

In paragraph 12, the speaker uses another signpost to introduce her third main point, dealing with the treatment of anorexia (paragraphs 12–14). As in other parts of the speech, the speaker uses credible sources to support her ideas, and she identifies the sources for her audience. The quotation from Dr. Katherine Halmi in paragraph 12 dispels the notion that anorexia can be cured by personal willpower, while the statistic in paragraph 14 reinforces the fact that, for many anorexics, there is no effective treatment.

Although the topic of anorexia is far from novel, the speaker does a good job of keeping the audience interested. She avoids technical language, explains ideas clearly, and uses a variety of supporting materials. By returning to the story of Julie at the end of each main point, she personalizes the topic and reinforces its tragic consequences.

Conclusion: The conclusion consists of the final paragraph. After restating her central idea, the speaker ends by completing the story of her friend Julie. The emotional appeal of this story is unusual for an informative speech, but it is extremely effective. When delivered in class, it had a powerful impact.

Cryonics

---

1   The time is now. Imagine your mother or father has suffered a heart attack. Deprived of its vital blood supply, a part of their heart is dying. Or imagine your grandmother or grandfather lying nearly motionless in their nursing home bed. Advanced age, complicated by pneumonia, is about to end their lives. Or imagine a close friend has just entered the hospital with a massive system-wide infection. AIDS has left their body ravaged by multiple diseases.

2   For most people, these circumstances would herald the end of life. Today's medicine can no longer help them. But all of you may be able to meet again in the far future. Does this sound like science fiction? Perhaps. But it may one day be possible. How? Through the process of cryonics.

3   Cryonics is the process of freezing human beings after death in the hope that medical science will be able to revive them in the future. Intrigued by the prospect of being cryonically frozen, I've spent some time researching the subject of cryonics. After reading dozens of newspaper and magazine articles, I would like to give you a brief overview of the history, methods, and future of cryonics. Let's start with the development of cryonics.

4   Although the idea of freezing people is relatively new, the notion of preserving them is old. In the 1770s, for example, Ben Franklin wrote that he wanted to be "immersed in a cask of Madeira wine, 'til that time when he could be recalled to life." It was not to be, but Franklin's dream lived on to be revived in our time as cryonics.

5   Cryonics has been a staple of science fiction novels, the plot device in movies such as *Austin Powers* and *Sleeper*, and the subject of countless newspaper and magazine articles. Until 1964, however, cryonics remained firmly in the realm of fiction. It was at this time that physics professor Robert Ettinger argued in his book *The Prospect of Immortality* that cryonics was indeed possible. Three years later, on January 12, 1967, 73-year-old James H. Bedford became the first human being to be frozen.

6   Ever since Bedford was frozen, cryonics has steadily increased in popularity. Currently there are four cryonic institutions in the United States—two in California and one each in Michigan and Arizona. So far 80 people have been cryonically frozen from around the world, and another estimated 800 people have signed up to be frozen when they die. Their aim is to remain frozen in a state of suspended animation—perhaps for centuries—in the hope that medical science will be able to revive them in the future at a time when cures exist for virtually all of today's diseases and when restoration to full function and health is possible.

7   So you're probably wondering how will they do it? How does cryonics work?

8   Currently, when a person who has signed up to be cryonically suspended dies, a specific procedure, which was outlined in the book *Cryonics: Reaching for Tomorrow*, must be carried out. First, before death, an individual must decide whether to have his or her entire body frozen or just the head. If the whole body is to be frozen, it must be preserved upon death. Immediately after death—ideally within a matter of minutes—the patient is connected to a heart-lung machine, and chemicals such as glucose and heparin are circulated with the oxygenated blood to help minimize the freezing damage. At the same time, the patient's internal temperature is reduced as quickly as possible using cold packs.

9   If only the head will be frozen, a slightly different procedure must be carried out. The head must be surgically detached from the rest of the body and preserved in a separate container. You may be wondering why would I preserve only my head? The answer is, with some diseases the body is in a very poor condition. If this is the case and you choose to preserve your head only, you do so with the belief that medical science will be able to create a healthy new body for you in the future.

10   Once the head or body is ready for freezing, a liquid called a cryoprotectant, which works as an antifreeze of sorts to help prevent cell damage, is circulated through the body or head. Over a 20-day period, the patient is prepared for long-term storage by cooling the body or head to a temperature of negative 320 degrees Fahrenheit. When this temperature is reached, the patient is stored in a steel cylinder of liquid nitrogen. According to an article in Omni magazine, "At this temperature, biological function ceases and the patient will remain unchanged for hundreds of years."

11   Now that we have explored the development of cryonics and how the freezing process works, you may wonder about questions such as how much it costs and whether the people that are frozen can be rethawed.

12   According to an article in *Fortune* magazine, the cost of cryonic suspension ranges from $60,000 to $125,000. It can be creatively paid for by making the cryonics institution the beneficiary of your life insurance policy. These costs may be rather steep, but as one cryonics member states, "Facing my own mortality turned out to be much harder than coming up with the cash to pay for life insurance premiums."

13   But cost is not the only issue. Even if you can afford the cost of being cryonically frozen, scientists have not yet worked out all the details involved in freezing and rethawing. As explained by *New Scientist* magazine, the problem is that the freezing process itself inflicts a crippling amount of cellular damage by dehydrating cells and puncturing their delicate membranes. So far, there are only a few types of human tissue that can be successfully frozen and rethawed, including sperm, embryos, and bone marrow, which contain relatively few cells. It is not yet possible to freeze and rethaw complicated organs such as the heart or liver—not to mention a complete body or brain.

14   What scientists need is a procedure that will allow them to reduce the damage inflicted by the freezing process. And in fact scientists are currently working on this procedure. Research is being done in the hope of finding better cryoprotectants—or antifreezes—which will reduce the cell damage caused by freezing. According to the book *Cryonics: Reaching for Tomorrow*, scientists are also developing microscopic machines that are capable of repairing cells at the molecular level. These machines might one day make it possible to repair the cell damage caused by the freezing process and thus bring frozen patients back to full life. Until that time, the people that are already frozen will have to remain in their current state of suspended animation in the hope that science will one day work out solutions to the problems involved with freezing and rethawing.

15   In closing, we have seen that cryonics is much more than a plot in a science fiction novel. It has developed from a wholly unrealistic fantasy to the point that 80 people have already been frozen and hundreds more have made the choice to be cryonically frozen when they die. If scientists can ever figure out how to rethaw people successfully, we can be sure that cryonics will become much more popular.

16   So think again of your father or mother suffering a heart attack, your grandmother or grandfather dying of pneumonia, or your close friend stricken with AIDS. If they chose to be buried or cremated in traditional fashion, their physical minds and bodies would be destroyed. That is absolutely certain. By contrast, being cryonically frozen offers some small chance that they may be revived in the future. Even if that chance is small, it's more than no chance at all.

Cryonics

Commentary

"Cryonics" is an excellent example of an informative speech that presents highly technical concepts and procedures in a simple, straightforward fashion. Through careful audience adaptation, the speaker is able to make the science-fiction-like procedure of cryonics a clear, personal matter for the listener. Below is a synopsis of the speech.

Specific Purpose: To inform my audience about the history, methods, and future of cryonics.

Central Idea: Although cryonics has moved in recent years from science fiction to scientific reality, it is still far from foolproof.

Method of Organization: Topical

Introduction: The introduction consists of the first three paragraphs. The speaker begins with a series of hypothetical scenarios designed to relate the subject directly to the audience. In paragraph 2, the speaker further arouses the audience's interest by linking those hypothetical scenarios with the contemporary state of medicine, which serves as a nice foray into the central issue of the speech—informing the audience of the potential of cryonics to extend human life. Paragraph 3 accomplishes a number of important tasks, as the speaker defines cryonics, establishes her credibility, and previews the main points to be discussed in the body of the speech.

Body: Organized topically, the body of the speech contains three main points. The first main point, which considers the history of cryonics, runs from paragraph 4 through paragraph 6. In paragraph 4, the speaker shows the historic roots of the idea of cryonics, citing Benjamin Franklin's wish to suspend his own life until a future age. This citation accomplishes a number of purposes. It lends the speaker credibility, enhances the stature of her topic, and unveils the long history of the idea of cryonics. In paragraph 5, the speaker separates fact from fiction, distinguishing movies such as *Austin Powers* and *Sleeper* from Robert Ettinger's book *The Prospect of Immortality*. In paragraph 6, the speaker shows the extent to which cryonics has grown in only a few decades.

After a brief transition in paragraph 7, the speaker moves into the second main point of her speech, which she covers in paragraphs 8–10. In these paragraphs the speaker does an excellent job of translating scientific concepts into everyday, nontechnical language. In paragraph 8, she illustrates the process of cryonic freezing from the point of view of the cryonics patient. As in other parts of the speech, she is careful to cite her sources, thereby reinforcing her credibility and making clear that she has done the research needed to speak on this topic. In paragraph 9, the speaker shows the options available to a possible cryonics patient—freezing the whole body or freezing only one's head—and in paragraph 10 she explains key technical concepts in vivid, straightforward language.

Paragraph 11 provides a transition to the third main point, which the speaker begins discussing in paragraph 12 by juxtaposing the cost of cryonics with its apparent benefits. In paragraph 13, the speaker elaborates on the scientific difficulties of cryonics by citing New Scientist magazine on the potential cellular damage of cryonic freezing. In paragraph 14, she shows how scientists are working to overcome the difficulties of cryonic freezing. She ends paragraph 14 with a strong sentence that conveys both the hope and the dangers of cryonics.

Conclusion: The phrase "In closing" signals that the speaker is moving into her conclusion, which consists of paragraphs 15 and 16. Paragraph 15 reviews the main points of the speech, while paragraph 16 again relates the topic to the audience. The hypothetical scenarios of paragraph 16 mirror those of the introduction and reinforce the manner in which cryonics could potentially affect members of the audience. The final line of the speech makes clear the speaker's view that even though cryonics, in its current state of development, offers only a small chance of reviving people in the future, it represents "more than no chance at all."

––––––––––––––––––––

Dandelions: The Uncommon Weed

---

1   What starts out yellow and ends up as a fluffy white ball? If I told you it was *Taraxacum officinale*, would that ring a bell? What if I told you it was of the family *Compositae*—would that excite your senses?

2   If you haven't figured it out by now, the subject of which I am speaking is none other than the common, ordinary dandelion. Yes, those bright, yellow flowers which we all, as kids, eagerly snapped off the stems while chanting the words, "Mama had a baby and its head popped off!" I'm sure all of us remember having blown the fluffy white tufts into the air above.

3   Although we have these pleasant memories from our childhoods, most home-owners consider the dandelion as the most irritating and troublesome of all the weeds—partly because their deep root system makes them almost impossible to get rid of. However, from a botany class, I learned that the dandelion, in reality, is a very useful plant. From further research, I discovered that the dandelion has both wide medical and culinary uses. Today, I will explain these uses to you. We'll start by looking at the dandelion's medicinal value.

4   The scientific name of the dandelion, *Taraxacum officinale*, testifies to its value as a medicine. According to Edward Spencer, in his book *All About Dandelions*, *Taraxacum* refers to medical properties of a plant found in Persia. *Officinale*, the species name, when given to any plant, indicates that it is used by druggists and pharmacists.

5   Throughout history, dandelions have been used to help cure various medical ailments. Dandelions were reportedly used by the ancient Egyptians to treat kidney and stomach disorders. The dandelion's many cures were recorded by Arabian physicians in the tenth century. And in sixteenth-century England, dandelion waters were used in the treatment of illness among the nobility.

6   Today, scientists know as a fact that the dandelion has great medicinal value. According to Mea Allan, in her book *Weeds*, the plant contains chemicals that stimulate blood circulation, the liver, digestive organs, and especially the kidneys and bladder—which has gained the dandelion fame as a so-called "potty herb." Audrey Hatfield, in her book *How to Enjoy Your Weeds*, says that a tea made from dandelion roots or leaves is helpful in relieving many conditions. It helps relieve liver and lung disorders, and it helps treat anemia. In addition, it serves as a mild laxative and is helpful in aiding digestion. Hatfield also suggests that dandelion tea is highly effective in cases of eczema, scurvy, and similar skin conditions. So valuable is the dandelion in treating medical ailments that 100,000 pounds are imported into the United States each year for this purpose.

7   If you have no interest in using dandelions for your health, you can still find them of use in the kitchen. Historically, dandelions have been used as food for thousands of years. According to an article in *National Wildlife* magazine, they were among the original bitter herbs of Passover, a Jewish holiday which commemorates the Hebrews' liberation from slavery in Egypt. The English have been using dandelions in salads since the Middle Ages. And currently, many ethnic groups in the United States—such as Greeks, Poles, French, Italians, and even the Amish—all eat dandelions.

8   ll parts of the dandelion can be utilized to make a variety of delicious foods. Its bitter leaves, if picked before the yellow flowers appear, can be added to a salad. The leaves are usually mixed with other vegetables to vary their flavor. The dandelion's roots may be roasted in an oven, then ground and used as a caffeine-free coffee substitute. The golden yellow flowers can be steeped in water and then used to produce a delicious wine. And the entire dandelion plant may be used to make beer.

9   In addition to being tasty, dandelions are extremely nutritious. According to Peter Gail, a professor of economic botany at Cleveland State University, "The dandelion's nutrient qualities read almost like a One-a-Day vitamin." Dandelion greens have 50 percent more vitamin C than tomatoes, twice as much protein as eggplant, and double the fiber of asparagus. They have as much iron as spinach and more potassium than bananas.

10   All of this may sound strange to you, but not to the people of Vineland, New Jersey, the official Dandelion Capital of the World. In Vineland, the dandelion has grown from being a $68,000 crop in 1977 to almost a half-million-dollar crop today. At the beginning of the season, dandelions sell for as much as $1.25 a pound. Most of Vineland's dandelion crop ends up in restaurants and markets in Baltimore, Philadelphia, and New York City.

11   Every March the town hosts its annual seven-course dandelion dinner. The menu consists of dandelion soup, dandelion salad, dandelion sausage, dandelions and vegetables, dandelion beef roulade, dandelion sweet cup, and dandelion wine. Tickets for the dinner sell for $25 apiece, with people coming from as far away as Ohio. Former Vineland mayor Patrick Fiorilli has humorously summed up Vineland's position in the dandelion world: "In your yard, you go out and pull the dandelions out of the grass. Our farmers pull the grass out of the dandelions."

12   As we have seen, then, the dandelion is a greatly misunderstood plant. Despite its reputation as an irritating weed, in reality it is a very useful plant. Having various medical and culinary uses, the dandelion stands as one of the most underrated and least appreciated plants in the world. Hopefully, in the future, more people will come to recognize the usefulness of the dandelion, thereby reestablishing this "common" weed as a truly uncommon plant.

Dandelions: The Uncommon Weed

Commentary

Creative, crisply organized, and packed with fascinating supporting materials, "Dandelions: The Uncommon Weed" is a fine example of how to produce a captivating informative speech on a seemingly ordinary topic. Here is a synopsis of the speech.

Specific Purpose: To inform my audience about the medical and culinary uses of dandelions.

Central Idea: Despite its reputation as an irritating weed, the dandelion's medical and culinary properties make it a very useful plant.

Method of Organization: Topical

Introduction: The speaker opens with a series of three rhetorical questions that capture attention by arousing the audience's curiosity. She follows, in paragraph 2, by revealing the subject of her speech and by relating it directly to the audience. In paragraph 3, she establishes her credibility and previews the main points to be discussed in the body. All in all, this is an excellent example of an introduction for a speech to inform.

Body: Organized in topical order, the body of this speech contains two main points. The first, running from paragraph 4 through paragraph 6, explores the medical uses of dandelions. After explaining that the scientific name of the dandelion, *Taraxacum officinale*, indicates that the plant is used by druggists and pharmacists (paragraph 4), the speaker notes some of the ways it has been employed throughout history to cure medical ailments (paragraph 5). In paragraph 6, she relates what modern medical science knows about the medical value of dandelions. Because she is not a medical expert, she is careful to identify the sources of her information.

In paragraph 7, the speaker turns to her second main point, which continues through paragraph 11. This point deals with the culinary uses of dandelions and, like the first main point, is brought to life with a variety of intriguing supporting materials. In paragraph 7, the speaker provides historical facts about some of the ways different cultures have used dandelions as food through the years. In paragraph 8, she notes how dandelions can be used in salads, as the basis for a caffeine-free coffee substitute, and to produce wine or beer. In paragraph 9, she cites Peter Gail, a professor of economic botany at Cleveland State University, to establish the nutritional value of dandelions.

Paragraphs 10–11 present the story of Vineland, New Jersey, "Dandelion Capital of the World." Entertaining as well as informative, the story brings the speaker's ideas to life and gives them human interest. Its details about the size of Vineland's dandelion crop, the price per pound of dandelions, and the seven-course dandelion dinner are crucial. One way to communicate this to students is to have them imagine how much less effective the speech would have been if the speaker had merely said, "Dandelions are very important to the people of Vineland, New Jersey."

It is also worth noting how clearly the body of the speech is organized and how the speaker uses ample connectives to help listeners keep track of her ideas. Equally important, those ideas are presented in straightforward, nontechnical language.

Conclusion: The conclusion consists of paragraph 12 and is short and to the point. The phrase "As we have seen" cues listeners that the speech is coming to an end. The speaker then summarizes her main points and ends by restating her central idea—that, despite its negative reputation, the dandelion is a very useful plant.

Edible Insects

1   As the days of summer descend upon us, we await lazy days, beach parties, deep suntans, and, of course, insects. We may look forward to seeing grasshoppers jump through meadows and admiring backyard butterflies fluttering through flowers, yet we dread being stung by those yellow and black villains. But the future may bring insects an extra step closer to us—not so much for their stings, but for their food value.

2   I realize this idea of consuming those small, creepy and sometimes hairy creatures might turn one's stomach and boggle the mind. However the idea may not seem too unusual once we understand what it involves.

3   As a biology major, I have been enrolled in a course entitled "Insects as Food" in which I learned about edible insects people can and do consume. Today I'd like to share some of this information with you by first exposing the presence of insects in our everyday foods. Then we'll consider a history of edible insects. Next their nutritional value. Finally we'll see what the possibilities are for making insects a more prevalent part of our diet.

4   To begin, we must realize that while the idea of eating insects may be a new one, we unconsciously consume them with our everyday foods. Ronald Taylor's *Butterflies in My Stomach* informs us that lettuce, bread, corn, peanut butter, tomato sauces, and fruit juices contain insects or insect fragments. However, these small defects or, if you will, bugs in the food system should probably not be considered as dangerous as chicken salmonella or other food poisoning. As entomologist Gene DeFoliart, head of the food insect research division program here on campus, explains, "Unlike the dangerous chemicals in our foods, sometimes the insects in food are more nutritious than the food they are in."

5   In fact, our ancestors relied on insects for mere survival. Taylor describes a time—one and a quarter million years ago—when we were supposedly apes in the African continent, surviving by eating insects during droughts. More recently, the 1855 Dakota and Utah settlers survived by consuming the very grasshoppers that had plagued their crops. And today Dr. DeFoliart indicates that in some of the world's tropical areas, people consume insects as part of their daily diet. For example, insects comprise 40 percent of the protein intake in southern Zaire, caterpillars are an inexpensive agricultural alternative in China, and the University of Mexico documents 270 insects consumed regularly among rich and poor alike in that country. These and at least 60 other countries use insects in their diets.

6   The insects' taste and nutritional value make them an excellent food source. Their nutritional value is supported by figures from the consumer and food economic research division. As you can see on this chart, if we take 100 grams or a quarter pound or a hamburger size portion of cooked meats such as chicken, perch, ham, and beef, the average

protein content is 23 grams and the energy content is 240 calories. If we take an equivalent serving portion of cooked caterpillars, termites, and weevils, the average protein content is 15 grams higher and the energy content is nearly double that of our usual meats.

7   What is more striking is that, except for niacin, these insects also surpass the traditional meats in mineral content. In our usual meats, the mineral content might be a few or up to a couple dozen milligrams, whereas in these insects, it may be several or even hundreds of milligrams.

8   However, this idea of using insects for their nutritional value is only that—an idea—unless a market is created. Dr. DeFoliart, who in the next few years plans to introduce edible insects to the American market, realizes the stomach-turning nature of such topics. Indeed, while individuals who sampled edible insects accepted their taste, the fact that they looked like insects was the major complaint.

9   Therefore, to his team of twenty-five scientific advisors, DeFoliart has added food engineers who can pellet and flake insects into more desirable looking snack foods. Some of his candidates include dried acheta crickets, the honey bee pupae, and the *galleria* larvae, a small caterpillar which tastes like bacon. He will probably also emphasize to the health-minded population that unlike potato chips and french fries, which contain saturated fats, these insects contain the healthier unsaturated fats.

10   Most important, Dr. DeFoliart strategically intends to introduce edible insects not only to the general public but to those upper echelons who can afford other odd foods like escargot and caviar, which are no more than snails and fish eggs. The belief is that this approach will cause people to treat edible insects as a status food as opposed to denouncing them as pet food. Edible insects might also be legitimized by books such as Ronald Taylor and Barbara Carter's *Entertaining with Insects*, which includes 95 recipes for hors d'oeuvres, entrées, and other uses of insects.

11   In conclusion, I'll admit that the idea may indeed bother some people. Yet we should bear in mind that insects are consumed unconsciously with our everyday foods, historically they ensured the survival of some of our most distant ancestors, and currently they nourish many people in various parts of the world.

12   In the future, the possibility of expanding insects as a food source might not receive an available space at every single dinner table. But when we sit down and consider options for feeding the world's hungry, insects are likely to be on the table. Given these possibilities, the animal kingdom might eventually experience sibling rivalry between dogs and insects over who really is humanity's best friend.

Edible Insects

Commentary

Superbly researched, crisply organized, and engagingly delivered, "Edible Insects" is an exceptional informative speech. Here is a synopsis.

Specific Purpose: To inform my audience about the history, current use, nutritional value, and future of insects as a human food source.

Central Idea: Edible insects have long been consumed by people in various parts of the world, are high in nutritional value, and may one day find their way onto our own dinner plates.

Method of Organization: Topical

Introduction: Running through paragraph 3, the introduction begins in a fairly leisurely fashion as the speaker arouses curiosity about his topic by discussing the upcoming days of summer. After revealing his topic at the end of paragraph 1, he uses paragraph 2 to calm the queasiness some listeners might feel about the prospect of using insects as a food source. In paragraph 3 he establishes his credibility by referring to the class he is taking on "Insects as Food." He also provides an excellent preview statement that lets the audience know exactly what to listen for in the body of the speech.

Body: "Edible Insects" contains four main points. The first, developed in paragraph 4, explains that we unconsciously consume insects with our everyday foods—especially in items such as lettuce, bread, corn, peanut butter, tomato sauces, and fruit juices. Recognizing that this might be disturbing to some listeners, the speaker notes that the presence of insects in our food is far less problematic than such things as chicken salmonella and food poisoning. The quotation at the end of the paragraph provides a bit of wry humor and is consistent with the light touch the speaker employs throughout the speech.

In paragraph 5 the speaker turns to his second main point, in which he shows that humans have long used insects as a food source. The series of brief examples at the end of the paragraph is especially effective because it demonstrates that many people in the world today consciously consume insects as part of their daily diet. It is also worth noting how the speaker takes care, here and elsewhere, to document the sources of his information.

The speaker's third main point is that the nutritional value of insects makes them an excellent food source (paragraphs 6–7). Using figures he had found in his research, he shows that many insects are higher in protein and energy content than are beef, fish, and poultry. He also shows that insects are higher in minerals such as zinc, magnesium, and calcium.

In his fourth main point, the speaker explores current efforts to develop a market for edible insects in the United States (paragraphs 8–10). His primary source here is Dr.

Gene DeFoliart, the speaker's biology professor and an internationally recognized expert on the subject of edible insects. In addition to taking Dr. DeFoliart's course on "Insects as Food," the speaker interviewed him outside of class. Indeed, this speech provides a fine example of how students can use information gained from classes and interviews in their speeches—as long as they augment that information with additional research.

Conclusion: The speaker begins his conclusion in paragraph 11 with a concise summary of his main points. In paragraph 12 he reinforces the central idea and brings the speech to an end with a clever closing line.

Nothing to Sneeze At

1   You feel it welling up inside you, this delicate tingling, as if your every nerve were firing at once. You want to grope for the newspaper, your homework—anything—but you no longer control your body.

2   These seconds of helpless anticipation seem like an eternity, but then the spell is broken. You crash forward, your muscles contracting like a fist, and you can't even see that people are running away from you because something has forced your eyes shut.

3   And then it's over. You relax. Your head is clear, your body under control.

4   I'm talking, of course, about sneezing. I come from a long line of sneezers. My father sneezed, and his father and his father's father before him were all men for whom a blast from the nose was every bit as bracing as a plunge into the snow following a sauna.

5   This involuntary reflex known as the sneeze is not one of the burning mysteries of our time, but I'd like to tell you about some superstitions that have sprung up around sneezing and also let you know what's actually happening when you sneeze. Finally, in the interests of social harmony, I'll tell you how to sneeze safely and politely.

6   Sneezing is old. Citizens of the Roman Empire sneezed, but they were only following the tradition of the ancient Greeks, among them Aristotle, who considered the sneeze a favorable omen.

7   A sneeze worked wonders for Xenophon, the Greek historian and general. According to the *Concise Dictionary of Ancient History*, in 400 B.C. Xenophon, while still a mere foot-soldier, marched with the Greek army deep into hostile Persia, where the enemy slew all the Greek leaders and threatened to do the same to the confused troops when nightfall postponed the slaughter.

8   The desperate Greeks spent the night debating who should lead them in battle the next day. Xenophon rose to give a dramatic oration exhorting the men to follow him to liberty or to death. He spoke for an hour in the flickering firelight until a soldier to his right seconded his conclusion with a sneeze. Thinking this sneeze a favorable sign from the gods, the Greeks made Xenophon general, and when the sun rose the next morning, they marched to safety 10,000 strong behind their new leader.

9   Sneezing is seldom this dramatic, but many cultures echo the Greeks in their praise of the nose's most conspicuous function. Indeed, the *Encyclopedia of Occult Sciences, Superstitions, and Folklore* devotes eleven tightly spaced, oversized pages to the subject. For example, a Zulu who has just sneezed proclaims, "I am now blessed; the ancestral spirit is with me. It has come to me. Let me salute it, for it is he who causes me to sneeze."

10   Sneezing in India provokes a shorter, but no less salutary, response. If you were walking down the dusty streets of Karim Nagar, for instance, and you sneezed, bystanders would shout, "Live!" and you, as a polite tourist, must reply, "Live with you!" Most Indians consider sneezing healthy, if not supernatural; it is the inability to sneeze that is cause for alarm. Science magazine reports Indian scientists have labeled this malady "asneezia" and are currently researching ways to artificially induce the healthy sneeze.

11   In the West, despite the cheerful, almost compulsive blessing we give anyone experiencing spontaneous nasal expulsion, the sneeze has long been regarded with suspicion. Some people, my grandmother among them, believe we say "Bless you" because the heart skips a beat when you sneeze. It's true your eyes must close when you sneeze, but the heartbeat remains steady. I used to think we say "Bless you" because of the superstition that when you sneeze the soul exits through your nostrils. If no one blesses you, evil beings with a penchant for nasal drip will snatch your spiritual essence. Natives of Motlan and Mota in the South Pacific believe this, but our European blessing has a grimmer origin.

12   The Black Death of 590 A.D. left one half of Europe's population dead. The bubonic plague responsible for this holocaust didn't kill its victims without warning. Instead, it signified its presence by rosy rashes, swelling, and, as any medical student can tell you, telltale fits of sneezing. Since death so frequently followed sneezing, people began to say "Bless you"—a final blessing.

13   However differently a sneeze is reacted to throughout the world, its cause is generally the same: nasal irritation. Pollens from grass, trees, house dust, and a dozen other sources are basically harmless, but when they irritate the nose your body responds as if they were rampaging predators. In a case of mistaken identity and overkill, you inhale sharply and exhale with explosive force—up to 104 miles per hour.

14   Pollen is not the only culprit, though. The nose mistakes strong odors, sudden chills, and even bright lights for more dangerous parasites, and it tries to defend itself by banishing the intruders with a sneeze.

15   In addition to its physical causes, the *New York Times* reports a sneeze can also be brought on by psychological and emotional factors. If a man lunged at you with a knife, fear might make you sneeze. Once he left, your anguish and frustration over losing your valuables could cause you to sneeze again. If you decide to chase the criminal, bring along some tissues—the excitement could give you another sneezing fit.

16   In each of these cases, sneezing is assisting the nose in reaching equilibrium. Strong emotions can cause your nasal membranes to shrink or expand, and a sneeze brings you back to normal quickly and forcefully.

17   Occasionally, someone is blessed with an overly active equilibrating mechanism. In 1966 June Clark had a fit in which she sneezed every twelve seconds for 174 days. Before she finally stopped, doctors had tried tranquilizers, narcotics, x-rays, muscle relaxants, shock treatment, and even hypnosis, which almost worked until she sneezed and broke the trance.

18 Sneezing will probably never give you the trouble it gave June Clark, but the odds are that sooner or later you'll have to sneeze in a social setting. This can be especially uncomfortable given that no one carries a handkerchief any more—at least not in my social circle. Nevertheless, when you're in a crowded room, don't try to stifle or abort your sneeze in the interests of social propriety—you don't want to stop a force going over 100 miles per hour. With the air pressure that builds up from a stifled sneeze, people have been known to get nosebleeds, pop blood vessels, or even go blind.

19 Instead, open your mouth while you sneeze so your nose doesn't take all your force. Most important, cover your nose. Jane Brody writes in the *New York Times* that "An unimpeded sneeze sends two to five thousand bacteria-filled droplets into the air." With a single sneeze, any one of us could raise this room's bacterial count for the next forty-five minutes. Understandably, every etiquette theorist from Lord Chesterfield and Amy Vanderbilt to Eleanor Roosevelt and Miss Manners advocates being a quick draw with a handkerchief. Failing this, hold the hankie over your nose after the sneeze—it shows good faith.

20 Whatever the cause and whichever country you're sneezing in, with practice and luck you'll be able to cover your sneeze quickly and effectively. Then you can sit back and relax, waiting for someone to bless you, wish you *gesundheit*, or, if you're in the right place at the right time, appoint you to high military command.

Nothing to Sneeze At

Commentary

"Nothing To Sneeze At" is a top-notch informative speech. It is interesting, clearly organized, fits well with the guidelines discussed in Chapter 15 of the textbook, and is short enough to be discussed in a single class session. Here is a synopsis of the speech.

Specific Purpose: To inform my audience about the superstitions associated with sneezing, the causes of sneezing, and the proper way to sneeze.

Central Idea: Sneezing has long been the subject of superstition, has a number of causes from pollen to strong emotions, and should be done safely and politely.

Method of Organization: Topical

Introduction: The introduction consists of paragraphs 1–5. After cleverly arousing curiosity and relating the topic to the audience in paragraphs 1–3, the speaker reveals his topic in paragraph 4 and previews the body of the speech in paragraph 5. His tongue-in-cheek approach to establishing credibility in paragraph 4 is consistent with the overall tone of the speech, but some listeners felt it should have been supplemented by a brief reference to the speaker's research.

Body: The body is arranged topically and contains three main points, the first of which deals with superstitions that have sprung up around sneezing (paragraphs 6–12). This point is particularly effective because it casts new and interesting light on what would appear to be a mundane subject. The story about Xenophon (paragraphs 7–8) is a model of clear explanation. Rather than assuming the audience knew about Xenophon before the speech, the speaker provides all the necessary details. Yet he does so in a way that does not oversimplify the story for someone already familiar with it.

The statement in paragraph 9 that "the *Encyclopedia of Occult Sciences, Superstitions, and Folklore* devotes eleven tightly-spaced, oversized pages to the subject" of sneezing not only identifies the speaker's source, but reinforces the importance of the subject. The final example of this section—about sneezing and the bubonic plague (paragraph 12)—is highly effective. Notice especially the dramatic impact of the final sentence: "Since death so frequently followed sneezing, people began to say, 'Bless you'—a final blessing."

The second main point in the body deals with the causes of sneezing (paragraphs 13–17). While the information about pollen is fairly ordinary, the speaker brings it alive through his use of colorful language. He follows this with the interesting observation that sneezing can also be caused by psychological and emotional factors. Rather than getting overly technical, however, he explains with a hypothetical example that personalizes the subject for his listeners (paragraph 15). The story of June Clark (paragraph 17) ends this section on a strong note.

It should also be noted how well the speaker uses connectives here (and throughout the speech) to help listeners keep track of his ideas. At the beginning of paragraph 13 he introduces the second main point with an excellent transition ("However differently a sneeze is reacted to throughout the world, its cause is generally the same: nasal irritation"). He then has a signpost ("Pollen is not the only culprit, though") at the start of paragraph 14. Another transition at the start of paragraph 15 leads listeners from the physical causes of sneezing to its psychological and emotional causes.

The third main point explains how to sneeze politely and safely in a social setting (paragraphs 18–19). Its first observation—that stifling a sneeze can cause nosebleeds, popped blood vessels, even blindness (paragraph 18)—is an important bit of information that was new to most members of the audience. Indeed, it was so new that some thought the speaker should have presented a source here. Although the second observation—that a person should cover his or her nose when sneezing (paragraph 19)—is common-place, it could not have been left out of the speech. Fortunately, rather than just saying, "You should cover your nose when you sneeze," the speaker provides a wealth of colorful information that keeps the audience's attention.

Conclusion: The conclusion consists of only two sentences (paragraph 20). The first sentence subtly reminds the audience of the main points discussed in the body. A good question for discussion is whether the speaker should have provided a more detailed summary here. One point of view holds that he did not need such a summary because the body of the speech was sufficiently clear and nontechnical. Another point of view holds that a summary is always helpful in the conclusion of an informative speech because it helps the audience remember what the speaker has said. Whatever one's position on this question, there can be no doubt that the final sentence of the speech brings everything together and concludes on a spirited, upbeat note that gives the speech a sense of psychological unity.

It is also important to note that the conclusion—like so much of the speech—is related directly to the audience. One of the strongest features of this speech is that the speaker consistently personalizes his ideas. Rather than talking in abstract terms, he gets the audience involved by employing the terms "you" and "your." Particularly effective examples of this occur in paragraphs 1–3, 10–11, 15, and 18–20. Indeed, by my count, the words "you" or "your" occur sixty times in the full speech. In addition, there are a number of references to "us," "we," and "our"—all of which reinforce the personal tone of the speech.

Making a Difference Through the Special Olympics

1   In Seattle, nine young athletes gathered at the starting line for the 100-yard dash. At the gun, they all started off, not exactly in a dash, but with a desire to run the race to the finish and win. All except one little boy who stumbled on the asphalt, tumbled over a couple of times, and began to cry. The other runners heard the boy cry. They stopped; they looked back. Then they all went back to the boy's side—every single one of them. One girl with Down syndrome kissed him and said, "This will make it better." Then all nine linked arms and walked to the finish line—together.

2   These athletes were not competing on national television. They were not sponsored or idolized. But they were given the opportunity to flourish under the glow of their own spotlight, to feel the brush of the ribbon cross their chests as they ran through their own finish line in their own Olympics—the Special Olympics.

3   Founded in 1968, Special Olympics invited the world to let go of limiting views, unyielding prejudices, and ignorant misconceptions about people with cognitive disabilities and to embrace the idea that they can be respected, valued, contributing members of society. Just think, one of the kids who ran through that finish line could have fallen into your arms. Or, maybe one day, could be your own child.

4   After working as a volunteer for the Special Olympics and doing additional research for this speech, I'd like to encourage you to become involved as a volunteer for the Special Olympics. We'll start by looking at the need for volunteers.

5   According to the Special Olympics Web site, more than 1.3 million people compete in Special Olympics around the world. Participants must be at least eight years old and be identified as having a cognitive or intellectual disability. There are currently 200 Special Olympics programs running in over 150 countries.

6   As the Special Olympics continues to grow, so does the need for volunteers. Here in Wisconsin, there are 10,000 athletes and 3,500 volunteer coaches. But because of all the individual attention required by Special Olympics athletes, there's always a need for more volunteer coaches, or for loads of other volunteers as well.

7   Now you know the need for Special Olympics volunteers. So the question is: What can you do to help? The answer is: Become a volunteer. The most obvious way to become a volunteer is to become a coach. Now, you don't have to be a great athlete. You don't have to have any prior coaching experience. Special Olympics offers a general course on the principles of coaching, in addition to a mentoring program in which the new coaches receive guidance from the experienced coaches.

8   If you don't want to be a coach, there are other ways to help out as well. You can work behind the scenes by assisting with fund-raising or organizing events or any of the other countless details involved in running a huge organization such as Special Olympics. It's also very important that you know that your contribution to Special Olympics can last from a day to a year to a lifetime, depending on the level of commitment that you're ready to make.

9   No matter how you decide to help, I guarantee you that working with the Special Olympics will be immensely rewarding. As a coach, your instruction and support will help your athletes develop physical skills, while your interaction and friendship will help them develop socially. Ronna Vanderslice, author of the article "Special Olympics: Beneficial to All," reports that individuals who get involved in sports and recreation through Special Olympics develop larger networks of friends, are more likely to socialize with others, and receive more social support.

10   But it's not just the athletes who benefit from Special Olympics. In my case, working with Special Olympics is one of the most gratifying things I have ever done in my life. Not only do I have the satisfaction that comes from helping others improve the quality of their lives, but I've met so many amazing people and met so many great friends that, really, I would not trade the experience for anything.

11   Now you know the need for Special Olympics volunteers, some ways that you can help out, and the benefits to the volunteers and athletes alike, so now I'd like to ask you to take the step of getting involved with the Special Olympics. If you want more information, you can check out the Web site for the Special Olympics or visit the local headquarters located on Monona Drive here in Madison. I also have brochures with contact information that I'll be handing out after the speech.

12   I know you may not have a lot of time available right now, but you can volunteer for the time that fits your schedule. The most important thing is to get involved in some capacity, for whatever amount of time you can manage.

13   Remember the nine children I mentioned at the beginning of this speech. Think of their happiness and their support for one another. Think of how much they gained from running in that race. And think of how you can help others experience the same benefits as they strive to fulfill the motto of the Special Olympics: "Let me win. But if I can't win, let me be brave in the attempt."

Making a Difference Through the Special Olympics

Commentary

"Making a Difference Through the Special Olympics" is an excellent example of how a student can utilize emotional appeals responsibly and to enhance the persuasiveness of his or her message. The speech is available online and on the DVD of student speeches that accompanies this edition of The Art of Public Speaking. Below is a synopsis that focuses on how the speaker employs the methods of persuasion discussed in Chapter 17.

Specific Purpose: To persuade my audience to volunteer for the Special Olympics.

Central Idea: Volunteering for the Special Olympics supports a worthy cause and is rewarding for athletes and volunteers alike.

Method of Organization: Monroe's motivated sequence

Credibility: The speaker establishes her credibility in paragraph 4 by stating that she has worked as a volunteer for the Special Olympics. The fact that she has personal experience with the Special Olympics frames everything she says in the rest of the speech and makes her ideas much more persuasive. This is especially true with regard to her explanation in paragraph 10 of how gratifying it is to work with the Special Olympics. This paragraph would not have nearly the same impact if the speaker had to rely on quoting a secondary source. We believe her because she is speaking from firsthand experience.

If you watch the video of the speech, you will see that the speaker's credibility is enhanced by her delivery. Not only does she speak with the voice of experience, but she speaks with a powerful sense of sincerity, conviction, and goodwill. She is, in essence, speaking from the heart, and she reaches out to the audience at a personal level.

Evidence: The speaker begins with an extended example about a race of Special Olympics athletes in Seattle. Vivid in its detail and moving in its description, the example illustrates the spirit of Special Olympics at the same time that it gains the attention and interest of the audience. It is hard to imagine a more effective way of beginning the speech.

In fact, this extended example is so effective that it raises the question of whether the speaker could have used a second extended example, especially in paragraphs 9–10, where she discusses the benefits of the Special Olympics. The quotation from Ronna Vanderslice in paragraph 9 is well chosen to support the speaker's point, but a story about the manner in which a particular individual benefited from participating in the Special Olympics would have reinforced the point and might have added to the emotional appeal of the speech. On the other hand, adding a second extended example would have required the speaker to delete something from the speech. If this issue comes up in class, it can provide a good opportunity to explore the strategic decisions a persuasive speaker must make in deciding what to include in a speech and what to leave out.

In paragraph 5, the speaker uses statistics from the Special Olympics Web site to quantify the extent of the organization's activities around the globe. Even though the figures come from the Special Olympics rather than from an outside source, they are non-controversial, and there is no reason to doubt their accuracy. The same is true of the statistics in paragraph 6 about the need for Special Olympics volunteers. Because the speech was delivered in Wisconsin, the speaker presents statistics about the situation in that state, thereby relating the topic directly to her audience.

If the speaker had more time, she could have presented additional statistics about the number of Special Olympics participants and the continuing need for volunteers, but she knew from her class survey that most of her audience already understood that charitable organizations such as Special Olympics can always use new volunteers. As a result, the speaker was able to cover the need point fairly quickly, thereby giving her more time to focus on the satisfaction and visualization steps of Monroe's motivated sequence.

The speaker uses one piece of expert testimony—the quotation in paragraph 9 from Ronna Vanderslice reporting that the athletes who participate in Special Olympics have larger networks of friends and develop stronger social skills. This is an important quotation because it deals with an aspect of the Special Olympics that requires professional expertise the speaker does not possess.

For the most part, however, the speaker is able to rely on her personal experience as a major source of evidence throughout the speech. In a sense, this is a kind of peer testimony that comes from the speaker herself. We are prepared to accept that testimony because the speaker has worked as a Special Olympics volunteer. Absent that experience, she would have had to rely much more on outside sources. It is also worth noting that the speech would have been less effective if the speaker had not taken the time to establish her credibility in the introduction. If you have students who wonder why they need to include a credibility statement in their introductions, this speech provides a perfect example of its importance.

Reasoning: The primary method of reasoning in this speech is causal. The speaker argues that volunteering for the Special Olympics benefits both the athletes and the volunteers. To put the position more formally, the speaker claims that if a particular cause occurs (in this case, volunteering for the Special Olympics), a particular effect will ensue (benefits will accrue to the athletes and volunteers alike).

Less explicit is the speaker's use of reasoning from principle. Underlying the speech is the following unstated syllogism: One should volunteer to support worthy causes; the Special Olympics is a worthy cause; therefore, one should volunteer to support the Special Olympics. In fact, a similar unstated syllogism underlies almost every appeal for support by any charitable organization. Because few people would contest the major and minor premises, they are likely to accept the conclusion as valid.

This does not mean, however, that they will automatically take the step of volunteering. To move an audience to action, a speaker must visualize the personal benefits of volunteering, answer questions about the time commitment and other practical issues, and reach the audience on an emotional as well as a logical level.

Emotional appeal: "Making a Difference Through the Special Olympics" provides an excellent example of how students can use emotional appeal in a persuasive speech that seeks immediate action. The poignant opening example establishes an emotional tone that runs throughout the entire speech and is brought full circle with the quotation of the Special Olympics' motto in the closing sentence.

Other parts of the speech that carry strong emotional impact include the following: Paragraph 2, in which the speaker talks about Special Olympics athletes having the opportunity to "flourish under the glow of their own spotlight" as they run "through their own finish line in their own Olympics." Paragraph 3, which relates the topic directly to the audience and asks them to visualize themselves greeting a Special Olympics runner at the finish line. Paragraph 10, in which the speaker talks about the personal gratification she has received from working with the Special Olympics. Paragraph 13, in which the speaker precedes her quotation of the Special Olympics' motto by referring back to her opening example and reminding the audience of its emotional connotations.

Finally, there is the speaker's delivery, which adds greatly to her emotional appeal even as it boosts her credibility. Her delivery is animated, direct, and extemporaneous. She has excellent eye contact, establishes a strong communicative bond with the audience, and exudes goodwill throughout. She does not use a great deal of overtly emotional language, but the substance of her ideas, in combination with her heartfelt delivery, produces a speech that is notable both for its emotional appeal and its ethical value.

Putting the Brakes on Teenage Driving

1   On a chilly November night two years ago, a Ford Explorer was charging down a California highway. The 16-year-old driver and three of his friends were returning from a concert in Los Angeles. These young people were good students, gifted athletes, talented artists and musicians. And none were drunk or impaired by drugs.

2   They were, however, driving too fast, and the driver lost control of the car. The car went into a ditch and hit a tree. The driver and one passenger were killed. The other two passengers escaped with severe injuries. One of these passengers was my nephew. Today he is finishing high school in a wheelchair, a wheelchair he will occupy for the rest of his life.

3   Unfortunately, tragic auto accidents involving teenage drivers are much too common in all parts of the United States. After researching the subject for my speech, I have come to the same conclusion as the experts—that the best way to prevent such accidents is to raise the age for full driving privileges to 18 or older.

4   I know from my audience-analysis questionnaire that most of you oppose such a plan. But I also know from my questionnaires that most of you recognize that 16- and 17-year-old drivers are less skilled and less responsible than older drivers. So I ask you to listen with an open mind while we discuss some of the problems associated with teenage driving, the major causes of the problems, and a plan that will go a long way toward solving the problems.

5   No matter how one looks at the evidence, it all leads to one fact: There are too many motor vehicle accidents, deaths, and injuries involving teenage drivers. According to the National Highway Traffic Safety Administration, while teenagers make up 7 percent of the nation's licensed drivers, they represent 14 percent of all motor vehicle fatalities. The NHTSA reports that last year 3,657 drivers aged 16 to 20 were killed in automobile accidents. In addition to killing the drivers, these same accidents took the lives of 2,384 teenage passengers. But these accidents didn't affect teenagers alone. They also took the lives of 2,625 people aged 21 or older. So the total number of people killed last year in automobile accidents involving teenage drivers was 8,666—almost exactly the number of full-time students at this campus.

6   Evidence also shows that the younger the driver, the greater the risk. According to the Insurance Institute for Highway Safety, 16-year-olds have "the highest percentage of crashes involving speeding, the highest percentage of single-vehicle crashes, and the highest percentage of crashes involving driver error." Moreover, as *USA Today* reports, 16-year-olds are three times more likely to be involved in fatal crashes than are older drivers.

7   Now that we've seen the extent of the problem, we can explore its causes. One of the causes is inexperience. New drivers just haven't had enough time on the road to develop their driving skills. But inexperience is far from the only cause of the problem. After all, there will always be inexperienced drivers—even if the driving age is raised to 21 or even to 25.

8   A second cause is revealed by brain research. Findings from the National Institute of Mental Health show that the brain of an average 16-year-old has not developed to the point where he or she is able to effectively judge the risk of a given situation. Dr. Jay Giedd, who led the research team that conducted the study, states: "When a smart, talented, and very mature teen does something that a parent might call 'stupid,' it's this underdeveloped part of the brain that has most likely failed." Steven Lowenstein, a medical professor at the University of Colorado, has just finished a five-year study comparing the traffic records of 16-year-old drivers to drivers aged 25 to 49. His conclusion? "Deliberate risk taking and dangerous and aggressive driving behaviors predominated" among the 16-year-olds.

9   A third cause of motor vehicle fatalities among teenage drivers is night driving. According to the *Washington Post*, when 16-year-olds get behind the wheel of a car after dark, the likelihood of having an accident increases several times over. Of course, nighttime driving is less safe for everyone, but it becomes particularly dangerous when combined with a young driver's inexperience and reduced ability to gauge risk.

10   Finally, there is the presence of teenage passengers in the car. We all know what it's like to drive with our friends—the stereo is up loud, cell phones are ringing, everybody's laughing and having a good time. The problem is that all these factors create distractions, distractions that too often result in accidents, injury, and death. Allan Williams, chief scientist at the Insurance Institute for Highway Safety, reports that one teenage passenger doubles the risk of a fatal crash. With two or more passengers, the risk is five times greater. Remember my nephew's accident I mentioned at the start of my speech? There were three passengers in the car.

11   So the extent of the problem is clear. So, too, are its causes. What steps can we take to help bring about a solution? First, we need a national policy that no one can receive a learner's permit until age 16, and no one can receive full driving privileges until age 18. This will allow 16-year-olds time to gain driving experience before having an unrestricted license and to reach a stage of brain development where they are better able to handle the risk and responsibility of driving.

12   Second, we need to restrict nighttime driving so as to keep younger drivers off the road when conditions are riskiest. Some states have tried to address this problem by banning teenagers from driving after midnight or 1 a.m., but as the Insurance Institute for Highway Safety reports, these laws don't go far enough. According to the Institute, we need a 9:00 p.m. or 10:00 p.m. limit until drivers reach the age of 18.

13   Third, we need to restrict the number of teenage passengers in cars driven by younger drivers. In fact, says Kevin Quinlan from the National Transportation Safety Board, "passenger restriction is the first and foremost measure you can take" to reduce teenage driving fatalities. According to Quinlan, the optimal policy would be to bar drivers age 17 or younger from having any passengers in the car unless the riders are adults or family members. Drivers from the age of 17 to 18 should not be allowed to carry more than one teenage passenger.

14   Now I know all of this might sound harsh and perhaps inconvenient, but the evidence is clear that it would save a significant number of lives. "If you want to discuss harsh," said one father whose 17-year-old son died in an accident three years ago, "I can talk to you about harsh. It's being awakened at 2:30 in the morning by the State Patrol telling you that your son has just been killed."

15   Everyone in this room has lived to college age. But this year alone, thousands of teenage drivers will not live that long. And they won't live that long due to factors that we can prevent. There's no way to solve all the problems we encounter on the road, but we can do something to help save the lives of younger drivers and make the road safer for all of us. As I said earlier, this might sound harsh or inconvenient, but I know my nephew would gladly trade both for the chance to walk again.

Putting the Brakes on Teenage Driving

Commentary

"Putting the Brakes on Teenage Driving" is an instructive example of a persuasive speech on a question of policy. Because it deals with a controversial issue that may draw the opposition of some students, be sure to focus class discussion on the organization, supporting materials, and persuasive methods of the speech rather than on the merits or demerits of the speaker's proposal. Here is an analysis.

Specific Purpose: To persuade my audience that the age for full driving privileges should be raised to 18.

Central Idea: Raising the age for full driving privileges to 18 will help reduce the large number of accidents and deaths among teenage drivers.

Method of Organization: Problem-cause-solution

Introduction: Consisting of paragraphs 1–4, the introduction opens with a story about an automobile accident that claimed the lives of two teenagers and seriously injured two others, including the speaker's nephew. The fact that the speaker's nephew will have to spend the rest of his life in a wheelchair makes clear why the speaker feels so strongly about the subject of teenage driving and increases the likelihood that the audience will pay close attention to her ideas. In paragraph 4, the speaker explicitly asks her classmates to listen with an open mind. This is always a good strategy when the audience is overtly opposed to a speaker's position.

Body: There are three main points in the body of this speech, the first of which argues that there are far too many motor vehicle accidents, injuries, and deaths involving teenage drivers. In paragraph 5, the speaker presents statistics from the National Highway Traffic Safety Administration to show the seriousness of the problem. It is worth noting how she relates the statistics directly to her listeners by stating that the total number of people killed last year in accidents involving teenage drivers is almost exactly the same as the number of full-time students at the school attended by the speaker and her classmates.

In paragraph 6, the speaker turns from teenage drivers in general to 16-year-olds, who constitute by far the highest risk group. She supports her claim with strong evidence from the Insurance Institute for Highway Safety and *USA Today*. In the light of this evidence, it would be hard for even the most skeptical listener to deny that there is a substantially higher risk of accidents and deaths among 16-year-old drivers than among any other group of drivers.

Having established the existence of a serious problem, the speaker devotes paragraphs 7–10 to exploring the causes of the problem. One of the advantages of using problem-cause-solution order is that it helps ensure that a speaker's plan will actually get at the causes of the problem rather than merely addressing its symptoms. In this speech, it has the added benefit of demonstrating that the problem stems primarily from the age of young drivers, rather than from other factors that are not directly associated with age.

The speaker begins her discussion of the causes in paragraph 7 by pointing to the inexperience of younger drivers. Anticipating the mental response of her listeners, however, she also notes that inexperience is far from the only cause of the problem. After all, there will always be inexperienced drivers no matter what the driving age may be. This is a good example of how persuasive speakers should anticipate and answer objections that are likely to arise in the audience's mind.

In paragraph 8, the speaker relies on brain research to show that most 16-year-olds are inherently more likely to engage in risk taking and other dangerous behaviors on the road than are older drivers. In paragraph 9, she notes that younger drivers are particularly prone to accidents when driving after dark, and in paragraph 10, she documents the fact that the presence of teenage passengers in a car driven by a teenager dramatically increases the risk of a fatal accident. In each case, the speaker documents her claim with evidence from reliable, high-quality sources. Although a listener might ultimately disagree with the speaker about her proposal to raise the driving age, it is difficult for a reasonable listener to deny the weight of the evidence in the problem and cause sections of the speech.

In paragraphs 11–13, the speaker presents a three-part solution. First, she calls for a national policy in which no one could receive full driving privileges before age 18 (paragraph 11). Second, she proposes limiting nighttime driving by teenagers (paragraph 12). Third, she recommends restricting the number of teenage passengers in cars driven by younger drivers (paragraph 13). Taken together, these proposals address all four of the causes of the problem discussed in main point two. Because the speaker is not an authority on highway safety, she uses expert testimony to show that her plan will in fact reduce teenage driving fatalities.

She ends the solution section of her speech in paragraph 14 by addressing the objection that her plan is harsh and inconvenient. She confronts the issue with a powerful quotation from a father whose son died in a traffic accident. This quotation adds emotional appeal and forces listeners to think about the tradeoff between convenience and saving lives.

Conclusion: The speaker begins her conclusion (paragraph 15) by encouraging her classmates to reflect on their lives relative to the thousands of teenage drivers who will be killed this year alone and will never have the chance to attend college. She then summarizes her main points, reinforces her central idea, and builds upon the emotional appeal of the quotation in paragraph 14. In the final sentence she refers again to her nephew's accident, noting that he would gladly accept the inconvenience caused by her policy for the chance to walk again. The appeal here is powerful, dramatic, and personal—an excellent example of how to craft a memorable, hard-hitting conclusion.

The Ultimate Gift

1   Are you at least 17 years old? Do you weigh more than 110 pounds? Do you consider yourself fairly healthy?

2   If you answered yes to all of these questions, you should be donating blood every two months. In my survey of the class, I found that only 50 percent of you have ever donated blood and that only 1 out of 13 of you donate on a regular basis. The lack of participation of eligible donors is a serious problem that requires immediate action. Through extensive research and two years of faithfully donating blood, I have come to realize the magnitude of this problem and just how easy the solution can be.

3   Today I would like to show why blood donors are in such desperate need and encourage you to take action to combat this need. Let's first take a look at the overwhelming need for blood donors.

4   The lack of participation of eligible blood donors poses a threat to the lives of many Americans. According to the American Red Cross Web pages, where I obtained an enormous amount of information, in the United States alone someone undergoes a blood transfusion once every three seconds, which amounts to 3,000 gallons of blood every hour, day and night. People who benefit from donations range from cancer patients to organ transplant patients to surgical patients; even premature infants and trauma victims benefit from donations. The need for blood never takes a vacation and neither should donors.

5   Let me tell you about Brooke, a three-year-old girl with long, curly blond hair and bright blue eyes. Brooke is a victim of cancer and had major surgery to remove a large tumor in her abdomen. She has spent approximately half of her life in the hospital receiving chemotherapy and other treatments for infections that resulted from a decrease in her white blood cell count after each session.

6   According to Texas Children's Hospital, Brooke's treatment will require blood products with a replacement value of 508 units of blood, of which only 250 units have been replaced. She still needs more than 250 units of blood to continue her treatment. If she doesn't receive this blood, she will not live to attend kindergarten, to go to the prom in high school, or to get married— luxuries we all too often take for granted.

7   Cases like Brooke's are becoming all too common these days, with only 1 in 20 eligible Americans donating blood and the donor rate dropping steadily at 2 percent annually. These facts are particularly distressing considering that nearly half of us here will receive blood sometime in our lives.

8   You can now see the magnitude of the problem with the lack of blood donations. Fortunately, it is a problem that can be easily solved. Each and every one of you can be part of the solution. All you have to do to save priceless lives is go to the nearest Red Cross and donate your blood.

9   For those of you who have never donated blood before, the process is so simple and easy. First, you fill out a donor information form that asks you questions about your sexual history and health. You will then receive a mini-physical. They will take a drop of blood from your finger to measure the percent of red cells in your blood. Then they will take your blood pressure, as well as your temperature and pulse. So not only are you saving lives by donating blood, you are also checking on your own.

10   After your physical, you will be asked from which arm you prefer to donate. Then you will be asked to lie on a donor chair. A staff member will clean your arm and insert a sterile, nonreusable needle, so there is no way to contract AIDS from donating blood. After a pint of your blood has been taken, which usually takes about 10 minutes, you will be asked to rest for 10 to 15 minutes while you enjoy juice and cookies. The process is over, and in eight weeks you can donate again.

11   Many of you may be scared at the thought of the anticipated pain and needles. I admit I was terrified the first time I gave blood, but then I realized I was scared over nothing. The extent of the pain as they insert the needle is equivalent to someone scratching your arm for a brief second, and while the needle is in your arm, you don't feel a thing. And as I stated before, it is impossible to contract AIDS from donating blood.

12   Now that you know how easy and safe the solution is to the lack of blood donations, let's take a look at just how much difference your donations can make. Every unit of blood you donate can help save up to three lives. You see, the blood you donate is divided three ways—into red blood cells, white blood cells, and platelets. Each of these are stored separately and used for different types of treatment. Red blood cells are used to treat anemia. White blood cells are used to fight infections, while platelets are important to control bleeding and are used in patients with leukemia and other forms of cancer.

13   The joy you get from helping three people can be increased many times over. You see, you can donate blood six times in a year. Those six donations could help as many as 18 people. Just think, if you donated for 10 years, you could help save the lives of nearly 180 people. Who knows—one of those lives could be that of a friend, a family member, or even your own, since you can now donate in advance of your own surgery.

14   Now that you know what a difference just one donation can make, I want to encourage you to take action. I urge you to take a stand and become a regular blood donor. Forty-five minutes out of your day is a small price to pay for the lifetime of satisfaction you receive by knowing you may have saved a life. If you have never donated blood before, pull deep inside yourself to find some courage and become a proud wearer of the "I am a first time blood donor" sticker. If you have donated before, think back to the feeling of pride you received from making your donation.

15   Finally, I ask all of you to think of a loved one you hold so dear to your heart. Imagine they need a blood transfusion and there is a shortage of donations that day so they can't receive the treatment they so desperately need—just like Brooke, the three-year-old girl I talked about earlier. Go to the nearest Red Cross in Madison, which is on Sheboygan Avenue, or attend the next blood drive here on campus. These drives are held in various parts of campus, including the dorms. In fact, the next drive will be held in the Ogg Residence Hall in two weeks.

16   Please take this opportunity to save lives and make yourself feel like a million bucks. Give the ultimate gift—the gift of life. Donate blood!

The Ultimate Gift

Commentary

"The Ultimate Gift," a speech urging the audience to become regular blood donors, provides an excellent model of Monroe's motivated sequence. Here is a synopsis of the speech that focuses on its use of the motivated sequence.

Specific Purpose: To persuade my audience to become regular blood donors.

Central Idea: By becoming regular blood donors, college students can help save lives and replenish the shrinking U.S. blood supply.

Method of Organization: Monroe's motivated sequence

Attention: The attention section of the speech can be found in the introduction, which consists of paragraphs 1–3. The opening sequence of three rhetorical questions in paragraph 1 gets the audience involved right at the outset, while the first sentence of paragraph 2 moves from the opening questions to the topic of blood donation. After pulling the audience further into the speech by referring to her audience-analysis questionnaire, the speaker establishes her credibility by noting that she has been a regular blood donor for the past two years. A concise preview statement in paragraph 3 completes the introduction and provides a strong lead-in to the next section of the speech.

Need: The need section, which comprises the first main point in the body of the speech, runs from paragraph 4 through paragraph 7. In this section, the speaker supports her claim that the lack of participation by eligible blood donors is a serious problem. She begins in paragraph 4 by presenting statistics from the American Red Cross and by noting some of the medical conditions that require blood donations for treatment. In paragraphs 5–6, she presents an extended example of a three-year-old child named Brooke who requires massive amounts of blood for her cancer treatments. Paragraph 7 completes the need section by moving from the example of Brooke to additional quantitative evidence about the shortage of blood donors nationally.

Satisfaction: An excellent transition at the beginning of paragraph 8 moves the speaker from the need section to the satisfaction section, which constitutes the second main point in the body. After stating her policy in paragraph 8, the speaker devotes paragraphs 9–11 to explaining the process of donating blood. In doing so, she addresses three concerns that many of her classmates had mentioned on their audience-analysis questionnaires. First, she spells out the details of the process so people will know exactly what to expect when they go to donate blood. Second, she notes that all blood is drawn with sterile, nonreusable needles, so one need not fear contracting AIDS from donating. Third, she reassures listeners that despite many people's fear of needles, the process of donating blood is virtually painless.

Clear, crisp, and detailed, this section of the speech provides a model satisfaction section. One of the best ways to communicate this to students is to ask them to imagine the speech without paragraphs 9–11. Most will see at once how much weaker the speech would be if these paragraphs were not present. It is also worth noting how the speaker relates her ideas directly to the audience by talking in terms of "you" and "your" throughout paragraphs 9–11.

Visualization: After completing the satisfaction section, the speaker shifts to the visualization section with a transition at the start of paragraph 12. Consisting of paragraphs 12–13, this section comprises the third main point in the body. Here the speaker visualizes for her audience the benefits that will accrue if her policy is adopted.

She begins in paragraph 12 by explaining that because every unit of donated blood is divided three ways, it is possible to help as many as three people with a single donation. In paragraph 13, she builds upon this analysis by noting that since a person can donate blood six times annually, it is possible to help as many as 18 different people in a single year and up to 180 over ten years. The final sentence of paragraph 13 does an excellent job of relating these figures to the speaker's classmates by stating that their donations could benefit a friend, a family member, or even themselves.

Action: Another excellent transition, at the beginning of paragraph 14, marks the beginning of the action section, which constitutes the conclusion and runs through the end of the speech in paragraph 16. As with the other parts of the speech, this section is extremely well developed. Rather than cursorily stating that her classmates should start donating blood, the speaker steadily builds her call for action throughout paragraphs 14–16.

In paragraph 14, she appeals both to first-time blood donors and to people who have donated before. In paragraph 15, she uses emotional appeal by asking the audience to think of someone dear to them who might be denied blood when they urgently need it—just like the three-year-old girl discussed earlier in the speech. The speaker then tells her classmates exactly where they can go to donate blood, including the location of the next blood drive on campus. She ends in paragraph 16 with three sentences that become progressively shorter and more imperative in tone. As in the rest of the speech, she brings her ideas home to her classmates throughout the action section by addressing them directly as "you."

Self-Defense on Campus

1   You're tired; you're hungry. You've just spent a long day at College Library and you can't wait to get back to your room. Glancing outside, you remember how quickly it becomes dark. You don't think much of it, though, as you bundle up and head out into the gusty wind. Not until you spy the shadows on the sidewalk or hear the leaves rustling beside you do you wish you weren't alone. You walk quickly, trying to stop your imagination from thinking of murderers and rapists. Only when you are safely inside your room do you relax and try to stop your heart from pounding out of your chest.

2   Can you remember a time when you felt this way? I would be surprised if you never have. The FBI reported last year that there were three murders, approximately 430 aggravated assaults, 1,400 burglaries, and 80 rapes here in Madison alone. And while these statistics are quite alarming, they don't even compare to the numbers of larger metropolitan areas.

3   No matter where we live, crime affects us all—men and women, students and instructors, young and old. We need to stop being the victims. One way we can do this is by enrolling in a self-defense course. There are many times I can remember when my heart seemed to pound out of my chest, but because I took an introductory course in self-defense, I feel more confident and more prepared to deal with potentially dangerous situations. Today I would like to encourage all of you to enroll in a self-defense course. Let's start by looking at the dangers of crime we face as college students.

4   College students face many crime issues, both as members of society and as students on campus. These crimes endanger our money, our property, our self-confidence, our psychological well-being, and even our lives. According to the Foundation for Crime Prevention Education, violence and crime have dramatically increased. An American is six times more likely to be assaulted with a weapon today than in 1960. The FBI reports that someone either is murdered, raped, assaulted, or robbed every 16 seconds. This means today, at the end of our 50-minute class period, approximately 187 people will have been victims of a violent crime.

5   College students, many of whom are away from home for the first time, are especially easy targets for crime. Students often look at campus housing as a secure place. But according to the book *Street Wisdom for Women*, precautions must be taken in a dorm or Greek house, just as in any house or apartment. How many of these bad habits do you have? How often do you leave your room without locking your door, forgetting how easily accessible your room is to anyone? How often do you fall asleep without locking your door? Or how often do you open your door without first checking to see who is there? As the Wake Forest University Police Crime Prevention Web site states, "Each of us must become aware of the precautions necessary to reduce the likelihood that we will become victims of crime." Those who forget to take these precautions invite trouble.

6   Although students must watch themselves in campus housing, they must also take care elsewhere. Prevalent use of drugs and alcohol, especially on college campuses, increases the chance of crime. Using drugs or alcohol makes you an easier target because, as we all know, it affects your judgment, influencing your decisions on safety. According to the Pacific Center for Violence Prevention, in 42 percent of all violent crimes, either the assailant, the victim, or both had been drinking. Specifically on campus, 90 percent of all violent crimes involve drugs and/or alcohol. This problem is so serious that testimony by law enforcement officials reprinted on the Security on Campus Web site indicates that many college campuses are the highest crime areas in their communities.

7   So now that we see the dangers we face as students, what can we do to protect ourselves? Although there are many ways of dealing with crime, I recommend that you and every college student enroll in a self-defense course. You can choose from a variety of self-defense courses offered right here in Madison. You can find one to fit your schedule and your pocketbook. On campus, the university has a club sport called Shorin Ryu Karate, which emphasizes practical self-defense. They hold their meetings in the evening, after classes, right on campus, and they're open to all university students, faculty, and staff.

8   Another option is Villari's Self-Defense and Tai Chi Center, which not only offers courses in self-defense, but in tai chi, karate, and kung-fu. Villari's location on State Street is convenient for all university students. To find a class that fits your needs, you can also search over the Internet or through the Yellow Pages. I also brought along some brochures today, so if you are interested, please see me after class.

9   After enrolling in a self-defense course, you will find yourself much better prepared to deal with an emergency situation. Patrick Lee, an instructor for a course called "Self-Defense for Women: Victim or Survivor," claims the biggest thing he teaches in his courses is that you must decide from the beginning whether you want to be the victim or the survivor. Repeating over and over again that "I am a survivor" not only increases your self-confidence but helps you think more clearly in a difficult situation.

10   I didn't realize the importance of this myself until I took an introductory course in self-defense in my high school physical education class. After a few days of practice, each of us faced the notorious padded attacker. Expecting to enjoy fighting the attacker, I prepared to yell "No; stop; back off" as forcefully as possible. But before I knew it, this man, twice my size, had put me in a hold I could not get out of. My mind was so overcome with fear that I could barely muster out a "No." Immediately, I pictured this as a real situation, one which I probably would not have survived.

11   But after a few more days of practice, we were able to go against the padded attacker one more time. This time, I no longer felt fear. I felt anger. I was angry that this

man felt he could take advantage of me. This time, using what I learned, I yelled "No; back off" and successfully escaped his move. And this time I survived.

12   I'm not the only example showing the benefits of taking self-defense. If you're interested, check out "Stories From Self-Defense Classes" posted to the Internet by the Assault Prevention Information Network. Although I don't have the time to share with you the dozens of success stories, I can sum them up with a quote by Cindy, a 23-year-old woman who used her self-defense knowledge to scare off an assailant. Cindy says, "I know deep inside, where it matters most, that I have what it takes to defend myself if need be, and this feeling is one of pure joy." As you can see, self-defense is time and money well invested.

13   So I encourage you to enroll in a self-defense course, whether it be through a physical education class or through a private organization and whether you do it here or back in your hometown. Even if you do not enroll right away, I encourage you to do so in the near future. Taking such a course could mean keeping your money, protecting your property, defending yourself, your boyfriend or girlfriend, husband or wife. It could even mean the difference between life and death.

14   Don't ever think, "It could never happen to me." Why not be prepared? As Patrick Lee said, "Ask yourself, do you want to be the victim or the survivor?"

Self-Defense on Campus

Commentary

"Self-Defense on Campus" is an excellent speech that illustrates how students can utilize all the methods of persuasion discussed in the textbook. Here is a synopsis that focuses on how the speaker employs the methods of persuasion.

Specific Purpose: To persuade my audience to enroll in a self-defense class.

Central Idea: Enrolling in a self-defense class is an effective way for students to help protect themselves against the dangers of crime they face on campus and in society at large.

Method of Organization: Monroe's motivated sequence

Credibility: In keeping with the functions of a speech introduction discussed in Chapter 10 of the textbook, the speaker establishes her credibility in paragraph 3 by noting that because she has taken a self-defense class, she feels more prepared to deal with potentially dangerous situations. The audience is more likely to listen carefully to the rest of the speech knowing that the speaker has firsthand experience on the topic.

The speaker turns to her experience again in paragraphs 10–11 when she presents an extended example showing how she learned to protect herself in her self-defense class. Although this example is used to demonstrate the practicality of the speaker's policy, it also reinforces her credibility and strengthens the persuasiveness of the entire speech. So, too, do the speaker's sincerity, command of the topic, and goodwill toward the audience— all of which are evident throughout her presentation.

Evidence: The speaker uses two extended examples to excellent effect. The hypothetical example that opens the speech gains attention and relates the topic to the audience. Its impact is reinforced by the statistics in paragraph 2 that connect the example directly to the college community in which the speech was delivered. In paragraphs 10–11, the speaker uses an extended example based on her own experience to demonstrate how taking a class in self-defense can increase one's confidence and ability to respond properly in a dangerous situation. These two examples are among the most memorable parts of the speech and are central to its persuasive appeal.

The speaker is equally adept in her use of statistics. Those in paragraph 2 show that the hypothetical example presented in paragraph 1 is not far-fetched, while those in paragraph 4 reinforce the point that crime is a serious problem in American society. It should also be noted how, in paragraph 4, the speaker translates her numbers into terms that relate directly to her classmates by noting that, during the 50 minutes of their speech class, 187 people will have been the victims of a violent crime. In paragraph 6, the speaker presents figures that show the correlation between violent crimes and the use of alcohol and/or illegal drugs. Here, as elsewhere, the speaker's statistics come from reputable sources, and she identifies those sources for the audience.

As with examples and statistics, testimony plays an important role in this speech. The speaker uses testimony twice in paragraph 5 to underscore the importance of taking precautions against crime—first, when she paraphrases the book Street Wisdom for Women, and second, when she quotes the Wake Forest University Crime Prevention Web site. In paragraph 7, she cites the Security on Campus Web site to support her point that many college campuses are the highest crime areas in their communities. In paragraph 9, she presents expert testimony from Patrick Lee, a self-defense instructor, and in paragraph 12 she employs peer testimony from a woman named Cindy who used her self-defense knowledge to scare off an assailant. Finally, in paragraph 14, the speaker concludes with a quotation from Patrick Lee asking, "Do you want to be the victim or the survivor?"

Reasoning: The primary method of reasoning in this speech is causal. The speaker does not claim that lack of training in self-defense causes crime or that taking a self-defense class will produce a reduction in crime. Rather, she argues that lack of training in self-defense makes a person more vulnerable to crime and that taking a self-defense course will make a person more confident and more prepared to deal with potentially dangerous situations.

What makes the reasoning of this speech persuasive, however, is less the structure of the speaker's argument than the strength of her evidence. All of her main points are backed up with excellent supporting materials, and she does an especially good job in paragraphs 9–12 of demonstrating that taking a self-defense course will in fact produce the benefits she claims for it. Given the speaker's evidence, most listeners are prepared to accept her reasoning.

Emotional Appeal: Although "Self-Defense on Campus" does not employ a great deal of overtly emotional language, it still generates fairly strong emotional appeal. One of the emotions it taps is the fear of becoming a crime victim. This is especially evident in the vivid hypothetical example that opens the speech, but it is reinforced by the speaker's statistics and testimony throughout the problem section (paragraphs 4–6). The speaker's use of fear appeals can also be seen in paragraph 10, in which she narrates her experience of being unable to fight off the padded attacker at the beginning of her self-defense class.

In addition to presenting fear appeals, the speaker provides a specific course of action through which her listeners can combat the source of fear. Research has demonstrated that this is the most effective way to use fear appeals in a persuasive speech. Having aroused the audience's concern about being able to protect themselves in a dangerous situation, the speaker then discusses the sense of security, confidence, and even happiness that come from receiving training in self-defense. In paragraph 11, she explains how she learned to thwart the padded attacker by the end of her self-defense class, and in paragraph 12 she quotes the feeling of "pure joy" described by one woman who used her self-defense training to scare off an assailant.

In all these cases, the emotional appeal grows naturally out of the speech content and is strengthened by the speaker's sincerity and conviction. It is also worth noting that there is a strongly gendered dimension to the emotional appeal in this speech. Although the speaker makes a concerted effort in several places to relate her subject to the men in her audience, there is no doubt that the fear of crime—and especially of personal assault—is greater among women than among men. It is also true that the speaker's extended examples—both the hypothetical example in paragraph 1 and the personal example in paragraphs 10–11—tend to resonate most powerfully with women. This is not a weakness in the speech, but it does provide an interesting point for discussion about the nature of emotional appeal and the manner in which it can vary from audience to audience.

To Save a Child

1   For every morning that you wake up and eat breakfast, there are 840 million people beginning their daily struggle with chronic, persistent hunger. For every morning that you have the privilege of going to class, 250 million children head off to work where many will make less than $1 a day. And for every day that this vicious cycle continues, there are 24,000 fewer people in our world.

2   Millions of children living in developing countries cannot depend on their parents to support them. Rather, they live each day with little more than the hope that someone more fortunate than them might take compassion on them. By sponsoring a child for two years through an organization called Compassion International, I have seen the difference that $28 a month can make in a child's life.

3   Today, I'd like to encourage you to become involved with Compassion International. First, I will look at the desperate help children worldwide need. Second, I want to explain Compassion International and what it is they are doing to help meet the needs of these children. And finally, I will show you that Compassion International is an upstanding, legitimate organization that will put your money to work saving the lives of children. Let's start by looking at the need for this organization.

4   The demand for organizations such as Compassion International in developing countries is so great because of two main reasons: poverty and poor education. According to the World Bank Web site, it is poverty that causes 250 million children to work full- or part-time jobs while they should be receiving an education. In Thailand, for example, the typical 11- to 15-year-old boy or girl is forced to work an average of 50 hours every week. Similarly, in Bangladesh, children who do not attend school work as long, if not longer, hours than adults by the time they reach just 13 years of age.

5   According to a brochure sent to me by Compassion International, the average family income in Central America is $50 per month. Unfortunately, the cost of food in Central America is the same as in the United States. Because so few families can afford the cost of groceries, half of all children living in Central America are malnourished. Twenty percent of them are so severely malnourished that improved diet alone will not cure them.

6   Of course the problem isn't limited to Central America. The Hunger Project Web site claims that worldwide "about 24,000 people die from hunger or hunger-related causes every day, and three-fourths of them are children under the age of five." To put this in perspective, 24,000 deaths is equivalent to more than half the students on this campus dying every day. To think of it another way, it means that more children lose their lives to hunger every week than the number of Americans that lose their lives to cancer in an entire year.

7   According to the Hunger Project, "the best way to reduce hunger is through education because the educated are best able to break out of the cycle of poverty that causes hunger." Once again, let's look at Central America. Most of the children in Central America are not required to go to school. And if they do go, it is rare that they ever make it past the 6th grade because even public education is too expensive. This cycle is never-ending. If children do not become educated, they will never be able to make enough money to break out of the cycle of poverty. However, this vicious cycle can be broken with the help of Compassion International.

8   Compassion International was founded in 1952 by the Reverend Everett Swanson as a result of working with orphans in Korea. Swanson established a program through which people could sponsor needy Korean children for a few dollars a month. Those children would receive benefits that included food, clothing, education, shelter, and health care. Since then, Compassion International has expanded to 22 countries and has assisted more than 500,000 children across the globe.

9   Compassion International works in this way: In each community where they sponsor children, there is a place called the project. This is where the children go to receive nutritious meals and additional schooling. The projects are small, usually 150 children, and the local staff works hard to become personally acquainted with each sponsored child and his or her individual needs. Through providing them with an education now, Compassion is helping children to support themselves and their families in the future.

10   When you sponsor a child, it is usually for several years until the child is either 18 or has completed their schooling. You can sponsor a child for just $28 a month and even have the option of paying several months to a year in advance. Compassion International understands that there may be a time when you can't support your child. This is why there is no obligation to continue your sponsorship. Compassion International claims that they will immediately look for a new sponsor for your child and he or she will have continued support without interruption.

11   I have been sponsoring a little boy named Jose Francisco for two years. He lives in Ecuador with a family of seven and is ten years old. I get about three letters a year from Jose, and it's clear from those letters that he has had new opportunities to learn and grow—both physically and mentally. Being Jose's sponsor has been incredibly rewarding and is something that every one of us has the opportunity to do.

12   At this point, most of you are probably thinking, "How much of my money actually goes to helping my child?" Any true skeptic would feel the same way. From my class survey, more than 50 percent of you thought that less than half of your money would go directly to your child. And I, too, was reluctant to sponsor a child at first for the same reason.

13   Because of this, I read a report on Compassion conducted by the Better Business Bureau. This report shows that 78 percent of your money goes directly to your child. Of the rest of your money, 9 percent goes toward fund-raising. The other 13 percent is for administration purposes and includes the increase in net assets.

14   Another reassuring factor for me was that when I went to Compassion International's Web site, I discovered that they are audited both internally on a periodical basis and externally every year. Both of these audits help to ensure that funds are properly received, tracked, and managed for each child. From this evidence it's clear that Compassion International is an upstanding organization and is deserving of its rank from *Smart Money* magazine as "one of the top ten charitable organizations in the entire country."

15   So today I'd like to encourage you to sponsor a child of your own through Compassion International. When you consider that $28 a month amounts to less than one dollar a day, is this really too much to give to provide a child with an education, food, and health care that will help break the cycle of poverty? If $28 a month, every month, is still too much, I encourage you to provide a child with a one-time gift of $28.

16   Your $28, whether you give it just once or every month, can help save a child's life and fill them with hope for the future. This is why the time to start thinking about sponsoring a child is right now, and the time to take action is today. If you are interested in sponsoring a child or want to find out more information, I'll be distributing brochures for Compassion International after my speech.

17   May your compassion for the well being of the world's children encourage you to open your heart and maybe even your checkbook. Because as Compassion International states, "while we cannot individually change the world, we can change the world for one child."

To Save a Child

Commentary

A persuasive speech seeking immediate action, "To Save a Child" is an excellent example of how to use Monroe's motivated sequence. Here is a synopsis of the speech.

Specific Purpose: To persuade my audience to help children worldwide by contributing to Compassion International.

Central Idea: Contributing to an organization such as Compassion International can help break the cycle of poverty that affects millions of children.

Method of Organization: Monroe's motivated sequence

Introduction: The introduction consists of paragraphs 1–3. In paragraph 1, the speaker accomplishes the attention step of Monroe's motivated sequence by relating the plight of millions of impoverished children around the world to the daily activities of her audience. Paragraph 2 introduces the topic of the speech and establishes the speaker's credibility by noting that she has sponsored a child through Compassion International for the past two years. The introduction ends in paragraph 3 with a detailed preview statement that provides an excellent lead-in to the body.

Body: In the first main point of the body, the speaker demonstrates the need to help impoverished children around the world (paragraphs 4–7). Drawing on sources such as the World Bank and the Hunger Project, she uses statistics and testimony to argue that poverty, hunger, and poor education create a need for charitable organizations such as Compassion International. The speaker does a fine job translating statistics into terms that can be readily understood by her classmates when she states that the 24,000 hunger-related deaths that occur in the world every day are equivalent to half the students on her campus dying every day. She also draws a comparison between the number of daily hunger-related deaths and the number of Americans who die of cancer every year.

After providing a brief transition at the end of paragraph 7, the speaker moves to the satisfaction step of Monroe's motivated sequence, which constitutes the second main point in the body of her speech. Paragraph 8 provides information about the founding and growth of Compassion International. Paragraph 9 provides details about the activities of Compassion International in the communities where it sponsors children. Paragraph 10 explains the options for donating to Compassion International, with special emphasis upon a monthly gift of $28. Paragraph 11 concludes the satisfaction step of Monroe's motivated sequence with the speaker explaining her personal involvement in Compassion International.

In paragraphs 12–14, the speaker moves to the visualization step of Monroe's motivated sequence. Knowing from her class survey that many of her classmates were skeptical about the extent to which money donated to charitable organizations actually goes to the people it is intended to help, the speaker provides evidence to document the financial integrity of Compassion International. In paragraph 13, she cites figures from the Better Business Bureau to show that 78 percent of the money donated to Compassion International goes directly to helping needy children. In paragraph 14, she explains how Compassion International is audited on a regular basis to help ensure that its funds are properly received, tracked, and managed. She ends paragraph 14 with a quotation from Smart Money magazine indicating that Compassion International is one of the top 10 charitable organizations in the United States. All in all, paragraphs 12–14 provide an excellent example of how to develop the visualization step when using Monroe's motivated sequence.

Conclusion: Consisting of paragraphs 15–17, the conclusion presents the action step in the motivated sequence. In paragraph 15, the speaker asks listeners to donate $28 a month. If they can't afford that, she encourages them to make a one-time gift of $28. In paragraph 16, she calls for immediate action and explains that she will distribute brochures from Compassion International after her speech. Paragraph 17 reinforces the call for action and ends the speech with a moving quotation about the manner in which each individual can make a difference in the life of a child.

The Problem with Pennies

1   "A nickel for your thoughts." "A nickel saved is a nickel earned." "Nickels from heaven."

2   Okay, maybe these phrases don't have quite the same ring as the original sayings—"A penny for your thoughts," "A penny saved is a penny earned," and "Pennies from heaven." But it's a fact of our nation's economic life that the penny is becoming obsolete. Inflation over the past few decades has been the death of penny candy, penny arcades, and penny bubble gum. The fact is that pennies don't buy much of anything anymore. The age of the penny is over. It's time to let this dinosaur of our economy go extinct.

3   Sure, most of you say, pennies can be annoying. But why do we have to get rid of them? Why must we change something that's worked for so long? And what would we do without pennies? I had the same questions when I started work on this speech. But as a result of my research, I'm convinced that the continued use of pennies is a costly problem and that we can get along just fine without them. Today, I hope to convince you of the same thing.

4   The place to begin is by noting that pennies cause problems for individuals, for businesses, and for the nation as a whole. Many Americans consider pennies a useless annoyance. According to my class survey, about two-thirds of you find pennies bothersome. They take up space and add weight to your pockets, wallets, and purses. They get in the way when you're trying to find other coins. They slow down checkout lines when you have to search for exact change. And most of the time when you really need coins—for copy machines, pay phones, and vending machines—you can't use pennies anyway.

5   In fact, many people don't use pennies. A survey by the U.S. Mint showed that only half of the 12,000 people questioned use pennies on a daily basis. Most of the other half collect pennies around the house, waiting until they have enough to cash in at the bank. It can be a long wait. In a *Los Angeles Times* article, writer Noel Gunther explained that during his last two years in college, he and his roommate saved all their pennies so they could throw a "Pennies from Heaven" party for graduation. They filled six jars with what looked like a fortune. The day before graduation, they emptied the jars and counted out $21.56—barely enough to buy beverages!

6   Pennies are a nuisance for the business community as well as for individuals. The National Association of Convenience Stores estimates that an average of two seconds is spent handling pennies during each of its members' 10 billion annual cash transactions. That comes out to a total of 5.5 million hours spent handling pennies—at an annual cost of $22 million. According to *Fortune* magazine, some banks charge up to 30 cents for every

dollar's worth of pennies they process. This makes it very costly for some businesses to accept pennies.

7   Keeping pennies in circulation also costs the nation as a whole. Every year the Treasury Department takes about 7 billion pennies out of circulation because they are bent or worn out. According to the Treasury Department, several billion more pennies go into mayonnaise jars, coffee cans, piggy banks, and dresser drawers. Or they are simply thrown away. In the survey mentioned earlier in my speech, the U.S. Mint reported that 6 percent of American adults simply jettison their pennies with the trash!

8   To keep an adequate supply of pennies in circulation, the U.S. Mint creates approximately 12 billion new pennies each year. The cost of manufacturing these new pennies is .66 of a cent apiece, which adds up to almost $80 million a year. As Treasury officials told *U.S. News & World Report*, when you add on storage and handling expenses, it costs our society considerably more than a penny to transact a penny's worth of business.

9   You can now see the magnitude of the problem with pennies. Fortunately, it's a problem that can be easily solved.

10   The solution I recommend is similar to a plan supported by the Coin Coalition, a group working to eliminate pennies from our economy. The plan has four basic steps. First, the federal government should legalize and standardize the rounding off of all purchases to the nearest nickel. This rounding off should take place after all items in a given transaction are totaled but before the sales tax is added. Because the number of purchases rounded up would roughly equal the number rounded down, this would not cause any increased cost to consumers.

11   Second, the sales tax should also be rounded off to the nearest nickel. Both the customer and the state would stand an equal chance of gaining or losing a maximum of two cents on each purchase. In essence, this is no different from what you do when you file your income taxes—except that in computing your income taxes, you round everything off to the nearest dollar.

12   Because the first two steps of this plan will eliminate the need for pennies, the third step is for the U.S. Mint to stop making new pennies. As we have seen, this will save the taxpayers some $80 million a year in minting costs alone.

13   The fourth step of this plan is for people to cash in the pennies already in circulation, thereby removing pennies entirely from the money supply.

14   I admit that it may be hard to imagine a world without pennies, but there is plenty of evidence that this plan will work. James Benfield, Executive Director of the Coin Coalition, notes that when the U.S. stopped minting half-cent coins in 1857, a similar procedure of rounding off purchases and phasing out the coins worked extremely well. None of us miss the half-cent, and in a few years none of us will miss the penny.

15   Whether we realize it or not, many of us already round off some of our purchases to the nearest nickel. Think for a moment of the "Take a Penny, Leave a Penny" containers next to the cash registers at local convenience stores. Every time you take a few pennies from the box to pay for your purchase or leave a few pennies from your change, you are actually rounding off the amount you pay to the nearest nickel.

16   In conclusion, pennies create problems for individuals, for businesses, and for the nation as a whole. The time and money currently wasted in using and minting pennies could be put to more productive ends. By rounding off purchases and sales taxes to the nearest nickel, by ending production of new pennies, and by letting old pennies drop out of use, the problems created by pennies could be eliminated without upsetting the economy. And just as we have gotten used to life without penny candy, penny arcades, and penny bubble gum, so I think, given time, we will also get used to the phrase "a nickel saved is a nickel earned."

The Problem with Pennies

Commentary

"The Problem with Pennies" is an excellent persuasive speech on a question of policy and provides an instructive model for students who are preparing their own speeches. The commentary below deals with the questions one must always ask of a policy speech: Does the speaker present a convincing case that a serious problem exists? Does the speaker offer a clear plan to solve the problem? Does the speaker demonstrate that the plan is practical?

Specific Purpose: To persuade my audience that pennies should be eliminated from the United States money supply.

Central Idea: Because pennies cause problems for individuals, businesses, and the economy as a whole, they should be eliminated from the U.S. money supply.

Method of Organization: Problem-solution

Need: The speaker deals with the need for change in the first main point of the body, which runs from paragraph 4 through paragraph 8. In paragraphs 4–5, she shows that pennies are such an annoyance that many people simply don't use them. After citing the results of her class survey, in which two-thirds of the class said they found pennies bothersome, the speaker presents a series of specific situations in which pennies are a nuisance. Her repeated use of "you" in paragraph 4 gives the speech a personal tone and relates it directly to the audience. So, too, does the story from writer Noel Gunther in paragraph 5 about his experience collecting pennies while in college.

In paragraph 6, the speaker claims that pennies are a nuisance for businesses as well as for individuals. She supports the claim with an arresting set of figures from Fortune magazine and the National Association of Convenience Stores. Here, as elsewhere, the speaker's evidence is from reliable sources, which she identifies for the audience.

Paragraphs 7 and 8 present a combination of statistics and testimony to demonstrate the problems created for the nation as a whole by keeping pennies in circulation. The evidence in paragraph 8 is particularly strong and builds cumulatively to the statement, based on testimony from U.S. Treasury officials, that "it costs our society considerably more than a penny to transact a penny's worth of business." All in all, the need section of this speech is extremely well developed.

Plan: After a transition in paragraph 9, the speaker moves to her second main point, in which she presents her plan and demonstrates its practicality. The plan has four steps, which are presented in paragraphs 10–13. Each step is explained clearly and concisely so listeners will understand exactly what the speaker is proposing. This is especially notable in paragraphs 10 and 11. Notice how much less effective the speech would have been if the speaker had failed in those paragraphs to explain the procedures by which purchases and sales taxes will be rounded off to the nearest nickel.

Practicality: The speaker demonstrates the practicality of her plan in paragraphs 14 and 15. Dealing with questions of practicality is especially crucial in a speech such as "The Problem with Pennies," in which listeners are likely to be skeptical about a speaker's plan. As discussed in Chapter 16 of the textbook, persuasive speakers must think of their speech as a kind of mental dialogue with the audience. The speaker must anticipate the possible objections listeners will raise to the speaker's point of view and answer those objections in the speech.

"The Problem with Pennies" provides an excellent example of how to do this. In paragraph 14, the speaker reasons analogically in showing that her plan is similar to that by which half-pennies were abolished during the nineteenth century. "None of us miss the half-cent," she explains, "and in a few years none of us will miss the penny." (For a discussion of analogical reasoning and its role in persuasive speaking, see Chapter 17 of the textbook.)

In paragraph 15, the speaker deals with possible reservations about the feasibility of rounding off purchases to the nearest nickel by showing that most people already do exactly that when they use the "Take a Penny, Leave a Penny" containers at local convenience stores. It is also important to note how the speaker relates her ideas in paragraphs 14 and 15 directly to her audience by using words such as "us," "we," and "you." Because the speaker is trying to answer the objections of her Immediate listeners, it only makes sense for her to bring her ideas home to those listeners in personal terms.

Multicultural, Multilingual

---

1   *Perdóneme señor; me perdí. Podría decirme cómo ir al Hotel del Sol?*

2   A few of you may know what I just said, "Excuse me, sir. I'm lost. Could you tell me how to get to the Sun Hotel?" However, some of you may not, even though you had three to four years of Spanish in high school. I have one question for you: Would you be able to get around in a foreign country where the language you studied was spoken?

3   According to a class survey I conducted, all of you said that you studied a foreign language in high school, the majority of you for three to four years. Yet most of you do not have enough knowledge of the language to use it correctly. In addition, 92 percent of you said you thought it would have been more helpful to have started your foreign language study earlier.

4   Today I hope to convince you that knowledge of a foreign language is important and that it would be more beneficial to begin foreign language study earlier in our education. With the world economy globalizing and our country becoming increasingly multilingual, knowledge of a foreign language is now a necessity. Through my own experience and research, I have discovered that starting foreign language instruction in elementary school is most advantageous because our language-acquisition skills are the sharpest at that time. Let's begin with why knowledge of a second language is critical for the world today.

5   The first reason such knowledge is critical is because it is essential for global communication. According to an article in *Current* magazine, Americans both in and out of government proclaim the new global economy the defining reality of our age. With technology growing faster and faster, we have now become closer to our global neighbors than ever before. Governments and businesses will increasingly need workers who can communicate with our global partners in Latin America, Africa, and Europe.

6   According to an article in the *Foreign Language Annals*, "The number of foreign-based industries doing business in the United States has tripled in the last ten years, while the U.S. has doubled overseas business." A recent issue of *Career World* states that some accountants at Chase Manhattan Bank and National City Bank must have a good grasp of foreign languages because these banks have branched out abroad. One study in the *Journal of Education for Business* showed that among both United States and foreign firms, 51 percent of the responding firms would give hiring preferences to those accounting and business majors skilled in a foreign language.

7   Not only is knowledge of a foreign language necessary for business communication, but the United States itself is a country of mixed cultures, nationalities, and tongues and is growing more multilingual every day.

8   According to Table 57 in the *Statistical Abstract of the United States*, people born in another country make up 9 percent of the American population. An article in the *Population Bulletin* states that 32 million people reported to last United States Census that they spoke a language other than English at home. This number is larger than the populations of New York, Pennsylvania, and Colorado combined and is six times larger than the number of people that live here in Wisconsin.

9   According to the Census Bureau, more than 17 million people in the U.S. speak Spanish as their primary language. In many parts of the country, knowledge of Spanish has become a vital day-to-day issue. Kathy Lemmons, chairwoman of the foreign language department at Fayetteville High School in Arkansas, says, "When I talk to doctors, they wish they would have taken Spanish; when I talk to lawyers and business people, they say the same thing."

10   But whether Spanish, Japanese, German, Italian, Chinese, or Polish, it is obvious that proficiency in another tongue is needed. To meet this need, I propose a solution that mandates state governments to require foreign language instruction in all elementary schools. The program I advocate is called FLES, the Foreign Languages in Elementary Schools Program. This program is based mostly on the spoken word versus writing and interpretation, and it starts teaching foreign languages as early as the first grade or even kindergarten.

11   It's important to note that much of the foreign language instruction done in this program is very basic. Olwen Bell, a French teacher at an Arkansas elementary school that has implemented the program, states that "There's a lot of role playing, singing, and chanting." Classroom teachers can easily take courses to learn how and what to teach the kids. It's not necessary for teachers to go back to school to get a degree in a foreign language. However, teachers should take instructional courses so they have opportunities for continued professional growth.

12   This program is working in Arkansas and other states. North Carolina, Oklahoma, Montana, and Arizona either have or are planning to institute similar programs. It is time for the rest of the U.S. to follow their lead. This would be a huge change in American education, but it's something that is vital if students are to be prepared for the world they will live in.

13   For years European and Asian countries have begun mandatory English in early grades. Other English-speaking countries such as Australia do extensive foreign language training in the early grades of their schools. Foreign language instruction works in these countries, and it can work in the U.S. as well.

14   In fact, there is abundant evidence that the optimum time to learn a foreign language is before the age of 10 because the brain is most receptive at this time. According to the book *Teaching Foreign Languages to the Very Young*, specific skills such as the ability to distinguish between foreign sounds and to reproduce them are more effective before the age of 10. The same book states that after the age of six the capabilities for pronunciation rapidly begin to deteriorate.

15   John Silber, Chancellor of Boston University and Chairman of the Massachusetts Board of Education, remarks, "It is quite clear that remarkable competence in a language can be achieved in three years—if these years are the ages three, four, and five. There is no question that for the average child trying to become bilingual, the earlier the better."

16   Finally, although some people wonder whether early foreign language instruction gets in the way of learning other subjects, according to the book *Foreign Languages and the Elementary School Child*, experiments done in public schools in Minnesota, Pennsylvania, and New York showed that learning foreign languages had no adverse effects on achievement in subject areas such as math and social studies. In some cases, kids who had foreign language instruction performed better in subjects such as spelling, reading, arithmetic, and language usage.

17   Furthermore, studying a language can help students better understand those outside their own culture and aid them in becoming more tolerant.

18   *Cuándo visitamos un país extranjero, estamos suponiendo que alguien habla Inglés? Depende de un diccionario?* To put it in English, "When we visit a foreign country, are we to expect that someone will speak English? Depend on a foreign language dictionary?"

19   People from other countries know to expect little from Americans as far as speaking foreign languages is concerned. However, it is time to stop this stereotype.

20   As we have seen, there is strong evidence that knowledge of a second language is vital for interaction both within the United States and on a global scale. We can provide that knowledge by instituting foreign language study in all elementary schools. Evidence shows that this is the best time to begin foreign language acquisition and that instruction in a second language can even help in learning other subjects.

21   With this in mind, hopefully one day when our children are lost somewhere in a foreign country, unlike their parents before them, they will know exactly what to say and do.

Multicultural, Multilingual

Commentary

By analyzing the use of supporting materials in a speech, students often get a better idea of how to use them in their own speeches. "Multicultural, Multilingual" has a variety of supporting materials and illustrates how they can be employed to clarify and bolster a speaker's ideas. It also provides an opportunity for students to discuss how the speaker could have employed supporting materials more effectively. Here is a synopsis of the speech.

Specific Purpose: To persuade my audience that foreign language instruction should be mandatory in all U.S. elementary schools.

Central Idea: Mandatory foreign language instruction in all U.S. elementary schools will help prepare today's students for interaction in the global economy and in the increasingly multicultural context of the United States itself.

Method of Organization: Problem-solution

Introduction: The introduction consists of paragraphs 1–4. Posing the opening question in Spanish is an excellent attention-getter. In paragraph 2, the speaker relates the question to her audience, and in paragraph 3 she mentions the results of her audience-analysis questionnaire, which showed that the great bulk of her classmates concurred that current foreign language instruction at the high school level is insufficient to provide a working knowledge of a language. Paragraph 4 provides a clear overview of the speech and reinforces the speaker's credibility.

Body: There are two main points in the body of this speech. The first explains why knowledge of a second language is vital for the world today and is developed in paragraphs 5–9. The speaker begins by demonstrating that being able to communicate in a foreign tongue is a great advantage in the global economy (paragraphs 5–6). After an excellent transition in paragraph 7, she then shows that the United States itself is growing more multilingual day by day (paragraphs 8–9).

The second main point presents the speaker's solution and runs from paragraph 10 through paragraph 17. In paragraphs 10–11, the speaker introduces her policy of mandatory foreign language instruction in all U.S. elementary schools. Paragraphs 12–17 are devoted to discussing the policy's practicality. The speaker notes that a similar policy is already working in a few U.S. states (paragraph 12) and has worked in other countries for years (paragraph 13). She also shows that foreign language instruction is most effective when begun at an early age (paragraphs 14–15), that it has no adverse effects on the learning of other subjects (paragraph 16), and that it can help students become more tolerant in dealing with people outside their own culture (paragraph 17).

Conclusion: The conclusion consists of paragraphs 18–21. In paragraph 18, the speaker gives a sense of psychological unity to the speech and subtly lets the audience know that it is coming to an end by echoing the introduction with another question posed in Spanish. Paragraphs 19–20 reinforce the central idea by summarizing the speaker's main points, while paragraph 22 ends the speech with a strong closing line.

Supporting Materials: The speaker uses a number of brief examples to reinforce her ideas. One example appears in the problem section when the speaker observes that some accountants at firms such as Chase Manhattan Bank and National City Bank need a second language to better serve the banks' international clients (paragraph 6). This example is especially effective because most people would assume that accounting is a technical subject that does not require knowledge of a foreign language.

The heaviest concentration of brief examples in this speech occurs in the solution section, and especially in the paragraphs devoted to showing the practicality of the speaker's policy. In paragraph 12, she cites several states that have successfully instituted a program similar to the one she recommends. In paragraph 13, she mentions that European and Asian nations have long begun foreign language instruction in the early grades, and in the same paragraph she specifies Australia as an example of an English-speaking nation that requires extensive foreign language training in elementary school. In paragraph 16, she points to the experience of public schools in New York, Minnesota, and Pennsylvania to show that studying a foreign language can actually enhance performance in other subjects.

The speaker does not present any extended examples. Although it is easy to envision how one or two might have helped reinforce her argument, it is difficult to point to anything currently in the speech that could easily be deleted so as to make room for an extended example or two. The key to using supporting materials effectively is to choose those that will best strengthen the speaker's ideas given the topic, purpose, audience, and length of the speech. In this case, the speaker appears to have chosen wisely for the most part.

This can be seen as well in her use of statistics. In paragraph 3, she cites the results of her class survey to show that 92 percent of her classmates agree that they would have been better served by starting foreign language instruction earlier in their education. In paragraph 6, she presents figures from the Foreign Language Annals about the growth of international business. In the same paragraph she draws from a survey in the *Journal of Education for Business* to note that 51 percent of the responding firms would give hiring preferences to accounting and business majors skilled in a foreign language. As in other parts of the speech, her figures here are drawn from credible, clearly identified sources.

Statistics are also important to the speaker's argument about the increasingly multilingual nature of U.S. society. In the first sentence of paragraph 8 she references Table 57 in the *Statistical Abstract of the United States* to document the fact that 9 percent of the U.S. population was born in another country. In the next sentence she presents figures from the Population Bulletin about the 32 million people in the U.S. that speak a language other than English at home. She then translates that figure into more meaningful terms for her audience by showing that it is larger than the populations of New York, Pennsylvania, and Colorado combined and is six times greater than the population of Wisconsin, where the speech was presented. Finally, in paragraph 9 the speaker cites statistics from the Census Bureau showing that 17 million people in the U.S. speak Spanish as their primary language.

It is worth noting that all of the speaker's statistics occur in the need section of the speech, while most of her examples occur in the practicality section. This is not unusual in a persuasive speech on a question of policy. When demonstrating the need for a change from current policy, a speaker will typically seek to quantify the extent of the problem that needs solving. When showing that his or her policy will solve the problem, a speaker will most often turn to examples that illustrate how the policy, or something close to it, has worked when implemented in other circumstances.

Some students will identify the speaker's citations in paragraph 6 of the *Foreign Language Annals*, *Career World*, and the *Journal of Education for Business* as instances of testimony. In each of these cases, however, the speaker is citing a source either for statistics or for brief examples. Testimony, in the strict sense of the term, refers to the expression of opinion and can come from either an expert source or a peer source. Although it is easy to think of cases in which the lines among testimony, examples, and statistics can begin to blur, students usually find it helpful when the distinctions among them are clearly established. Problematic cases can then be dealt with on an individual basis as they arise.

There are a number of clear cases of testimony in this speech. In paragraph 9, the speaker presents a quotation from Kathy Lemmons, chairwoman of the foreign language department at Fayetteville High School, about the need for knowledge of Spanish among doctors, lawyers, and business people. Although the speaker does not say so explicitly, this quotation is especially important because Arkansas is not usually thought of as a state with a large Spanish-speaking population. If there is a need for knowledge of Spanish in Arkansas, that need is doubtless many times greater in states like California, Texas, Florida, and Arizona.

Testimony also figures prominently in the solution section of the speech. In paragraph 11, the speaker presents a quotation from Olwen Bell, a French teacher who has worked with the FLES program that the speaker advocates. In paragraphs 14 and 16, she paraphrases two books—the first about the effectiveness of foreign language instruction for children of young ages, the second to show that early foreign language instruction does not interfere with learning in other subjects. Paragraph 15 contains what is probably the most effective piece of testimony in the entire speech—a quotation from John Silber underscoring the point that early instruction is the best way for a child to acquire fluency in a second language.

The only point in the speech that is not documented occurs in paragraph 17, where the speaker asserts that studying a foreign language helps students become more tolerant and more understanding of people outside their own culture. While this point would appear more or less self-evident, it certainly would have carried more force had it been backed up by testimony or some other kind of evidence. All in all, however, the speech provides an instructive example of how students can increase both the clarity and persuasiveness of their ideas by the skillful use of supporting materials.

The Dangers of Chewing Tobacco

---

1   On March 30, Tom, a twenty-three-year-old man from northern Wisconsin, went in for his yearly dental checkup. As far as he could tell, there were no real problems except maybe the one or two usual cavities that the dentist always seems to find. The dentist began poking around at Tom's teeth, but soon became more interested in Tom's lower lip and gums. The dentist noticed an unusual growth on Tom's lower lip and asked if Tom was a regular user of chewing tobacco. Tom answered yes.

2   After a series of tests, Tom was diagnosed as having a deadly type of oral cancer. Just one week after Tom's dental checkup, he had surgery to remove the cancer. This photograph shows Tom after his surgery. As you can see, a large portion of Tom's lower lip was removed and the area was drawn together by stitches. The surgery left Tom disfigured and looking quite grotesque, but it was not the worst part. Tom died just one month later. Chewing tobacco caused Tom's death.

3   Due to the fact that I am currently studying to be a dentist, and because my father is a dentist and I have worked for him as an assistant for over four years, I have actually seen cases similar to Tom's which result from chewing tobacco. I have also attended a number of seminars on this topic, and today I'd like to persuade each of you to feel as strongly as I do about the dangers of chewing tobacco.

4   In my speech, I'd like to show you the many problems that can result from chewing tobacco. Then I'd like to persuade each of you to take action and help change the lenient laws governing the use of chewing tobacco in our society. Let's begin by looking at how widespread the problem of chewing tobacco really is.

5   Chewing tobacco is more common than you may think. According to the American Cancer Society, one in every twelve Americans is a regular user of chewing tobacco. The average age of first use is just ten years old, which means that many children are chewing tobacco when they are in fourth grade. The American Cancer Society also reports that 40 percent of high school boys have tried chewing tobacco—and, what's worse, 21 percent of kindergartners have tried it. Children are using chewing tobacco before they can even read the warning labels!

6   Now you know that chewing tobacco is widespread, but you may wonder what could possibly happen when a person uses chewing tobacco. Well, smokeless tobacco has multiple dangers according to the American Dental Association and the American Cancer Society. First, tooth decay and tooth loss can occur. Chewing tobacco contains grit and sand, which wear away at the teeth. It also contains added sugars to improve the taste—but they also wear away at the teeth, leading to cavities and tooth loss.

7   Another effect of chewing tobacco is gum disease. Regular use of chewing tobacco causes visual gum damage in less than two to three months. According to the American Dental Association, about half of all teenage users have some type of gum problem. But what's wrong with gum disease? Well, it causes the gums to pull away from the teeth, which further increases the risk of tooth decay and loss.

8   Gum disease and tooth loss are serious enough, but as we saw at the beginning in the story about Tom, chewing tobacco can have most serious consequences. According to the American Dental Association, those who use chewing tobacco just once in a while have four times the risk of developing oral cancer than do nonusers. And if that isn't bad enough, those who use chewing tobacco three or more times a week for over a year have fifty times the risk of developing cancer than do nonusers. This risk is even greater than that of smoking cigarettes. But unlike smoking cigarettes, where cancer develops slowly over time, chewing tobacco can cause cancer in teens and young adults.

9   For example, Sean Marsee, a nineteen-year-old high school student from Oklahoma, was one of the most well-liked students in his senior class. Sean used chewing tobacco from age twelve to age eighteen, when he was diagnosed as having oral cancer during his senior year in high school. As a result, Sean had to have a series of disfiguring operations. First three-fourths of his tongue was removed. Then all the muscles and lymph nodes on the right side of Sean's face and neck were removed. And lastly his jawbone was removed from her to here. As you can imagine, Sean was left looking quite grotesque. But this was not the worst part. As extreme as the surgery was, it could not stop Sean's cancer from spreading, and he died just one year later. There can be no doubt that chewing tobacco caused Sean's death.

10   I know this is a terrible thought, but the point I'm trying to make is an important one. You must be aware of the terrible consequences of chewing tobacco because next time it could happen to you or to someone you love.

11   Let's look, then, at what can be done to diminish the use of chewing tobacco. First, the laws in Wisconsin pertaining to the age at which chewing tobacco can be bought must be strengthened. The law in Wisconsin states that chewing tobacco can be purchased at age eighteen, but according to the Department of Law Enforcement, the laws on chewing tobacco sales have been ineffective. To be effective, the laws must be enforced and have adequate penalties.

12   A number of other states, including California, set the fine for selling chewing tobacco to minors at $1,500 for the first offense and $6,000 for the second offense. According to the American Dental Association, this law has cut the use of chewing tobacco by minors by almost 60 percent. I would like you to help pass a law resembling this in Wisconsin. You must help stop people from selling cancer to our children. You can make a difference. You can write to our legislators urging that a bill like this be created here in Wisconsin.

13   Second, use of chewing tobacco during all professional sporting events should be banned. According to the American Dental Association, the primary reason children develop an interest in chewing tobacco is because they see their role models doing it. These role models include parents, relatives, and friends, but more importantly, they include sports stars. Children see athletes as role models. Children think if it's all right for athletes to use chewing tobacco, it must be all right for me to do it too. If these role models would stand up and say chewing is wrong, many of our children would change their minds about the drug.

14   What we need, then, is a ban on chewing tobacco use during professional sporting events. You may think this is impractical, but already one baseball team, the Kansas City Royals, has taken a stand. They have switched from chewing tobacco to bubble gum. You can help influence other teams to do the same. I urge you to write to your favorite team or to your favorite athlete urging them, individually or as a team, to take a stand against chewing tobacco as the Royals did.

15   In conclusion, then, I am pleading with each of you to take action against the use of chewing tobacco. When you think of this subject, remember the problems of chewing tobacco. Remember Tom—and remember Sean. By adopting the measures I have discussed today, you can help stop what happened to Tom and Sean from happening to others.

The Dangers of Chewing Tobacco

Commentary

"The Dangers of Chewing Tobacco" is an excellent persuasive speech that illustrates how students can make effective use of all the methods of persuasion discussed in Chapter 17 of the textbook. Here is a synopsis that focuses on how the speaker employs the methods of persuasion presented in Chapter 17.

Specific Purpose: To persuade my audience that the laws governing the sale of chewing tobacco should be strengthened and that professional athletes should refrain from using chewing tobacco during games in order to reduce the problem of chewing tobacco use among young adults.

Central Idea: The dangers of chewing tobacco pose a serious problem that can be curbed by state legislation and by banning the use of chewing tobacco during professional sporting events.

Method of Organization: Problem-Solution

Introduction: The introduction consists of paragraphs 1–4. The speaker begins with an extended example that does an excellent job pulling the audience into the speech (paragraphs 1–2). A color photograph enlarged to 11 x 17 inches and mounted on posterboard adds to the story's drama and impact. In paragraph 3, the speaker establishes her credibility, and in paragraph 4 she provides a clear preview statement that lets the audience know what to listen for in the body of the speech.

Body: There are two main points in the body. The first demonstrates that the use of chewing tobacco is a serious problem in the United States (paragraphs 5–10). After showing how widespread that use is, the speaker demonstrates that chewing tobacco poses a number of dangers, including tooth decay and tooth loss, gum disease, and, most deadly, oral cancer. The speaker then turns to her second main point, in which she presents a two-part solution to the problem (paragraphs 11–14). The first part deals with the laws governing the sale of chewing tobacco to minors (paragraph 11–12). Because the speaker is a student at the University of Wisconsin, she focuses on the laws in that state. The second part of the speaker's plan calls for banning chewing tobacco in all professional sports events (paragraphs 13–14).

Conclusion: Brief and hard-hitting, the conclusion is presented in paragraph 15. After restating the need for action against chewing tobacco, the speaker ends by referring back to the two extended examples presented earlier in the speech. This helps reinforce the central idea and ends the speech on a strong note.

Credibility: Paragraph 3, in which the speaker explains her professional training and personal experience on the topic, provides an excellent model of how students can establish their credibility in classroom speeches. In addition, as the speech progresses, the speaker's command of the topic and her obvious sincerity reinforce the audience's perception of her competence and good will.

Evidence: The speaker does an excellent job of using evidence to persuade her listeners. The extended examples of Tom in paragraphs 1–2 and of Sean Marsee in paragraph 9 dramatize the speaker's claim about the dangers of chewing tobacco. Both examples are vivid and richly textured, and both deal with people in the same age group as most members of the speaker's audience. These examples alone make up almost 25 percent of the speech, and they are crucial to its impact. In addition, the speaker uses brief examples to good effect in paragraphs 12 and 14 to demonstrate the practicality of her plan.

The speaker's use of examples is complemented by her use of statistics in paragraphs 5, 7, 8, and 12. In each case, the speaker employs statistics from credible sources and identifies those sources for her audience. She also does an excellent job of translating her statistics into human terms. The most dramatic instance of this is the extended example of Sean Marsee in paragraph 9 that gives a personal dimension to the statistics cited in paragraph 8. Less dramatic, but equally effective, is the speaker's method in paragraph 5. After stating that the average age of first use of chewing tobacco is "just ten years old," she explains that this means "many children are chewing tobacco when they are in fourth grade." Then, after noting that 21 percent of kindergartners have tried chewing tobacco, she exclaims, "Children are using chewing tobacco before they can even read the warning labels!"

Testimony plays less of a role in this speech than do examples and statistics. The speaker uses testimony in three places. In paragraph 6, she cites the American Dental Society and the American Cancer Society on the multiple dangers of chewing tobacco. In paragraph 11, she cites the Department of Law Enforcement to note that laws regulating the sale of chewing tobacco in Wisconsin have been ineffective. In paragraph 13, she cites a statement from the American Dental Association that the use of chewing tobacco by role models is the primary reason children develop an interest in it. In all three cases, the speaker uses credible sources and identifies them in the speech.

Reasoning: The speaker relies primarily on causal reasoning and analogical reasoning. She uses causal reasoning in paragraphs 6–9, where she argues that chewing tobacco is a cause of tooth decay, tooth loss, gum disease, and oral cancer. She does not claim that chewing tobacco is the sole cause of these conditions, only that it is an important contributing factor. In each case, she supports her claim with credible evidence of a causal connection. The speaker also uses causal reasoning in paragraphs 13–14, when she claims that many children start chewing tobacco because they see athletes chewing. If the athletes stopped chewing in games, she reasons, then children would be less likely to chew themselves.

The speaker employs analogical reasoning in paragraph 12. Her argument there is that because tougher laws against selling chewing tobacco have worked in California and other states, similar laws would work in the speaker's state of Wisconsin. Analogical reasoning is often used in this way by speakers to demonstrate the practicality of their proposed policy.

Emotional Appeal: For the most part, the speaker allows her emotional appeal to grow naturally out of her speech content. Vivid and richly detailed, the extended examples of Tom (paragraph 1) and Sean Marsee (paragraph 9) help to encourage a strong emotional reaction against chewing tobacco. When the speaker delivered the speech, she used a visual aid to show what Tom's face looked like after his surgery. The visual aid was an oversized color photograph, 11 inches by 17 inches that had been enlarged for the speaker at a local copy service. To enhance the visibility of the photograph, the speaker mounted it on a large piece of white poster board. The effect was quite dramatic and powerfully reinforced the emotional impact of the speaker's words.

The speaker also does a fine job in paragraphs 10 and 15 of relating the examples of Tom and Sean to her listeners and of appealing to the fear that they, or someone they love, could be victimized by chewing tobacco.

Boxing: The Most Dangerous Sport

1   "I killed a man. Afterward, they told me that it wasn't my fault, and that anyway it was nothing new. It had happened before. It has happened since. And, believe me, it will happen again."

2   This quote was uttered by boxer Roger Donoghue after he fought fellow boxer George Flores. During the fight, Donoghue punched Flores so mercilessly and with such force that shortly after the bout was over, Flores went into a coma. He never woke up again.

3   This horrifying scenario, the sight of one man literally beating another man's brains out, is what boxing is all about. What's even more frightening is that many, many other fighters have suffered the same fate as George Flores. In fact, as *Time* magazine reported, in the last decade over seventy boxers have died from boxing-related causes. Moreover, at least 15 percent of all boxers, even if they don't die, incur irreversible brain damage.

4   Growing up, like most of you, I watched boxing, and sometimes I even enjoyed it. But as I recently watched Mike Tyson pummel Frank Bruno into submission in a heavyweight championship fight, I began to wonder what possessed one man to beat another with such force and without remorse.

5   In answering my audience analysis questionnaire, most of you said the sport of boxing was violent but that the decision to fight should be left up to the individual. However, I'm here to show you that the choice cannot be left up to the individual, who probably has been swayed by the chance for fame and fortune. The evidence against boxing is shocking and overwhelming, and tonight I hope to convince you that all states should ban the sport of boxing because it damages its participants and our society.

6   For decades, experts have warned us about the dangers of boxing. As long ago as 1928, Dr. Harrison Martland published the first article regarding the dangers of fighting in the *Journal of the American Medical Association*. Today the American Medical Association argues that "The principal purpose of a boxing match is for one opponent to render the other injured, defenseless, incapacitated, and unconscious. Boxing, as a throwback to uncivilized man, should not be sanctioned by any civilized society."

7   Even heavyweight champion Mike Tyson says, "This is a hurt business. When you see guys like Trump, Kennedy, and Rockefeller come to a fight, regardless of what they may represent, they come to see someone get hurt, and my objective is to inflict as much punishment as possible."

8   But why all the warnings? Because boxing can cause irreparable physical damage to its participants. A punch thrown by a heavyweight can land with a force exceeding 1,000 pounds, which causes the head to snap back or twist violently, forcing the soft brain to be rammed into the rigid skull like a yolk slammed into the side of an egg. The nerve cells and blood vessels in the brain are then twisted, ruptured, and stretched, which causes swelling and results in the brain pressing against the inside of the skull. A blow to the head so that consciousness is lost causes minute or larger hemorrhages, contusions at the base of the brain, and a tearing of nerve fibers that cannot be easily identified. These symptoms are not detectable by the victim of the beating.

9   Neurologist MacDonald Critchley states that a boxer's chances of suffering brain damage increase in proportion with the number of bouts fought. Another neurologist, Dr. Jan Corsellis, examined the brains of fifteen boxers who died of natural causes. He observed a pattern of abnormal cerebral changes not present in nonboxers.

10   Subsequent studies have shown that boxers are also far more likely to suffer from another type of brain damage called *cavum septi pellucidi*, which occurs when a boxer receives a blow to the brain and a cave or space develops between the two membranes that divide the brain. Many boxers who have this ailment suffer permanently with symptoms similar to the brain disorder Parkinson's disease. This disease develops when the brain ceases to produce sufficient amounts of dopamine, a substance that helps in the transmission of nerve impulses involved in motor control.

11   Perhaps the most poignant example, because he was so admired for his once-strong body, is the case of Muhammad Ali. In his prime, Ali was glamorized, but now he suffers from a severe case of Parkinson's disease. Ali's side effects are impaired hand-eye coordination, slurred, unintelligible speech, reduced muscle strength, and chronic fatigue. Ironically, Ali became a victim of the sport he once saved. Ali, once the unbeatable heavyweight champion, the force who claimed that "boxing never scarred his pretty face," has been reduced to a mere shell of a man, a shaking, silent reminder of the brutality of boxing, a brutality which does not discriminate on the basis of race, creed, or religion.

12   Not only is boxing dangerous to its participants, but it can hurt our society as well. Boxing influences how violent some spectators become. According to David Phillips, a sociologist at the University of California, homicides increase dramatically after every nationally televised broadcast fight.

13   Sadly, inner-city minority teens are the real victims who learn that the way to success is to emulate the violence condoned by boxing. According to the *Saturday Evening Post*, kids even drop out of school to become professional fighters. What awaits them is a future filled with punishment and abuse, while only a handful of fighters go on to make the millions of dollars that are so glorified by our society.

14   Of all athletes to emulate, the last ones should be boxers, who get rich without an education and achieve heroic status through violence. Of all sports to emulate, why boxing, where the object is to move your opponent closer to death?

15   You've heard how boxing causes physical and mental damage to its participants, and about the negative effects it has on our society, so now let's take a look at the solutions.

16   The best solution is to ban the sport of boxing. All fifty states should pass resolutions to abolish this barbaric sport. Granted, there is a lot of money invested in the sport, but can we put a price on human life?

17   The American Medical Association strongly supports this proposal and has attempted time and again to eliminate boxing. AMA president Dr. Joseph Boyle called their resolution to abolish the sport "a statement that's about as strong as it can get."

18   Elsewhere, people have also recognized the need to eliminate this dangerous sport. In 1969 Sweden banned pro boxing, but the U.S. has done nothing despite all the evidence that has been levied against boxing. Just as Sweden has survived without it, so can we.

19   Even world-renowned sportscaster Dick Enberg, who has spent his career watching sporting events of all kinds, couldn't think of a reason to continue boxing. In fact, in a speech given last week here on campus, Enberg said that while the goal in other sports is to defeat the opponent by scoring more points, the goal in boxing is to hurt, knock out, and incapacitate the other competitor. Though he professed admiration for the fighters, Enberg felt there was no justification for the sport.

20   For the sake of fighters, and for the sake of our society, it's important for us to take a stand against this brutal activity.

21   So in conclusion, boxing is unquestionably a dangerous and often deadly sport and must be banned. The goal of a boxer is to destroy another human being. How many more fighters must be rendered permanently injured or killed in the ring before we put an end to this deadly sport?

22   The next time you turn on the television or read the paper, you just might hear of someone suffering the same tragic fate as George Flores. But unlike the other deaths we read about, this one will have been different. It will have been endorsed by our society, and thousands of people will have cheered for the killer and paid big money to watch the killing happen—all in the name of sports entertainment.

23   As we've seen, in boxing there are no winners. Let's stop the madness before someone else loses. Let's ban boxing before someone else dies.

Boxing: The Most Dangerous Sport

Commentary

"Boxing: The Most Dangerous Sport" is a persuasive speech on a question of policy. In addition to illustrating many of the principles discussed in Chapters 16–17 of the textbook, it provides a useful speech for discussion because of its use of supporting materials. Most members of the audience opposed the speaker's position, and he knew he would have to provide persuasive evidence if he were to have any hope of getting people to reassess their attitudes on the topic. Here is a synopsis of the speech.

Specific Purpose: To persuade my audience that professional boxing should be banned in the United States.

Central Idea: Professional boxing should be banned in the United States because it is harmful to society and causes irreparable physical damage to its participants.

Method of Organization: Problem-Solution

Introduction: The introduction consists of paragraphs 1–3. It begins with an attention-getting quotation from boxer Roger Donoghue about a fight in which he killed fellow boxer George Flores. Although the quotation was uttered in 1951, the speaker presents statistics in paragraph 3 to show that boxing remains a deadly sport to this day. Although the speaker seeks to establish his credibility and good will in paragraph 4 by stating that his opinions about boxing have changed over time, he could have done a better job if he had mentioned the great amount of research he put into researching the speech. In paragraph 5, he refers to his audience-analysis questionnaires and provides a clear preview statement of the ideas to be developed in the body of the speech.

Body: The body of this speech contains two main points. The first, which explains the need to abolish professional boxing, runs from paragraph 6 through paragraph 14. In these paragraphs, the speaker devotes most of his attention to showing that boxing causes irreparable physical damage to its participants (paragraphs 6–11). He also argues that it harms society in general (paragraphs 12–14). After an excellent transition in paragraph 15, the speaker moves into his second main point (paragraphs 16–20), in which he presents his plan that all fifty states should pass legislation banning the sport of boxing.

Conclusion: The conclusion consists of paragraphs 21–23 and does an excellent job of strengthening the speaker's central idea. After ending paragraph 21 with a pointed rhetorical question, in paragraph 22 the speaker returns to the opening story of George Flores to reinforce the brutal nature of boxing. He ends in paragraph 23 with a series of sharp, dramatic sentences.

Supporting Materials: The speaker uses two extended examples. The first is that of boxer George Flores, who was killed in a fight with Roger Donoghue. This example, accompanied by testimony from Donoghue, is developed in paragraphs 1–2 and is mentioned again in the conclusion. Although there are many other examples of fighters dying in the ring, the speaker had time to develop only this one. To show that the example is not unrepresentative, in paragraph 3 the speaker presents statistics from *Time* magazine on the number of fighters who have died from boxing-related causes in the past decade.

The speaker's second extended example is that of Muhammad Ali, who suffers from Parkinson's disease as a result of his boxing career (paragraph 11). This example is especially well-chosen because Ali is a well-known figure even to people who are not boxing fans. The effectiveness of the example is heightened by the speaker's vivid portrayal of Ali as "a mere shell of a man, a shaking, silent reminder of the brutality of boxing, a brutality which does not discriminate on the basis of race, creed, or religion."

In addition to these extended examples, the speaker presents a brief example in paragraph 18 to support the practicality of his plan. He notes that Sweden eliminated pro boxing in 1969 and has survived just fine. Arguing analogically, he infers that the U.S. would also do just fine without boxing.

Unlike some topics for persuasive speeches, this one does not lend itself to heavy use of statistics. In contrast to issues such as gun control or drunk driving, there are not so many professional boxers in the U.S. as to produce thousands of deaths or serious injuries every year. Although the speaker seeks, in paragraph 3, to quantify the seriousness of the number of deaths caused by boxing, he could have strengthened his argument by adding a few more statistics. He might also have strengthened his argument by saying something like, "Although the number of professional boxers is small compared to some sports, we should not tolerate any sport that produces such a high proportion of deaths and brain injuries among its participants. Certainly, we would not find it acceptable if a comparable number of players in professional baseball or professional football were killed each year."

The only figures in the body of the speech occur in paragraphs 8 and 9. In paragraph 8, the speaker states that a punch thrown by a heavyweight boxer can land with a force exceeding 1,000 pounds. Although it is debatable whether this is a statistic in the strict sense of the term, many students will identify it as such. Many will also note that the speaker does not identify the source of the figure. He could have avoided this problem by preceding the figure with a statement such as "According to *Sports Illustrated*, a punch thrown by a heavyweight. . . ." On the positive side, the speaker's use of vivid language to explain the impact of a 1,000-pound force when applied to the human skull is highly effective. If not for this explanation, the 1,000-pound figure would have had little meaning for the audience.

In paragraph 9, the speaker cites the research of neurologist Jan Corsellis, who detected a pattern of abnormal cerebral changes in the brains of fifteen boxers who died of natural causes. Unlike the figure in paragraph 8, however, this one is neither explained fully nor related to the audience.

Given all the testimony that has been advanced against boxing over the years, it is not surprising that the speaker relies above all on this form of supporting material. In addition to the quotation from Roger Donoghue in paragraph 1, he presents testimony from the American Medical Association (paragraph 6), boxer Mike Tyson (paragraph 7), neurologist MacDonald Critchley (paragraph 9), sociologist David Phillips (paragraph 12), the *Saturday Evening Post* (paragraph 13), AMA president Joseph Boyle (paragraph 17), and sportscaster Dick Enberg (paragraph 19). All of these are credible sources, and all are identified in the speech.

Seatbelts: A Habit That Could Save Your Life

1   As you may have noticed, I was on crutches for two months this semester. I had already been on crutches for three months before that, and last year I was on them for seven months. You see, I've had hip surgery three times in the last year and a half.

2   It all started when I experienced my first serious car accident. I swerved off the road to avoid a head-on collision with another car. My car rolled over and struck a large tree. I was not wearing a seatbelt. In the process of being thrown back and forth across the car, I chipped a tooth, cut the back of my head, broke my hip, and cracked three ribs, which resulted in a punctured lung and massive internal bleeding. When they got me to the hospital, my blood pressure was down from a normal 120-over-70 to 50-over-30 as a result of all the internal and external bleeding and as a result of shock. The doctors waited more than twenty-four hours to do surgery to repair my hip because they didn't think I was going to survive all of my other injuries.

3   Somehow I survived, and now a year and a half later I am finally walking normally, though I will be walking around for the rest of my life with a piece of metal this long in my hip, and I'm not allowed to do any athletic activities that require running.

4   All that pain and suffering could have been avoided if only I had been in the habit of wearing a seatbelt. But I wasn't in that habit, and I know from my class survey that 40 percent of you do not usually wear a seatbelt, and 75 percent of you do not always wear one. Yet the National Highway Traffic Safety Administration tells us that each person stands a one-in-three chance of being in a serious car accident at some time in his or her life. So we can possibly predict that one-third of you will be in a serious accident at some point. And it may sound corny, but I mean it, so I'm going to say it—I don't want what happened to me to happen to any of you.

5   So I want to talk to you about wearing seatbelts. First I'm going to tell you to what extent you will be protected by wearing a seatbelt. Then I'm going to look at some of the reasons why people don't wear seatbelts and point out the problems with those reasons. And after I've given you the evidence, I am going to ask you all to make a habit of wearing seatbelts.

6   So first, to what extent will you be protected by wearing a seatbelt? Well, the Wisconsin Department of Transportation says if you are in an accident and are not wearing a seatbelt, you are four times more likely to be killed than if you are wearing one. Furthermore, consider this—there are 35,000 deaths each year in the United States as a result of traffic accidents. The National Highway Traffic Safety Administration, the National Child Passenger Safety Association, and the Wisconsin Department

of Transportation all estimate that traffic deaths would decrease from 35,000 to around 17,000 annually if everyone wore seatbelts.

7   So our most knowledgeable and reliable sources of information on seatbelts have all come to the same conclusion—that we would cut traffic deaths in half if everyone wore seatbelts, and that we would save 18,000 lives each year. Now let me put that number into perspective—18,000 people, or the equivalent of more than half the undergraduates on this campus, are needlessly killed every year because they do not wear seatbelts.

8   But why is this true? What does a seatbelt do to protect you? Well, in a head-on collision, which is usually the worst type, your body will be thrown forward into the steering wheel, into the dashboard, or through the windshield with incredible force. Imagine falling headfirst from the top of a three-story building. The force with which you would land on the ground is equal to the force with which you would be thrown forward in only a 30 mile-per-hour collision. But a seatbelt will absorb that force and prevent you from slamming into the interior of the car.

9   In my own experience there is little doubt that a seatbelt would have minimized my injuries. I looked at pictures of the car after my accident. The car was totaled, and it was an ugly mess, but the two front seats and the entire driving compartment were completely intact. I have to believe that if I had been strapped into that seat, I would have walked away from my accident with minor bruises. But remember I used the word "if"—if I had worn a safety belt.

10   So the evidence is strongly in favor of wearing seatbelts. That brings me to the next question—why don't people wear seatbelts?

11   People often say that in an accident they would rather be thrown free of the car, or at least be able to get out of the car in case of fire or submersion in water. Well, according to the Wisconsin Department of Transportation, accidents involving fire and submersion make up less than one out of every 200 auto accidents. Furthermore, you are actually more likely to be able to get out of the car if you are wearing a seatbelt, because you are more likely to be conscious and not seriously injured. And with regard to being thrown free of the car, the Wisconsin Department of Transportation says you are 25 times more likely to be killed if you are thrown out of the car, because you can be thrown onto hard pavement, thrown into stationary objects, or struck by other cars. Clearly you are safer being strapped in than being thrown around.

12   The other major reason why people don't wear seatbelts is that seatbelts are uncomfortable and restrict movement. Now, if this is your reason for not wearing a seatbelt, let me ask you to do something right now. Imagine in your mind a two-sided scale. On one side of the scale, put the value that you place on being completely comfortable while driving. And on the other side of the scale, put the value that you place on your life and your health. Which side is heavier? If your life and your health mean more to you than a little bit of extra comfort while driving, then it only makes sense to wear a seatbelt.

13   So I'm here today to ask all of you to make a habit of wearing seatbelts. The statistics are simple—chances are that about one-third of you will be in a serious auto accident at some time in your life. It could happen fifty years from now, and it could happen tomorrow. And if you are in an accident, you are four times more likely to be killed if you are not wearing a seatbelt than if you are wearing one.

14   So if you think you are safer not wearing a seatbelt, you're betting against heavy odds. And if you still won't wear a seatbelt, because a seatbelt is uncomfortable and inconvenient, then you're placing your momentary comfort ahead of your life and your health. So tell yourself that you are going to make a habit of wearing seatbelts. Then do it.

15   There is nothing I can do about my accident now, and I don't plan to go around for the rest of my life kicking myself because I didn't wear a seatbelt that day. What's important is that I learned something from the experience. I've made a habit of wearing seatbelts when I ride in a car, and I'm hoping that each of you will do the same if you haven't already.

16   I will never be able to play basketball or go downhill skiing again, but at least I'm here and at least I can walk. I was a lot luckier than 35,000 other Americans that year.

Seatbelts: A Habit That Could Save Your Life

Commentary

A persuasive speech on a question of policy, "Seatbelts: A Habit That Could Save Your Life" is notable for its sharp organization, for the manner in which the speaker establishes his credibility by drawing on his personal experience, and for the way he relates the topic directly to his classmates throughout the speech. Here is a synopsis of it.

Specific Purpose: To persuade my audience to use seatbelts every time they drive or ride in an automobile.

Central Idea: Because seatbelts are proven lifesavers and there are no good reasons not to wear seatbelts, everyone should get in the habit of wearing seatbelts whenever they drive or ride in an automobile.

Method of Organization: Topical

Introduction: The introduction consists of paragraphs 1–5 and does a superb job of fulfilling the functions of a speech introduction. Paragraphs 1–3 gain attention with a dramatic story based on the speaker's personal experience. The story is especially effective because of its specific details about the speaker's injuries and how close he came to dying. In contrast, imagine if the speaker had merely said, "A year and a half ago I was in a serious automobile accident." This would not have had nearly the same impact. Nor would it have done as much to establish the speaker's credibility and good will.

In paragraph 4, the speaker moves from his opening story to reveal the topic of his speech and to relate it directly to his audience. The final sentence of this paragraph—in which the speaker says, "I don't want what happened to me to happen to any of you"—had a strong emotional impact when delivered in class. In paragraph 5, the speaker ends his introduction by previewing the main points to be discussed in the body. Although it is longer than usual, the introduction of this speech is extremely effective in preparing the audience for the persuasive appeals that follow.

Body: The body of the speech runs from paragraph 6 through paragraph 14 and has three main points. The first main point, developed in paragraphs 6–9, is that seatbelts are a proven way to reduce the chances of injury and death in an automobile accident. In paragraph 6, the speaker presents statistics to show that traffic deaths in the U.S. would be reduced from 35,000 per year to 17,000 per year if everyone wore seatbelts. In paragraph 7, he adroitly translates those statistics into terms that relate directly to his audience.

The speaker continues with his first main point in paragraph 8 by explaining why seatbelts are so valuable in helping to prevent injuries. He compares the force of a 30-mile-per-hour collision to falling headfirst from a three-story building. In paragraph 9, he draws on his own experience to reinforce his point about the value of wearing a seatbelt. The final sentence of this paragraph is especially effective.

After a transition in paragraph 10, the speaker moves into his second main point, which consists of paragraphs 11–12. These paragraphs are extremely important, for they answer the audience's two major objections to wearing seatbelts. Had the speaker ignored these objections, his speech would have been much less effective. In paragraph 11, he supports his position with statistics from the Wisconsin Department of Transportation. While this would not have been the best source of statistics for a speaker in another state, it was an excellent source for this speech, which was presented to a class at the University of Wisconsin.

In paragraph 12, the speaker deals with the fact that many people find seatbelts uncomfortable by asking his audience to imagine a two-sided scale on which they weigh the value of personal comfort versus their lives and health. Which do you value more, he asks, your life and health or "a little bit of extra comfort"? If you value your life and health more, he notes, it only makes sense to wear a seatbelt.

Paragraphs 13–14 develop the speaker's third main point, in which he calls for the audience to make a habit of wearing seatbelts. He begins the point in paragraph 13 by reiterating key statistics from earlier in the speech. This is an excellent technique. Rather than overwhelming listeners with a barrage of figures, the speaker uses a few well-chosen statistics to drive home his message. In paragraph 14, the speaker makes a direct call for action. Here, as elsewhere, his appeal is enhanced by his clear, forceful language.

It is also important to note that the speaker's appeal throughout the body of the speech is strengthened by his use of the words "you" and "your" to relate the topic directly to his listeners. In addition to increasing audience involvement, this gives the speech a strong conversational quality.

Conclusion: The speaker begins his conclusion in paragraph 15 by referring to the accident he had discussed in the introduction and by reiterating his call for action. Paragraph 16 ends the speech on a strong emotional note. The speaker's sincerity here and throughout the speech did much to strengthen his credibility and persuasiveness.

———————————————————————

Capital Punishment

---

1   Imagine being ready to die. On January 7, 1988, at 3:19 a.m., Texas began to execute convicted murderer Robert Streetland by pumping lethal drugs into his veins. Before he was pronounced dead seven minutes later, the telephone rang in the death chamber. The governor's office had received word that the United States Supreme Court was ready to consider a new motion of appeal. In the words of a prison spokesman, "The Supreme Court wanted to know where we were in the process, but by then it was too late."

2   I stand before you today to discuss the issue of capital punishment. Should the death penalty be administered to those who are deemed guilty of murder in a court of law? Based upon your answers to my class survey, if this decision were left up to this class, 75 percent of you would sentence the guilty defendant to death by way of lethal gas, lethal injection, hanging, or electrocution.

3   In my speech, I want to persuade you to reassess your view of capital punishment. My arguments will address the following issues relative to capital punishment: the injustice of capital punishment, the immorality of capital punishment, and capital punishment as a deterrent to crime. First of all, allow me to discuss the injustice of capital punishment.

4   Evidence shows that capital punishment is a discriminatory means of punishment. Some refer to capital punishment as the poor man's justice. In other words, those without the capital get the punishment. As criminologist Hugo Adam Bedeau has stated, often people are sentenced to death and executed not because they have been found to be uncontrollably violent, but because they are too poor to purchase a first-rate lawyer to defend them. To quote Bedeau, "People who have been executed for capital crimes have historically been the losers in an arbitrary lottery, the victims of the disadvantages that almost always come with poverty."

5   This discrimination is not only economic, but is also racial. As Supreme Court Justice William Brennan has stated, "Race casts a lot of shadows on the capital sentencing process." The most compelling evidence of this comes from a study conducted by Professor David Baldus of the University of Iowa. After studying nearly 2,500 murders in Georgia, Baldus concluded that no matter whether the killer be black or white, when it came to sentencing, the victim's race held firm as a primary determinant of life or death. People convicted of murdering whites, Baldus concluded, were eleven times more likely to be sentenced to death row than people convicted of killing blacks. This tends to confirm the analysis of Welsh White, of the University of Pittsburgh Law School, that it is built into the system that those in the predominant race will be more concerned about crime victims of their own race. Justice? I think not.

6   In addition to being discriminatory, capital punishment is also immoral. In fact, one reason why capital punishment is immoral is because it is discriminatory. This was stated especially well by Daniel Hoye, General Secretary of the United States Catholic Conference. "The system under which criminals are sentenced," he says, "is such that race often plays a prominent role in determining whether they will live or die. The fact that capital punishment is applied in a racially discriminatory way has been one of the reasons for our continued opposition on moral grounds to the application of the death penalty."

7   The immorality of capital punishment is not a matter of statistics or hard scientific fact. Instead, it is a matter of belief. The Bible says, "Thou shalt not kill." The Bible does not say, "Thou shalt not kill except in cases of murder, treason or capital crimes." It simply says, "Thou shalt not kill."

8   Proponents of the death penalty maintain that anyone who is lowly enough to commit murder deserves to die. But I ask you, how can we show that killing is wrong by killing someone ourselves? When we execute people, we are telling the rest of the world, and our children, that murder is acceptable. How can we maintain that murder is wrong if we are committing the same act that we allegedly denounce? In other words, two wrongs don't constitute a right. I agree with Dr. Rupert Theobald, a criminologist and statistician from the Wisconsin Legislative Reference Bureau, who stated that the message that capital punishment sends is that vengeance is acceptable. Morality? I think not.

9   But there is yet a third issue that we must confront, and that is whether capital punishment is an effective deterrent to crime. And this is a very controversial point with strong opinions on both sides. In truth, the small number of executions in the United States in recent years makes it hard to judge the value of capital punishment as a deterrent. It may be that the death penalty deters crime, but there is no clear-cut evidence which proves that it does. As the National Academy of Science concluded in its analysis of the death penalty, and I quote, "Available studies provide no useful evidence on the deterrent effect of capital punishment."

10   Indeed, there is at least one strong reason to believe that capital punishment does not work as a deterrent. As the Wisconsin Legislative Reference Bureau recently reported in its report on capital punishment, a major problem with the concept of deterrence is that it requires the would-be murderer to contemplate the consequences of his or her crime. In other words, if the murderer is not likely to think about the prospect of capital punishment before committing a crime, or is not able to think about it, then capital punishment cannot logically work as a deterrent to the commission of that crime. As the *Columbia Law Review* reports, "Many people who commit murder may not be able because of mental illness, mental retardation, or excessive emotion to realistically accept the danger of being caught, convicted, and executed. It is very unlikely that capital punishment would deter many of the people who are committing capital crimes." Deterrent? I think not.

11   In conclusion, we must realize that capital punishment is discriminatory. We must realize that capital punishment is immoral. And finally, we must realize that capital punishment is not an effective deterrent to crime. I would urge all of you who support capital punishment to reassess your views and to see its injustice, its immorality, and its ineffectiveness as a deterrent to crime.

Capital Punishment

Commentary

A thoughtful speech on a highly controversial topic, "Capital Punishment" illustrates many of the principles of effective persuasion and is especially notable for the speaker's audience analysis and adaptation. Knowing from his class questionnaires that most of his listeners opposed his position, he takes care to address their objections and to answer them with evidence. He also does an excellent job of organizing the speech and uses plenty of transitions and signposts to help listeners grasp the connections among his ideas. Here is a synopsis of the speech.

Specific Purpose: To persuade my audience that capital punishment should be abolished.

Central Idea: Capital punishment should be abolished because it is unjust, immoral, and ineffective as a deterrent to crime.

Method of Organization: Topical

Introduction: Although the speaker does not establish his credibility on the topic of capital punishment, his introduction is exemplary in all other respects. The opening sentence commands attention and leads into the story about the execution of convicted murderer Robert Streetman. After relating this story, the speaker announces his topic, relates it to his listeners by referring to their responses to his class survey, and ends the introduction with a concise preview of the main points to be discussed in the body.

Body: Organized in topical order, the body of this speech contains three main points, each of which takes up a major issue relative to capital punishment. The first, developed in paragraphs 4–5, argues that capital punishment is economically and racially discriminatory. The speaker's statement in paragraph 4 that "those without the capital get the punishment" is especially compelling and is followed by a quotation from criminologist Hugo Adam Bedeau that points to the fact that having the financial resources to hire a first-rate defense lawyer is a critical factor in avoiding capital punishment. The claim of racial discrimination, presented in paragraph 5, is supported with a brief quotation from Supreme Court Justice William Brennan, with statistical evidence from University of Iowa professor David Baldus, and with testimony from University of Pittsburgh Law School professor Welsh White. Main point one ends with the biting statement: "Justice? I think not."

An excellent transition at the start of paragraph 6 introduces main point two, which deals with the immorality of capital punishment. The speaker advances three subpoints. First, he states that capital punishment is immoral because it is discriminatory, a claim he supports with a quotation from Daniel Hoye of the U.S. Catholic Conference (paragraph 6). Second, the speaker contends that there are no limitations on the Biblical injunction, "Thou shalt not kill" (paragraph 7). Third, he holds that killing someone through capital punishment is just as wrong as killing someone through murder (paragraph 8). The last words of paragraph 8—"Morality? I think not"—parallel the end of main point one and end the second main point on a powerful note.

The third main point addresses the value of capital punishment as a deterrent to crime (paragraphs 9–10). After noting that this is a difficult issue to assess because of the limited number of executions in recent years, the speaker quotes the National Academy of Science's judgment that there is "no useful evidence on the deterrent effect of capital punishment." He then turns to a report from the Wisconsin Legislative Reference Bureau to explain that there are logical reasons to believe that, in many cases, capital punishment is not likely to deter people from committing murder. As in other parts of the speech, the speaker's evidence here does not prove that he is right in an absolute sense—capital punishment is too complex and contentious an issue to admit of perfect proof on either side—but it does enhance both the credibility and potential persuasiveness of his arguments. The final words of main point three—"Deterrence? I think not"—reinforce the speaker's position and lend artistic unity to the speech by echoing the language used to end both of the preceding main points.

Conclusion: Brief and hard-hitting, the conclusion (paragraph 11) succinctly signals the end of the speech and reinforces the central idea.

Responsible Drinking

1   "This Bud's for you." "Buy that man a Miller." "It's the right beer now." The message you get from beer companies is that you deserve that ice-cold beer when you're having a good time.

2   On the other hand, you hear, "Drinking and driving can kill a friendship" and "Friends don't let friends drive drunk." You easily get the impression that it's no problem to drink to excess as long as you don't drive. But I've seen students who didn't drive get carried out of parties on stretchers because they drank until they passed out. I've had to put friends in cabs or have them stay over at my home because they drank too much to be able to make it home safely.

3   As a student at this and another university, I've seen firsthand that drinking too much is a problem and my research shows that it's a growing problem on college campuses. Tonight, I will tell you of the serious problem of excessive drinking by college students. I'll discuss some causes and I'll propose a solution.

4   Let's first examine the problem when college students drink to excess. From my in-class survey, I learned that eleven of you agree that excessive drinking by college students causes serious problems for the university community, while only four of you are either undecided or disagree. We're probably all aware of the dangers of drinking and driving, and we're becoming increasingly aware of the role of alcohol in acquaintance rape, but let's turn to some problems you may not have thought about.

5   First, students may use a community's medical resources if they drink too much. According to an article published in *Newsweek*, the number of students from Boston University hospitalized for alcohol-related illnesses doubled this year. Hospitals and police are valuable community resources being used by students who drink too much.

6   In addition to causing problems for the community, students may cause problems for themselves if they drink too much. A student may skip class, work, or studying due to a hangover. Now you might be thinking, what's a skipped class here and there? Well, it adds up. According to the Office for Substance Abuse Prevention in Washington, D. C., alcohol is a factor in 21 percent of all college dropouts.

7   Next, students who drink to excess sometimes injure themselves or others. I found from my in-class survey that eight of you have had an alcohol-related injury or you know someone who has had an alcohol-related injury. Much more tragic are student deaths caused by alcohol. In February of this year, a student at Princeton University climbed on top of a train that was stopped at the station. This student was electrocuted when he touched the train's live wire, and he had been drinking heavily at a campus party.

8   According to the Office for Substance Abuse Prevention, alcohol is the leading cause of death among young adults. Furthermore, of college students currently enrolled in the United States, more than 240,000 will eventually lose their lives to alcohol. Two hundred and forty thousand—that's the current student population of this university, six times over.

9   Now that we've seen how drinking too much is a serious problem for students and their communities, let's look at some causes. Of course, there are many general causes—from the glorification of drinking that we see in the media, to the tradition of drinking heavily as a rite of passage. But I'd like to discuss some causes that are more specific to college life. I'll tell you how alcohol-centered activities and social pressure can lead to excessive student drinking.

10   Now, college has many activities that are alcohol-centered. Many parties may have drinking as a main event or feature drinking games, and we all know that the purpose of a bar located within walking distance of a campus is for people to purchase and to consume alcohol. If alcohol is the thrust of the activity, then most people who attend that activity will drink, and no one is setting limits as to how much they should drink. All around the country, Spring Break has become such an alcohol-centered activity that the Surgeon General said, "Spring Break used to be where the boys are, now, it's where the booze is."

11   In addition to alcohol-centered activities, social pressure is a cause. I remember well my initiation into an eating club at Princeton University when I first started in college. Most of my friends were getting initiated that night as well, and we got the message clearly—from each other and from the club—that if we wanted to make it into the club that night, we would have to drink, and drink heavily. Everyone I knew drank a great deal that night. Many of you have also experienced social pressure, because I found from my survey that nine of you feel that social pressure has an impact on the amount you drink.

12   Now that we've seen how social pressure and alcohol-centered activities can lead to excessive student drinking, I'd like to discuss solutions that address these causes. These are simple solutions that are within your power to use right away.

13   First, you can choose fun activities that are not alcohol-centered. For a friend's twenty-first birthday, rather than just taking them out for drinks, take them shopping for a special gift. You can go for walks, go to sporting events, or go for bicycle rides to see the view of the city rather than just the view from the bar. You can choose parties and clubs that are alcohol-free. You may say, "Nobody wants to go to activities that don't involve alcohol," but this year the Wisconsin Union Directorate offered students a chance to help the poor in Florida, North Carolina, and Texas as an alternative to Spring Break. There were only 40 positions available, but over 120 people applied.

14   Choosing activities is important, but the choice not to drink too much is equally important. So if you attend activities that do involve alcohol, make a decision before the event that you will not drink too much. You can use the buddy system and say to a friend,

"Tonight at the party I've decided only to have three drinks. If you help me maintain my limit, I'll help you maintain your limit."

15   In social situations where there is a lot of pressure to constantly have a drink in your hand, you can alternate an alcoholic drink with a nonalcoholic drink. For instance, I like to drink rum and coke, so what I'll do is I'll have one rum and coke and then for my next drink I'll ask the bartender to fill that same glass with just Coca-Cola. I can easily maintain my limit, and no one else at the party needs to know that I'm not always consuming alcohol. If we recognize that social pressure is a factor in our drinking, we can use it to our advantage to help us drink responsibly.

16   Tonight we have learned about the serious problem of excessive drinking by college students and some of its causes, and I do hope you realize that solutions are within your power. Please don't think I'm against alcohol, but I am advocating responsible use of the drug—and we must recognize alcohol's power as a drug.

17   Let's go beyond "Friends don't let friends drive drunk" to "Friends don't let friends get drunk." Be a good friend to the most important person of all—yourself—and if you choose to drink, please don't drink to excess.

Responsible Drinking

Commentary

Presented in an introductory public speaking class at the University of Wisconsin, "Responsible Drinking" is a persuasive speech on a question of policy. Although students have heard so much about the problem of excessive drinking on college campuses that they often tune out part way through speeches on the subject, in this case everyone listened intently. A returning student, the speaker presents her ideas clearly and forcefully but without sounding morally superior to her classmates. Here is a synopsis of the speech.

Specific Purpose: To persuade my audience that, if they choose to drink, they should take action to drink responsibly.

Central Idea: Excessive drinking among college students is a serious problem that can be combated by choosing social activities that are not alcohol-centered and by overcoming social pressure for excessive drinking.

Method of Organization: Problem-Cause-Solution

Introduction: Consisting of paragraphs 1–3, the introduction captures attention with a series of well-known slogans from beer companies. After presenting the slogans, the speaker suggests that the problem of drinking on college campuses involves much more than drunk driving—a theme she will develop in detail as the speech progresses. She also establishes her credibility and provides a succinct preview of the main points to be discussed in the body.

Body: This speech provides an excellent example of problem-cause-solution order. Main point one (paragraphs 4–8) deals with the problem of excessive drinking by college students. Rather than focusing on such familiar issues as drunk driving and the role of alcohol in acquaintance rape, the speaker mentions these in passing and spends the bulk of her time discussing equally important but less publicized aspects of student drinking. Main point two (paragraphs 9–11) focuses on two major causes of the problem unique to college life: the large number of alcohol-centered activities on and around campus and the social pressure on students to drink to excess. Main point three (paragraphs 12–15) presents solutions to the problem.

It is important, when using problem-cause-solution order, to make sure the solution deals directly with what the speaker identifies as the cause of the problem. In this case, the first part of the speaker's solution, choosing social activities that are not alcohol-centered (paragraph 13), addresses the first of the causes she had discussed in main point two. The second part of her solution, coping with the social pressure to drink excessively (paragraphs 14–15), addresses the second cause she had mentioned in main point two. Here, as throughout the body, the impact of the speech is strengthened by the excellent use of transitions and signposts to ensure that the audience can follow the speaker's reasoning and progression of ideas.

Conclusion: The conclusion consists of paragraphs 16–17. After summarizing her main points in paragraph 16, the speaker ties the whole speech together in paragraph 17 by referring back to the quotations she had used in the introduction. The closing line reinforces the central idea and ends the speech with a final appeal for individual action.

Making Campus Accessible for Disabled Students

---

1   I'd like to ask you to use your imaginations and think how it would feel if you'd spent an evening studying for an exam. You get up in the morning all set to go to classes, you go down, you get to your door, and it won't open. You think, "Oh, I can just use my back door." But you go to your back door, and that won't open either.

2   It would be pretty frustrating, wouldn't it? That's the kind of frustration handicapped students feel when they can't get to class because of the snow. And that's the same kind of frustration I found when I tried to get my scooter through the snow and it short-circuited because it got so wet from the snow.

3   Now there are many reasons that campuses could be inaccessible, but what I would like to address today is the inaccessibility of this campus due to the uncleared snow. You may think, "This is never going to affect me," but sadly it could. By accident or illness, it could become a problem for you.

4   As you can see, I use a scooter to get around campus, and I have found that this campus is inaccessible due to the uncleared snow. I'd like to share that problem with you and then share my solution. Let's start with the problem.

5   As I see it, the problem faced by handicapped students has two components: the uncleared snow and the violation of the Americans with Disabilities Act. The first component is the inaccessibility of this campus due to the uncleared snow that creates a barrier for wheelchairs and scooters to pass through. Here in Wisconsin, we get an average of 43 inches of snow in any winter and an average of thirteen days of snowfall over one inch or more. As you can see, that would create a significant barrier for those of us who have to use scooters or wheelchairs to get around.

6   A fellow handicapped student shared his story with me. He is a quadriplegic; he has no use of his arms or his legs. He directs his scooter with a wand by his chin. He tried to get through the snow this winter, and he tipped over and was hurt. This is unfair, and it's dangerous. Why should he have to jeopardize his life just to try to get to class? And why is it fair for him to be kept out of class when he has paid for classes out of his pocket just like you and just like me? I've heard the same kinds of horror stories from several handicapped students. The fact remains that the snow creates a barrier that we just cannot pass through, and that barrier really creates a significant problem for us.

7   The second component of this problem is that the Americans with Disabilities Act, a civil rights act that was passed by Congress and signed by President Bush in 1990, prohibits discrimination and requires that barrier-free access to any public accommodation be given to the handicapped students. The university is in violation of this act. Let me read part of it for you: "People with disabilities have the right to full and equal access to any facility or accommodation of any public place. They have the right to make a request for acceptable services by that public accommodation." I believe that language is clear: "full and equal access." And we're not getting that. That's why I believe the university is violating the Americans with Disabilities Act.

8   Now that we have a clear understanding of the problem, let me share my solution with you. An effective solution could have three components. The first component is that the university should adopt a policy of snow removal similar to the ordinance that the city of Madison has. That ordinance reads: "Sidewalks must be cleared of all ice and snow whenever it accumulates to one-half inch or more and the walks must be cleared by noon the day following the snowfall." I think the university should adopt this as a campus policy.

9   Second, the university should set priorities to the areas that the handicapped students need. In an interview with Gene Turk of the Grounds Department, I learned of the university's priorities. He says that first the stairs and the hills are taken care of. Then the parking lots and the sidewalks are cleared by the plows. There was never any mention of the ramps or the curb cutaways that we handicapped students need. We're not getting a fair deal here. That's why I think the university is violating the Americans with Disabilities Act. The university needs to set as priorities the areas that we need—the ramps and the curb cutaways.

10   The third component of my solution would address the lack of personnel in the Grounds Department. The university should hire a staff member who could focus on those areas that handicapped individuals need to get around. Some of you may be wondering, "How much would this cost?" A forty-hour week, at eight dollars an hour, would be $15,000 dollars a year, plus benefits. The official published university budget is $1 billion. Surely, they can find, in a budget that big, funding for $15,000 to hire someone who could make this campus accessible to all of us.

11   In closing, I really believe this is a workable solution. If the university were to go ahead and adopt this policy, it would fulfill the requirements of the Americans with Disabilities Act and make this campus accessible, providing full and equal enjoyment for those of us who are the handicapped students. Won't you help me effectuate this change? Please consider signing a petition that would encourage this university to change its snow removal plan. I will have those petitions in the back of the room when this speech is finished.

12   To end, let me share with you a quote out of the book *Access: The Guide to a Better Life for Disabled Americans*: "The disabled minority is not a closed society. While nobody would ever change skin color, anyone can join this minority by accident or by illness." Disability does not respect age, sex, religion or social status. Every American should see himself or herself as an ally for the disabled person who is just seeking a fair deal. Thank you.

Making Campus Accessible for Disabled Students

Commentary

"Making Campus Accessible for Disabled Students" shows how students can construct speeches on matters of local concern. The speaker, who suffers from multiple sclerosis, addressed the audience while seated in her scooter. Here is a synopsis of the speech, with special attention to how it utilizes the methods of persuasion discussed in Chapter 17 of the textbook.

Specific Purpose: To persuade my audience that the University of Wisconsin-Madison should change its snow removal policy to make campus more accessible to handicapped students.

Central Idea: The University of Wisconsin should change its snow removal policies to solve the problem of inaccessibility to handicapped students.

Method of Organization: Problem-Solution

Introduction: Consisting of paragraphs 1–4, the introduction begins with a hypothetical scenario that allows students who are not disabled to imagine themselves in a situation akin to that of a handicapped student who cannot get to class because of the snow. The speaker then tells her audience: "You might think this never is going to affect you, but, sadly, it could. By accident or illness, it could become a problem for you." She ends the introduction by previewing the main points she will discuss in the body.

The introduction also plays a crucial role in establishing the speaker's credibility. The fact that she suffers from multiple sclerosis and has to get around campus in a scooter gives her high initial credibility. She reinforces that credibility by noting that she, like other handicapped students, has experienced problems getting to class because of the university's failure to clear snow in a timely fashion. Moreover, as the speech progresses, she continues to build her credibility by exhibiting sincerity and good will and by delivering the speech with genuine conviction.

Body: Organized in problem-solution order, the body of this speech contains two main points. The first details the problem of inaccessibility to campus for handicapped students because of the uncleared snow (paragraphs 5–7). The second presents the speaker's solution to the problem (paragraphs 8–10).

Both points are amply supported with evidence. In the problem section, the speaker uses statistics and examples to demonstrate that there is a need to change the university's snow removal priorities. In the solution section, she uses testimony from a member of the Grounds Department to reinforce her claim that ramps and curb cutaways are not currently a priority for snow removal on campus. She also presents statistics to show that the university can afford to hire additional personnel to clear snow from ramps, curb cutaways, and other areas needed by handicapped students. This is important because a potential objection to the speaker's plan is that it might be too costly. Anticipating the objection and answering it with evidence makes her position more persuasive.

The speaker also makes effective use of reasoning in both main points. In the first, she reasons from principle in arguing that the university is violating the Americans with Disabilities Act. Her reasoning is as follows:

a. The Americans with Disabilities Act requires equal access to all public facilities for people with physical disabilities.

b. The university's policy of snow removal does not provide equal access for students with physical disabilities.

c. Therefore, the university's policy of snow removal violates the Americans with Disabilities Act.

In her second main point, the speaker reasons from analogy by contending that the city of Madison's snow removal policy is also appropriate for the university. If that policy works in the city, she suggests, it should be workable on campus as well.

Although the speaker does not employ a great deal of emotional language, her personal involvement with the topic, the sincerity and conviction of her delivery, and her examples of handicapped students who have had trouble getting around campus because of the snow all combine to give her speech a degree of emotional appeal and to enhance its persuasiveness.

Conclusion: The conclusion consists of paragraphs 11–12. Paragraph 11 summarizes the main points and calls upon listeners to sign the petition that the speaker will have available after the speech. The closing paragraph reemphasizes the fact that anyone can become disabled at any time and encourages all members of the audience to see themselves as allies for the disabled.

A Whisper of AIDS

Mary Fisher

---

1   Less than three months ago, at platform hearings in Salt Lake City, I asked the Republican Party to lift the shroud of silence which has been draped over the issue of HIV and AIDS. I have come tonight to bring our silence to an end.

2   I bear a message of challenge, not self-congratulation. I want your attention, not your applause. I would never have asked to be HIV-positive. But I believe that in all things there is a purpose, and I stand before you and before the nation, gladly.

3   The reality of AIDS is brutally clear. Two hundred thousand Americans are dead or dying; a million more are infected. Worldwide 40 million, 60 million, or 100 million infections will be counted in the coming few years. But despite science and research, White House meetings and congressional hearings, despite good intentions and bold initiatives, campaign slogans and hopeful promises—it is, despite it all, the epidemic which is winning tonight.

4   In the context of an election year, I ask you—here in this great hall or listening in the quiet of your home—to recognize that the AIDS virus is not a political creature. It does not care whether you are Democrat or Republican. It does not ask whether you are black or white, male or female, gay or straight, young or old.

5   Tonight, I represent an AIDS community whose members have been reluctantly drafted from every segment of American society. Though I am white and a mother, I am one with a black infant struggling with tubes in a Philadelphia hospital. Though I am female and contracted this disease in marriage and enjoy the warm support of my family, I am one with the lonely gay man sheltering a flickering candle from the cold wind of his family's rejection.

6   This is not a distant threat; it is a present danger. The rate of infection is increasing fastest among women and children. Largely unknown a decade ago, AIDS is the third leading killer of young adult Americans today—but it won't be third for long. Because, unlike other diseases, this one travels. Adolescents don't give each other cancer or heart disease because they believe they are in love. But HIV is different, and we have helped it along. We have killed each other with our ignorance, our prejudice, and our silence.

7   We may take refuge in our stereotypes, but we cannot hide there long. Because HIV asks only one thing of those it attacks: Are you human? And this is the right question: Are you human? Because people with HIV have not entered some alien state of being. They are human. They have not earned cruelty and they do not deserve meanness. They don't benefit from being isolated or treated as outcasts. Each of them is exactly what God made—a person. Not evil, deserving of our judgment; not victims, longing for our pity. People: Ready for support and worthy of compassion.

8   My call to you, my party, is to take a public stand no less compassionate than that of the President and Mrs. Bush. They have embraced me and my family in memorable ways. In the place of judgment, they have shown affection. In difficult moments, they have raised our spirits. In the darkest hours, I have seen them reaching not only to me but also to my parents, armed with that stunning grief and special grace that comes only to parents who have themselves leaned too long over the bedside of a dying child.

9   With the President's leadership, much good has been done; much of the good has gone unheralded; and, as the President has insisted, "Much remains to be done."

10   But we do the President's cause no good if we praise the American family but ignore a virus that destroys it. We must be consistent if we are to be believed. We cannot love justice and ignore prejudice, love our children and fear to teach them. Whatever our role, as parent or policy maker, we must act as eloquently as we speak—else we have no integrity.

11   My call to the nation is a plea for awareness. If you believe you are safe, you are in danger. Because I was not hemophiliac, I was not at risk. Because I was not gay, I was not at risk. Because I did not inject drugs, I was not at risk.

12   My father has devoted much of his lifetime guarding against another Holocaust. He is part of the generation who heard Pastor Niemoeller come out of the Nazi death camps to say: "They came after the Jews, and I was not a Jew, so I did not protest. They came after the trade unionists, and I was not a trade unionist, so I did not protest. Then they came after the Roman Catholics, and I was not a Roman Catholic, so I did not protest. Then they came after me, and there was no one left to protest."

13   The lesson history teaches is this: If you believe you are safe, you are at risk. If you do not see this killer stalking your children, look again. There is no family or community, no race or religion, no place left in America that is safe. Until we genuinely embrace this message, we are a nation at risk.

14   Tonight, HIV marches resolutely toward AIDS in more than a million American homes, littering its pathway with the bodies of the young—young men, young women, young parents, and young children. One of the families is mine. If it is true that HIV inevitably turns to AIDS, then my children will inevitably turn to orphans.

15   My family has been a rock of support. My eighty-four-year-old father, who has pursued the healing of the nations, will not accept the premise that he cannot heal his daughter. My mother refuses to be broken; she still calls at midnight to tell wonderful jokes that make me laugh. Sisters and friends and my brother Phillip, whose birthday is today—all have helped carry me over the hardest places. I am blessed, richly and deeply blessed, to have such a family.

16   But not all of you have been so blessed. You are HIV-positive but dare not say it. You have lost loved ones, but you dared not whisper the word AIDS. You weep silently; you grieve alone.

17   I have a message for you: It is not you who should feel shame. It is we—we who tolerate ignorance and practice prejudice, we who have taught you to fear. We must lift our shroud of silence, making it safe for you to reach out for compassion. It is our task to seek safety for our children, not in quiet denial but in effective action.

18   Someday our children will be grown. My son Max, now four, will take the measure of his mother. My son Zachary, now two, will sort through his memories. I may not be here to hear their judgments, but I know already what I hope they are.

19   I want my children to know that their mother was not a victim. She was a messenger. I do not want them to think, as I once did, that courage is the absence of fear. I want them to know that courage is the strength to act wisely when most we are afraid. I want them to have the courage to step forward when called by their nation or their party and give leadership, no matter what the personal cost. I ask no more of you than I ask of myself or of my children.

20   To the millions of you who are grieving, who are frightened, who have suffered the ravages of AIDS firsthand: Have courage and you will find support.

21   To the millions who are strong, I issue the plea: Set aside prejudice and politics to make room for compassion and sound policy.

22   To my children, I make this pledge: I will not give in, Zachary, because I draw my courage from you. Your silly giggle gives me hope. Your gentle prayers give me strength. And you, my child, give me the reason to say to America: "You are at risk." And I will not rest, Max, until I have done all I can to make your world safe. I will seek a place where intimacy is not the prelude to suffering.

23   I will not hurry to leave you, my children. But when I go, I pray that you will not suffer shame on my account.

24   To all within sound of my voice, I appeal: Learn with me the lessons of history and of grace, so my children will not be afraid to say the word AIDS when I am gone. Then their children, and yours, may not need to whisper it at all.

25   God bless the children and God bless us all. Good night.

A Whisper of AIDS *by Mary Fisher*

Commentary

"A Whisper of AIDS" was delivered at the Republican National Convention in Houston, Texas, on August 19, 1992. Only a year earlier Mary Fisher had learned that she had contracted the HIV virus from her ex-husband. Resolving to do all she could to fight the disease, she became an outspoken advocate of the need for public understanding and resources in the battle against AIDS. After telling her story to the Republican Platform Committee in May 1992, Fisher, a former staff assistant to President Gerald Ford, was invited to address the party's national convention that summer.

Feeling, as she said later, like "the only HIV-positive Republican," she was deeply concerned how her message of compassion and awareness would be received. It did not take long, however, for Fisher's audience to realize that they were hearing a very special speech. Within a few minutes, the Astrodome turned virtually silent as the delegates stopped their chatting and gave Fisher their undivided attention. Some were moved to tears. Across the United States, millions watched on television, captivated by Fisher's somber words and heartfelt delivery. The *New York Times* deemed the address "exceptional for its deep emotion and sharp message." It was ranked 52nd in the survey Professor Martin J. Medhurst and I conducted of 137 communication scholars to determine top 100 American speeches of the 20th century.

Here is a synopsis of the speech.

Specific Purpose: To persuade my audience to adopt attitudes of awareness toward the AIDS epidemic and of compassion toward people who are HIV-positive.

Central Idea: Because AIDS can strike anyone at any time, we must do all we can to combat it and to be compassionate toward people who are HIV-positive.

Method of Organization: Spatial

Introduction: The introduction of Fisher's speech consists of paragraphs 1–2, in which she succinctly states her aim to "lift the shroud of silence" that has covered the issue of HIV/AIDS in the Republican Party. Because her speech was preceded by a brief video that established her credentials as a traditional Republican despite her status as HIV-positive, she did not need a longer introduction.

Body: The body of the speech falls into four main sections, the first of which runs from paragraph 3 through paragraph 6. In these paragraphs Fisher discusses the seriousness of the AIDS crisis in an effort to convince Republicans that neither they—nor anyone else—is immune from the disease. After giving statistics on the extent of the epidemic, she notes that AIDS is not a political creature—it attacks people regardless of age, gender, race, political affiliation, or sexual orientation. And, she stresses, despite everything that has been done to combat AIDS, "it's the epidemic that is winning."

The second section of the body consists of paragraphs 7–10, in which Fisher issues a call to the Republican Party to treat AIDS victims with the compassion they deserve. People who are HIV-positive, she tells her audience, do not merit shame or condemnation. After praising President and Mrs. Bush for their personal compassion toward her, she urges the Party as a whole to act with similar compassion toward AIDS victims in general. It is not possible, she pointedly remarks, to "praise the American family but ignore a virus that destroys it."

In the third section of the body, paragraphs 11–14, Fisher issues a powerful plea to the nation for awareness. Reasoning analogically, she compares people who shrug their shoulders over AIDS to people who did not protest against Hitler's concentration camps in Nazi Germany. No matter what we may think, she warns, "There is no family or community, no race or religion, no place left in America that is safe." Until the U.S. comes to terms with this fact, she warns, it will continue to be a nation at risk.

The fourth—and longest—section of the body runs from paragraph 15 through paragraph 24. In this section Fisher moves back and forth between personal observations about her condition and her family and comments directed to various portions of her audience. After thanking her family in paragraph 15 for their support and compassion, she speaks in paragraphs 16–17 to HIV-positive people who lack support and compassion. It is not you who should feel shame, she says, but those of us who "tolerate ignorance and practice prejudice."

In paragraphs 18–19, Fisher speaks movingly of her two sons—how she hopes they will remember her and how she hopes they will act with courage and leadership when she is gone. Then Fisher urges her audience to act with courage and leadership as well. Turning in paragraph 20 to AIDS sufferers, she tells them that if they have courage, they will find comfort. In paragraph 21, she calls on people who do not have AIDS to exercise leadership by setting aside "prejudice and politics to make room for compassion and sound policy."

Bringing the speech to an emotional climax, Fisher returns to her children in paragraphs 22–23, addresses them by name, and expresses the hope that they will not suffer shame on her account. Then she moves back to her general audience and appeals one last time for awareness and compassion so "my children will not be afraid to say the word AIDS when I am gone."

Conclusion: If there is a clearly identifiable conclusion to Fisher's speech, it is the brief words of paragraph 25—"God bless the children, and God bless us all"—and even those words are so closely connected to the content of paragraph 24 that they can be considered an extension of that paragraph rather than a distinct conclusion. As with Martin Luther King's "I Have a Dream," the most meaningful question to ask about the end of Fisher's speech is not whether it has an explicit conclusion, but whether it concludes effectively—which it unquestionably does.

Credibility: Fisher faced two problems with respect to her credibility. The first was to be seen as someone with substantial enough Republican credentials to be taken seriously by the convention audience. Because of the repeated praise of "family values" and the negative tone toward people who are HIV-positive by previous speakers at the convention, there was no guarantee that Fisher's immediate audience would pay much heed to her message.

To boost Fisher's credibility as a Republican, her speech was preceded by a video stressing her family's long-time connections with the Republican Party, including her work as a staff assistant to President Ford and her father's activities as a Republican fundraiser. During the speech itself, Fisher reminded the audience of her Republican credentials by mentioning her testimony before the platform committee three months earlier (paragraph 1), her family's close relationship with President and Mrs. Bush (paragraph 8), and her commitment to the President's cause (paragraph 10).

Fisher's second concern with respect to credibility was to be seen as a bona fide spokesperson for the AIDS community. The video before her speech helped, as it explained the circumstances by which she had become HIV-positive and projected a positive personal image of her as a mother and as an AIDS activist. Whatever positive impact the film had, however, could easily have been destroyed by a poor speech. As it turned out, everything Fisher said and did in her address boosted her terminal credibility far above her initial credibility. Perhaps most important in this regard were her lack of self-pity, her compassion and good will, her poignant emotional appeals, and her eloquent language.

Evidence and Reasoning: Although Fisher does not employ a great deal of statistical evidence, she does present telling figures in paragraphs 3 and 6 about the extent of the AIDS epidemic. These figures are necessary to establish her point that AIDS is on the march in the United States and the world. However, had she presented too many statistics, she would have changed the tone of her speech and may have undermined its personal, emotional appeal.

Fisher's strongest use of testimony comes in paragraph 12, in which she quotes Pastor Niemoeller about the consequences of not protesting against the Nazi death camps during World War II. She then uses this quotation as the basis for the analogy, in paragraph 13, between the tragic results of ignoring the concentration camps and the tragic consequences of ignoring the explosive growth of the AIDS epidemic.

Fisher uses two extended examples in her speech. The first comes in paragraph 8 and describes the compassionate response she has received from President and Mrs. Bush. The moral, of course, is that Republicans in general should respond compassionately to all people who are HIV-positive. The second extended example occurs in paragraph 15, where Fisher explains the support she has received from her family. She then contrasts that support, in paragraphs 16–17, with the prejudice faced by many people who are HIV-positive.

As in both of these examples, most of the evidence in Fisher's speech comes from her personal experience. Not only is this appropriate given her status as HIV-positive, but it is sound rhetorical strategy. To be successful, Fisher had to move the AIDS debate beyond the level of statistics and experts and relate it to the lives of ordinary Americans. By drawing on her own experience, Fisher personalizes the issue and gives it an immediacy it had previously lacked for most of her audience.

Emotional Appeal: Fisher's speech offers a splendid example of the power of emotional appeal in persuasive speaking. Much of her emotional appeal comes, of course, from the highly personal nature of the speech, which was reinforced by Fisher's direct, unaffected delivery. As we shall see shortly, the eloquence, simplicity, and genuine pathos of Fisher's language also contribute to her emotional appeal.

As the speech progresses, Fisher appeals primarily to two contrasting emotions—fear and compassion. The most notable fear appeals are in paragraphs 3–6 and 11–14, in which Fisher explains the brutal reality of the AIDS epidemic and seeks to convince her audience that no one is immune from it. The most extended appeals to compassion are in paragraphs 7–10, 15–17, and 21–25, but the need for compassion runs through the entire speech as a theme in a symphony.

Language: As effective as Fisher's speech is in other respects, it is distinguished above all by its use of language. Just as Martin Luther King's "I Have a Dream" stands out from the thousands of speeches delivered during the civil rights movement, so the artistry and eloquence of Fisher's address make it the most memorable public discourse to date of the struggle against AIDS.

As in most speeches noted for their eloquence, Fisher's language is clear, familiar, and concrete. She creates sharp visual images—often of great poignancy and emotional power, and often in combination with repetition and parallel structure. Examples of this occur in the affecting imagery of paragraphs 4–5, the "Because I was not . . ." series of paragraph 11, the uncompromising insistence of paragraphs 13–14, and the gentle compassion of paragraph 16. It is also worth noting how Fisher uses repetition and parallelism to build the cadence and power of her address as she builds to her conclusion in paragraphs 19–25.

Fisher also makes effective use of antithesis. Thematically she juxtaposes the contrasting impulses of fear and compassion, ignorance and awareness, silence and speech. This thematic antithesis is reinforced by the heavy use of stylistic antithesis. In paragraph 2, for example, Fisher says, "I bear a message of challenge, not self-congratulation. I want your attention, not your applause." In paragraph 6, she cautions that AIDS "is not a distant threat; it is a present danger." In paragraph 10, she counsels that "We cannot love justice and ignore prejudice, love our children and fear to teach them." In paragraph 13, she warns, "If you think you are safe, you are at risk." In paragraph 17, she tells AIDS victims, "It is not you who should feel shame; it is we." Indeed, antithesis occurs so frequently that one can find examples of it throughout the address.

Choices and Change

Barbara Bush

1   Thank you very, very much, President Keohane; Mrs. Gorbachev; trustees; faculty; parents; and, I should say, Julia Porter, class president; and certainly my new best friend, Christine Bicknell. And, of course, the Class of 1990. I'm really thrilled to be here today and very excited, as I know all of you must be, that Mrs. Gorbachev could join us. These, these are exciting times. They're exciting in Washington, and I had really looked forward to coming to Wellesley. I thought it was gonna be fun; I never dreamt it would be this much fun. So thank you for that.

2   More than ten years ago, when I was invited here to talk about our experiences in the People's Republic of China, I was struck by both the natural beauty of your campus and the spirit of this place.

3   Wellesley, you see, is not just a place, but an idea—an experiment in excellence in which diversity is not just tolerated but is embraced.

4   The essence of this spirit was captured in a moving speech about tolerance given last year by a student body president of one of your sister colleges. She related the story by Robert Fulghum about a young pastor [who], finding himself in charge of some very energetic children, hits upon the game called Giants, Wizards, and Dwarfs. "You have to decide now," the pastor instructed the children, "which you are—a giant, a wizard or a dwarf." At that, a small girl tugging at his pants leg asks, "But where do the mermaids stand?"

5   And the pastor tells her there are no mermaids. And she says, "Oh yes there are; I am a mermaid."

6   Now, this little girl knew what she was, and she was not about to give up on either her identity or the game. She intended to take her place wherever mermaids fit into the scheme of things. Where do the mermaids stand—all of those who are different, those who do not fit the boxes and the pigeonholes? "Answer that question," wrote Fulghum, "and you can build a school, a nation, or a whole world."

7   As that very wise young woman said, "Diversity, like anything worth having, requires effort." Effort to learn about and respect difference, to be compassionate with one another, to cherish our own identity, and to accept unconditionally the same in others. You should all be very proud that this is the Wellesley spirit.

8   Now, I know your first choice today was Alice Walker—guess how I know!—known for *The Color Purple*. Instead you got me—known for the color of my hair. Alice Walker's book has a special resonance here. At Wellesley, each class is known by a special color.

For four years the class of '90 has worn the color purple. Today you meet on Severance Green to say goodbye to all of that, to begin a new and a very personal journey to search for your own true colors.

9   In the world that awaits you beyond the shores of Lake Waban, no one can say what your true colors will be. But this I do know: You have a first-class education from a first-class school. And so you need not, probably cannot, live a paint-by-numbers life. Decisions are not irrevocable. Choices do come back. And as you set off from Wellesley, I hope that many of you will consider making three very special choices.

10   The first is to believe in something larger than yourself, to get involved in some of the big ideas of our time. I chose literacy because I honestly believe that if more people could read, write, and comprehend, we would be that much closer to solving so many of the problems that plague our nation and our society.

11   And early on I made another choice which I hope you'll make as well. Whether you're talking about education, career, or service, you're talking about life, and life really must have joy. It's supposed to be fun.

12   One of the reasons I made the most important decision of my life—to marry George Bush—is because he made me laugh. It's true, sometimes we've laughed through our tears, but that shared laughter has been one of our strongest bonds. Find the joy in life because, as Ferris Bueller said on his day off, "Life moves pretty fast, and [if] you don't stop and look around once in a while, you're gonna miss it." (I'm not gonna tell George you clapped more for Ferris than you clapped for George!)

13   The third choice that must not be missed is to cherish your human connections, your relationships with family and friends. For several years you've had impressed upon you the importance to your career of dedication and hard work—and, of course, that's true. But as important as your obligations as a doctor, a lawyer, a business leader will be, you are a human being first, and those human connections—with spouses, with children, with friends—are the most important investment you will ever make.

14   At the end of your life, you will never regret not having passed one more test, winning one more verdict, or not closing one more deal. You will regret time not spent with a husband, a child, a friend, or a parent.

15   We are in a transitional period right now. We are in a transitional period right now, fascinating and exhilarating times, learning to adjust to changes and the choices we—men and women—are facing. As an example, I remember what a friend said on hearing her husband complain to his buddies that he had to baby sit. Quickly setting him straight, my friend told her husband that when it's your own kids, it's not called baby sitting.

16   Now, maybe we should adjust faster; maybe we should adjust slower. But whatever the era, whatever the times, one thing will never change: Fathers and mothers, if you have children, they must come first. You must read to your children and you must

hug your children and you must love your children. Your success as a family, our success as a society, depends not on what happens in the White House, but on what happens inside your house.

17   For over fifty years, it was said that the winner of Wellesley's annual hoop race would be the first to get married. Now they say the winner will be the first to become a CEO. Both of those stereotypes show too little tolerance for those who want to know where the mermaids stand. So, so I want to offer a new legend: The winner of the hoop race will be the first to realize her dream. Not society's dreams—her own personal dream. And who knows? Somewhere out in this audience may even be someone who will one day follow in my footsteps and preside over the White House as the President's spouse. And I wish him well!

18   Well, the controversy ends here, but our conversation is only beginning. And a worthwhile conversation it has been. So as you leave Wellesley today, take with you deep thanks for the courtesy and the honor you have shared with Mrs. Gorbachev and with me. Thank you. God bless you. And may your future be worthy of your dreams.

Choices and Change *by Barbara Bush*

Commentary

Barbara Bush's commencement address at Wellesley College on June 1, 1990, is one of the best known speeches of recent years. Bush was invited to speak by the senior class when their first choice, Alice Walker, author of The Color Purple, could not attend. In protest, 150 Wellesley seniors—about one-fourth of the graduating class—signed a petition charging that Bush was not a good role model for career-oriented students at a women's college and has been chosen because of the man she married rather than for her own achievements.

The petition touched off a storm of controversy. Throughout the month before Bush's speech, educators, newspaper columnists, and others debated the petition and the larger issue of women's role in American society. The media spotlight became so intense that Bush's speech was broadcast live by all the major television networks.

Instead of pretending there was no controversy, Bush acknowledged it and turned it to her advantage with a deft blend of humor and goodwill. She did not abandon her own views on the issues facing women in American society, but neither did she disparage listeners who held different views. The result is a speech that students find interesting both for its approach to audience adaptation and for its message about the role of women in the United States. Expect a lively discussion on both aspects of the speech.

Here is a synopsis of the speech:

Introduction: The introduction consists of paragraph 1, in which Bush acknowledges other dignitaries as well as members of her audience. Christine Bicknell, whom Bush calls her "new best friend," was the student speaker who had preceded her on the podium.

Body: The body runs from paragraph 2 through paragraph 17 and contains two main points. The first is developed in paragraphs 2–7. In this section of the speech, Bush praises Wellesley's commitment to diversity, but she does not define diversity in racial, ethnic, or sexual terms. Rather, she characterizes it in general terms as requiring the effort "to learn about and respect difference, to be compassionate with one another, to cherish our own identity, and to accept unconditionally the same in others" (paragraph 7). This is a crucial move, for it allows Bush to identify with a value shared by most of her listeners while at the same time implying that the people opposed to her appearance have not been acting in the true spirit of diversity.

Any potential conflict over this move, however, is quickly dissipated by Bush's good-natured treatment, in paragraph 8, of the fact that Alice Walker had been the senior class's first choice for commencement speaker. In the second half of paragraph 8, Bush introduces her second main point—that Wellesley's seniors will have crucial choices to make as they begin the journey for their own true colors.

As Bush develops this point in paragraphs 9–17, she urges her listeners to make three choices—to get involved in major social issues (paragraph 10), to keep in mind that life is supposed to be fun (paragraphs 11–12), and to cherish their human relationships with family and friends (paragraphs 13–16). Bush spends most of her time on the third choice, and in doing so presents a number of lines that were widely quoted afterward by commentators on the speech.

Paragraph 17 brings the second main point to a close and contains the best known line of the speech, in which Bush says: "Somewhere out in this audience may even be someone who will one day follow in my footsteps, and preside over the White House as the president's spouse. And I wish him well!" Although Bush had used this line in previous speeches, it was new to the audience at Wellesley, and they responded with cheering and prolonged applause. Paragraph 17 is also noteworthy for the way it links the two main points of the speech by referring back to the story in main point one about where the mermaids stand.

Conclusion: The conclusion consists of paragraph 18, in which Bush states that the controversy over her appearance is over but that the conversation on women's issues is only beginning. After thanking the seniors for the "courtesy and honor" of addressing them, Bush closes by saying to the seniors, "may your future be worthy of your dreams."

The Massachusetts 54th

1   Staring at a once beautiful valley now filled with bodies that serve only as a reminder of the morning's gruesome events, a lonely grave digger thinks to himself. Unable to fight in the Civil War because he is black, he can only bury the soldiers that fight and die for his freedom, wondering when he will get his chance to fight.

2   In the movie *Glory*, this grave digger is played by Morgan Freeman, and he is given his chance to fight as a member of the 54th Regiment of the Massachusetts Volunteer Infantry. The Massachusetts 54th was the first black regiment of the Civil War. Led by Colonel Robert Gould Shaw, the 54th showed remarkable bravery, patriotism, and sacrifice.

3   Even though the North was opposed to slavery, many Northerners held on to anti-black attitudes. Because of these attitudes, the Massachusetts 54th was given dangerous assignments and equipped with substandard, or even broken, equipment. Wearing shoes no better than wrapped cloth, tattered uniforms that did little or nothing to ward off the cold, and using guns that would misfire every other shot, the 54th still proved to be one of the bravest regiments in the Civil War.

4   On top of their bravery, the members of the Massachusetts 54th exhibited the highest levels of patriotism. Despite the racism and other struggles they faced, they were proud to wear their uniforms and to carry the Union flag into battle. Their patriotism can best be seen when one observes the number of deserters from this regiment—none. Despite the thousands of desertions suffered by many other regiments on the Northern side, not a single soldier deserted from the Massachusetts 54th.

5   I have spoken so far of bravery and of patriotism, but it is the sacrifice of the 54th that has etched them into the pages of history. That sacrifice occurred during the assault on Fort Wagner in 1863. This heavily guarded Confederate fort lay on the beaches of South Carolina, nearly unapproachable. A frontal assault was needed to weaken the fort enough to allow for a full-scale attack. It was a suicidal mission, but the 54th volunteered for it.

6   They were the first regiment to storm Fort Wagner, and so would suffer the highest casualties. Rushing forward, they reached the fort well before any reinforcements that were supposed to back them up. Believing the reinforcements to be close behind, the 54th attacked Fort Wagner and found nothing but the enemy. When the charge was over, more than 250 soldiers from the regiment had been killed, wounded, or captured.

7   To join an army that didn't believe in you. To fight with an army who didn't like you. To die for an army that didn't respect you. This was the Massachusetts 54th. Today they lay where they died, on the beaches of South Carolina. Colonel Shaw and his men were piled together in a mass grave, which has since been covered by the shifting tides of the Atlantic. A small statue stands in Boston—a reminder of their sacrifice.

8   Bravery, patriotism, and sacrifice. These are qualities of the Massachusetts 54th. With the help of their efforts, along with all the other black regiments that followed them, slavery did eventually come to an end.

9   In the movie *Glory*, Morgan Freeman talks of his chance to fight for the freedom of his own people. The 54th grasped this chance, they fought for it, and they eventually died for it. In the words of Union General Truman Seymour, "On every inch of the sands in front of Fort Wagner will be forever traced in undying glory the story of the determination and courage of the Massachusetts 54th."

The Massachusetts 54th

Commentary

An excellent commemorative speech, "The Massachusetts 54th" pays tribute to the first African-American regiment in the U.S. Civil War. In keeping with the goals of a commemorative speech, the speaker provides enough information about the Massachusetts 54th for his listeners to understand its accomplishments, but he focuses above all on engendering admiration and respect for those accomplishments. The speech also shows how students can use the stylistic devices of imagery, parallelism, and repetition to heighten the impact of their ideas. In addition to discussing this speech in class, you may want to show the video of it, which is available online and on the DVD of student speeches that accompanies this edition of *The Art of Public Speaking*. Here is a synopsis of the speech.

Introduction: Paragraphs 1–2 constitute the speech's introduction. The speaker gains attention by using vivid language to create an image of the grave digger played by Morgan Freeman in the film *Glory*. He then moves quickly to reveal his topic (the Massachusetts 54th) and its significance as the first black regiment of the Civil War. The speaker ends his introduction by previewing the three traits of the Massachusetts 54th that he will concentrate on in the body—bravery, patriotism, and courage. As with the rest of the speech, the language of the introduction is crisp, forceful, and uncluttered.

Body: The body of the speech runs from paragraph 3 through paragraph 7. Paragraph 3 deals with the bravery of the Massachusetts 54th, paragraph 4 with its patriotism, and paragraphs 5–7 with its sacrifice. As the speaker develops each point, he provides concrete examples and other details that allow the audience to visualize the tribulations and triumphs of the 54th. Particularly noteworthy are his description of the substandard equipment issued to the 54th (paragraph 3), his explanation of the lack of desertions from the 54th (paragraph 4), and his account of the assault on Fort Wagner (paragraphs 5–6). Paragraph 7 ends the body by stating that the soldiers of the 54th were buried in a mass grave which has since been covered by the "shifting tides of the Atlantic." The final sentence ("A small statue stands in Boston—a reminder of their sacrifice") is especially moving.

Throughout the body of the speech, the speaker uses the resources of language discussed in Chapter 12 to reinforce the impact of his ideas. The imagery at the end of paragraph 3 magnifies the contrast between the anti-black attitudes of most Northerners and the bravery of the Massachusetts 54th. The use of concrete language in paragraphs 5–6 to describe the 54th's heroism in the attack on Fort Wagner puts the scene vividly before the audience. The use of repetition and parallelism at the start of paragraph 7 is highly effective in reinforcing the speaker's ideas. So, too, are the transitions in paragraphs 4 and 5, both of which help listeners keep track of the speaker's main points as he moves through the body of the speech.

Conclusion: The conclusion begins in paragraph 8 by summarizing the three major traits of the Massachusetts 54th celebrated in the body of the speech—bravery, patriotism, and sacrifice—and noting how those traits helped contribute to the end of slavery in the United States. Paragraph 9 unifies the entire speech by returning to the story of the grave digger played by Morgan Freeman in the movie *Glory*, while the closing quotation from General Truman Seymour reinforces the central idea and ends the speech on a strong note.

———————————————

James "Cool Papa" Bell

1   In 1946 one of the greatest baseball players of all time retired after almost twenty-five years as a pro. No, it wasn't Babe Ruth, Joe DiMaggio, or any other star you've probably heard of. The man was James "Cool Papa" Bell, star of the Pittsburgh Crawfords of the Negro League.

2   The Negro League was the name of the league where black players were forced to play until 1947, when major league baseball became integrated. The Negro League had some of the best players never to be appreciated, and Cool Papa Bell headed that list.

3   Many say that Bell was the fastest player ever to play the game. This could very well be true. He led the league in stolen bases almost every year he played until he retired at age forty-one. Satchel Paige, a former teammate of his, said Cool Papa was so fast he could flip the switch and be in bed before the lights went out.

4   In fact, Jesse Owens, the Olympic sprinter who was known as the fastest man in the world, said he would race and beat anyone around the bases as long as that person wasn't Cool Papa Bell. At five feet, eleven inches tall and only 135 pounds, Bell was thin as a rail. But no one made fun of his slender size as he swiftly and smoothly stole second or scored from first on a single.

5   And Cool Papa was smooth. In his first game as a pro, the seventeen-year-old, then known as James, came into the game in the bottom of the ninth inning and struck out one of the league's best hitters on three straight pitches. Pretty smooth for a guy who wasn't even a pitcher. For playing with the savvy of a seasoned veteran even though he was only a kid, his manager called him "Cool Papa."

6   But to say that Cool Papa had style would be an injustice to him. Cool Papa was style. Whether in his baseball uniform or his Sunday best, Cool Papa had a flair all his own. Some of you may have seen flip-down sunglasses, a necessity and fashion statement for many major league players today. Flip-down sunglasses weren't unknown to Cool Papa. After all, he invented them.

7   But despite all of Cool Papa's baseball feats and the style with which he accomplished them, his greatest achievement was that he played at all. You see, James "Cool Papa" Bell was the victim of a disease known as racism—racism that kept him from playing in the same league as white players, racism that kept him from being in the same record books as white players, racism that kept him from earning the same money as white players. In fact, to make ends meet, Cool Papa would race home after each game just so he could change clothes and get to his second job as a nighttime security guard. This kind of thing would be unheard of for players today.

8   But despite the inequalities he faced, Cool Papa kept on playing the game he loved. He helped pave the way for Jackie Robinson, the first African American in the major leagues, and others who followed him. Cool Papa did this by fighting racism the same way he played baseball—stylishly but effectively. Despite knowing that he would never reach his dream of playing in the major leagues just because of his color, Cool Papa Bell, and many others for that matter, played on, hoping that someday there would be only one league—a league of professional baseball players, regardless of race.

9   So let's take a few moments, which is longer than it would take Cool Papa to steal second base, to appreciate James "Cool Papa" Bell—the speedy baseball star, the stylish innovator, the man who fought racism just by going to work every day.

James "Cool Papa" Bell

Commentary

"James 'Cool Papa' Bell" is a commemorative speech that deals with one of the greatest baseball players in the old Negro League, to which black players were relegated before the integration of major league baseball in 1947. The topic will probably be appreciated most by students who are baseball fans, but the speech transcends sports to focus on the larger issue of racism in U.S. society and the refusal of "Cool Papa" Bell to be ground down by it. The speech also illustrates the differences between a commemorative speech and an informative speech. Although the speaker provides information about Bell, he does not present a full view of Bell's life or even of his career as a baseball player. Rather, he focuses on Bell's most praiseworthy qualities and seeks to enhance his listeners' appreciation of those qualities. Here is a synopsis of the speech.

Introduction: The introduction consists of paragraphs 1–2. The speaker begins by arousing curiosity about the topic of his speech. He then reveals that his subject is James "Cool Papa" Bell, who played his entire baseball career in the Negro League because the major leagues were still segregated. The last sentence of paragraph 2 identifies Bell as the finest player in the Negro League and provides a deft lead-in to the body of the speech.

Body: Composed of paragraphs 3–8, the body of the speech develops three main points. The first is that Bell was the fastest baseball player of all time (paragraphs 3–4). The second is that Bell played the game with a style all his own (paragraphs 5–6). The third—and most important—is that Bell was a pioneer who helped pave the way for Jackie Robinson and other African Americans who would later play Major League Baseball (paragraphs 7–8).

Throughout the body of the speech, the speaker provides well-chosen supporting materials to illustrate Bell's athleticism and character. The speaker also makes effective use of the resources of language discussed in Chapter 12 to elevate and polish the style of the speech. At the end of paragraph 4, for example, he employs alliteration in the sentence, "But no one made fun of his slender size as he swiftly and smoothly stole second or scored from first on a single."

In paragraph 8, the speaker uses repetition and parallelism to emphasize the extent to which Bell was victimized by racism—"racism that kept him from playing in the same league as white players, racism that kept him from being in the same record book as white players, racism that kept him from earning the same money as white players." The dexterity of this passage, in combination with its sharp message about the evils of racism, gives the speaker's words special force.

Conclusion: The conclusion consists of the final paragraph. After subtly announcing that the speech is coming to an end by saying, "So let's take a few moments . . . ," the speaker closes by reminding the audience of Bell's accomplishments as "the speedy baseball star, the stylish innovator, the man who fought racism just by going to work every day." The parallel structure of these phrases enhances the cadence of the speaker's delivery, while the final words—"the man who fought racism just by going to work every day"—provide a sense of drama and reinforce what the speaker sees as Bell's most important attainment.

———————————————

The Survivors

1   "Work! Harder. Faster. Shovel! Don't just stand there. Shovel!"

2   And so he shoveled with all of his energy and all of his might. Hour after hour, he shoveled until his body could not shovel any more. Finally, he stopped working, leaned over on his shovel, and let his body limply rest, as his eyes stared at the ground.

3   The commander looked his way and hollered in a low and penetrating voice, "Shovel!" But the man did not move. The commander lifted his gun, loaded it with ammunition, and shot him. The man released his hands from the shovel and fell to the ground. He murmured his last words, "How could this happen?" The Nazi walked over, lifted his heel, and kicked the man into the mass grave, which he had been digging.

4   One more Jew was removed from this world. He was one of 6 million who was brought to his death by the Nazi policy to annihilate the Jewish race. The Nazis collected the Jews in the ghettos; they transported the Jews to the death camps; they worked the Jews until they could not work any more. Then they killed them—by gun and by gas, by starvation and sickness, by torture and terror.

5   Millions of Jews died in the death camps of Dachau, Buchenwald, Auschwitz, and Treblinka. It seems unfathomable that people could have survived the Nazis' wartime atrocities. Yet, by the grace of God, there were survivors. The survivors were the young and the strong, not the old and the meek. The survivors were the lucky and the few.

6   My grandparents are Holocaust survivors. They are each the only survivors in their families. They witnessed the deaths of their mothers and fathers, sisters and brothers, friends and neighbors. They witnessed the destruction of their lives and homes, towns and country, shops and synagogues. They lived through the ghettos. They lived through the death camps. They lived through the excruciating work. They lived to see liberation.

7   Since I was a little girl, my grandparents have told me about their lives during the Holocaust. They have told me about the persecution, the intolerance, and the injustice so that I could appreciate my freedom, my liberty, and my independence. It has always amazed me that my grandparents don't have spite or malice. After all they suffered, they have only hope and love. They don't want to hate any more.

8   During World War II, my grandparents were victims of anti-Semitism. Fifty years later, they are victims no longer. Today they fight against the "isms" which plague our communities, our states, our nation, and our world. They tell their story so that we, the younger generation, will understand the horrific force which anti-Semitism was in their lives. They relate their experiences to the struggles which so many people grapple with

today. They will tell their story, and they will not rest until all people can live without fear and without denial—until all people can live with pride and with dignity.

9   And when my grandparents are gone, I will continue to tell their story. I will tell my children about the men and women who were murdered for no cause. I will tell my children about the heroism of the Jews in the Warsaw ghetto who fought strength for strength against the Nazi militia. I will tell these stories to all who will listen.

10   And I hope that you, too, will tell stories. As the Holocaust survivor and writer Elie Wiesel, once said, "Not to transmit an experience is to betray it."

11   To the millions who died in the Holocaust, lie peacefully in your graves, for you have not been forgotten.

The Survivors

Commentary

An excellent commemorative speech, "The Survivors" functions at several levels. At one level, it pays tribute to the speaker's grandparents, who lived through Hitler's concentration camps in World War II. At another level, it honors those Jews who lost their lives in the camps. At yet another level, it is a celebration of human pride, freedom, and dignity in the face of tyranny and oppression. The speech also illustrates the differences between a commemorative speech and an informative speech. Although the speaker provides information about the Holocaust and her grandparents, she does not go into historical detail about either. Rather, she deals with her grandparents' experiences at a very general level and relates those experiences to larger issues of freedom and tolerance. Here is a synopsis of the speech.

Introduction: As in many commemorative speeches, there is no visible break between the introduction and the body of "The Survivors." The best way to parse the introduction of this speech is to see it as running through paragraph 5. This is an unusually long introduction, but it works well to get the audience involved in the speech. After opening with a story about a Jewish prisoner who is murdered by a Nazi guard (paragraphs 1–3), the speaker expands briefly upon the millions of Jews killed during the Holocaust (paragraph 4). Then, in paragraph 5, she shifts attention to "the lucky and the few" who survived the Holocaust. Had the speaker made this shift sooner, it would not have had the same effect. She needed to spend time discussing the victims of the Holocaust before mentioning its survivors.

Body: The body of the speech (paragraphs 6–10) focuses on the speaker's grandparents. In paragraph 6, she discusses her grandparents' experiences during the war. In paragraphs 7–8, she relates her grandparents' story to "the struggles which so many people grapple with today." In paragraph 9, she notes that she will continue to tell her grandparents' story so people will not forget the horrors of the Holocaust or the heroism of its victims. In paragraph 10, she ends the body with the oft-quoted statement of Elie Wiesel that "Not to transmit an experience is to betray it."

Throughout the body of the speech, the speaker uses repetition and parallelism with great effectiveness. Paragraph 6, for example, proceeds through seven consecutive sentences that begin with the word "They." The last four sentences are especially powerful: "They lived through the ghettos. They lived through the death camps. They lived through the excruciating work. They lived to see liberation." Also note the last three sentences of paragraph 9, which begin with "I will tell . . ." The restatement of these words in parallel structure reinforces the speaker's ideas and strengthens the rhythm of her speech.

Conclusion: The conclusion is made up of the last three paragraphs, the first two of which continue the speaker's use of repetition and parallelism and restate her tribute to the victims of the Holocaust. The final sentence gives a sense of unity to the entire speech by reiterating the dying words of the man in the opening story. It also ends the speech on a powerful note by reinforcing the speaker's opposition to tyranny wherever it might occur around the globe.

———————————————————

My Grandfather

---

1   Every day people are born and people die. Human beings come into this world and leave it—most without their names being immortalized in any history books. Millions of people have lived and worked and loved and died without making any great claims to fame or fortune.

2   But they aren't forgotten—not by their friends, not by their families. And some of these people, some very special people, are not forgotten even by those who hardly knew them. My grandfather was one of these very special people.

3   What made him so special? Why is he remembered not only by friends and family but even by casual acquaintances? Very simply, because he was the essence of love. More than that, he was the essence of what I think of as "active" love. Just as his heart was not empty, his words were not empty.

4   He didn't just speak of compassion. During the Great Depression he took homeless people off the street into his home when they needed a place to sleep. He gave them food when they needed something to eat. And though he wasn't a rich man by any means, he gave them money when they had none. Those people off the street will remember the man who had enough love in his heart to share with them all that he had.

5   He didn't just speak of tolerance. During the 1960s, when his peers were condemning those "long-haired hippies," I can remember riding in the car with my grandfather, picking up dozens and dozens of those "long-haired hippies" who were hitchhiking, and going miles out of our way to give them a ride somewhere. Those men and women will remember the man who had enough love in his heart to bridge the gap between his world and theirs and to practice the spirit of brotherhood.

6   And he didn't just speak of courage. He proved his courage time and time again. He proved it to a little girl who was trapped in the basement of a burning building. He pulled her out of the flames and gave her back her life. And that little girl, now a grown woman, will remember the man who had enough love in his heart to risk his life for a person he didn't even know.

7   He also proved his courage, in a more personal way, to his family. In 1966 he was told he had leukemia and only a year to live. He immediately started chemotherapy treatment, and I don't know which is worse—the effects of the disease or the effects of those treatments. In the ensuing year we saw his hair fall out, we saw his skin turn a pasty shade of gray, and we saw him lose so much weight that he seemed to shrivel up into half the size he had been. We didn't want to see him go out that way.

8   And we didn't. He fought that disease with all his strength and all his courage. And despite the pain he endured, he never complained. I think about him when I catch myself complaining about my "tons of homework" or a "terrible headache," and suddenly that homework or that headache doesn't seem so terrible after all.

9   He lived through that first year, and he lived through eight more. And that disease never stopped him from working, and it never stopped him from caring. All through those years of suffering, he continued to show compassion and tolerance and courage.

10   He died in 1975. And though he left this world without ever making the pages of a history book, he still left the world a great deal. He left to the people who knew him a spirit to exemplify life—a spirit of unconditional, selfless, and truly inspiring love.

My Grandfather

Commentary

Presented in an introductory public speaking class, "My Grandfather" illustrates how a commemorative speech should focus on the essence of its subject. Rather than presenting a biography that recounts the facts of her grandfather's life, the speaker deals with what she believes to be his most praiseworthy qualities. The speech also shows how students can use clear, simple language to convey meaning and to arouse emotion. Here is a synopsis of the speech:

Introduction: The introduction consists of paragraphs 1–3. Because many previous speakers had dealt with famous people, paragraphs 1–2 were especially effective in capturing the attention of the audience. At the end of paragraph 2 the speaker announces the exact topic of the speech, and in paragraph 3 she presents the central idea—that her grandfather was the essence of "active love." The last sentence of paragraph 3 helps to clarify what the speaker means by "active love" and provides a smooth bridge to the body of the speech.

Body: The body of the speech begins in paragraph 4 and runs through the next-to-last paragraph. Three main points are developed: "He didn't just speak of compassion" (paragraph 4); "He didn't just speak of tolerance" (paragraph 5); "He didn't just speak of courage" (paragraphs 6–9). The parallel wording of each main point reinforces the speaker's ideas and gives coherence to the body. So, too, does the repetition and parallelism in the last sentences of paragraphs 4–6. Throughout, the speaker gives her ideas life with specific examples that illustrate her grandfather's "active love." The language of the speech is clear, familiar, and concrete. Most of the words consist of one or two syllables, and there are few wasted words. The speech moves crisply from idea to idea. When delivered in class, it also picked up considerable emotional power as it proceeded.

Conclusion: The conclusion consists of the last paragraph. By stating that her grandfather "left this world without ever making the pages of a history book," the speaker relates back to her introduction. This gives the speech a sense of unity and signals that the speaker is about to conclude. The final sentence ties the entire speech together by rephrasing the central idea clearly and vividly.